START TO FIGURE:

FUGITIVE ESSAYS, SELECTED REVIEWS

# Start to Figure

*Fugitive Essays*

*Selected Reviews*

## Andrew DuBois

PALIMPSEST PRESS

Copyright © 2020 Andrew DuBois
All rights reserved

Palimpsest Press
1171 Eastlawn Ave.
Windsor, Ontario. N8S 3J1
www.palimpsestpress.ca

Printed and bound by Rapido Books in Ontario, Canada.
Edited by Katie Fewster-Yan. Series Editor is Jim Johnstone.
Cover art is a detail of "First Dance Class" by Susan Manchester.
Book typography and cover design by Carleton Wilson.

Palimpsest Press would like to thank the Canada Council for the Arts and the Ontario Arts Council for their support of our publishing program. We also acknowledge the assistance of the Government of Ontario through the Ontario Book Publishing Tax Credit.

LIBRARY AND ARCHIVES CANADA CATALOGUING IN PUBLICATION

Title: Start to figure : fugitive essays, selected reviews / Andrew DuBois.
Other titles: Works. Selections
Names: DuBois, Andrew (Andrew Lee), author.
Identifiers: Canadiana 20200183893 | ISBN 9781989287514 (softcover)
Subjects: LCSH: Canadian poetry—History and criticism. | LCSH: American poetry—History and criticism. | LCSH: Poetics. | LCSH: Poetry. | LCGFT: Reviews. | LCGFT: Essays.
Classification: LCC PS8143 .D83 2020 | DDC C811.009—dc23

# Contents

Acknowledgements . . . . . . . . . . . . . . . . . . . . . . . 9
Preface . . . . . . . . . . . . . . . . . . . . . . . . . . . . . 11

## I.

Amelia Curran: "I Am the Song" . . . . . . . . . . . . . . . 15
He Covers the Waterfront: The Music of Duane Andrews . . . . . . . . 22
Hollywood's Radio Edit: On *Straight Outta Compton* . . . . . . . . . 32
Melvillean Provocation and the Critical Art of Devotion . . . . . . . . 39
John Ashbery's Harvard Education, 1945–1949 . . . . . . . . . . . 55
Genteel Versifiers . . . . . . . . . . . . . . . . . . . . . . . 62
Ethics, Critics, Close Reading . . . . . . . . . . . . . . . . . . 70
Short Reviews . . . . . . . . . . . . . . . . . . . . . . . . . 83

## II.

Poetry: Letters in Canada 2018 . . . . . . . . . . . . . . . . . 133
Poetry: Letters in Canada 2017 . . . . . . . . . . . . . . . . . 158
Poetry: Letters in Canada 2016 . . . . . . . . . . . . . . . . . 181
Poetry: Letters in Canada 2015 . . . . . . . . . . . . . . . . . 192
Poetry: Letters in Canada 2010 . . . . . . . . . . . . . . . . . 207
Poetry: Letters in Canada 2009 . . . . . . . . . . . . . . . . . 273

Books Reviewed . . . . . . . . . . . . . . . . . . . . . . . 343
About the Author . . . . . . . . . . . . . . . . . . . . . . . 351

# Acknowledgements

Everything here has been printed before. The "Letters in Canada" essays appeared in the *University of Toronto Quarterly*. Old pals David Galbraith and Colin Hill were my accommodating editors for the omnibus reviews. "He Covers the Waterfront" came out in *Music & Literature* and was solicited by my friend Jesse Ruddock; she slapped it into shape. The essay on Amelia Curran is from *World Literature Today*. Thank you to Michelle Johnson for encouraging it and then seeing it through. "Hollywood's Radio Edit" appeared online at the *LA Review of Books*. It was a bit of a mess before Anna Shechtman fixed it. Thanks to Jeffrey Gray, "Genteel Versifiers" came together for *The Greenwood Encyclopedia of American Poets and Poetry*. The Melville essay appeared in *Melville and Aesthetics*, edited with tact and skill by Samuel Otter and Geoffrey Sanborn. "Ethics, Critics, Close Reading" is from a special issue of *UTQ*, edited by the nonpareil Marlene Goldman.

Of the short reviews, one is from the *New York Times Book Review*, one from *American Literary History Online*, and two from *UTQ*. Otherwise, all of them but one appeared in the *Harvard Review*. So did the essay on "John Ashbery's Harvard Education," the earliest thing here, which has now been superseded by a chapter in Karin Roffman's biography; still, I include it out of affection for my younger self. *Harvard Review*'s editor, Christina Thompson, shored up and pared down my prose in a way that had a big impact on my thinking and my style. More crucial, perhaps, was how it was always practically pastoral to go into the *Review*'s offices and graze the books to review. She made me feel most welcome. This one, then, is for editors who make us better, including the ones for this book, Ginger Pharand and Katie Fewster-Yan.

## Preface

Although I enjoy at least imagining that I enjoy what we used to call "theory," I am incapable of sustaining one; nor am I in particular ideological (though I would be the last to know, right?); in fact, I may almost be devoid of what we used to call "ideas." The main claim to coherence of this collection is that one person ostensibly wrote it.

Then again, as Hamlet says when he's backed himself into a corner, I'm not really the one responsible. That was all a different me. It is a feeling with which a person can relate in reading over a batch of one's fugitive work. Then it starts to come back: where you were when you were writing; where you were living and sometimes with whom; what else you were doing and reading at the time; the ego struggles of editing; the nervous anticipation preceding publication; most of the time, the sound of crickets; every once in a while, a pleasant response. In the meantime, there is a record of something that was observed, described, and thought through—a nice remainder. It exists, on paper; it is real, real as life. Now that I have most of those records in one place, I feel that the sum of them is a more coherent me than me myself.

"Grace to be born and live as variously as possible!" Frank O'Hara's beautiful exclamation has been something of a mantra, and I trust this collection honors the invocation of it, in its relative variety; naturally I gravitate toward particular things, and occasion often leads one not only toward but away from paths that one might have otherwise taken; but one does prefer to be open (within reason), a preference that is mollified by writing omnibus reviews and having omnivorous editors, teachers, colleagues, and friends, who have helped keep me from ever, ever being consistently bored.

As for being consistently boring, I don't think I'm that, either, but a couple of these pieces do run a tad long. The main thing when that seems to happen is not to try to read everything all at once. It's okay to take a break or to read a little bit while you're eating dinner. There's no rush or point of being in a hurry. For instance, it has become clear that my first two go-rounds at the big *UTQ* reviews are like a test of becoming Canadian that had the instructions in bold: *Show Your Work!* So that's one style. Others herein are more lapidary or sanguine, brisk or elliptical. As I am a weak maker of arguments, the only thing that need be followed is each letter in front of the other, which the reader will perhaps concede is the proper arrangement for moving forward, ever forward, for now.

I.

# Amelia Curran: "I Am the Song"

When you've flown as far east as you can fly over North America, the last place to land is St. John's, Newfoundland. Some people head straight from the airport to the lighthouse at Cape Spear, which is the continent's true most eastern point. Others hike or drive up Signal Hill, to stand where Marconi stood to receive the first transatlantic wireless message, sometimes texting from the top. Still others head toward Jellybean Row, to walk a stone's throw from St. John's Harbor, sauntering among the bright and whimsical saltbox shops and rowhouses of Duckworth Street and its steep, sloping environs.

Count me among the latter. It is not just that Duckworth satisfies the architectural sweet-tooth—though it is impossible not to light up at the purples, yellows, oranges, ochres, reds, pinks, greens, and blues that shine like a smile through even the foggiest harbor days. It's because that's where you find Fred's Records; and Fred's Records is where you go to get your Newfoundland music fix. No neophyte pop-up shop of the vinyl renaissance variety, the venerable Fred's has instead been around for some forty-five years. The space is full but not cramped, the staff resolutely unsnarky, and the recommendations astute. The store doesn't *only* sell local music, but it seems to sell *all* of it.

A curious observer can hardly help notice, placed at the front of the store, several albums by an artist named Amelia Curran, festooned with enthusiastic descriptions written by the staff in block letters and colorful pen. Curran, a St. John's native, is a songwriter-singer-guitarist, who, over the course of such albums as *War Brides* (2006/2008), *Hunter, Hunter* (2009), *Spectators* (2012), *They Promised You Mercy* (2014), and *Watershed* (2017), has made a name not only in this island province, but elsewhere in the country and beyond. (Her second album, for instance, won the prize for Best Roots and Traditional Album at the JUNO Awards, which is Canada's Grammys.) Drawn to its title and cover, a curious observer decides to try *They Promised You Mercy*. When he gets it home and puts it in his player, where it will stay unreplaced for weeks, he discovers that rarest of things: the perfect album. Later on, after further observation of her work, he will find it to be of a piece with the entire oeuvre.

\* \* \*

Amelia Curran is a tumble of paradoxes and ironies. She articulates her lyrics with total clarity, yet the persona she conveys floats in and out of distinctness; her songs are relentlessly first-person, yet there are so many self-definitions that some are self-cancelled and none coalesce; her music sounds old but sounds new; she's smack in your face but she hides. Her first words on *War Brides*, Curran's introduction to the world, come from a song called "Scattered and Small," and are strangely already posthumous: "I was so alive, I can only look back." This, of all things, at the start, words from the talking dead: beginnings containing their endings, nows resurrecting their thens. Time—as both fact and as concept—is truly of the essence for Curran and, respecting its mystery, she doesn't quite know what to make of it—other than art.

In her hands that turns out to be plenty. The second song on the album is called "Furious Curve" and it's a curious swerve indeed, not in its sound but in its sense of time. "Oh the future is flying too fast for the furious curve," she begins, speaking truly for us all, before ending, "What if someone subtracts from the sum of all fears?" At first I took that to mean: what if someone comes along who takes away from our fears, a benevolent arrival. (Lord knows we could use it.) Later I figured it might mean: what if a person, someone, anyone, in the face of all these fears, shrinks, subtracts, gets scattered and small.

"Time was the telltale factor for all of our fate." This, from a later song called "You've Changed," feels as old as alliterative verse, as fresh as bouncing syllables bouncing still. Curran's diction is spare, her poetics abstract and metaphorical, her rhetoric often anaphoric, her lines almost always end-stopped albeit with occasional rhythmic elisions of enjambment where the line just keeps on going. It is not devoid of the mystic. (She believes in "Devils," as a song of that title attests.) Hers is a poetry of archetypes and of figures, not elaborate images or developed conceits. Her lines have the aphorist's balance, the residual impact. You circle around them like a koan: "Time was a storybook, time was a thief." Even time can be turned by Curran into the past tense.

But when you have reverence for the past, nostalgia for the present, and fear of the future, you are experiencing a certain kind of totality of time.

Her second album, *Hunter, Hunter* (a play on "hunter-gatherer"), starts with a song saying *au revoir* as hello ("Bye, Bye Montreal": "If you're in town you'll look me up / We'll dance the days into the cups") and ends with a song called "Last Call." The latter sounds like a hazy vision of an actual night out on George Street, a classic port street, which is sort of a St. John's version of Beale Street, but with way less blues and barbecue, much more ocean air. Willie Nelson once wrote that "the night life ain't no good life, but it's my life," and given the proliferation of boozy evenings and painful mornings in her lyrics, Curran would likely concur:

> Those red-faced prophets, bartender, and me
> They're dancing in riddles on top of dead dreams
> I kissed a sailor, said he was the sea
> But he never knew it from me
>
> Last call
> Time is an invalid inside us all

Like the pub scene in *The Waste Land* ("Hurry up please, it's time"), the end of the night is the end of the line. In the same album's "Tiny Glass Houses," Curran imagines an opposite path, a Benjamin Button-esque dream of reversal (with just a touch of Auden): "Drink 'til you're sleeping, I love you that way / Like we are all babies, all our beds are unmade." Silently and sweetly slovenly, instead of dumb, dirty, and drunk—the melancholy barfly's dream.

Red-faced and face-down is not the only way to depict this persona, however. That version is too passive for Curran to rest on. She kicks off her wonderful list-song of self-definition, "I Am the Night" (from *They Promised You Mercy*), by owning the decision to stay out till all hours: "I am the queen of the closing bar." She *is* a musician, after all. She is an incredible number of things. Reading through *Relics and Tunes: The Songs of Amelia Curran*, published last year by Newfoundland's Breakwater Books, the "I am" construction yields up numerous things that Curran is:

> A factory
> A clarity
> A memory (1978, to be exact)
> A vision
> The matador coaxing your love to my core
> The shadow that heightens the light
> A wild abandoned ray of heat
> A lover's enemy
> Just a Tuesday in a world of Friday nights
> A fortune of fever and lust
> The wrecking ball
> Just a road

And then there is "I Am the Night" itself, with its repetition-powered insistence of being:

> I am the gravity that holds you down
> I am the jewel in the thorny crown
> I am the furthest from the madding crowd
> I am the seventh of the seven pounds
>
> I am the tremor in the nightmare deep
> I am the ceiling on your lifelong dreams
> I am the medicine that keeps you clean
> I am the fortune in the telling scheme

And yet this is not *clearly* just Curran herself speaking, of course, for the song is an apostrophe and it is Night herself who is speaking. This vacillation between the presence of the singer through her voice and her absenting herself in her figures makes for a foggy but brisk-winded vitalism in practically every verse.

★ ★ ★

The term "singer-songwriter" conjures a folkie sitting on a wooden stool on a bare stage, and although I'm sure she can play that and any other way, Curran as a maker of music is quiet yet slyly, lushly textured. She folds sounds up, kneads them. A cursory accounting of instruments heard on her albums includes acoustic and electric guitar, electric and upright bass, drums, percussion, cello, mandolin, harmonica, accordion, trombone, clarinet, banjo, bouzouki, trumpet, flugelhorn, French horn, tenor sax, lap steel guitar, violins and violas, dobro, piano, Hammond organ, and a good deal of vocal harmonizing. This paints a picture of Curran as a bandleader as much as a solo act. She can go up- or down-tempo and lose nothing in between. She edges up against the sweetness of good pop, on the one hand, and something rusty and clangy and rough on the other, without ever really veering too far either way.

As with most original artists, inside their originality you can hear echoes of their stellar predecessors. To use an overextended and hipsterized word, the true original is a great "curator" of her own influences. One critic called Curran a mix of Leonard Cohen and Patsy Cline, and while it wouldn't be my first choice, you could do well worse. When she writes "And you won't find me / Oh no, you won't find me" or "And you won't see me" or "And you won't catch me," one recalls the "He's Not Here" persona of Dylan; or the hiding behind a mask of Joni Mitchell on *Don Juan's Reckless Daughter*; or then again, one hears strains of the great country songsmith Cindy Walker, who proclaimed that "You don't know me." The maritime plaintiveness of the Newfoundland legend Ron Hynes comes through in her sadder laments. The chorus to "Fables & Troubles" could have come from Liz Phair's *Whip-Smart*. When Curran sings that "God's no rebel, he's a handyman," the spectral Judee Sill is there, echoing back that "Jesus was a crossmaker." Several lyrics sound like a juggling of the poems of Robert Frost: "I have made a promise that I have promised to keep," "There's no untaken road when nothing stays for long," "In brazen secret paradise / A carousel of fire and ice."

In the introduction to her collection of lyrics, there is a brief discussion regarding the difference between poetry and lyrics; like most such discussions, this one is circular and unsatisfying. Yet Shannon Webb-Cannon, a friend of Curran's who pens it, puts it nicely when she writes that Curran "illustrate[s] how words are married to the melody. Their relationship relies on vows made to one another." One can agree with Curran up to a point when she says, "Lyrics must have music to communicate. Poems must have a page." Yet as someone who reads roughly a hundred new books of poetry every year, and who has ingested much moribund verse in the name of historical scholarship, I can say without exaggeration that Curran's lyrics on the page are as successful as 75% of all that stuff in print. Naturally, having those lyrics set to music, played expertly, and having those words sung beautifully by their own composer, raises that percentage by far.

* * *

"Their relationship relies on vows made to one another." As coincidence would have it, not long after I had procured Curran's *War Brides*, I was up at a place called Grate's Cove. There are lots of rock walls there—they cover 150 acres—and if you drive a little way from there to Red Head Cove, you can get your best view of the birds on Baccalieu Island—petrels and puffins and kittiwaks and gannets and murres. My trips to Grate's Cove tend to involve stopping at an inn, studio, and restaurant there run by a friendly couple named Courtney and Terrance. Terrance is from around the cove and Courtney is from Louisiana and they met teaching English in South Korea. Thus, their food is an unexpected mixture of Creole, Korean, and local Newfoundland fare. I'm from North Alabama, and have retained a good deal of my accent. Eating my *jeon* and snow crab étouffée, I overheard two couples talking to one another. The one couple had accents like mine but with added syrup, so (very much out of character) I asked if they might be from Alabama or Georgia.

They *were* from Georgia, it turned out, and we asked each other how we'd come to be where we were. My story was boring: I was living in Carbonear, because I liked it there. Theirs contained more oomph. The wife in the couple was the daughter of a woman who had been a "war bride" from St. John's. Her mother, from a well-to-do city family—but not yet a Canadian family, as Newfoundland was not yet part of Canada—married an American serviceman who was stationed for a while on the island during WWII. After the war was over, she resettled in rural southern Georgia, following her husband back to his native home. The daughter, now in her seventies, said it was a big adjustment for her mother, from electric lights and indoor plumbing to back to candles and outhouses.

In "All the Ladies," Curran sings, "It's the same old story that I've heard ten times before / You're sending your love to war [ ... ] And all the war brides sing their soldiers' songs / The night is short, dear, but their love is long." I had always thought of the painful romance of longing, the worried wife left behind, the constant fear of the arrival of the fateful telegram. I had never considered what happened when that telegram thankfully never came, when a man essentially new to you returned, alive but not likely unscathed, to begin to dictate in part how your life would now be. On her newest album, *Watershed*, Curran says that "Time is only tireless, it cannot rewrite / Love is only heart strings that you will not untie / You have got each other[.]" To me she's the soldier and the wife, the country and the city, the present and the past—the melancholy, romantic past; the melancholy, realistic present. You can see her smiling and snapping her fingers: "You know I love the subtle silence." Then she shifts her bandmates into gear.

# He Covers the Waterfront:
# The Music of Duane Andrews

The island of Newfoundland seen from a map looks like fractal geography as printed fact. The island proper—the biggest part by far of the whole of what is sometimes called The Rock—has a kind of polyp on its southeastern-most side. The polyp looks like an island that looks roughly like the island from which it hangs; and hang it does, because it is not an island at all, but a peninsula. It's called the Avalon Peninsula—king and queen-fed courtly dreams of paradise in that name—and the closer and closer you read on the map, the more it looks like a living geological Mandelbrot Set. The ocean gives way to big bays, big bays to smaller ones, which give way to harbors and coves and little inlets; just like the Trans-Canada Highway, which starts here before stretching its ribbon of asphalt on for what seems like forever, gives way to smaller highways such as 70, 75, 80, which in turn become Main Streets and Water Streets and finally devolve into something called "drungs," which are rural Newfoundland lanes. Avalon looks from here like the claw of a crab—cartography is maritime destiny—or maybe, in the knuckles and muscles and bones of its towns and the blood and veins of its roads, it resembles a damaged, but very much living, human hand.

If you drive in a long, tight "U" from the capital St. John's (and you will have to drive—there is no bus, although there used to be) you are moving down around the eastern and then up along the western side of Conception Bay. Now, every bay is a conception bay necessarily; just as, given the womb-tomb conundrum, every bay is necessarily an end. As Donne said, in the voice of a navigator's compass, "Thy firmness makes my circle just, / And makes me end where I begun." And that is where this finds us, in a place called Carbonear, which is where Duane Andrews was born and raised. Like him and a lot of other folks with certain kinds of talents and dreams, we'll leave it, but we will be coming back to it soon.

* * *

Between the Klondike-inspired stories in rhyme of Robert Service and the macabre free-verse clarity of Margaret Atwood, E.J. Pratt is sandwiched in the years as a once-upon-a-time "most famous Canadian poet." Fewer people read him now, but Pratt was an interesting cat. He was born and raised in Western Bay—about 20 clicks north of Carbonear—where his father was a Methodist minister, as he himself later became ordained. A sign up the road marks the site of the first Methodist Church built in North America. Although Pratt spent most of his adulthood in Toronto teaching at the University that takes the city's name—and where a library, a poetry prize, and a professorship all now bear his—Pratt mined his Newfoundland roots from beginning to end in his poems. The Government of Canada in his honor has placed a nondescript plaque with a compact biography outside the Western Bay Post Office, though you would have to already know it was there to give it your notice.

There is a volume of Pratt's poetry from 1932, *Many Moods*, that reminds me of Duane Andrews's music, but especially of his relatively recent, delicately filigreed, and deeply textured release *Conception Bay* (2015). It is an album that catches the weather of its eponymous place—the dramatic seasons, the volatile shifts from fog to sun to dapples and shadows, the winds for which the word "bracing" was invented, the occasional profound stillnesses. In addition to the many moods are the many names of this place, a scattershot representation of dark humor and diverse pedigree, of the sea's centrality and the sentimental touch:

> *Mistaken Point*
> *Placentia*
> *Harbour Grace*
> *Old Perlican*
> *Ochre Pit Cove*
> *Butter Pot Park*

*Motion Head*
*Tinker Point*
*Burnt's Cove*
*Roaches Line*
*Low Point*
*Bald Head*
*Heart's Desire*
*Heart's Delight*
*Heart's Content*
*Turks Cove*
*Bay Bulls*
*Spaniard's Bay*
*Portugal Cove*
*The Spout*
*Witless Bay*
*Bay de Verde*
*Old Shop*
*South Dildo*
*Tickle Harbour*
*Shuffle Board*
*Ocean Pond*

For instrumental music, Andrews's has lots of linguistic pleasures. It must be strange to speak only with your fingers, some wood, and some string, though the titles also talk. In Newfoundland people are taciturn, until they turn voluble, but friendly, once they figure you are worth the effort. Great talkers are among them and there is music in what they say. It is not quite like the Deep South, where the oddball constructions and the elisions of the accent are mitigated by the syrup slowness of the delivery. Here people talk fast, and there is a different diction—the *Dictionary of Newfoundland English* runs to 700 pages of words that you never have heard—and for all I know, if you throw a half-case of India Beer into the mix (the slogan of which, under a picture of a Newfoundland dog, is "Man's Best Friend"), it makes it even harder to follow because you are always trying to go back and catch up to something you missed and is already gone.

The titles Duane Andrews makes up or appropriates are fun to read and give the same pleasures as those names on the map. There are the ones that ring of Newfoundland "itself": "Joe Batt's Arm Longliners," "The Sailor's Bonnet," "The Breakwater Boys," "Bell Island," "The Petty Harbour Bait Skiff," "Land and Sea Medley." Then there are the French titles, which come from both multiple drives and a singular source: "La Gitane," "Nantes," "Gigues," "Douce Ambiance," "Valse des Niglos." There are the remade, actually *classical*, classics ("Improvisations on Chopin's Opus 64 No. 2," "Improvisations on the First Movement of Mozart's String Quintet") and some classics of Americana and Tin Pan Alley and classic pop and classic country and classic rock: "Oh Susannah," "Sweet Georgia Brown," "Georgia on My Mind," "Mr. Sandman," "Tennessee Stud," and "Layla," for instance, the latter three on *Fretboard Journey* (2016), a killer hodge-podge of an album that is the work of a Newfoundland guitarists supergroup. (What other kind of group could reinvent "Layla" without asking for ridicule?) There, Andrews trades rhythms and licks in a well-woven tapestry with Sandy Morris, Gordon Quinton, and Craig Young, the latter with whom Andrews also made the album *Charlie's Boogie* (2013).

You have got to describe the songs that he plays to get a handle on their range and the easiest way to do that is to talk about genre or form. There are the reels, the jigs, and the waltzes:

>    *Pique Point Reel*
>    *Kelly Russell's Reel*
>    *Pipe Reels*
>    *Lisa's Jigs*
>    *The Portuguese Waltzes*
>    *St. John's Waltz*

The rags, the blues, and jazz:

>    *The Supermoon Rag*
>    *Ragtime Annie/Ragtime Rufus*
>    *Jamo's Blues*
>    *Tennessee Blues*
>    *Isaac's Blues*

*D.D.'s Blues*
*Four on Six*
*Fables of Faubus*
*Caravan*

At first, I figured just by looking at its title that another song, "Bartlett & Frissell," was an homage to the jazz guitarists Bill Frisell and Bruce Bartlett (*Modern Jazz Guitar Styles*: "Seeing Bruce Bartlett live at Ryle's in Boston was and is a required pilgrimage for guitar students at Berklee.") Maybe it is a palimpsestic homage, though, because the former guitarist's name has one "s," not two. Turns out there is another Bartlett and Fris[s]ell who have something in common besides the guitar. Bob Bartlett was a heroic sea captain and explorer born in Brigus, just south of Carbonear; Varick Frissell was an American filmmaker whose last film, *The Viking*, starred Captain Bartlett as the S.S. Viking's captain. Most of it was made in Quidi Vidi (just outside of St. John's) but during the filming of some action and iceberg sequences off the coast of Labrador, a cache of ice-breaking dynamite exploded. The film was Frissell's last because he was killed in the blast, along with over two dozen other men.

The interest of Andrews in film is evident too in more obvious ways. There is a load of soundtrack work—his website lists 29 titles. He also made a swing album for children with Laura Winter and Erin Power as The Swinging Belles, called *More Sheep, Less Sleep* (2015), which won the Juno Award in 2016 for "Children's Album of the Year." The collaborative drive is defining in Andrews, as it is with many musicians and artists at large, no doubt; but the way the single ego gets absorbed into the collective in his work reminds me of music played in places where the playing itself is the spine of social life, not an independent art project. It recalls a time when you could probably play *something*, and if you couldn't play something at least you could sing, and if you couldn't carry a tune perhaps you were nimble enough to dance, and if you could dance you needed pickers and fiddlers and somebody on a squeeze box and a washboard and an oil drum and maybe someone to snap and pop the spoons—virtuosity without pomposity sitting easily with anyone who can hang on a musical bell curve that finally excludes no one. How this is all conveyed so strongly in his oeuvre without devolving into rote reproductive nostalgia, how a corpus that could be a real Frankenstein's monster of clumsily-stitched, grotesquely disparate parts is, instead, a fully formed body, an organic whole, wholly him: this is the loveliest wonder of it.

To my mind, the most beautiful of the Newfoundland songs played by Andrews is "Let Me Fish Off Cape St. Mary's." He has recorded it twice—on *Conception Bay*, with a string quartet, and on *The Empress* (2012), the second of his albums with Dwayne Côté, a masterly fiddler. The song has been called Newfoundland's "unofficial anthem" and was written by an interesting man named Otto Kelland. Like his father before him, Kelland was a policeman, then became a warden and finally assistant superintendent of Her Majesty's Penitentiary in St. John's. After hanging up the badge in 1966 he taught boatbuilding for a decade, wrote multiple books of stories and verse, and ended up with the Order of Canada for his cultural contributions, before dying one month short of a century old.

Kelland put pen to paper in 1945 to write the words of "Cape St. Mary's," but according to his granddaughter, Sally Kelland-Dyer, who told it to Robert Doyle for the second edition of *Doyle's Almanac of Newfoundland*, and who had heard the story from her father: "The song was written in his head long before it was written down. He used to pace the hall at home with his violin and sing some words. As he was pacing he would spit his chewing tobacco in a bucket and then pace some more. Once [it was] written down, he spent some time playing with the words and making minor revisions…. He did not," she said, "have a singing note in his head," but he "was a great fiddler and organist" who "played music by ear." Knowing Kelland's creation by heart was de rigueur for the family: "Learning and singing the song was mandatory, so to speak, for all his many grandchildren. He felt it placed something in our hearts about the love of the province that would never leave, and he was right."

He *was* right, even if you are not Kelland's grandchild. I had heard Andrews's instrumental versions before I ever read the words and they seemed to capture several provincial spirits. The one with Côté is a couple of guys playing a lullaby to end a long night of revels, telling everybody without ever saying so that it is just about time to hit the sack. The one on *Conception Bay* is more of an aubade—it has been my favorite song for waking up to for over a year, replacing another favorite, Ahmad Jamal's "Morning of the Carnival"—but, like Sylvia Plath's "Morning Song," it is an aubade with a residual darkness. The way Andrews and the quartet play Kelland's tune is less about another sunny start to another fabulous day, than it is a kind of pleasant albeit exasperated prayer for having survived another night's tempest, yet again, at least for a while.

★ ★ ★

"Confederation with Canada is surely the greatest single event that has happened to us since our Island was discovered. One casts one's mind over the five centuries of our recorded history and finds nothing so great." So wrote The Honorable Joseph R. Smallwood in 1967, almost twenty years after the Confederation took place, which he more than anyone helped facilitate; you could say that he made it happen. It was a long time coming and a long time resisted and not everybody thought it was so great. A half-century after he wrote those words introducing the third-volume of *The Book of Newfoundland* as its ex-Prime Minister, I heard a couple of rancid but funny jokes told on Joey Smallwood's behalf within two days of staying in Carbonear. Such is one of the boons of Confederation, a partial lifeline and relinquishing of freedom about which the populace remains so ambivalent that only humor can begin to process the results.

I think Andrews tells a Smallwood joke himself. On his album *Raindrops* (2008), he has a song called "Bees and Flowers / Joe Smallwood's Reel." It is a short diptych of a track, a bit over two minutes, and at the crease where Smallwood's reel begins it does take a minor turn. When you put bees and flowers together something pollinates and you get something else and longer lasting, so perhaps that is Andrews being fair to what all was actually gained. That is more a measured piece of wit than an outright joke. The next song on the album, though, is Charles Mingus's "Fables of Faubus," and since it is obvious that his albums are immaculately sequenced, it is also obvious that reel and fable are the chiastic hinges that link Faubus and Smallwood.

You might not recall Governor Orval Faubus of Arkansas, whose refusal to integrate the public schools after *Brown vs. Board of Education* deserves the eternal enmity of decent people. Bringing out the state's National Guard to keep the Little Rock schools segregated and to bar the door to nine innocent children—and to implicitly suggest that it was publicly fine to smear them with racist bile—led the usually amenable, normally affable, ultimate greatest of greats Louis Armstrong to cancel a U.S.-sponsored tour of the Soviet

Union; to directly castigate President Eisenhower for his cowardice in not nipping Faubus's venality in the bud; and to refer to Faubus himself, in speaking to the student journalist Larry Lubenow, as a "no-good motherfucker," which they could hardly print in the paper, of course. Lubenow proposed "ignorant plowboy" instead and Armstrong said that it would do. So you tell me about the juxtaposition of Orval and Joe.

*   *   *

Through the magic of iTunes there was revealed one of those algorithmic quirks that, digital though they may be, manage to approximate on occasion what it is like randomly to browse in a library's physical stacks. Because everything is arranged alphabetically by the artist's first name, in my iTunes library all of my Duane Andrews albums are bookended by Duane Allman on the one side and Duane Eddy on the other. This serendipitous sonic non sequitur could be taken as a karmic divining rod. They have something in common besides the mere guitar, surely, but what is it? It must have something to do with individuality and hybridity and how to manage those dualities of ditties. Duane Eddy moves from Dylan to Ellington, from sock-hop to schlock, from "St. Louis Blues" to "Sioux City Sue" to "On Top of Old Smokey" to "Blueberry Hill," always playing Duane Eddy, picking out that reverberative rockabilly, that rolling, echoing, surfing sound. Duane Allman is that long-haired country cracker playing Black blues who rigs those blues with rock and electrically reinvests rock with the Southern soul from which it came and who stretches out in jazzy improvisations and helps devise a new kind of band that jams.

If I scroll up a bit in the iTunes alpha-bit there is another great guitarist, perhaps the greatest of them all, Django Reinhardt, where Andrews and Allman most meet, in the form of "Jessica," a song Dickey Betts wrote and on which the almost-whole Allman Brothers Band elaborated, an extendable vamp meant to be played with two fingers, in honor of the gypsy guitarist Reinhardt, whose fretting hand was badly burnt in a caravan fire, leaving him at a temporary loss but eternally alive. Duane Allman doesn't play on "Jessica," because Duane Allman was recently dead when it was written; in that sense, though, the absent presence of the song is not just the brilliant but damaged hand of Django, but a bygone brother from a surviving but damaged band.

Django Reinhardt is Duane Andrews's lodestone. The power of the pull is immense. The latter picker is an unabashed proselytizer for the former—the reverent words of the sermon are apparent in almost every note played, and I would wager that not a week goes by without Andrews saying Django's name out loud to someone he hopes will appreciate him. It is refreshing to hear mature artists secure enough to be so enthusiastic in their acknowledgement, not of something so etymologically insidious and casually described as mere "influence," but of something more like total possession. They are not a matter of ownership, mind you, these claims of Duane's; for in the way that the most loving art most vividly testifies, there is a strange temporal hiccup whereby Reinhardt, instead of being owned by Andrews, possesses, like a benevolent spirit, the music of Andrews through time.

As with Willie Nelson's "Trigger" (which has had "Nuages" played upon it who knows on how many occasions), Andrews's guitar is valued by its owner in a strong musical and personal relation to Django; as with the owner of Trigger, Andrews is, as the CBC reports, "a one-guitar man, as opposed to a collector." His vehicle of transport was made by a young luthier from Italy named Mauro Freschi, modeled on the kind of Selmer guitar played by Reinhardt. That is certainly one way to possess one's own possession, to own up to one's obsession, to make every session a resurrection. After studying jazz at St. Francis Xavier in Antigonish, Nova Scotia, Andrews moved to study composition at conservatories in Paris and Marseille. One wonders if it took moving away for him to look back more clearly on what music his native province had to offer; if being back in Newfoundland now leads him to look back ever more fondly to Reinhardt as mentor and France as a musical home; if there is not something of a gypsy existence whereby one is always travelling away from a place and finding oneself in new art, discovering the new in the old, recovering iterations of oneself in returning, of leaving and ever returning.

\* \* \*

If my rough math is right, Andrews must have begun his peregrinations around the time that the Newfoundland cod fishery was collapsing. The cod moratorium was instituted in 1992 and it was meant to last a year. There is still a moratorium. I don't know if the average Joe was ever financially well-to-do in

Conception Bay, but I cannot imagine the moratorium helped. No, it certainly hurt, for a long while at least. Probably it was just another reason to distrust "Canada," which is what some locals call the gargantuan part of the country that isn't Newfoundland. To put things in perspective, imagine if there was a venture capital moratorium in Silicon Valley; and that it lasted twenty-five years; and that instead of being peopled by a bunch of eager and well-heeled newcomers, it was deeply lived in by the children of children of children of children, who had been doing that one thing all their lives. This is the nature of a catastrophe, a turning of the verse.

In the Carbonear of Andrews's youth, a large portion of the town depended on Fred Earle's fish processing plant to make ends meet. Now the best relic of any halcyon days sits partially sunk in Harbour Grace, a stone's throw from Carbonear. It is the S.S. Kyle, a legend of a ship, owned by Fred and his brother, the dashing local hero Captain Guy. Fred's daughter used to swim out to the Kyle once a year in commemoration, but time seems to have recently ended that too. Across the way sits a lifesize statue of Amelia Earhart, another hero, who left from an airstrip in Harbour Grace to start her transatlantic flight. That venture was among the great successes of its kind. Yet the air taketh and giveth away, the memorial reminds us, just as the rusted and hulking Kyle reminds us, so does the sea. Whether you sail or fly back to the mainland, something ventured has led to something gained and likely to something lost; and for everything you take with you from Conception Bay, even more is left behind. No worries—you can recover some of it by listening to that Freschi guitar Duane Andrews steers through the fog.

# Hollywood's Radio Edit:
# On *Straight Outta Compton*

Now that the hosannas, jeremiads, and most of the money have rolled in, let's start with the music. The heroes of *Straight Outta Compton* —a mostly enjoyable, sometimes shaky, musical biopic—are the three main members of N.W.A. (Niggaz Wit Attitudes): Eazy-E, Dr. Dre, and Ice Cube. (DJ Yella and MC Ren are also in the group but don't merit much screen time.) The best of N.W.A.'s music is among the best of its kind. Indeed, they helped invent the kind, so-called "gangsta rap." Their relation to their own times (late-1980s, early-1990s Los Angeles), as well as to times today, is resonant. When they broke up after a short tenure that was long on impact, N.W.A. reigned as the most important hip-hop group ever to come from the West Coast. They've yet to relinquish that distinction.

Director F. Gary Gray, who helmed the dopehead haze of *Friday* in 1995, starts *Straight Outta Compton* with three vignettes introducing each of its heroes. The movie opens on a drug deal about to go bad. Eazy-E (Jason Mitchell) is the most "street" of the three, unafraid and pugnacious, even with guns pointed at him. A frenetic scene follows in which Eazy does an old-school sort of parkour over Compton's nighttime rooftops and fences, darting from cops who bust in like they're looking for bin Laden. An egregious pun presents itself: Eazy's hip to the cops, and he hops away. Hip-hop's kineticism is embodied here in a fitting beginning for a movie named for an album, which begins with one of the most kinetic tracks ever made.

From Eazy escaping apprehension, we move to Dr. Dre (Corey Hawkins). He is lying on a mosaic of music: LPs by Roy Ayers, Funkadelic, and Zapp. Fanned-out beneath this blissed-out fanboy, the album covers are a peacock's tail of stellar taste. The young Dre, a groove savant, wears headphones and is settled deep in the cut. That prophetic pair of not-yet-"beats-by-Dre" over his ears represents a release from the harsh noise of the outside world, while also suggesting the sound of the billions of dollars to come. When we meet him, though, Dre is still living with his mother, who is not impressed with the chump change that her son picks up playing records. She thinks that he should get a real job.

Cut to Ice Cube (O'Shea Jackson Jr., Ice Cube's real-life son) on the school bus, scratching ink into his rhyme book. Cube is being bussed back with his fellow Black students from a fancy school awash with preppies on the lawn. His real home is exemplified by the angry O.G. who stops and boards the bus after a couple of kids flash the wrong gang signs from the window. In addition to being good material for Cube the burgeoning poet, the menacing man, sporting a Blood red bandana, is a hulking reminder of the reasons for Cube to work harder on those raps. The scene is staged but spot-on. Ice Cube was, after all, barely out of short pants when he got with N.W.A., one of hip-hop's finest precocities.

At the time that the movie begins, the West Coast has little to no standing in the world of rap music, insofar as the world of rap music was New York City and environs. Los Angeles was dominated by an electro sound, in which Dre played a part as a member of the World Class Wreckin' Cru, a group that, at its best, made drum-machine-and-synthesizer-based dance music. There was also a good deal of fast, precise scratching, as when Dre—a "doctor," remember—performs "surgery" on a song of that name, cutting with a stylus instead of a scalpel. In fact, there was a whole local scene of other like-minded musicians: the collective Uncle Jamm's Army, Arabian Prince, Egyptian Lover, and even Bobby Jimmy, the Weird Al of rap, whose "Roaches" (1986) featured rapping critters in its video.

*Straight Outta Compton* is motivated to show that this music scene was largely corny, the better to suggest that Dre made a brave leap when he went in a different direction. And it's true that those polyester suits don't hold up well. New York never cottoned to L.A. electro, but it was big in the South, where it had a lot in common with Miami Bass. The two regional styles, however, were seen as largely unsophisticated when compared to East Coast rap. Lorded over by such stalwarts as KRS-One, Chuck D, Rakim, Big Daddy Kane, and Run-DMC, the East expected lyrics—real lyrics—not robot sounds or sex chants.

The West wasn't all for naught before N.W.A., though. Toddy Tee recorded a crucial 12-inch, "Batterram," in 1985. Too Short, "with dirty raps coming out my mouth / and you know damn well what I'm talking about," was "coming straight from Oakland." Ice-T of Los Angeles had briefly, almost accidentally, snuck into the mainstream with "Reckless" on the soundtrack to *Breakin'* (1984). And his song "6 'n the morning," all criminal picaresque, has much in common with the Ice Cube–penned, Dre-produced, Eazy-emceed "Boyz-n-the-Hood."

At the local level, then, something was brewing. Enter enterprising Eazy-E, who has some money to spend. Dre has the musical chops and convinces Eazy to go in on a record. They convene in a studio, where we find that Ice Cube has written some rhymes about your everyday Compton gangbanger. After some Kangol-wearing New York–lames can't catch that West Coast flow, the guys figure, "Why not let Eazy try it?" He is, after all, the most gangsta of the group, so into the booth he reluctantly steps. The scene of Dre coaching Eazy on how to rap should become a classic. In general, the early studio scenes are ripe with partnership, friendship, and the invigorating pleasures that youths can take in their own electric talent. You don't see many scenes like this in movies—young black guys having fun and being creative without the weight of the world bearing down on them. Instead, the making of "Boyz-n-the-Hood" is a good time had by all.

In addition to that iconic song, N.W.A.'s artistic legacy rests on four others: "Straight Outta Compton," "Gangsta, Gangsta," "Fuck Tha Police," and "Dopeman." These all appear on their 1988 *Straight Outta Compton* LP. "Express Yourself," from the same album, is catchy, it's true, but in its context, it's a fake: why should this anthem to self-expression be the only song on the LP without any cussing? It's an obvious ploy for radio play, and, at any rate, it didn't take. The better, more scabrous songs made the waves.

Musical biopics tend to depict their subjects as either survivors or martyrs. *Straight Outta Compton* does both. Ice Cube and Dr. Dre, the movie's multi-million-dollar producers, are the survivors. Eazy-E, who died of AIDS in 1995, is the martyr. Treated suspiciously fairly on screen, he was always something of a cipher, an impression that grew as Dre and Cube outpaced him. When he is diagnosed with HIV, the fictionalized Eazy is incredulous: "I'm no faggot," he explodes. In 1995? Four years after Magic Johnson's press conference? If the scene is accurate, it's a masterpiece of willful ignorance. Of course, one feels guilty speaking ill of the dead, and the movie sure doesn't risk it, no matter what his bandmates said about him in life.

Eazy's fate remains apt as a cautionary tale given the current apathy regarding HIV. That is not, however, why *Straight Outta Compton* has been marketed as *au courant* and "a movie for our time." As the Universal Pictures press copy has it: "As they spoke the truth that no one had before and exposed life in the hood, their voice ignited a social revolution that is still reverberating today." The movie includes several scenes of vicious cops exerting force, talking smack, pushing everybody around, and the blood boils.

When the members of N.W.A. are forced to the ground and then toyed with as if by brats who tear the legs off spiders, just for standing outside the studio in which they are recording, you can see why they made "Fuck Tha Police." It's rude, even incendiary, but it makes its point. The song leads to threats from the FBI and a warning from local police before a show in Detroit: play that song and you're toast. A well-filmed riot ensues. (But were there really so many white people at those shows? I doubt it.) Thus do the authorities turn a protest song—and it *is* a great American protest song—into a *cause célèbre*. Now we're talking about free speech.

*Straight Outta Compton* and its "movie for our times" marketing are simultaneously significant and opportunistic. But if it intended to tap into the social unrest associated with the #blacklivesmatter movement and the killing of unarmed African-Americans, it surely didn't intend to tap into unrest over the perpetual verbal and physical violence against women. As for verbal abuse, the group has no shelter on that score—if the brunt of their songs isn't misogynist, then the word is devoid of meaning. And, as everybody who was listening to N.W.A. back in the day knew, long before he had earned legendary status, Dr. Dre beat up the music journalist Dee Barnes. (Incidentally, F. Gary Gray once served as cameraman for Barnes.) I lived in the boonies and I knew about it—I was 14 or 15, and we didn't have MTV or, of course, the internet yet—so it clearly wasn't some secret. Nobody stopped listening to N.W.A. because of it, myself included.

Days after the movie's premiere, Gawker hosted Barnes's eloquent essay about how she was hit, choked, and then blackballed from the rap industry. All she got out of that beatdown—aside from unshakeable migraines, a thwarted career, and the proverbial "undisclosed settlement" (she discloses it; it's not that much)—was a mention in a Dre-produced song by Eminem, who, as usual, thinks that hurt women are funny. At the time, Eazy and Ren said that she got what was coming to her, and a lot of people agreed. Now that the movie is out, and after a bit of an internet stink, Dre said that he was sorry he "hurt those women." (Plural noted.) Ice Cube, on the other hand, is frankly intransigent when it comes to saying "bitch," but then he's never been known actually to beat anybody.

Some say that the acts of pain perpetrated against the women in Dre's life should have been depicted in the film, but that doesn't make much dramatic sense. Those incidents didn't impact Dre's growing success or that of N.W.A. Either way, common sense says that you don't commission an altarpiece and insist on an unbiased representation. This is not just a biopic, but a vanity project, and that's not Monopoly money behind it. In its own way, the movie is honest about how the group saw women. By its end, each of the three principals has a wife or something like it. One of them even plays a role in the plot—she took accounting in college and uncovers fiscal shenanigans on Eazy's behalf—but it's hard to remember their names. As if to remind us that N.W.A. matured in a culture of top–down misogyny, there's that opening scene again. The cops come in with a batterram, a tank that knocks down doors. (The LAPD was avant-garde when it came to militarization.) It slams right into a woman's chest, clearly killing her, but she's just another bitch sent flying in the angel/ho cosmology.

After all, the real relationships in *Straight Outta Compton* are between men. The friendships are deep, which makes the inevitable dissensions sink in. The group's trajectory is a narrative cliché: they start from the bottom, get more and more famous, and money gets in the way. The source of the money problems is a manager named Jerry Heller (Paul Giamatti). He's a stock villain, a shifty Jew who also happens to have genuine principles, seemingly viewing the guys of N.W.A. as his friends, cash cows though they be. Perhaps surprisingly, the portrait of Heller and Eazy's relationship makes this movie. It's more ambivalent, loving, and rich than anyone could have expected. Where Eazy is honest, sweetly sardonic, and devoted, Heller is a shield, a mentor, and a surrogate father who lets him down in the end.

Under Heller's management, the members of N.W.A. get incredibly famous, which is a manager's job. Except for Eazy, they don't get incredibly paid, which is a manager's problem. Ice Cube is the first to defect, and eventually Dre gets fed up, too. Suge Knight, cofounder of Death Row Records, has been looming in the background and now, in a red zoot suit, he sweeps in like Lucifer. He first leeches onto The D.O.C., a rapper affiliated with N.W.A.'s label. This subplot will mean nothing to most people, and is included in the film as a pretext to build up Suge's treachery. The first, Dre-produced D.O.C. album is an underheard gem, though—he's better than a cheap plot point. Dre sets up shop in Suge's studio. This period marks the apotheosis of gangsta rap, as Snoop Dogg (the natural) and Tupac (the prophet) come on the scene.

*Straight Outta Compton* catches the sadomasochistic aspect of the genre. Suge is a dungeon master surrounded by evil cronies who mimic him in being big and bad. It's pushed to the edge of parody when Dre steps from the studio to find a handsome, buff man almost naked, down on all fours, being forced to grovel like a cur while guns are waved around. Everybody finds this incredibly funny except for Dre. As for the masochism, try living for a week on blunts and malt liquor and tell me how you feel: this seems to be the Death Row diet.

"Gangsta rap" is a complex term, but as far as fully dispensing with it, that cat's out of the bag. It's here to stay and is generically useful as far as it goes. Like that other rap epithet, the difference here between –ers and –az is vast. In laying the foundation for gangsta rap, did N.W.A. influence a bunch of dismal art? Sure, why not. "Oh, it's all bitches and hoes and money and cars." It's not, of course, *all* about that at all. But let's say that it was. Recall what G. K. Chesterton said: "It is too often forgotten that just as a bad man is nevertheless a man, so a bad poet is nevertheless a poet." In gangsta rap, one often finds the quintessential bad man—as in that "bad man Stagolee"—reciting a bad poem. "Not bad meaning bad, but bad meaning good?" It depends. There are astonishing songs in the genre.

Boneheaded moves are made in this movie. The foreshadowing is so heavy that you can hardly see your hand in front of your face. We know, for instance, within 30 minutes that Dre's sweet younger brother is going to die because he wants to tag along with big bro on tour but is rebuffed. But when the group huddles up around their broken comrade after he hears the tragic news, the loss feels real. Its veracity is not, however, helped along by Eazy placing his hand on those of the others and saying, "We'll always be brothers." You know right away that the very words will be hurled back in his face, like a thrown drink that took half an hour to mix. Then there are the portentous, preposterous moments when a character—first Eazy, then Suge, then Dre—names his respective music label. Time slows down, and the pregnant words are uttered: Ruthless, Death Row, Aftermath. What could possibly go wrong?

Biopics aren't really where you go for brilliant moviemaking, though, especially musical versions. The genius is already in the music, and to try to match that genius on film is somewhat redundant, if not impossible. From the innumerable lives of the great composers, to three tries at Stephen Foster, to the tortured jazz legends and the dead rock and rollers, they all end up bio-pictured. So far, hip-hop has *Notorious* (2009) and will soon see the long-gestating Tupac picture.

For now, though, we've got *Straight Outta Compton*, a movie that, despite its compromised provenance, deserves to have been made, not only for N.W.A.'s great songs and compelling story, but for how much fine art Dr. Dre and Ice Cube kept making after the group's demise. So "their voice ignited a social revolution that is still reverberating today"—is that the takeaway? Nope, that's just the best, most potent selling point appropriate to the moment. But N.W.A. was never meant to be "appropriate." They didn't make a revolution. They just made music that makes you angry and makes you think, songs that pump you up or put you down, art that makes us talk and speaks for itself and that's plenty.

# Melvillean Provocation and the Critical Art of Devotion

If an American writer has provoked a greater range of experimentation in criticism than Herman Melville, the difference could hardly be by much. These experiments constitute a loose tradition at least 60 years old, one which begins with Charles Olson's *Call Me Ishmael* (1947) and extends to such works as C. L. R. James's *Mariners, Renegades and Castaways* (1953), Paul Metcalf's *Genoa* (1965), Susan Howe's "Melville's Marginalia" (1993), Frank Lentricchia's *Lucchesi and the Whale* (2001), and K. L. Evans's *Whale!* (2003). Although as dissimilar as experiments should be, they have a few features in common. First is generic hybridity; they draw on the conventions of novels, poems, plays, memoirs, confessions, politics, polemic, psychological case studies, and literary criticism. Such hybridity is unsurprising, if we assume the gravitational pull on these authors of Melville, who tried different genres across discrete works as well as inside them, and whose most famous novel was once classified as a work of cetology.

To discuss such strange critical stuff as Melville provokes is to become entangled in a peculiar problem, which is the entanglement of the critic and the object of art. The writing on Melville under discussion here is extreme in this regard, an extremity that seems to be personal in nature. What makes it a matter of aesthetic interest are those cases in which this extreme personal relationship is manifest as a matter of style. In these cases we don't merely infer the extremity that provoked the work; rather, the work itself is embodied extremity. This stylistic embodiment of extremity takes up, grapples with, sinks under, and rises out of Melville's own aesthetics. Unlike Poe, for instance, to name another writer who has provoked intense responses, Melville (with one exception) made only scattered statements on the subject. As often as not, his aesthetic positions and concerns must be derived from his aesthetic practice. One of the advantages of reading Melville-inspired critical oddities is seeing in them Melville's often obscure aesthetic concerns mirrored more clearly, as if the reflecting glass had focusing powers. These concerns include the fundamental aesthetic dialectic of imitation and originality; the role of institutions as a perceived threat to art; and the connection of writing to mental and physical health and disease.

* * *

In a review of two scholarly books and a new edition of *Moby-Dick* published five years after the completion of *Call Me Ishmael*, Charles Olson writes that Melville "is not solely an instrument for use. It is one of the losses of all the critique and scholarship which I am reviewing that the totality of Melville's effort is not dealt with as one. And so the very extraordinary contribution Melville did make still stays obscured. By his impeccable and continuous inquiries into what ways ideality... no longer fit modern reality in a form proper to its content, he drove further than any of his predecessors toward forcing totality of effort to yield some principle out of itself." For a certain kind of critic, the "form" of criticism likely to be considered "proper" to the "content" of Melville's corpus is insufficient, if by propriety we mean reasoned and relatively objective argumentation manifest in what we can call an academic style. It is clear from the rough repetition in the above passage that Olson believes critics of Melville must model themselves not on academic models but on Melville's own achievement.

For Olson, an original totality must be mirrored by a critical totality in order to convey the truth of the original. Olson's engagement was not so literal as to need to mimic Melville's forms exactly, especially his poetic forms. Both in his criticism and his poetry, Olson exhibits formal and stylistic methods gleaned instead from what he describes as Melville's sense of (in Olson's orthography) "SPACE," his sense that there were "no barriers to contain as restless a thing as Western man was becoming." Melville, writes Olson, "wanted a god. Space was the First... Space and time were not abstraction but the body of Melville's experience." Thus are spatial and historical representation linked in *Call Me Ishmael*, and thus is Melville linked by Olson to the latter's own "Projective" aesthetics.

Alongside the abiding concern with how space and time might be embodied in writing, *Call Me Ishmael*—especially in its work on Melville's reading—is concerned with literary influence and paternity. In a chapter called "The book of the law of the blood," Olson writes a quartet of sentences that apply to Melville and to his own relation to Melville: "Melville was agonized over paternity. He suffered as a son. He had lost the source. He demanded to know the father." Ahab's literary originality is also figured in such terms by Olson, insofar as his "birth was dark, uncanonical." The book even begins with an epigraph pointing to the problem of paternity: "O fahter, fahter gone among / O eeys that loke / Loke, fahter: your sone!" This little poem enacts much of what Olson sees Melville enacting. The suffering son is evidenced in the initial cry, "O fahter, fahter," while the father's status as "lost source" is seen in "gone among." The "eeys that loke" seem at first to fulfil the son's demand to know the father, but it is important that the line in which they appear is a hinge in the poem, for the son also demands the impossible—that the absent father know him: "Loke, fahter: your sone!" The urge to acknowledge one's origins and at the same time to have one's own originality acknowledged is an aesthetic paradox informing all of *Call Me Ishmael*. Even the provenance of the above epigraph playfully treats what elsewhere is suffered over, as reported by the editors of Olson's *Collected Prose*, who reproduce an exchange regarding the epigraph's archaism: "Frances Boldereff wrote Olson, May 20, 1949, 'I love very deeply—the lines at the opening of *Call Me Ishmael*. Are they early Swedish?' A return letter of May 23, 1949, answered, 'They are early Olson.'"

If for Olson the final measure of success in writing about Melville is reproducing Melville's totality, then there is no other option than to fail. Yet from its invented epigraph to its bizarre and inaccurate table of contents to the contents themselves to a final sentence that not only names a prophet but partakes in the rhetoric of prophecy ("The son of the father of Ocean was a prophet Proteus, of the changing shape, who, to evade philistine Aristaeus worried about bees, became first a fire, then a flood, and last a wild sea beast"), *Call Me Ishmael* is a daring performance. In *Whale!*, a more recent book which embarks on an Ahab-like quest to rehabilitate Ahab, a quest that owes much to *Call Me Ishmael*, K. L. Evans argues that "one reason why poets such as [...] Charles Olson have proved adept at reading Melville is because their poetics—the art of making—construct valuables in the desert. The tools of trade in traditional scholarship are designed for finding, rather than making, its treasures. Such scholarship offers a sort of archaeology of literary merit; reconstructing the shape of a thing from traces of the past has come to be what we call cultural, intellectual work [ ... ] What we lose, along with the transient matter of paper or expression, are the affinities of motive and preoccupation." One way to recover those "affinities" is through aesthetic risk, or by trying to find that place where an imitation of Melville's style meets critical originality. Evans herself is self-conscious enough about this strategy to repeat her adoption of it: "I am not producing an account of these texts so much as adopting the style of their approach;" "I am not trying to produce an account of *Moby-Dick* so much as adopt the style of its approach." But such self-consciousness also suggests a paradox, for the distinction between "finding" and "making" is difficult to maintain, insofar as Evans "makes" her unconventional critical approach out of the style of approach she "finds" in Melville. The same could be said of Olson, and not to either's discredit.

In terms that mirror his own poetics as described in the important essay of 1950, "Projective Verse," Olson also asserts in *Call Me Ishmael* that for Melville to take "an attitude, [or] the creative vantage" in relation to America is to "see her as OBJECT in MOTION, something to be shaped, for use." Creativity is connected here to use. What Olson is evaluating is not the fact of use itself, which in itself is neither good nor bad, but rather *how* Melville is being used. In his prosimetrum "Letter for Melville 1951," a scathing and mournful attack spurred by the Melville Society's conference on the hundredth anniversary of *Moby-Dick*, Olson asks, "Can anything be clearer, than how Melville is being used?" Those nefarious uses by assorted professors include professional advancement and an excuse to congregate on a pretty college campus over Labor Day. The critics who also take Melville as object but instead take what Olson sees as "the creative vantage" do so in part because Melville's creative vantage is distinctively literary-critical, at least to hear Olson tell it: "Melville's reading is a gauge of him, at all points of his life. He was a skald, and knew how to appropriate the work of others. He read to write [ ... ] Melville's books batten on other men's books."

As we can see in the ways Olson deals with Melville in *Call Me Ishmael*—through the book's challenging structure; its typographical and historical strangeness; its unpredictable movement between narrative, argument, grand claims, anecdotal minutiae, conventional citation, and singular research—"creative use" is a kind of use that seems to risk something at the level of form and style. It is obviously idiosyncratic, maybe even a little unhinged. If it is deliberately so, then Olson is only acting out what he sees acted out in Melville: "He knew how to take a chance [ ... ] The man made a mess of things [ ... ] He had to be wild or he was nothing in particular [ ... ] He knew the cost if he let his imagination loose." It is especially telling that Olson singles out Melville's most significant work of literary criticism, his essay on Hawthorne, as "a document of Melville's rights and perceptions, his declaration of the freedom of a man to fail." Taking this reading as a touchstone, if Olson in *Call Me Ishmael* ultimately and necessarily fails to reproduce Melville's "totality of effort," in another sense his risking and achieving such failure is the very model of success, for it follows the risk-taking model of Melville and adheres to one of Melville's most explicit aesthetic positions.

The texts in the tradition of response we're mapping follow Melville and Olson not only in taking risks and risking failure, but also in their ambivalent relationship to the aesthetic dialectic of imitation and originality. This dialectic is related to the above discussion of use, insofar as such texts tend to use Melville by imitating what Evans calls Melville's "style of approach," and yet the imitation is part of an effort to make original criticism. In this as in other matters, Melville's more adventurous critics have learned from Melville himself. Take, for instance, *Pierre*, the novel that followed *Moby-Dick*, in which a painted portrait of Pierre Glendinning's father initiates the eponymous figure's fatal descent from devoted son, destined to marry the good girl Lucy, to depraved writer, running off with the servant girl Isabel, whom young Pierre comes to believe was fathered by his late sire in a youthful indiscretion. It is the painted portrait that solidifies his belief, for he sees there, in the eyes of his father, the eyes of Isabel. One way to read the portrait is to see it as an artifact in which an Aristotelian notion of imitation as pleasure and a Platonic notion of imitation as danger meet. Certainly the results of Pierre's seeing the portrait as a proper imitation are both full of pleasure and fraught with danger, the former rendered euphemistically (being sexual and incestuous), the latter melodramatically. The relationship to imitation in *Pierre* is, to say the least, highly ambivalent.

This is addressed by Melville in Pierre's burning of the portrait. The problem with imitation for the writer, after all, is that it keeps him from being his own man. It means he has been fathered; the alternative is to be orphaned, or rather, to orphan oneself. Neither option is satisfying. In fact, being orphaned doesn't change the fact that you were fathered. It is no coincidence that Pierre can only truly go off on his own in order to make it as a writer once he has burned his father's portrait. And yet the problem is also that one can only assert one's originality against what is indisputably, chronologically original. Pierre *needs* the imitative portrait to spur his own attempt at originality, as heard in the exclamations that attend its burning: "'Now all is done, and all is ashes! Henceforth, cast-out Pierre hath no paternity, and no past; and since the Future is one blank to all; therefore, twice-disinherited Pierre stands untrammeledly his ever-present self!—free to do his own self-will and present fancy to whatever end!'" Melville's tackling of the matter in *Pierre* is no surprise, given the novel's status as what Sacvan Bercovitch calls "a major text not only in but about American literary history." If the treatment is oblique, this indirection points not to lack of interest, but to how deeply problems of imitation and originality are ingrained in Melville's entire conception of the status of the writer (especially the American writer) as both fathered figure and self-made orphan.

Leo Bersani hits the nail on the head by seeing orphanhood as central to Melville's idea of the American writer, which is also to say, his ideas of country, vocation, and self. "Should America be orphaned?" asks Bersani. "Can you become an orphan if you already know who your parents are? Put in these terms, the problems inherent in the resolve of nineteenth-century American writers to forge a great national literature freed from parental European influence may begin to seem not merely grave but unsolvable." Bersani also quotes the stunning passage from "Hawthorne and His Mosses" that begins, "But it is better to fail in originality, than to succeed in imitation," and ends, "Let us boldly contemn all imitation, though it comes to us graceful and fragrant as the morning; and foster all originality, though, at first, it be crabbed and ugly as our own pine knots." And when Melville, in chapter 44 of *The Confidence Man*, one of his most explicit discussions of the aesthetic problem of originality, says, "certainly, the sense of originality exists at its highest in an infant," we know that that sense would be heightened still more if that infant were an orphan.

Another consideration of the dilemma occurs in a book with its own fair share of meta-moments that give us insight into Melville's aesthetics. In his third novel, *Mardi*, the narrator exclaims: "And if it harder be than e'er before to find new climes, when now our seas have oft been circled by ten thousand prows, much more the glory!" Safe to say, this exclamation need not be taken to speak only of maritime exploration. The best-known moment of meta-commentary in *Mardi* is probably the extended episode in which the philosopher Babbalanja, the historian Mohi, the minstrel Yoomy, and the two kings, Abrazza and Media, discuss the epic poem of the isle of Mardi, a work called the *Koztanza* by a poet named Lombardo. The scene is full of talk of the relevance of the past to great authors, a scene set by King Abrazza, "who loved his antique ancestors, and loved old times, and would not talk of moderns." The conversation quickly turns to "old Homeric bards" and then to the *Koztanza*, which the King deems a "curious work, a very curious work."

Among the members of the group, it is Babbalanja who best knows the epic and its history. Early in the scene, then, prompted by a question from Media about what "originally impelled Lombardo to the undertaking," Babbalanja embarks on a tangent that touches the heart of the matter:

> We have had vast developments of parts of men, but none of manly wholes. Before a full-developed man, Mardi would fall down and worship. We are idiot, younger sons of gods, begotten in dotages divine; and our mothers all miscarry. Giants are in our germs, but we are dwarfs staggering under heads overgrown. Heaped, our measures burst. We die of too much life… We are full of ghosts and spirits; we are as graveyards full of buried dead that start to life before us. And all our dead sires, verily, are in us; *that* is their immortality. From sire to son, we go on multiplying corpses in ourselves, for all of which are resurrections. Every thought's a soul of some past poet, hero, sage. We are fuller than a city. Woe it is that reveals these things.

This is no happy admission of authorial belatedness; one suspects, given the ghoulish and morbid language, that not only Babbalanja, but also Melville, would have the situation be otherwise. In addition to declaring that "of ourselves, and in ourselves, we originate nothing," Babbalanja cites with approval a seemingly contradictory passage from Lombardo's autobiography: "'I have created the creative.'" One must, I can only imagine, have such moments of pragmatic forgetfulness to get great writing done. Perhaps the truer truth, however, is hinted at in a sentence uttered by Babbalanja that is all the more astonishing for its harsh and pregnant brevity: "Genius is full of trash."

It is impossible to say why this matter has such pride of place in the texts that follow Olson, but reasonable to think that such critics might have been doubly troubled insofar as they followed both Olson *and* Melville. No fathers are fully slain and non-mastery is the lived experience, as Paul Metcalf, in particular, knew quite well. For not only was Metcalf, as a poet, in an artistic lineage which includes Olson as a towering figure, he was also a family relation of Melville's. His mother, Eleanor Melville Metcalf, was Melville's granddaughter, a source of help to many early Melville scholars and the author of her own book about Melville. Along with her husband, Henry, she "very nearly adopted Olson during Olson's student years;" in a "note of thanks" deep into *Call Me Ishmael*, Olson writes that as far as Eleanor and Henry are concerned, "the Shakespeare was only a beginning"—they had provided him with Melville's own copy—"for they have made all Melville's things mine, indeed have made me a member of their family." Thus was Metcalf also in a "familial" relation to Olson.

Of all writers, Metcalf could thus be said to have a natural right to treat the topic. And indeed, in the opening of his novel-cum-critical-analysis *Genoa*, the narrator, Michael Mills, introduces his father, Paul B. Mills, as a man, a myth, a mere hindrance: "He would never tell us what the B. stood for." The true fathers in the book are Melville and Columbus, excerpts from whose writings make up half of *Genoa*'s bulk. The two men are linked in the mind of Michael Mills as explorers, and for him their various explorations provoke both exhilaration and depredation. If in *Moby-Dick*, for *Genoa*'s narrator Michael, "[c]ertain it is that Melville performed an act original and radical to himself," it is also certain that there is a connection between Melville and the figure that motivates *Genoa*'s plot, Michael's brother Carl, a troubled man who has seen and done unpalatable things and who is also obsessed with Melville. "I began to wonder when in his career he had read so much Melville," Michael writes, "read him so well that he had memorized whole passages. Or perhaps he had never actually read him [ ... ] maybe Melville, as history, had impressed himself into the fiber and cells of which Carl was made, had become part of his makeup." This passage occurs during Carl's declamations in a madhouse. If that "as history" is superfluous, it is because Metcalf has made it deeply clear by this point in the novel that there is little distinction between the terms "Melville," "history," and "family" in the narrator's mind. Carl even looks like the great white whale. But then Michael, who has a clubfoot, is a sort of an Ahab.

To find in their own characters analogues in the characters of Melville may seem like the most brazen form of imitation, but as Bersani writes, for Melville, "analogy authenticates originality." Frank Lentricchia's character Thomas Lucchesi rightly describes Melville as "addicted to the analogical habit." In *Mariners, Renegades and Castaways,* James follows it by seeing in Ahab an analogue for Hitler; he opens the book with a discussion of Nazism and Communism, speculating that Hitler would have ultimately become communist, and then concludes: "It is now that we can see in his full stature Ahab, embodiment of the totalitarian type." And in "Melville's Marginalia," Susan Howe sees in Bartleby a predecessor figure, an analogue, and in doing so makes a new Bartleby.

The epiphanic story of Howe's encounter with marginalia begins when she "saw the penciled trace of Herman Melville's passage through John Mitchel's introduction [to *Poems by James Clarence Mangan*] and knew by shock of poetry telepathy the real James Clarence Mangan is the progenitor of fictional Bartleby." Suffice it to say that "poetry telepathy" is not the strongest leg on which to stand in the average critical argument. Nevertheless, and despite the fact that Howe does go on to argue her case in more conventional ways—for instance, the work of Mangan would have been widely known in Melville's circles immediately prior to his writing of "Bartleby"—or through the assertion of linguistic echo—for instance, Mangan and Bartleby both use the word "stationary"—poetry telepathy in this case is fairly convincing.

"Melville's Marginalia" is about Melville imitating in Bartleby aspects of Mangan that resulted in the creation of an original character. It is also about Howe imitating aspects of Olson to original effect. The variety of typography, the use of the page as a field, the combination of "lyric" moments with discursive passages and historical anecdotes, the transformation of oneself into a character within the Melville matrix: these features her poem shares with

Olson's work. But the poem is her own; she writes there of a limitation that is ultimately overcome: "On earth I guess / I am bound by a definition of criticism." On earth that definition is inextricable from rational argument and institutional prerogatives, including the prerogative, as Howe sees it, to marginalize certain writers from the past (Mangan, "the man with the name so remarkably like *margin*") or, closer to home, the tendency to marginalize students. If the poem's titular link to Olson, who helped bring Melville's marginalia to scholarly light, can be inferred through method and style, Howe explains another, more direct link in expository prose; for the main source of the poem's title lies in the work of a late, little-known scholar, Wilson Walker Cowen, work that has become known by passing through other hands: "The extracts in *Melville's Marginalia* were collected, transcribed, and collated by a dedicated sub-sub-graduate student in a time before librarians, scholars, and authors relied on computers or Xerox machines. Perhaps his leviathan-dissertation exhausted him."

If the explicitness of the poem's critique of how professional and institutional prerogatives can be harmful both to the person and to their art is unique in the tradition I am mapping, the critique itself is not. Melville again is a model—think of his perverse relationship to the perversities of professional publishing; of Ishmael, whose whaleship was his Harvard or Yale, a profession weighed against two institutions; of Bartleby, preferring not to, to the point of professional then actual death; of "hate-shod" Pierre, prepared to murder, with a letter from his publisher under his shoe.

Olson, too, is a model—Robert Creeley writes that Olson's "attack" on critics who to his mind badly used Melville "is a constant throughout the early *Maximus Poems* and in others [such] as 'Letter for Melville 1951,' wherein all the accumulated anger prompted by such misappropriation finds a voice… Such perverse professionalism is a condition he attacks all his life, in every possible context." James ends *Mariners* with a blistering first-person critique of other institutions, the U.S. Departments of Immigration and of Justice, the latter accused of "violating the most elementary principles of justice," the former "in its policy-making echelons ridden with national arrogance." In *Lucchesi and the Whale*, Lentricchia's critically exegetical and critically ill fantasia on the hazards of being a writer, Thomas Lucchesi—described as an "obscure American novelist," a "rumored writer," a "relentless reader," a "recessed bachelor," and "the Scrooge-Christ of Art"—is obsessed with Melville and shares with him many obsessions. (One of these is the obsession with orphanhood.) He is also relegated to the special anonymity reserved for the recently unemployed. A teacher as well as a writer, Lucchesi is fired as a professor after one too many inappropriate remarks.

As in Howe's poem, the sense is pervasive in *Lucchesi* that academic institutions, as well as the arguments they value, fail the one who wants really to *know* Melville's work. Despite, or rather because of "subject[ing]" his students "to repeated and strenuous exercise in deep aesthetic immersion," nobody at the university sticks out his neck to retain Lucchesi. Under the heading "Advanced Moral Turpitude," which follows "Moral Turpitude 101," Lucchesi addresses the campus through a statement published in its student newspaper. (His own marginal relation as a creative writer to the institution at large is emphasized by the fact that the place is named "Central.") The crucial sentence of that statement I take to be the following: "In the hour of my need, my students, like the administrators, showed no concern whatsoever for my terrible Melville troubles." Nor does criticism as understood by the administrators and the indoctrinated students offer solace for those troubles. Making sustained arguments based on "the deadly territory of 'the example,'" for example, is for Lucchesi beneath contempt; naturally, however, he cannot help himself from making such arguments. This despite the fact that, as he notes parenthetically, "when I cite and explain examples I become sad, even nauseous, and my syntax goes down the toilet." That is to say, a certain kind of criticism makes him sick.

Plato called poets the imitative tribe; it was meant as a warning, a suggestion of the danger of representing *this* as *that*. Melville courts that danger, but is wary of imitation insofar as it weds him to his predecessors and compromises his originality (the stance of "Hawthorne and His Mosses"); at other times, he is wary of imitating popular forms for financial reasons (*Mardi* is the beginning of the record of this wariness, *Pierre* its climax, the decades of verse its denouement). And yet, in another mood, Melville can praise Greek architecture while also warning against a misapprehension of what constitutes originality: "Not innovating willfulness, / But reverence for the Archetype."

These vacillations are not *easy* ones in Melville, nor have they tended to be so in the critics under discussion and the characters they create. (Lucchesi's sickness over imitating academic forms of argumentation is exemplary in this regard.) Insofar as the dialectic of imitation and originality is central to what Bersani calls the "representation of Melville's America," then this dialectic is "inseparable from a crisis of meaning [ ... ] The interpretive faculty is associated with madness." This mad-making interpretive crisis has carried over to the critics; unsurprisingly, for texts that try stylistically to "embody" Melville's aesthetics, this crisis is often embodied as literally as possible, as manifest in a crisis of the brain and the body. If, as Terry Eagleton says, "aesthetics is born as a discourse of the body," in most of the creative responses to Melville this creation story of aesthetics is told as a story of a body wracked by deformity, illness, and insanity.

The narrator of Metcalf's *Genoa* is club-footed, as mentioned, while his brother Carl has a "monstrous, out-shapen head," just one in a "series of unique medical phenomena." A central figure of Howe's "Melville's Marginalia," Mangan, is characterized as "a spectral creature on a ladder" with "blanched hair / [that] was totally unkempt[,]" one with "corpse-like features" who was "no / stranger to hospitals" and who died of starvation; another, Cowen, is portrayed as having been worked to death. Evans begins *Whale!* with a preface by a "glaciologist" who calls the author a "queer fish among critics" and writes in her acknowledgements that she "was pushing a project, a rude, rough-cut kind of literary criticism that encouraged an 'unhealthy' proximity to its subject." And the eponymous Thomas of *Lucchesi* is "in between medical appointments, and Barnes-and-Noble happens to be located in between." This final citation, with its medico-literary chiasmus, carves in allegorical space the connection in these writings between deprivation, disability, or infirmity and a writer's body of writing in a world inhospitable to it.

The most extreme text under discussion in this regard is the book by James. For most of its seven chapters, *Mariners, Renegades, and Castaways* is closer to straightforward criticism than is the work of Olson and the others, as James steadily advances his thesis that "Melville's theme is totalitarianism, its rise and fall, its power and weakness." Around the fifth chapter, however, called "Neurosis and the Intellectuals," James writes that Melville, unlike Freud, found that the "preoccupation with personality" was "not human nature but disease, a horrible sickness." Both Ishmael and Pierre, he writes, "are sick to the heart with the modern sickness." This theme seems to pass, but in the final chapter, it re-emerges with a vengeance—only now it is James himself who is sick. The book's finale is an astonishing account of James's internment on Ellis Island awaiting trial on immigration charges. He had been contemplating writing a book on Melville when he "was arrested by the United States Government and sent to Ellis Island to be deported" back to his native Trinidad. His situation remade the nascent book:

> What form it might have taken had I written it according to my original plans I do not know. But what matters is that I am not an American citizen [ ... ] My case had been up for nearly five years. It had now reached the courts, and there would be some period before a final decision was arrived at. I therefore actually began the writing of this book on the Island, some of it was written there, what I did not write there was conceived and worked over in my mind there. And in the end I finally came to the conclusion that my experiences there have not only shaped this book, but are the most realistic commentary I could give on the validity of Melville's ideas today.

Of all the experiences on the island that led James to the critique of bureaucratic and institutional cruelty and incompetence, as well as those that led him to a deeper understanding of Melville, none was more formative (or receives more pages of treatment) than his experience of suffering from a duodenal ulcer while incarcerated. In great detail James recounts his horrible condition, one exacerbated by institutional contempt or disinterest. At times one forgets one is reading a book about Melville, but then, as James writes, echoing Olson, "I believe my total experience should be told."

If Melville's critics create characters who embody problems with the body, or make themselves characters in a Melvillean story of authorial affliction, it is in part because of Melville's having done so:

> My cheek blanches white while I write, I start at the scratch of my pen, my own mad brood of eagles devours me, fain would I unsay this audacity, but an iron-mailed hand clenches mine in a vice and prints down every letter in my spite. Fain would I hurl

off this Dionysius that rides me; my thoughts crush me down till I groan; in far fields I hear the song of the reaper while I slave and faint in this cell. The fever runs through me like lava; my hot brain burns like a coal; and like many a monarch, I am less to be envied than the veriest hind in the land.

So goes a message from the narrator of *Mardi*. At one point in *Genoa*, Metcalf cites a passage from Melville relevant to us now: "Strange! That so many of those who would fain minister to our own health should look so much like invalids themselves." Of course, and again citing Metcalf citing Melville, for the critic hunting the big game of aesthetic satisfaction and total response, "one's malady becomes [one's] most desired health." Lucchesi, connecting writerly pain and bodily suffering, says of Melville that he is "gravely ill with the disease of literary love." In an essay on *Pierre*, Stephen Rachman argues that "Melville considered professional writing disease-like, subjecting the practitioner to morbid stimulation." One may also quote in this regard another writer influenced by Melville, Norman Mailer, who speaks of existential and physiological facts together:

> Writing a novel over two or three years of the hardest work sometimes does the kind of damage to the body that is equal to obliging someone who has never smoked before to consume two or three packs a day for months. In reaction, I think, I've become an interested amateur about medicine; when you are a writer, you are, in a certain sense, doctor to yourself. You can always feel tensions and ailments creeping into you… [Y]ou become alert to the relation not only between yourself and other people but between yourself and your body. Writing impinges on that body; writing depends ultimately on that body.

I would add as pure speculation that not only does the writer become aware of the body; the writer also becomes aware that what he is writing is itself a kind of a body. If the work or the *corpus* is a body then there is no reason that it shouldn't be sick. Why? Because—before a body can get better, it has to be sick.

"Woe it is that reveals these things." So said Babbalanja in *Mardi* when discoursing on how our originality is compromised by those "corpses in ourselves," aesthetic woe figured as bodily fact. Just as the uneasy vacillations between imitation and originality consume and help make Melville the Melville we know, so too do the hard swerves between sickness and health. In an essay on Nietzsche, Gilles Deleuze tracks a similar vacillation. Nietzsche, he writes, "saw in illness a *point of view* on health; and in health, a *point of view* on illness [ ... ] Thus movement from health to sickness, from sickness to health, if only as an idea, this very mobility is the sign of superior health [ ... ] As long as Nietzsche could practice the art of shifting perspectives, from health to illness and back, he enjoyed, sick as he may have been, the 'great health' that made his work possible." Nietzsche himself, under the respective headings "Value of illness" and "Usefulness of sickliness," described in *Human, All Too Human* the pragmatics of such mobility:

> The man who lies ill in bed sometimes discovers that what he is ill from is usually his office, his business or his society and that through them he has lost all circumspection with regard to himself: he acquires this wisdom from the leisure to which his illness has compelled him.
>
> He who is often sick does not only have a much greater enjoyment of health on account of the frequency with which he gets well: he also has a greatly enhanced sense of what is healthy and what sick in works and actions, his own and those of others: so that it is precisely the sickliest writers, for example—and almost all the great writers are, unfortunately, among them—who usually evidence in their writings a much steadier and more certain tone of health.

Such a writer, too, is Pierre, who in contemplating his progenitors Dante and Hamlet is driven to sickness and mad despair as he finds the gloom in the light and the light in the gloom: "Now indeed did all the fiery floods in the *Inferno*, and all the rolling gloom in *Hamlet* suffocate him at once in flame and smoke. The cheeks of his soul collapsed in him: he dashed himself in blind fury and swift madness against the wall, and fell dabbling in the vomit of his loathed identity." The identity of the writer—it is split, and ever in motion. We are following Melville's model when we see the movement between sickness and health as analogous to and inextricable from the movement between imitation and originality. That the tradition of response to these aspects of Melville's aesthetics should be embodied in hybrid texts displaying formal and stylistic mobility finally comes as no surprise—an antidote, pleasure, and partial cure, perhaps, but surely not a surprise.

# John Ashbery's Harvard Education, 1945–1949

A few years after John Ashbery, Class Poet of 1949, graduated from Harvard University, William Bentinck-Smith wrote that, like it or not, "any entering Harvard freshman is subject to what might be called collegiate predestination [...] The Harvard man is bound to be thought something he is not and that handicap should have some subconscious effect on his writing." Ashbery, with his associative skeins of language, is celebrated for his "subconscious effect" as a writer, and his potential for success in that vocation was already evident when he got to college in the fall of 1945. But no success is assured and, as Bentinck-Smith wisely warns, "Harvard has had its Ella Wheeler Wilcoxes as well as its Shelleys." Before he is counted among the Shelleys, let us recall that John Ashbery is the only Harvard man to have published his own "Variations, Calypso, and Fugue on a Theme of Ella Wheeler Wilcox."

Ashbery was a prodigious imitator and borrower and a reader of catholic taste. Evidence of the reading he did for his undergraduate classes often crops up in his poetry. As a junior at Harvard he took English 130b ("Metaphysical Poets: Donne to Marvell") from Professor Douglas Bush, the great humanist whose province was practically all of English poetry and expository prose, and whose fabled memory held intact all 11,000 lines of *Paradise Lost*. For his paper "Nature Images in the Poetry of Vaughan and Marvell," Ashbery earned an A-minus, but his reading of Marvell led, in 1951, to his own "The Picture of Little J. A. in a Prospect of Flowers," after Marvell's pastoral of virtually the same name, and to the beautiful first poem of *Self-Portrait in a Convex Mirror* (1975), "As One Put Drunk into the Packet-Boat," whose title comes from the first line of Marvell's verse satire in heroic couplets, "Tom May's Death."

The young Ashbery was also taught by the formidable F. O. Matthiessen, whose *American Renaissance* (1941) arguably remains the major study of mid-nineteenth century American literature. Ashbery wrote on Wallace Stevens for Matthiessen's course, English 278 ("Twentieth Century American Poetry"), in addition to producing a precis for an anthology of W. H. Auden and Marianne Moore that shows how widely he had read in the work of those two poets. His breadth in the latter assignment is balanced by moments of almost indifferent critical precision ("the 'idea' is in most cases a sort of Christmas tree on which Miss Moore hangs her wonderful objects") characteristic of his later criticism. Sadly, two years after Ashbery took the class, Matthiessen took his own life by jumping from a window. In his book *On the Outside Looking Out*, John Shoptaw implies that Ashbery's poem "Illustration" (written in the fall of 1950), in which a "novice [ ... ] on a cornice" drifts "softly downward / Out of the angels' tenderness and the minds of men," is in part a response to the death of his erstwhile teacher.

Ashbery's Harvard curriculum ultimately benefited from an institutional change that took place after his freshman year. In 1946-47 "Comparative Literature" first appeared, alphabetically nestled between "Classics" and "Comparative Philology." The new department, chaired by then-Associate Professor Harry Levin, was an addition that surely facilitated Ashbery's continental interests. He enrolled in Levin's Comp. Lit. 161 ("Proust, Joyce, and Mann") in the fall of 1948, and the next semester tried Comp. Lit. 251, Associate Professor Renato Poggioli's class on "European Romanticism." Poggioli had yet to publish his important *Teoria dell'arte d'avanguardia* (1962), but it is fascinating to imagine the transplanted Italian teaching the young American, whose criticism and poetry both show signs of having benefited from Poggioli's historical understanding of radical aesthetic traditions.

In a review essay written for Poggioli on Arthur Symons's *The Romantic Movement in English Poetry*, Ashbery offers a criticism of Symons that some detractors might apply to Ashbery's own work: "The fault of this book may be its all-inclusiveness." This criticism is then recuperated as a compliment, however, for though the author "discusses a great many poets who deserve to be forgotten," he is "witty or just, as the occasion demands, and often a minor poet [ ... ] becomes the grain of sand around which Mr. Symons secretes a pearl of critical insight which may have a far wider application than the importance of the poetry would seem to indicate." With a mere change of names, this remark could serve as an accurate description of the Norton Lectures delivered by Ashbery at Harvard some forty years later. Those lectures, published as *Other Traditions* (2000), lovingly discuss six minor writers important to his poetry.

Ashbery's presence in Levin's class on Proust, Joyce, and Mann is also intriguing, for not only was Ashbery being instructed there by a worldly and masterful critic on the work of three masters of Modernist prose, but he was also being graded by a graduate student teaching fellow, John Simon, who would go on to become a critic in his own right. And as a critic, Simon has undervalued Ashbery. In a 1962 review of Ashbery's second volume, *The Tennis Court Oath*, Simon declares it "non-poetry" of "not even honest free association," and says of Ashbery (along with Kenneth Koch and Barbara Guest), in a judgement that has not held up well, that "these abstract expressionists in words are every bit as undistinguished and indistinguishable as their confreres of the drip, dribble and squirt." Simon continues to denounce the poet in print, writing in a recent essay that Ashbery has "never written a single poem of any importance." This critical antipathy, if it existed during Simon's and Ashbery's Harvard days—the two were widely published in *The Harvard Advocate*, twice together in the same issue—did not affect Simon's objectivity as a grader. For although, in the margins of an Ashbery paper on *Remembrance of Things Past*, Simon chastises the younger student for referring to Proust's Odette as a "stupid woman," Ashbery ultimately received an A from him in Levin's class.

The labyrinthine, soporific subordinations of Proust have often been named as a source for Ashbery's dreamy lines, another reason the course with Levin is of special interest. Other of his courses relate in more general ways to his subsequent career. For years Ashbery earned money as an art critic, writing reviews for the *Paris Herald Tribune*, *ARTnews*, *New York*, and *Newsweek*; his criticism was collected in *Reported Sightings: Art Chronicles 1957-1987*. For the final of "Modern Art," a course which he took early in his undergraduate career, Ashbery wrote in part on Picasso, which perhaps paved the way for a comparison made in his senior honours thesis on "The Poetic Medium of W. H. Auden." Ashbery there writes that Auden "does not have periods in the sense an artist like Picasso does; he has merely gone on steadily improving his original gifts."

As an undergraduate essayist, Ashbery exhibited what might be called spiritual concerns in tones mixing irony with melancholy. For a course on "The Epic" taught by the renowned classicist John Huston Finley, Ashbery in a paper on the "Modern Implications of Dante's *Inferno*" notes with nostalgia that "though we know that the earth revolves around the sun, we are worse off than Dante, for we cannot make the fact significant." Like many an undergraduate, Ashbery was flirting with the insignificance of belief, a game of wilful diminishment instigated here in confrontation with Dante's powerful vision of Hell: "Nowadays sin has disappeared; we regard it as an object for pity or curiosity [ ... ] Those of us who reject sin do so on moral grounds." And though this rejection of sin is deemed moral, it is a morality grounded not in holiness, but in modernity's self-satisfying altruism—a heady sentiment made almost funny in the prolixity and local colour of Ashbery's summary, oratorical statement: "Therefore if we practice stern morals without true faith let us never assume that we are thus rendered holier than the Australian bushman, but recognize that the good for which we toil is society's, and ultimately, our own."

The voice in these essays is not significantly different from the voice in Ashbery's mature criticism: the sophisticated nonchalance, the ease of accurate evaluation, the sense that we are in the midst of a strong, if open, sensibility. But the real interest in his academic labours lies in the light they might shed on the poetry of his adulthood. The same, of course, is more or less true of Ashbery's undergraduate poems, most of which illuminate in their relative weakness the strength of the poems of his maturity.

Just as the young Ashbery's intellectual interests were served by the establishment of a Comparative Literature department, and by being instructed by some of the era's great scholars of English and American literature, his needs as a budding poet were served by the re-establishment of the *Advocate*. The University's preeminent literary magazine had endured "a wartime lapse of almost four years," as it explained, but resumed publication in the spring of 1947. The propitious beginning again gave Ashbery a campus forum, and he placed a poem in the "new" *Advocate*'s first issue. While the *Advocate* was not the first magazine to feature Ashbery's work, it at least featured his work together with his name. As David Lehman tells it in *The Last Avant-Garde*, two of Ashbery's high school poems appeared in *Poetry* magazine in November 1945. A classmate of Ashbery's, unbeknownst to him, had copied his poems, given them a pseudonymous source, and placed them with Deerfield Academy's poet-in-residence, who was impressed and sent them to *Poetry*, where they were published as "Lost Cove" and "Poem," by one "John Michael Symington."

The first poem Ashbery published in the *Advocate*, "A Sermon: Amos 8:11-14," shares a concern with his essay on Dante. There he had pondered the divine father figure with suspicious breeziness: "God has come to be a just, scholarly man in spectacles; difficult to persuade but in most respects very like ourselves. We do not think about him very much." In "A Sermon," he took as his text a Biblical passage in which God is very much on the minds of those denied access to Him. The poem's epigraph from Amos reads: "And they shall wander from sea to sea, and from the north even to the east; they shall run to and fro to seek the word of Jehovah, and shall not find it. In that day shall the fair virgins and the young men faint for thirst." The "sermon" on this text involves primarily a series of injunctions, which perhaps led Ashbery to consider it an appropriate selection for the class poem of 1949. One wonders whether his classmates took to heart the alternately sensible and strange suggestions of the first two stanzas: "In this land travel light / And lightly: keep rude hands from sight / Nor with speech design fidelities. / Break vows as fagots: ignore / Promises, prayers, lusting before the door, / Nor press the sinning Tartar to his knees. // Move as water: soon gone / Lightly girdling the dry stone. / Touch nothing long: involve / Nothing ever. Your fate and history / Meet in geometry / And in radiant law dissolve."

Of his thirteen contributions to the *Advocate*, one ("Fête Galante") is a prose piece of conscious banality, slightly alienating, of the kind that would show up scattered in fragments throughout *The Tennis Court Oath*. It is a well-written imitation with no show of virtuosity, as it mimics the romance genre's false enthusiasms ("The eightieth birthday of Andrew E. Wylie! That old reprobate still alive! Imagine!"), its heavy-petting dialogue, and its description purpled by bruising similes:

> "Darling," somebody says, and wraps her in a pair of strong arms. His mouth descends over hers like absolute night.
> "Oh stop," Lucy says presently, "You don't know how physically revolting you are to me."

Otherwise, Ashbery's *Advocate* contributions (apart from a collaged cover he co-designed) are more or less formal poems, usually featuring rhyme and regular stanzas. In addition to his exegetical "Sermon," he attempts two elegies (one titled "Elegy," the other, using a variation on Tennyson's *In Memoriam* stanza, titled "Grandma"); "A Fable"; a kind of ironic eclogue ("A Perfect Orange"); several almost-but-not-quite-covert love poems, like "For A European Child," in which "[t]he conceit, pulled tight as a mask across // The obvious bone, altered but could not hide / Love's aching premise"; a surrealistic "Song From a Play"; and lilting trivialities like "Waltz King," in which Ashbery's dactyls recall the dance of his title's one-two-three, one-two-three: "Roses whirled up from the south." If reconciling this young formalist modernist with the later practitioner of postmodern free verse seems too difficult, perhaps the best solution is to cite the young Ashbery himself, from his senior honours thesis: "It seems unnecessary to discuss in detail Auden's metrical innovations [and] his rhyme schemes; in *Poems* he uses as many different forms as possible, which signifies in most cases merely juvenile high spirits."

Ashbery's early poems are often precious (a none-too-damning flaw in a young poet), and are too tightly controlled to allow room for the metaphysical drift of thought that characterizes his most wonderful work. Yet they manage to be both obscure and aestheticized without being off-putting. For all the differences from the later work, the early poems also contain in kernel many of Ashbery's most recognizable features, like romantic pathos filtered through the mind: "And the departure of love does not / Happen on this planet, it is a kind of action / Not permitted by the imagination." Or, as in this reworking of the auctioneer's call or the flight of a home-run ball, his democratic facility for transforming our clichés: "Foregoing, foregoing, / It seems we have foregone[.]" His early work even includes an *ars poetica* that gives an opaque but poignant peek at his ultimate *raison d'être* as a writer. In "Some Trees," his first volume's eponymous poem and the best poem of his Harvard career, Ashbery, as Harold Bloom writes, "had found already his largest aesthetic principle, the notion that every day the world consented to be shaped into a poem." It is this generous and hopeful aesthetic that helps place Ashbery among the great American poets, and the fact that this aesthetic was made explicit from his writerly beginning is just short of astonishing.

In "Some Trees," Ashbery perhaps came too easily to what he calls there the "comeliness" of the world—though that kind of ease is surely the rightful province of the young. He would move from such gentle homiletics to the destruction of *The Tennis Court Oath*, before reaching his characteristic astute expansiveness. And yet young Ashbery's trees truly "are amazing," as they try to tell us "that their merely being there / Means something; that soon / We may touch, love, explain." The early poems and papers of Ashbery are revelatory not for their precocious brilliance (though some, like "Some Trees" and his thesis on Auden, are highly accomplished), but for their prophetic status. The hints of the future therein, coupled with Ashbery's later creations of genius, give them the glow of importance. With a little digging, these historical curiosities can be touched, loved, and explained. As for the trees to which the poet referred, you can still see some of them in Harvard Yard today.

## NOTE:

The citations of Ashbery's critical prose are from the Ashbery Papers, AM6 (Box 31, E), Houghton Library of the Harvard College Library. Citations of Ashbery's undergraduate poems are from the *Harvard Advocate*, vols. CXXX–CXXXIL.

# Genteel Versifiers

The genteel tradition in American letters spans the years between the "American Renaissance" of the mid-19th century and that period marked by the movement toward literary realism and modernist experimentation that came to fruition in the early decades of the 20th. This "Indian summer of the mind," as one writer termed it, seems conservative and sometimes cloying to readers of our era, just as it often did to those realists and modernists whose artistic practice and aesthetic theories helped supplant it. Yet the genteel versifiers of the period wrote much that remains of interest. Their facility for traditional forms commands respect; devoted craftsmen, they were models of poetic labour, if not of unique inspiration or personal vision. A generic idealism leads much genteel verse into abstraction, and in such work an approach is favoured that militates against the subjective insight we post-Romantics tend to value in poetry. The genteel poets, however, played an important role in the development of a national literature. Not only did their commitment to the art of verse sustain much of the momentum gained by their true native progenitors, the Fireside Poets; their work as anthologists, editors, and critics also gave voice to the American aspect of a late-Victorian milieu. In diverse ways these now-maligned figures served the growth of American writing, both as negative example and positive force.

The term "genteel tradition" gained its prominence through the writings of George Santayana. In such essays as "The Genteel Tradition in American Philosophy" (1911), "Genteel American Poetry" (1915), and "The Genteel Tradition at Bay" (1931), Santayana described a dominant mode of American mental life and culture. The original basis for this genteel way of being—namely, Calvinism—had always been present in American life; yet as the 19th century progressed, and as Calvinism merged with Transcendentalism, Santayana, writing from the 20th century, found that "the hereditary philosophy has grown stale, and that the academic philosophy afterwards developed has caught the stale odor from it." Indeed, many aspects of American intellectual life seemed stale to Santayana. For example, writing of how the "agonized conscience" that Calvinism originally expressed was being denied available outlets, the philosopher-poet (and Spanish-American Catholic) remarks that "when a genteel tradition forbids people to confess that they are unhappy, serious poetry and profound religion are closed to them by that." The genteel tradition thus described was abstract, enervated, and effete; it was one half of a dual American ethos, and not the stronger half: "The American Will inhabits the sky-scraper, the American Intellect inhabits the colonial mansion. The one is the sphere of the American man; the other, at least predominantly, of the American woman. The one is all aggressive enterprise; the other is all genteel tradition." An aggressive, masculine modernity against a docile, feminine Victorianism, tepid intellect against dominating will: a set of terms that stood as a lens through which to see not only the contemporary scene, but also the several decades that preceded it.

If Santayana's philosophical work could be said to diagnose these symptoms of a washed-out culture, his poetry cannot be said to cure them. Perhaps he had in mind his own verse and that of other so-called "Harvard poets"— George Cabot Lodge, William Vaughn Moody, Trumbull Stickney—when he essentially lamented that American culture as it stood could neither produce nor accept work of serious, naturalistic, a-systematic originality. (On the other hand, Edmund Wilson thought highly of Stickney and lamented his early death in print.) Perhaps, too, Santayana's sense of the effete nature of the genteel mode was exacerbated by the work of such women poets as Anna Hempstead Branch, Louise Chandler Moulton, Josephine Preston Peabody, and Lizette Woodworth Reese—work, it must be said, that cannot be radically differentiated from that of their genteel male counterparts.

In fact, the era, as David Perkins demonstrates in *A History of Modern Poetry*, produced no shortage of poets working in the genteel mode, as well as many who were working against it, for (as Perkins writes) "inevitably the Genteel Tradition engendered countertendencies." Equally inevitable was the engendering of countertendencies within the practice of some of the genteel versifiers themselves. Such can be seen in the career of George Henry Boker (1823–1890), who, although certainly an adherent to genteel norms, also imperfectly resisted them. The author of several plays, mostly historical dramas—the two volume *Plays and Poems* was published by Ticknor and Fields in 1856—Boker also wrote a sequence called *The Book of the Dead* (1882), an elegy for his father. While the form itself is "genteel" enough, as is much of the language, the poem seems to violate decorum in expressing outrage over the treatment his father experienced in a lawsuit resulting from his role in the failure of a bank. This material would be suited for a realist novel, although Boker's formal handling of it would not.

The same might be said for Boker's *Poems of the War* (1864) and *Sonnets: A Sequence on Profane Love* (1929). The former, inspired in part by firsthand accounts of the Civil War, as well as by Boker's Unionist sympathies, purports often to place us at the scene of battle. Such poems as "The Ride to Camp," "The Crossing at Fredericksburg," and "Before Vicksburg" do not, however, recall the intimate touch of Whitman or the cold eye of Melville in those war poems of theirs that still seem modern. It is true that in a poem such as "Before Vicksburg," Boker resists total abstraction; in fact, we encounter such concrete things as "bomb-shells," "grape-shot," "case-shot," and fifty-four caliber cartridges. Yet at its core "Before Vicksburg" is a historical variation on that pathetic Victorian genre, the good-child-who-must-die poem, for in it a little drummer boy—"Weeping and sorely lame, / The merest child, the youngest face / Man ever saw in such a fearful place"—makes his final way to Sherman, to insist that the General get more bullets to his troops. Not yet seen as a butcher who burned his way through the civilian South, or even as an opportunistically vicious and thus victorious commander, Sherman instead is a sensitive soul "[s]hocked at his doleful case," especially at the "pool of bright, young blood" pouring from the boy; naturally "a drop, / Angels might envy, dimmed his eye," just as it must have dimmed the eye of many a reader.

*Sonnets: A Sequence on Profane Love*, which has been called the first attempt to write a sonnet sequence by an American poet taking Elizabethan practice as a model, was not published until three decades after Boker's death. Although in his own time Boker had been considered an eminent sonneteer, the 313 sonnets collected in the 1929 volume were (with two exceptions) unknown until a biographer found them squirreled away in the cupboard of Boker's daughter-in-law. The volume's subtitle is apt so far as goes the inspiration and theme of the sequence, for these poems, written over a thirty-year span, chronicle three separate love affairs carried on by Boker while he was married. It's no wonder they went unpublished during his lifetime. Reading these sonnets today, one feels that their profane foundations are rather masked by an admittedly skillful but nonetheless unadventurous adherence to formal convention; a poem beginning "Love stirs the pulses of my deeper thought" fails itself to stir the pulse. The volume does contain some interesting moments, however, such as Boker's re-working of the convention of courtship via meta-commentary, whereby he turns the self-referential trope into an indictment of his poetic contemporaries.

Two of Boker's closest friends, Bayard Taylor (1825-1878) and Richard Henry Stoddard (1825-1903), were also significant genteel writers. Stoddard gained early attention as a contributor to *Knickerbocker* magazine, although neither these contributions nor his first two volumes of verse, *Footprints* (1849) and *Poems* (1852), could earn him a living; with the help of Hawthorne he got a job in a New York custom-house, where he worked until 1870. Stoddard wrote much literary-critical work and edited such collections as *Female Poets of America* (1872–73) and *English Verse* (1883). The complete *Poems* (1880) contains among its five hundred pages a long narrative poem in heroic couplets ("The King's Bell"); a collection of ostensibly Persian, Arab, Tartar, and Chinese songs (originally appearing as *Book of the East* [1871]); elegies to leaders and friends; and a slew of shorter lyrics.

Bayard Taylor, like his friend Boker the author of many plays, also tried his hand several times at the novel, writing four of them in the 1860s alone. His peripatetic life, including appointments as secretary to the legation in Russia and as United States minister to Germany, furnished material for a number of travel narratives. His 1870 translation of Goethe's *Faust* sold strongly. Above all Taylor was known as a poet; indeed, he receives his own, surprisingly even-handed chapter in an important critical book, *Poets of America* (1885), by his genteel peer and acquaintance Edmund Clarence Stedman (1833-1908). Calling him "the most versatile of authors," Stedman writes of Taylor: "He let nothing go by him, he essayed everything, and he furnishes examples of what to do—and what to avoid." The remark after the dash is uncharacteristic of many genteel poets in their critical mode, since the stance most often encountered is one of mutual, total admiration. In his *Recollections* (1903), for instance, Stoddard writes of "the young Taylor and the young Boker, who were handsome, manly fellows, with mobile faces, alert eyes, and crowns of the clustering ringlets that made the head of Byron so beautiful." Stoddard puts Boker among august company—"He had one quality which is the distinction of most great writers, of masterminds like Shakespeare, Byron, Scott, Browning—fecundity of conception and rapidity of execution"—and Boker and Stoddard wrote sonnets to Taylor.

Helping a friend get a leg up was perhaps necessary in the genteel era (to say nothing of our own), for, although the work of these writers was widely disseminated, that work alone could not always pay the bills. Stoddard's long stint in the custom-house has been mentioned; Stedman, writing all the while, toiled away on Wall Street for years, unhappy and financially insecure. Several of the genteel versifiers did significant work as editors of the major periodicals of the day.

One such was Thomas Bailey Aldrich (1836-1907), who edited the *Atlantic Monthly* from 1881 to 1890. As a poet, Aldrich's first publication was *The Bells: A Collection of Chimes* (1855), which received little notice apart from that of Whitman, who later kidded Aldrich by telling him that he had enjoyed his volume of "tinkles." Aldrich did have popular success, however, with his bathetic "Ballad of Baby Bell," which was printed first in the *Journal of Commerce* and then reprinted in the weekly *Home Journal*, which Aldrich would soon help to edit. The inevitable fate of the ballad's titular figure—equal to "Christ's self in purity"—was death, and through the death of Baby Bell, the career of her nineteen-year-old creator was born. Ten years later, after a decade of freelance literary work, *The Poems of Thomas Bailey Aldrich* (1865) was brought out by the distinguished house of Ticknor and Fields. Eight volumes of collected works appeared in 1896.

Aldrich tried his hand at many types of verse. In *Cloth of Gold and Other Poems* (1874) he mined the Orientalist vein, as such titles as "An Arab Welcome," "A Turkish Legend," and "When the Sultan Goes to Ispahan" attest. "The Crescent and the Cross" is a comparative consideration of Islam and Christianity: "Here do they lie, two symbols of two creeds, / Each with deep meaning to our human needs." Unsurprisingly, he finally (albeit mildly) sides with his native faith: "That for the Moslem is, but this for me." Two blank verse narratives, "Wyndham Towers" (1890) and "Judith and Holofernes" (1896), are also of foreign origin, though the former is less exotically so. Closer to home is the ode "Spring in New England." Aldrich, who was born in Portsmouth, New Hampshire, concedes that not he, but the "bluebird" with his "venturous strain," is "New England's poet laureate / Telling us spring has come again!" One source of influence on Aldrich was an actual (if non-native) laureate, as we see in his poem "Tennyson," the inaugural question of which is answered in the title: "Shakespeare and Milton—what third blazoned name / Shall lips of after-ages link to these?" However, as Charles Samuels has convincingly argued, Aldrich might most profitably be considered less a Tennysonian than as a 19th century Herrick. His most pleasurable verses are the self-consciously minor, often witty lyrics, such as the series of quatrains he called "Footnotes." One of these, "A Hint from Herrick," more than hints at his indebtedness:

> No slightest golden rhyme he wrote
> That held not something men must quote;
> Thus by design or chance did he
> Drop anchors to posterity.

In addition to his numerous poems, Aldrich was also a prolific writer of prose. The title story of his collection *Marjorie Daw and Other People* (1873) was widely read and reprinted for years. Among Aldrich's several novels, the most notable is *The Story of a Bad Boy* (1869), a largely autobiographical tale.

Another important editor-poet of the period was Richard Watson Gilder (1844–1909). As a young man Gilder showed a sincere commitment to verse, and he was encouraged early on by Stedman, a life-long friend. Gilder was hardly out of step with his era in at first approaching poetry as a fine, disembodied abstraction. However, as Herbert Smith notes, Gilder as he got older "was no longer attempting to distill that ineffable, poetry, from thought; he became instead a formalist, considering himself something of an expert on the construction of the sonnet and the irregular ode." That his sense of his own poetic expertise was shared by his contemporaries is suggested by his being chosen as the first living author to be published by Houghton Mifflin—alongside such revered figures as William Cullen Bryant, Henry Wadsworth Longfellow, and John Greenleaf Whittier—in the "American Household Poets" series. The volume appeared in 1908, one year before his death.

Gilder's adherence as a poet to conventional form, as well as his inoffensive subject matter, does not tell the full story of his work. First as managing editor of *Scribner's Monthly*, where he worked from 1870 to 1881, and then as editor of the *Century*, Gilder published many writers we could hardly consider "genteel." Among these were writers of the burgeoning realist movement. In his poem "Realism," fellow poet Aldrich exhibited the disgust many writers of the time felt for such work, lamenting that

> Today we breathe a commonplace,
> Polemic, scientific air:
> We strip Illusion of her veil;
> We vivisect the nightingale
> To probe the secret of his note.

Gilder must not have felt so strongly about changes in the age, helping as he did to effect them. Although they are certainly not realists on the order of Dreiser, Southern regionalists such as George Washington Cable, Joel Chandler Harris, and Thomas Nelson Page, who all found a home in Gilder's magazines, are far from the New England genteel ideal. Gilder's careful exchanges with the midwestern realist Hamlin Garland suggest an editor who has a commitment to the new writing but who also understands the taste of his often easily offended readership.

Other writers published by Gilder include Edwin Arlington Robinson, William Dean Howells, Mark Twain, and, posthumously, Herman Melville, whose poems at the time were little remembered. Gilder was also a great champion of Whitman, at whose 70th birthday celebration he gave a speech, praising in particular the old grey-beard's formal innovation at a time when many critics denied that Whitman's work had any form at all. Some years earlier, as managing editor of *Scribner's* under J.G. Holland, Gilder had pushed hard for the publication of Stedman's survey of contemporary American poets, in which Stedman did not plan from the outset to excoriate Whitman, but rather to be judicious. Since Holland actively despised Whitman, he considered this approach unacceptable, but Gilder ultimately had his way. Another of Gilder's important enthusiasms was his dedicated lobbying for the passage of international copyright, largely to protect American authors from the pirating of their work by British publishers.

Although the genteel versifiers may be best remembered today as what David Perkins calls "a negative influence," since for the modernists that followed them "[t]he need to repudiate the conventional, usually insipid, see-no-evil verse of this time acted as a motive and spur," they may also be remembered as workhorses of American letters. If they were careful in their self-expression, they were also promiscuous in the kinds of writing they did. They were committed to American art, even if they too often looked abroad for their forms. Their relationship to the experimental writing of the day was skittish at best, but so was their writerly relationship to their own feelings, for which they may be afforded a touch of sympathy. In short, while we may not find the finest of the nation's poems among the work of the genteel poets, we will certainly find much that reveals the national soul.

# Ethics, Critics, Close Reading

Why a turn to ethics in Canadian criticism? One is hesitant to risk an answer, no matter how tentative, especially if one is neither officially nor yet sufficiently Canadian. For my part, I came from the States to Canada on Canada Day in the year 2004. The timing was propitious. My first cross-cultural revelation was that Americans are arrogant and Canadians are smug. No doubt it was partially provoked by the Americans and Canadians I knew asking me too soon and too frequently about the differences between Canadians and Americans. It was imperative to say something and if it was pithy so much the better. After the inadequacy of my response sank in, I relaxed into more dialectical ways of thinking. Having left one country at a time of much sloganeering, I preferred to avoid entering the new one in the pseudo-intellectual bumper-sticker trade.

Nevertheless, there may be something about Canada conducive not only to writing an ethical criticism, but also to writing criticism that can deal with both ethics and aesthetics without getting too chippy about it. Such criticism is obviously possible elsewhere—indeed, one would hope, anywhere. Still, my initial impression is that the aesthetics/ethics divide is undivided here more or less satisfactorily; or perhaps it is merely (as another immigrant put it) pretty to think so. In this case, however, the prettiness of the assertion is not at odds with its veracity. One corollary to the surge of interest in ethics of late among many literary critics (not only those living in Canada) is a similar surge of interest in aesthetics. The coupling may seem odd, especially given that aesthetics and ethics are often pitched as antithetical. Then again, one cannot help feeling that the two are somehow connected. "It may be true that one has to choose between ethics and aesthetics, but it is no less true that whichever one chooses, one will always find the other at the end of the road." So Susan Sontag began her essay "Godard," quoting her subject.

One also feels, however, that here there is less choosing between the two than choosing to take them together. When I say "here," I mean Canada, of course. But it would be disingenuous not to specify further, for "here" is also Toronto—which, as one is often reminded, is only a part of the whole—as well as the university that takes its name from the city. The specifics are relevant. First, there is the local, professional fact, for me at least, that when one moves to a new place and in one swoop gains a new group of colleagues, one hastens his intellectual and even personal acclimation by reading the work of those colleagues; indeed, such a subjective course of reading has made possible the following speculations. Second, staying with the local and professional but growing less subjective, there is the fact of the centrality, not only at the University of Toronto but also in Canadian cultural life, of Northrop Frye, whose influence as a mediatory figure in the putative ethics/aesthetics divide can still be ascertained. Third, there is a fact that I will not belabour but will merely conclude by remarking upon, namely, that this place, this city, this country is experiencing a rich period of immigration, one that is being theorized while it is happening, as well as one that suggests practical models for letting the ethics we adhere to and the art that we create exist not as sheer antitheses, but as partners of a sort, with the ethics and aesthetics of others affecting our own and vice versa.

To make the modest arguments I intend to pursue, it is necessary to begin by establishing once again the vexed relationship of ethics and aesthetics in the recent history of our profession. Limiting ourselves to the twentieth century and the first few years of the twenty-first, we find that, even in this relatively short span of time, the connections between aesthetics and ethics, if not exactly perspicuous, are deep and many. The catalogue for an exhibition demonstrating this finding might include such more or less randomly chosen entries as Gayley and Scott's *Methods and Materials of Literary Criticism: The Bases in Aesthetics and Poetics* (1899), which can serve as a summa of where literary criticism begins in the twentieth century. The terms of its title indicate that criticism does not count among its materials and methods those derived from a consideration of ethics; but of course for literary critics of the day, aesthetics and poetics were indebted heavily to Plato, Aristotle, Kant, and Arnold, among others, none of whom can be considered averse to matters of ethics. Furthermore, we may remark that wherever the old rhetorical tradition persists in twentieth-century criticism, the link between aesthetics and ethics persists.

Consider, too, the crucial fact that, despite rumours to the contrary, an interest in aesthetic matters has never been successfully exorcised from such genres of criticism as feminist, postcolonialist, and race and queer studies, which obviously incline towards the ethical. Nor did the various formalisms ever successfully exorcise ethics. For the purposes of the present essay, the formalism of greatest interest is New Criticism. This is the case because, for Anglo-American criticism of the past century, New Criticism exerted such a strong influence as a critical practice, especially as a practice of reading; and because, as we will see, aspects of that practice are returning in deliberate ways in the work of a host of scholars who would never be described first as formalists.

The New Criticism has been taken by many to signify that which in literary criticism is a- or anti-historical, a- or anti-political, a- or anti-psychological, a- or anti-moral (ethical)—in short, given critical fashion of late, that which is critically moribund. Rey Chow—who through the magic of tense hastens the lingering death, embalms the corpse, and brings the mummy back to life—sets the scene for the rejection of that practice of reading: "In the Anglo-American world the literary-theoretical avant-garde of the twentieth century was represented by New Criticism, which specializes in the discernment of a literary work's specificity through close reading... New Criticism is still invested in a kind of time-less reading of the work of literature, a reading that circumvents temporality by the ideological projection of the work's organic wholeness" (176). The story told by Chow has other tellers, too; and even if one disagreed with some of the facts of the story, it would be unwise to discredit tales of personal experience. Consider the souvenirs of Martha Nussbaum, who recounts finding as a graduate student of Classics at Harvard in 1969 that New Critics were disengaged not only from history and psychology but from ethics as well: "In the broader world of literary study to which Classics was occasionally linked, aesthetic issues were understood (following, on the whole, standards set by New Critical formalism) to be more or less divorced from ethical and practical issues" (12–13).

There are also interventions that corroborate the stories of Chow and Nussbaum at the same time that they revise them. Chow describes New Criticism as *the* "literary-theoretical avant-garde of the twentieth century" in

Anglo-America; nevertheless, the New Critical avant-garde was supplanted by other critical avant-gardes, the latter of which attacked or rejected the former, just as New Criticism had rejected the critical avant-garde (historical criticism à la Taine) that preceded it. Given this latter fact, one might, when reading Marshall Brown's exposé of the incomplete "rejection of 'close reading'" (804) by several prime movers of New Historicism, grudgingly mutter that turnabout is fair play. As Douglas Mao writes in a reading that rescues Cleanth Brooks and John Crowe Ransom for an age of extrinsic-minded criticism (and finds similarities in Ransom and Adorno), "the most popular form of attack upon the New Criticism has proven to be the assertion that in treating the literary text as an autonomous aesthetic object it severs it irretrievably from both psychology and history" (227). Moving back a few years, an encyclopedia essay written right after the New Critical heyday by Brewster Rogerson notes that New Critical "analysis at its strictest, being unconcerned with any hierarchy of values outside the poem, confines itself to judging internal relations, and thus at most to distinguishing good poems from bad"; however, "In practice, of course, the method is often yoked to some independent set of standards, moral or social...by which the critic relates the poem to a wider area of experience" (165). The situation thus seems to be this: there are numerous voices describing New Criticism as a practice that made a fetish of autonomy and the object of art, one that favoured aesthetics and form to the absolute exclusion of social content or context; then, there are numerous voices repeating this description in an attempt to revise it. The numbers of voices probably break down ten to one, respectively. The effect is somewhat like experiencing feedback at a concert of critics.

One whose work moderates the sound is Northrop Frye, who reacts to and sometimes against New Criticism, but who nevertheless can be fairer to it than many of the critics following him. (He can also be less fair than funny, as when he asserts that one of the "goals" available to those who walk the "way of pedantry" is "delicate learning, or 'new' criticism" (Frye, *Anatomy*, 72)). Frye is also a figure who moderates between aesthetics and ethics. It is in the "Ethical Criticism" essay of *Anatomy of Criticism*, after all, that Frye makes his distinction between centrifugal and centripetal reading: "Whenever we read anything, we find our attention moving in two directions at once. One direction is outward or centrifugal, in which we keep going outside our reading....

The other direction is inward or centripetal, in which we try to develop from the words a sense of the larger verbal pattern they make" (73). This binary finds an analogue two pages later in the post-Sidney distinction between that which "instructs" and that which "delights." As Frye remarks, again moderately (or with immoderate moderation), "Neither factor can, of course, ever be eliminated from any kind of writing" (75). In *The Critical Path*, subtitled "An Essay on the Social Context of Literary Criticism," Frye discusses Arnold's conception of "Culture" and of the culture that could achieve it. For such a culture, Frye writes, "moral and aesthetic standards are inseparable, united in the conception of good taste.... The impossibility of separating moral and aesthetic criteria indicates the importance of the critical function in society" (73). In the same book Frye suggests, in discussing the New Critics, how even in their practice the distinction between the intrinsic and extrinsic has been greatly exaggerated: "By the time I began writing criticism, the so-called 'new criticism' had established itself as a technique of explication.... The great merit of explicatory criticism was that it accepted poetic language and form as the basis for poetic meaning. On the basis it built up a resistance to all 'background' criticism that explained the literary in terms of the non-literary. At the same time, it deprived itself of the great strength of documentary criticism: the sense of context.... The limitations of this approach soon became obvious, and most of the new critics sooner or later fell back on one of the established documentary contexts, generally the historical one, although they were regarded at first as anti-historical" (20–21). To my mind, Frye's position is not really that such criteria as form and content (and content as context) cannot be separated (he separates them himself), but that they are not antithetical; they differ in emphasis, but are complementary.

My goal here, though—following but diverging from Frye—is not necessarily to preach moderation, but to consider why, and identify where, vestiges of New Critical practice, spars of New Critical interest, float up in our current sea. Of such spars I will focus on two: the notion of form and the notion of close reading. The latter will receive closer treatment than the former; however, the former holds a key to how the latter can be invoked by the newer ethical critics with so little of the customary defensiveness. In a powerful way the current discussion is defined by a binary—that old Janus, content and form. The ability to deconstruct or historicize the binary does little to dispel its pre-eminence in criticism; it only changes how the binary is treated. In critical discussion the content/form binary is connected to other binary terms; one might also say that these other terms are sometimes loose, sometimes strict subsidiaries of content and form. Thus, for Anglo-American literary criticism, aesthetics tends to fall under form, while ethics, politics, psychology, and history are classed under content. Some of the quotations above prove this well enough.

To call the content side of things ideological or didactic is possible but perhaps unwise, given the meanings associated with these terms. The aforementioned Rogerson reminds us that "the most pervasive of ideological standards in the critical tradition have been *ethical* standards" and suggests that between "the two extremes of outright didacticism and 'art for art's sake' there has traditionally been a wide range of argument; to disagree with Tolstoi is by no means to agree with Oscar Wilde" (172). Nor, to choose two names for a roughly symbolic purpose, is to disagree with Antonio Gramsci to agree with Cleanth Brooks. In the same encyclopedia quoted above, Brooks writes an entry on "New Criticism" in which he claims that one of the few things the various New Critics have in common "is a profound distrust of the old dualism of form and content, and a real sense of the failure of an ornamentalist rhetoric to do justice to the inter-penetration of the form and matter achieved in a really well-written work" (568). This implies that form and content are not such distinct entities after all at the same time that it suggests that form is the primary term of value.

There is a similar but much more explicit moment in Gramsci: "To grant that content and form are the same thing does not mean that we cannot distinguish between them." He goes on to ask and to answer a straightforward question:

> Can one speak of a priority of content over form? One can in this sense: that the work of art is a process and that changes of content are also changes of form. It is 'easier,' though, to talk about content than about form because content can be logically 'summarized.' When one says that content precedes form, one simply means that in the process of elaboration successive attempts are presented under the name of content and that is

all. The first content that was unsatisfactory was also form and, in reality, when one arrives at a satisfying 'form,' the content has also changed. It is true that often those who go on about form, at the expense of content, are saying precisely nothing. (203)

We are indebted to Gramsci for the proleptic suggestion that speaking of content may appeal to some for its ease; no doubt the same could be said of a prior generation's interminable explications of form. It seems to be the case that many of the strongest writers with an inclination towards ethics have absorbed the related messages of Gramsci and Brooks, which is that content and form can in one sense collapse into each other, and in another can be studied with profit as separate entities that might organize aspects of critical practice. The triple critical lesson to be derived is the necessity of using these terms with some self-consciousness, the necessity of not being defensive in using these terms, and the necessity of using these terms in a way that clarifies the critic's object of inquiry.

Of the aspects of New Criticism assimilated and used by ethically minded literary critics without being overly beholden or resistant to them, close reading is the example of most importance. People, of course, have been reading closely for a long, long time. In one recent history of reading in the West, the authors interpret nuances in archaic verbs that signify "reading," claiming that in Greece, between the fifth and fourth centuries BC, a style was first arrived at "capable of reading 'through' a text and permitting attentive consideration, examination and probing of what was being read" (Cavallo and Chartier, 9). On the other hand, people have been "close reading" for less than a century. The term is New Critical jargon that has come to be used more generally at the same time that it retains its history, which is to say, its New Critical birthright.

Given how close reading and what it conveys has often been described as antithetical to a range of matters ethical, historical, political, and psychological, it is surprising to see it turning up in unexpected places. Gayatri Spivak's short essay in the October 2006 *PMLA* is a case in point. It is titled "Close Reading"—ironically so, I suspected, at first; nothing therein reminded this reader of the kind of close reading "close reading" usually signifies. But then I read more closely. The essay is about contemporary language rights, the current teaching of language, and the impossibility of translation. What is the title

"Close Reading" in this context if it is not an ironic remark about a critical past that is unable to respond to present needs? Perhaps the title is instead an ironic remark about a critical past that both haunts and is used by the critical present; perhaps it is both the undefensive recuperation of a term and the wresting away of one. Primarily, given the essay's juxtaposition of current concerns and the recent critical past, the title bolsters Spivak's argument that "[b]ad globalization" "must destroy linguistic and cultural variety" (shades of Ransom) and that translation also always runs the risk of such destruction. To see a link between Spivak and New Criticism one need only read the following passage from her essay while considering, say, poetry itself to be one of the "world's languages," or to consider each poet's oeuvre to be a "language": "In the humanities disciplines, it is as if the world's languages, most especially the endangered ones, claim a right to be taught, in depth. I repeat, this is different from saying that you get ethical practice if you learn to read the text of the other, though I hold on to that as well" (1613). Here the interdiction against translation recalls an earlier generation's concept of the "heresy of paraphrase." Furthermore, New Criticism serves as a model of critical practice that won, as Spivak calls for, a "fight in the schools."

The term "close reading" appears with utmost prominence in the work of another postcolonial critic with an interest in ethics, Ato Quayson. His *Calibrations: Reading for the Social* begins with a startling sentence: "This book is about close reading" (xi). The sentence is startling for many of the reasons that Spivak's title is: first, postcolonial criticism is not usually associated with formalist practice; second, such practice is not usually given such pride of place in current criticism of any type; third, close reading traditionally did not treat the same texts as those read by Spivak and Quayson. This much is fairly apparent. What is not so apparent is how the term "close reading," which one might have expected to be divisive in the context of an extrinsic-minded criticism ("Reading for the Social"), operates quite otherwise.

In a partially autobiographical essay entitled "Incessant Particularities: *Calibrations* as Close Reading," Quayson describes his education as a reader and critic from the late 1970s through the late 1980s, an education that included New Critical practices. To this story is connected the fact that during the same time, "Ghana was in political turmoil." "The problem then," he writes, "was how to combine a respect for the text as an aesthetic object with a vigorous attention to the many dramatic things that were unfolding all around us" ("Incessant," 124). Close reading turned out to facilitate, not prevent, such a critical combination:

> For me close reading involves not just reading for specific details as a means of identifying interacting heterogeneities that, taken as a configuration, illustrate the parameters of a literary structure in the first place. But this reading for heterogeneity in the literary field is at once correlated to a reading of the social itself, my argument being that what allows literature to represent the social is not any straightforward mimetic relationship between the two but the degree to which literature encapsulates an image of the social via a configuration of heterogeneities. The task I set myself then was to elaborate a method of reading that could be replicated in relation to different literary and social contexts. ("Incessant," 126)

Quayson resists any simple translation of the literary text into the social, in that he rejects mining-by-paraphrase the literary text for nuggets of social content. We instead find in literature an *image* of the social; that image has a practical value insofar as it comes into being as "a configuration of heterogeneities," which suggests that literature is a practice site from which to begin to learn how to handle critically the actual heterogeneity that persists outside of literature. Perhaps to "calibrate" our readings is after all to discard the very notion of "outside of literature" and to replace it with the notion of "between the literary and the social." One reason Quayson's elaboration of his method in *Calibrations* is successful is that the commitment to "close reading," in large part derived from New Critical precedent, is well complemented by his strength as a post-Marxist; it is in this marriage of prior methods (both arguably "formalist") that we see how crucial it is for literary criticism to have a sophisticated and varied understanding of *form*, one that considers the aesthetic and the social dialectically.

One way that such a dialectical consideration can prove fruitful is to think through the social, somewhat paradoxically, as a political space that is determined in large part psychologically. Here, too, New Critical practice may prove crucial, for even where the term "close reading" itself is not used, something clearly analogous is. I am thinking of Sara Salih's "Introduction" to *The Judith Butler Reader*, where she writes, on the first page, that:

> The ethical-political stance Butler takes up... requires patience from readers who may well find the absence (indeed, the removal) of epistemological anchors disorienting. So, like Nietzsche, Butler semi-humorously advises her readers to follow the example of cows and learn "the art of slow rumination" in their textual practices. As Nietzsche puts it, reading is an art for which one must place oneself in a state that is "practically bovine," but this by no means implies an attitude of passivity and contentment; rather, readers should learn not to expect what Butler calls "radical accessibility" when they encounter texts that have set themselves the difficult task of rethinking and reconfiguring the possible within political theorizing. (1)

Close reading and bovine reading are not the same thing when considered historically (or zoologically). One can't help but laugh if one imagines a herd of Southern Agrarians chewing aesthetic cud. Maybe they would have appreciated the connection between the bovine metaphor and the social context that helps give it its significance, its reality, its referents. Salih, in emphasizing from the outset the need to practise "patience" in reading Butler, as well as in emphasizing that such readerly patience is for Butler what constitutes "critique" itself, suggests that practices of patient reading, whatever name they may take, both constitute critique and serve as a foundation for "ethical-political" stances.

Methodological cross-currents and the active, creative relation to the world and the text that they often imply are finally unsurprising, given that there are still critics who want to respond to the way things are and to shape how things are by showing us how to read. As Uzoma Esowanne writes at the end of an essay about Quayson on "Literary Reference and the Ethics of Reading," "we read *for* [the social] precisely because... we perceive ourselves as subjects who, through the act of reading, actively produce meaning by articulating our perception of the open-ended, unstable, and profoundly paradoxical dimensions of the social against and alongside those of the aesthetic" (120). Esowanne's remarks recall Frye's because we are reminded how Frye's practice mediated so well between the social and the aesthetic and so often did so in the service of a *Canadian* literature, a *Canadian* culture. As we can see, perhaps especially in the "Letters in Canada" omnibus reviews he wrote for *UTQ*, formal and evaluative work that would make a New Critic jealous is not at odds in Frye's practice with his assertion of a social (in this case, a national) dimension to the literature being critiqued.

In part because Canada is a locus of a great deal of actual, physical migration, what constitutes "Canada" or what makes a person or thing "Canadian" is in a great deal of flux; many people who live here, both from here and otherwise, are exceptionally self-conscious about that flux. It is inevitable that this social situation be reflected in contemporary Canadian writing, critical writing included, a point made to me in specifics by my colleague Neil ten Kortenaar. For a literary critic with a literary-historical inclination and an especial interest in poetry like myself, it is also significant that from the point of view of a "national" literature, Canadian poetry has apparently always exhibited a self-consciousness concerning the movement of people as a subject of literary interest; indeed, it seems a central subject—as in, for instance, *The Emigrant* of Standish O'Grady and of Alexander McLachlan, respectively, or Joseph Howe's "Acadia," or, in a more fantastical mode, John Hunter-Duvar's *The Emigration of the Fairies*. An awareness of the settler-invader history and of subsequent waves of immigration that have given rise to the particular structure of the Canadian nation-state lends support to the link between aesthetics and ethics. The influx of critics from different places to Canada serves as a suggestive analogy—but just as an analogy—to the influx of people to Canada. Where different people must deal with one another, moderation is a virtue. It may not be a virtue unique to criticism written in Canada, but any critic new to Canada might begin to see it manifested here. As our profession continues to consider ethics, it is heartening to see that some critics are wise enough not to discard our profession's critical past and to see that aesthetics and ethics are not enemies, to see that reading in regard to the other is not at odds with reading closely. It is heartening to see that despite all their potential tensions, our various modes of reading can learn to get along, helping us learn along the way.

## WORKS CITED

Brooks, Cleanth. "New Criticism." *Princeton Encyclopedia of Poetry and Poetics*. Enlarged edition. Ed. Alex Preminger. Princeton: Princeton University Press 1974, 567–68.

Brown, Marshall. *"Le Style est l'homme même*: The Action of Literature." *College English* 59:7 (November 1997), 801–9.

Cavallo, Guglielmo, and Roger Chartier. "Introduction." Trans. Lydia G. Cochrane. *A History of Reading in the West*. Ed. Guglielmo Cavallo and Roger Chartier. Amherst: University of Massachusetts Press 1999, 1–36.

Chow, Rey. "The Interruption of Referentiality: Poststructuralism and the Conundrum of Critical Multiculturalism." *South Atlantic Quarterly* 101:1 (Winter 2002), 171–86.

Esowanne, Uzoma. "*Calibrations*: Literary Reference and the Ethics of Reading." *Research in African Literatures* 36:2 (2005), 112–21.

Frye, Northrop. *Anatomy of Criticism*. Princeton: Princeton University Press, 1957.

— *The Critical Path*. Bloomington: Indiana University Press, 1971.

Gayley, Charles Mills, and Fred Newton Scott. *Methods and Materials of Literary Criticism: The Bases in Aesthetics and Poetics*. Boston: Ginn 1899.

Gramsci, Antonio. *Selections from Cultural Writings*. Ed. David Forgacs and Geoffrey Nowell-Smith. Trans. William Boelhower. Cambridge: Harvard University Press 1985.

Mao, Douglas. "The New Critics and the Text-Object." *English Language History* 63:1 (1996), 227–54.

Nussbaum, Martha. "Form and Content, Philosophy and Literature." *Love's Knowledge*. Oxford: Oxford University Press 1990, 2–53.

Quayson, Ato. *Calibrations: Reading for the Social*. Minneapolis: University of Minnesota Press 2003.

— "Incessant Particularities: *Calibrations* as Close Reading." *Research in African Literatures* 36:2 (2005), 122–31.

Rogerson, Brewster. "Criticism (Types)." *Princeton Encyclopedia of Poetry and Poetics*, Enlarged edition. Ed. Alex Preminger. Princeton: Princeton University Press 1974, 163–73.

Salih, Sara. "Introduction." *The Judith Butler Reader*. Ed. Sara Salih with Judith Butler. Oxford: Blackwell 2004, 1–17.

Sontag, Susan. "Godard." *Styles of Radical Will*. New York: Farrar, Straus and Giroux 1969, 147–89.

Spivak, Gayatri Chakravorty. "Close Reading." *PMLA* 121:5 (October 2006), 1608–17.

# Short Reviews

*The Way We Argue Now* by Amanda Anderson, Princeton University Press, 2006.

Subtitled "A Study in the Cultures of Theory," this collection of essays contradicts recent obituaries by showing that there are many theories yet breathing in academia. Anderson recalls us to detachment as a proper critical posture, argues that the cultivation of character can be an ethical act, and asserts that "the dominant paradigms within literary and cultural studies have had an adverse effect on the fostering of public-sphere argument precisely insofar as identity has come to seem the strongest argument of all." As this quote suggests, the book's reigning style is dry and its reigning stance nonconformist. If you dislike academic writing, you will dislike this book; if not, there is much here to learn.

After a helpful introduction, the book is divided into three sections ascending in strength. The first consists of an essay on a debate between Seyla Benhabib and Judith Butler, as well as one on performances of "aggrandized agency" in Victorianist feminist scholarship. Although the essential point of the former could be made with greater dispatch, the essay is still worth reading; it is also the book's most adversarial. Butler, writes Anderson, "requires a trumped-up version of normative critical theory in order to secure the pedigree of her politics." Benhabib needs "a more capacious model of dialogue, one that can accommodate different forms of political practice, particularly the disruptions of spectacle, performance, and...'theatrical rage.'" In Anderson's account of their differences, Benhabib and her call for norms of reciprocity and respect beats Butler and her belief that norms of whatever type are inherently insidious.

The next essay considers the faults of those who imagine feminine agency as "continuous with unreflective forms of power that are simply transmitted by culturally embedded subjects," while also insisting that "strange exceptions occur, wherein certain historical subjects are exempted from networks of power." Here Anderson begins in earnest her defence of detachment. "Indeed," she writes, "incoherence about critical detachment itself shadows much of contemporary theoretical debate." Her second section, "Living Universalisms," begins by arguing for "a term that throughout its long...history has been used to denote cultivated detachment from restrictive forms of identity"—namely, cosmopolitanism. In addition to its interest as a critique of our critical norms, the essay may also be educational for those who associate the term "cosmopolitan" merely with someone who has lived in several cities.

The final section, "Ethos and Argument," is exceptionally strong. Even the writing becomes more engaging. Although Anderson is not an interesting stylist, and there is no escaping the proliferation of jargon, her arguments on style and character are made with brio. The essay "Pragmatism and Character" considers Stanley Fish, Richard Rorty, and Barbara Herrnstein Smith, arguing that when "pragmatists make appeal to character," they "move toward a descriptive thickness that evokes the literary, and often they can be situated with regard to generic literary modes, such as irony or comedy." Smith, for one, is more ironist than comedian, and Anderson's description of the former's (self)-characterization of the "postmodern skeptic" is fun to read, even if the essay over-extrapolates a comprehensive argument from an isolated moment.

In the penultimate essay, on the so-called Foucault-Habermas debate, Anderson emphasizes how often character and ethos are intertwined. Here the allusion to Trollope in her title bears fruit, for who knew this better than Trollope? Given the much mentioned "turn to ethics" in the humanities, one cannot ignore Anderson's idea that ethos, which "can loosely mean habit, custom, practice, or manner" can produce (especially in critics inspired by Foucault) a "pronounced mystification" that "allows one to assign honorific status or moral resonance" without ever getting specific. Habermas resists ethos as a primary term, considering it a self-justifying refusal of "rational coherence." Unexplored in Anderson's analysis is a fact she nevertheless implies: although their followers respond to the character of Foucault and Habermas, the followers themselves are less compelling, for they can only take on, like an ill-fitting cloak, the authority and style of their masters.

Writing in her final essay that "argument informed by universalistic principles might itself become an ethos," Anderson uses the Norton Lectures of Lionel Trilling as a wall against which to bounce the ball of "communicative action" theory. In juxtaposing Trilling and Habermas, she asserts that the latter is not an elitist whose story is politically thin in the telling, but rather a deliberate thinker who values concepts of procedure, rationality, and argument over the concept of identity. Anderson suggests that his work on communication in the public sphere can be made to communicate *with* the public sphere. Because of its intensely academic style, her own book is unlikely to do so. However, for those interested in current critical debates and not allergic to dense, jargon-filled sentences, this book is indeed a powerful overview of the way we argue now.

\* \* \*

*Where Shall I Wander* by John Ashbery, Ecco Press, 2005.

"The lot of the long-lived artist in this country is hazardous." Thus Whitney Balliett began a consideration of Duke Ellington in 1963, although he could have been discussing John Ashbery of late. Such staying power as Ashbery's presents, among other problems, that of volume; when a poet is as prolific as Peyps, Proust, or Oates, readers can hardly keep up. This leads to the hazard of few people having read what they nevertheless have an opinion about. The new book of poems really is just more Ashbery, after all. Because of his prolixity, but also because of his difficulty, Ashbery not only endures hazards but also inflicts them on his readers. This relationship between poet and reader has always been a close one, however vexed. From the reader's side you can see it in the work of such critics as Harold Bloom, Marjorie Perloff, John Shoptaw, and Helen Vendler; in the poems of most postmodern poets worth their salt; and in the intensely Oedipal remarks, spurred by cheap white wine, of young writers and readers made after poetry readings, some of which are probably going on as we speak. From Ashbery's side, the closeness of the relationship is obvious, largely because Ashbery in his poems, Whitmanic as ever, *is* the reader. He irritates, then aggravates, then consoles the reader, imagines the eyes of the reader as daily amanuensis, and, as he himself is so often taken for granted, so too does he take the reader for granted.

All the familiar aspects of "typical Ashbery" appear in *Where Shall I Wander*. One finds an inconsistency in pronouns, an intermixture of loose verse and prose, a deployment of rudimentary form for ironic effect ("It's really quite a thrill / when the moon rises above the hill"), and reported and found speech, including high-toned allusions and everyday junk. There are also features that were always in the poems but now occur more frequently: deliberately recherché vocabulary, shaggy dog stories, mock joviality. The poems even look familiar, except for "Hölderlin Marginalia," which from a distance, seeing only the title, could be confused with a Susan Howe poem.

The soothing breeziness, however, is cut by a sharp poignancy. (One poem, titled "Novelty Love Trot," ends: "I must get back to my elegy.") It is a duality one sees in the relation of title to poem, of line to line; it is also one that takes structural form, as poems that begin as a melange of apparent nonsense end in a Romantic mode. "O Fortuna," for instance, begins in pretend exclamatory excess ("Good luck! Best wishes! The best of luck! / The very best! Godspeed! God bless you! / Peace be with you! / May your shadow never be less!") and closes with a couple of over-arching "all"s that bracket a distancing double-simile: "All hell didn't break loose, it was like a rising psalm / materializing like snow on an unseen mountain. / All that was underfoot was good, but lost." Elsewhere, in "Lost Footage," Ashbery ends again with "all" before reporting a literal vision that is also mythological and ekphrastic: "All was silent except the pedals / of the loom, from which a tapestry streams / in bits and pieces. 'I don't care how you do it.' // I can see the subject: an eagle with Ganymede / in his razor-clam claws, against a sky / of mottled sun and storm clouds. // From that, much vexation."

In many of the poems (as in these lines), "a tapestry streams in bits and pieces." Indeed, the form that dominates the spirit of the volume is arguably the cento, a patchwork poem made up of the scraps of other authors. The potential "authors" here are numerous and widely defined, potentially including anyone who ever said anything, and include Ashbery himself, using himself: "our pleated longevity mimics us." And how is he used today, by his readers? Is it we who are being addressed at the end of "The Snow-Stained Petals Aren't Pretty Anymore"? That prose poem, one of several in the volume, closes thus: "No one had paid attention. Such, my friends, is the reward of study and laborious attempts to communicate with the dead. In the end it all falls to pieces."

Ashbery's recent poems cause consternation in some of his readers. These poems can seem especially incoherent and necessarily tossed-off. ("Let's drink to that, / and the tenacity of just seeming.") Yet they are and they aren't. A patchwork is finally coherent in a tossed-off way. And Ashbery, who gathered and assembled the scraps in the present case, can count—of course, as always—among his astonishing virtues: a gargantuan vocabulary deftly employed, a knowledge of and talent for a wide array of forms, a witty and generous nature, a wide-ranging and well-exercised capacity for critical judgement, a fine mind, a painter's eye, a singer's ear, and the ability to write amazing sentences of all sorts within the hard-to-see confines of loosey-goosey stanzas, most of them, ultimately, with some good, old-fashioned meaning attached or attachable. Rich as ever, as ever worth our attention—just more Ashbery, after all, and thank goodness.

\* \* \*

*Word of Mouth: Gossip and American Poetry* by Chad Bennett, Johns Hopkins University Press, 2018.

Here is an original study with some unoriginal—that is to say, common imperfections. Bennett's intuition that gossip is not inconsequential but central to poetry, and that both gossip and poetry are eccentrically central to life, marks an ironic, mature, and observant mind. The intuition is brought to fruition as Bennett picks ripe and juicy examples. He is a talented noticer (the kind of guy good at *overhearing*) and a mostly persuasive close reader; at any rate, it is in his closer readings that his personality most comes out, where even the prose picks up. His rhetoric is unaggressive but his point is provocative. The point is that although not all gossip is queer, there is something potentially queer about gossip itself; and it is the very queerness of gossip that makes gossip a positive phenomenon (ethically, politically, socially speaking), not really as negative as its reputation suggests.

This reader is less sanguine than Bennett about the upside of gossip, or is rather more bullish on its downside. Ignoring, however, the harm that often comes when lips loosely flapped with bad intent meet ears widely opened in pernicious delight, one can appreciate how he best makes his case: through judicious selecting, biographical buttressing, citational covering, careful (and spry) close reading. His case is less well made when argument is really just blunt repetition, primarily repetition of a straw man version of lyric. Yet it is those readers with a stake in the history and theory of the lyric who will likely find in *Word of Mouth* the most to value, along with queer studies scholars.

"In framing my study's understanding of queer gossip," writes Bennett, "I should clarify that by 'queer' I mean not so much the expression or representation of gay, lesbian, bisexual, or transgender identities as the baffling of sexual or gender identity categories and of normative categorization more broadly." It is a definition difficult to test against the book's own evidence, given that the writers under discussion are Gertrude Stein, Langston Hughes, Frank O'Hara, and James Merrill. If "queer gossip" means gossip not by queer gossipers, but gossip to which something more amorphously queer adheres, then the poets under discussion needn't *necessarily* be queer. But as we've seen, this is about the "baffling" of a range of categories, which, although it can be confusing for the reviewer, gives a lot of leeway to the writer.

So too does the notion of the normative, against which Bennett's version of gossip gets its strength. He writes early on of gossip's "interest in the nonnormative" and of how "gossip's ability to meld saying and doing suggests a vital source of transformative, nonnormative energy." Yet the book's first two sentences are thus: "Ours is an age of gossip. Buzz, chatter, dish, gab, hearsay, schmooze, tittle-tattle: proliferating social scientific research on idle talk has ensured we have it on good authority that such various species of gossip account for at least two-thirds of everyday conversation." If this statistic—characteristically scrupulously footnoted—doesn't show that gossip is normal, normalizing, or normative, then it must be there to suggest that this otherwise smartly circumscribed and careful scholarly study is *widely relevant* to a *range of readers*.

It's not, after all, on the whole, at least not in practical terms; but there are many choice observations that would have heads shaking in assent from porch or stoop, to shed or boudoir, if they were phrased a different way. His discussion of "gossip as tape recorder" will ring true for any voluble sneaks whose words have been "replayed" to them in front of other people (*Hey, that was between us!*), leading to egg on the face. A plump digression out of Hughes on the nature of the old party line is hardly out of date, given the way that cellphones let us in on conversations that are none of our business. ("Like gossip, and in some senses like the lyric poem, party-line telephony occupied a liminal space in which private talk circulated publicly.") Bennett's explanation that Hughes is not "simple" in a pejorative sense ought to be unnecessary by now, but his concomitant sense that the latter's "seldom-remarked obscurity" shows "a sociality shared by both the vernacular and the lyrical" would be familiar to listeners of, say, the Wu-Tang Clan, where an elaborate slang and gossipy real-world references are the grit in the lyrical sandpaper. Elsewhere, "[i]n thinking about the relationship between poetry and gossip" in Merrill's *The Changing Light at Sandover*, "one could do worse than to begin with a formidable occasion for both: the poetry reading." Oh, could one ever!

Lyric in this book is portrayed as limited, so it can be shown to have its own transgressor inside itself. His four authors "each recalibrate the poetics and politics of lyric selfhood by grounding it not in a subject's autonomous self-expression, as modern ideas of the lyric would lead us to expect, but instead in the ambiguous or suspended agency effected by gossip's winged words." They exhibit "ambivalence toward the powers and aesthetic of autonomous selfhood so often accorded to the modern lyric poem." The modern lyric, "usually understood at midcentury as ahistorical," has "ideals of transparent universality"—yes, the *lyric* has its own ideals—from which (the popular) Hughes "and other marginalized poets" are "excluded." That same Hughes "resists a midcentury lyrical ideal of transparent universality that would exclude the irreducible singularities of black or queer experience." Perhaps somebody, somewhere at midcentury said that all lyric poetry should be these things (universal, ahistorical, autonomous), but if so, they were spitting in the wind. Such a poetry in practice has never existed, and we all know it, as did the poets themselves, so why rehearse these moribund versions of lyric?

For the sake of a sense of transgression is why. Frankly, it's unnecessary. We don't need those versions to know that Bennett is right about O'Hara's "self-gossip," a lovely discussion that radiates out toward poetry in general, and ever outward, toward your latest Facebook post or most immodest humble-brag; or that he is astute on Stein's conception of "gossip as a style of listening," reminding us with clarity that with gossip, it takes two to tango. To see, as does Bennett, Picasso depict the goddess of Fame in an homage to Stein is to see with acuity, as he also does when he locates the sexual congress of the Ouija board from Norman Rockwell and an early advertisement to the spectral shoptalk of Merrill and his partner David Jackson. His connection of gossip to a "poetics of aurality" adds a needed layer to concepts of a poetics of orality: "What does gossip sound like?" What are "the correspondences of gossip and music"? Good questions, asked in part in relation to recent work on the lyric by Jonathan Culler, Virginia Jackson, and others. In that regard, Bennett pretty much covers his bases, which is hard because he plows a lot of ground. The only references missing that might help further flesh things out are John Gruen's *The Party's Over Now* (1989) and Joe LeSeur's *Digressions on Some Poems by Frank O'Hara* (2004), which exemplify the relation of O'Hara to gossip; and John Emil Vincent's *Queer Lyrics* (2002), for obvious reasons.

*Word of Mouth* closes with a coda treating Juliana Spahr, John Keene, Eileen Myles, and D.A. Powell, as if to remind us that gossip poetry, or poetry gossip, is ever renewing itself—and so it is. John Updike may have called reviewing "a higher form of gossip," but Bennett shows that in that regard, poetry takes the prize.

★   ★   ★

*Mr. West* by Sarah Blake, Wesleyan University Press, 2015.

The cynic (or is it the realist?) may look at Sarah Blake's first volume of poetry with a skeptical eye toward its interest in pop culture: the book is about Kanye West. It is also about contemporary media, motherhood, appropriation, infatuation and race. But it is mainly about Kanye West. Yet neither the cynic nor the realist need worry that Blake is merely using that mercurial genius as an attention-grabbing gimmick. No, *Mr. West* is a book that is in utterly good faith. That doesn't quite make it a good book, however.

The first poem, a prologue, is titled (with characteristically prosaic plainness) "'Runaway' Premieres in Los Angeles on October 18, 2010." It begins with an epigraph from MTV.com in which Kanye speaks about the dearth of women in his life after the death of his mother. Next follow the first words from Blake herself, and they are not propitious: "Kanye is 33. If he were Jesus, he would die this year, / and be resurrected." In a self-dialogue, Blake responds portentously: "I can't unthink this thought." That's too bad, because the emphasis on Kanye as a martyr and a divine figure is the least compelling part of the book.

Near the end of the poem Blake reveals, "I am two months pregnant," and answers herself in a final line: "The two of you, tied to this week in my life." But this is to start *in medias res*. Blake's real beginning, after the prologue, is a strong one. Most people who write about rap feel the need to share their origin story, situating themselves in a culture—where you were when you first heard what. In "Like the Poems Do" there is a brisk naïve version of this tradition that brings dry humor to its honesty: "I grew up saying, I listen to everything but country / and rap."

Blake's status as a novice has its advantages, all the more so as she is undefensive about it. For one, she avoids the corny use of hip-hop slang out of context. For another, she is engaged in discovering her subject, rather than insinuating, as does many a putative expert, that she already knows it all: "Another / way to say beautiful things that I have learned tonight." Everything reminds her of Kanye: Italy, musical terms beginning with *con*, Horus and Paris and Hades, Adam and Eve and the Minotaur. (She is good at lists.) A drive "along the Juniata" yields "a rock face / following a bend in the road," which brings forth talk of God—"But first I thought of Kanye's head / singing, singing, singing into that rock." When she "can't draw a parallel today between you and the branch I saw on the sidewalk," she realizes "some days I shouldn't write about you."

The central connection Blake makes (and the main strength of the book) is between herself, as impending mother to a son, and Kanye's mother, Dr. Donda West. A touching elegiac strain is evident throughout these poems of motherhood, although in this triangle of affection, with the two women as the base, Kanye is still the uppermost point: "Donda made it seem easy in her memoir. / To love Kanye. To unconditionally love him." There is Donda's concern for Kanye after his infamous post-Katrina remark ("George Bush doesn't care about black people") and the delicacy with which she holds his head after his car accident, not letting on how bad his swollen face looks: "She controlled her expressions.... / Women are familiar with how not to scare / someone who's in danger." Dr. West's example brings Blake some prenatal fears: "I'm afraid I will be a horrible mother because / I am a horrible woman."

The correspondence that the poet sees between the growth of her baby and the growth of her interest in Kanye has a downside, however; namely, an overemphasis on the body. It is one thing to anatomize your own fetus, to say "Inside, fingernails grow this week" or to write "First, a baby will have a skeleton completely / of cartilage." It is another thing to anatomize a man, a Black man, given the way Black bodies are so often used and abused. The problem is not as dire as if, say, one were to take Michael Brown's autopsy and "repurpose" it, since Kanye, unlike Brown, is a consciously public figure, and also not a tragic one. There will doubtless be differing levels of tolerance for what Blake is doing in poems like "Kanye's Skeletal System" and "Kanye's Circulatory System," differing senses of how political a lens applies. To me it seems presumptuous and creepy.

"Kanye knows what appropriation is," Blake writes, justifying (rather, *attempting* to justify) his invocation of Emmett Till in relation to himself. Whether Blake also knows what appropriation is, at least in relation to race, is hard to parse—but then again, who does? Supposed authorities on the subject are hollow. There is a poem about various forms of "privilege" (the word of the day), and even in something as stupid as the Kanye vs. Taylor Swift brouhaha, she can find the racial angle. ("Taylor Doesn't Speak Out Against Racism" is a fine form of blame-the-unsympathetic-victim.) But it all feels perfunctory, or self-involved: "I wonder what you would think of me, vitreous, near translucent in my skin," she addresses Donda at one point. Blake is more concerned with cultural appropriation in general, as exemplified in Internet aesthetics; indeed, large chunks of the book are copied and pasted from online sources, from biographical boilerplate to vitriolic chat. She claims to be "surprised at the racism and violence and hate" of the comments, which suggests she and I have been surfing different webs.

What can and can't be copied, what constitutes authorship and ownership these days, is of the essence here, but again, the matter is underdeveloped. No actual Kanye lyrics were harmed in the making of this book—they are all covered over by gray boxes—and endnotes tell us this is because Blake either couldn't get permission to print them or couldn't afford the $466 fee required for each quote, which would have added up. She would have done better to start a lyrics website, where she could reproduce thousands and thousands of verses, and which, far from landing her in trouble, would generate advertising revenue and venture capital. But this curious reality is only implied by the book's absences, with the facts relegated to the back matter.

What is most importantly absent, however, is insight into Kanye's music. There is a concern for media context ("The Internet winds around[,]" "The first tweet when I visit today"), with images of Kanye online and in videos. Blake is better at describing the visual than the sonic, perhaps because in a poem the sonic has so much to be enacted. And while there are alliterative effects ("Bones break, fracture. They bruise. Sometimes, / kissing contusions"), nice rhythms now and again ("A language once written in Arabic script, now written with letters like ours") and some conception of how structure accentuates sound ("I can think, have thought, of great line breaks for that quote"), all in all it's too prosaic, too flat, to give a sense of why Kanye, for many of his fans, most matters. One wishes him well in design, in fashion, in fatherhood, in marriage, in whatever endeavor he undertakes. (Maybe not in politics.) But the Mr. West who has never made a boring album, whose masterpiece ratio is exceedingly high, is the Mr. West about whom I most want to read. And if *Mr. West*, in what it is missing, leads me back to listen again, some purpose has been served.

\* \* \*

*Northrop Frye and Others, Volume II: The Order of Words* by Robert D. Denham, University of Ottawa Press, 2017.

Now that all those luscious blue volumes of Northrop Frye's books and notebooks and letters and diaries and miscellaneous essays and interviews have come out, there is some fascinating and likely near-final trawling to be done. Not that the work won't keep on giving—it does and it will—but there are lacuna and minutiae that can now be filled in and figured out. Continuing to get down to the nitty-gritty, Robert D. Denham—a Frye careerist and polymath who has written or edited 32 books by or about the great critic—returns with the second volume in a three-part set. As with Volume I, this installment of *Northrop Frye and Others* considers a double handful of writers and thinkers whom Frye considered in his unpublished work, but whom he never discussed at length in print.

The book is an odd hodge-podge, which is welcome, as the more randomness one locates and brings to bear in reading Frye, the better. In an awesome understatement, Denham at one point notes, "As has often been observed, Frye is a schematic thinker[,]" but one of the best things about the publication of the *Collected Works* is to realize from how many places the schemes came and just how much got sieved out from the classic books in their composing. Some folks you would expect to see here, namely, the systemitizers and theorists and archetypal completists: Boehme, Carlyle, Coleridge, Hegel, Rabelais. Others wouldn't have been on the tip of my tongue but make sense: the Mahayana Sutras, John Stuart Mill (Frye mined from *On Liberty*), Machiavelli. ("Frye believes that hypocrisy can be a virtue if it is seen not as a moral principle but as a tactical one.") Two influences most of us won't know: Elizabeth Fraser and Jane Ellen Harrison, the latter a Cambridge classicist who died in 1928, the former a talented visual artist, travel companion, and friend with whom Frye even went on a self-described "pub-crawl;" their stories in relation to his close the book in a curious way (Fraser's winning letters and sketches to Frye are included and are a high point) that makes one anticipate the cast of characters awaiting us in the third part of this series.

You could do worse than assigning Denham's *Others* in one of those courses where they teach you Great Books—the first volume covered Kierkegaard, Lewis Carroll, Mallarmé, Aristotle, Longinus, and (the following five of whom I've never read and three of whom I'd never heard) Giordano Bruno, Paul Tillich, Henry Reynolds, Frances Yates, and Joachim of Floris—but they don't really teach courses like that anymore; everybody's too smart, specialized, googled-up, or woke; but there's a pleasant old-fashionedness here. These books have the spirit of a survey of intellectual history, but filtered through a Frye obsession: "His personal library contained forty-four books on Eastern philosophy and religion, forty-two of which have his marginal markings and annotations [ ... ] [T]here are forty-eight entries in the diaries and notebooks where he records his observations on the *Lankavatara* and the *Avatamsaka* Sutras." "He made twenty-five marginal markings and annotations in [the *Diamond Sutra*] and twenty in his copy of the *Lotus Sutra*." "Hegel makes more than twenty cameo appearances in *Northrop Frye's Student Essays* [ ... ] In two of the essays, [ ... ] Frye engages in more than just casual reference." "As for Harrison, Frye owned and read three of her books, the first two of which he annotated[.]" Books by and about Coleridge are counted as buttressing the later master's sense that (as he wrote in his diary) "any speculative work on criticism, such as the one I'm contemplating, has to involve a pretty thorough knowledge of Coleridge."

Speaking of "pretty thorough knowledge," that of Denham is impressive, as it must be to elucidate Frye so completely and with such prolixity and longevity. Frye's knowledge, of course, remains practically unfathomable, but my favorite nugget from the book just proves that almost all is never enough: "[Peter] Fisher was one of Frye's students, who, after graduating from college, had approached Frye about doing an MA thesis on Blake. As Frye reports this episode [ ... ], Fisher 'nearly walked out again when he discovered that I had not read the Bhagavadgita in Sanskrit, which he took for granted that any serious student of Blake would have done as a matter of course.'" (Well, naturally—and they say that the kids *these* days are entitled!) In the final analysis, a fun full book for the Frye fanatic.

\* \* \*

*The Vehement Passions* by Philip Fisher, Princeton University Press, 2002.

Philip Fisher is a professor of literature whose recent books are not the modest and specialized efforts characteristic of much current criticism. His topics range from America's culture of creative destruction to art in an age of museums to wonder and what he terms the aesthetics of rare experience. Readers should therefore not expect from its title that Fisher's latest book will merely explain why women once swooned in novels and fiery gentlemen once fought duels.

What readers will encounter instead is a book capable of leaving them changed, even shaken. *The Vehement Passions* reasserts the forgotten power of a partially lost vocabulary, a loss that has perhaps enfeebled human lives. Although passions such as anger, fear, grief, and shame are still psychic reference points in our culture, these impassioned states have been supplanted, Fisher argues, by categories that are more easily controlled. The extremity of impassioned states imperils a modern world of emotions, feelings, and moods (our preferred templates for the inner life).

The passions must therefore be domesticated, in part by the adoption of a new set of terms:

>In combination, the political term "insanity," the temperamental stance of irony, the civic virtue of tolerance, and the psychological conviction that most deep feelings are marked by ambivalence act together to police so successfully the borders of ordinary life within modern consciousness that the passions are not merely excluded; they appear quaint and archaic.

The civilizing victories that attend this process—for instance, the "triumph of impersonal justice over retaliation" in our legal system—are matched by more subtle defeats. Drawing powerfully on Aristotle, Fisher reconstructs a system in which anger (a model for impassioned states) is ethically desirable and "lies at the root of an intuitive and manageable sense of daily justice." Such desirability is the case not only because anger spurs us to action, but also because it, along with other passions, marks off for us the domain of what precisely in our life is worth fighting for.

The part such "marking off" plays in Fisher's argument is the strongest aspect of the book. "What lies within our power?" he asks. "What does not lie in our power? Where does the border between the two realms lie?" That border Fisher calls "the radius of the will," inside of which sits everything we believe to be in our control. According to Fisher, it is the passions that show us the otherwise ambiguous boundary that circumscribes our will:

>The passions mark the point of injury to the will by the unexpected, the unwanted, and the threatening. By signalling that an insult or injury to the will has taken place, the passions mark out for us a point where we expected the will to be able to succeed. The passions are therefore a sign that passivity, powerlessness, and an attitude of hopeless acceptance of whatever will come are not endemic to our reading of the world. The passions occur around an active will, one that expects to fare well in the world and can, for that very reason, be startled, surprised, even angered by insults or injuries to the will and its expectations about the future.

The passions similarly describe for us the boundaries of our social world. Grief felt over the death of a loved one, or the anger one feels for a wronged friend:

these passions allow us to know who in our life truly matters, just as the absence of felt passion lets us know who does not.

Both the argument and the style of *The Vehement Passions* are free from the sentimentality or mystification that might easily follow such a topic. Fisher's rigorous prose avoids pretentious obscurity, and as his argument gains strength in sedimentary fashion, the seriousness and scope of his project become ever more apparent. A concluding, characteristically muted encomium to literature as "our most important anti-Kantian domain" that "defends the priority of [ ... ] person-centered experiences in time" seems at first to come out of nowhere. Reflection, however, suggests that all through the book Fisher uses literature as a tool for genuine insight, not as a site from which to trumpet his own virtuosity. His constant recourse to Homer, Shakespeare, and other imaginative writers melds with his philosophical citations and the reader's own experiential knowledge to forge a coherent and far-reaching thesis. The resulting critical achievement proves that an ethical, responsible and full modern life can still be—perhaps must be—a life lived with passion.

\* \* \*

*A New Theory for American Poetry* by Angus Fletcher, Harvard University Press, 2004.

Almost forty years ago, in an essay written in implicit praise of Northrop Frye and his *Anatomy of Criticism*, the then-young scholar Angus Fletcher remarked that "any theorist who would free the traffic of criticism must harmonize variant and even discordant interests." Decades later, in *A New Theory for American Poetry*, Fletcher has done just that. If the literary parameters of Fletcher's theory are less expansive than those of the *Anatomy*, the prose of the former is livelier, its extra-literary concerns more immediate. Only time can tell the effects of this theory not "of" but "for" American lyric. Even in the present, however, it is clear that Fletcher has produced a book worthy of Frye's great work of theoretical harmony.

The largest claim made by Fletcher is generic: he argues that with American poetry we see the advent of what he calls the "environment poem." This new genre seeks neither to be about the surrounding world nor to represent it analytically; rather, it strives to be a world. Such poems, writes Fletcher, "aspire to surround the reader, such that to read them is to have an experience much like suddenly recognizing that one actually has an environment, instead of not perceiving the surround at all." The eponymous theory, an impressive apparatus that stabilizes the generic claim, has six parts: "concept of horizon," "the poet's way of being in the world," "poetry as environmental form," "the power of underlying rhythms," "the poetry of becoming," and a "theory of coherence."

Although there are dozens of rich asides on a wide range of topics, the work of three poets—John Clare, Walt Whitman, John Ashbery—best exemplifies the theory. There has been a resurgence of interest in John Clare of late, and the sympathetic critique of the poet here suggests that such interest is not misplaced. The starring role of this British Romantic in a theory of American poetry needs some explaining, however. Given the links between American poetry and British Romanticism, to reconceive the latter affects our picture of the former. Clare comes in because of his penchant for description (more pronounced than in Coleridge or Wordsworth, for instance), which urges Fletcher to ask a question with "numerous consequences," namely, "what is the formal, historical, and factual relationship between description and our knowledge of the environment?" Description, "the humblest of intelligent symbolic acts," is so common, writes Fletcher, that "its possible range eludes us." Yet it is through description that we are best able to grasp and expand our perceptual limits. Using Clare's descriptions to explore the "almost genetic connection between poetry and natural fact," Fletcher recalibrates the Romantic dialectic, which becomes in his theory "not the dialectic of nature and self—as many have thought—but the dialectic of natural fact and philosophical idea."

This leads us to Whitman, who, Fletcher claims, invented the environment-poem. Whitman was able to integrate natural fact and philosophical idea in heretofore unseen ways. At a political level, he made manifest the connection between the American scene and Jacksonian democracy. The rise of Andrew Jackson served not just America, but also Whitman's poems as "a unifying fact, the ordering of a vast social environment." For the country's founding planter class, Jacksonian tenets may have seemed chaotic and inconsistent with responsible governance. For Whitman, these tenets brought coherence both to America and to its poetry (indistinguishable in Whitman's vision), because, to paraphrase Fletcher, only inconsistency is truly coherent. Fletcher also shows how Whitman's poetics took cues from the natural world. His discussion of the Whitmanian phrase and the poet's harnessing of the power of waves—a theory of "undulant form"—is virtuosic formalist criticism.

In fact, Fletcher's book is a model both for treating large theoretical issues and for moving "beyond the vice of slavish thematics" by looking closely at actual poems. Although quite an achievement, it is perhaps not coincidental that such ostensibly divergent approaches are taken by a critic who asserts that "scale-shifting has a spiritual aspect." Nor is it coincidental that Fletcher, with his overwhelming but expressive theory, is so compelling a critic of Ashbery, the last in his trio of poets, for Ashbery is truly one who has created "a language capable of expressing the common fact of being perpetually overwhelmed." Fletcher asks, what "looks like chaos, but is not?" His answer—an Ashbery poem—is rhetorical and true and gets to the heart of an oeuvre in which perceptions are "crowding each other for simultaneous recognition like children at a birthday party."

The simile reminds the reader not only that Fletcher is smart, but also that his writing is lovely. It achieves perhaps its loveliest pitch in the following paragraph:

> To read Whitman you need to think like certain Thomas Nelson editions of my childhood. Printed on exquisitely fine India paper, these books were bound in what was called "limp leather." Reading Whitman is like holding a book bound in limp leather. You savor the creamy texture of the binding; you can almost eat the letterpress print; though most books are common enough, this one is a rare thing. You gaze on its soft green color, tracing pliant thoughts. Today scholars may believe they have explained everything. But our explanations and glosses, even in paperback, are thick, stiff, and heavy; they do not bend.

The "our" in "our explanations and glosses" is far too modest. In *A New Theory for American Poetry*, Fletcher may not have explained everything about his subject, but what he has explained is enough to occupy most minds for a long time. By being so pliant itself, the book bends us with brilliance toward the work of the poets it reads. Such a humble, attentive approach is only proper; many thanks to Fletcher for reshaping our critical posture.

\* \* \*

*The Children of Children Keep Coming: An Epic Griotsong* by Russell L. Goings, Simon and Schuster, 2009.

If the epic, to paraphrase Pound, is a poem that includes history, then such a poem might also include the recent history of the epic. The masterpieces of Modernism trail behind them a train of poetic and political vexations; postmodern aesthetics put epics of ostensible progress through the ringer, deconstructing a hoped-for coherence of fragments into knowing piles of pastiche; critiques of master narratives arose as an era's own counter-epics, meant through theory to supplant those of art; and the inevitable end-of-history that spelled the necessary end of the epic never quite materialized. Into this arena of upheavals, disavowals, and reversals enters Russell L. Goings with *The Children of Children Keep Coming: An Epic Griotsong*.

Because the song and the epic occupy opposite ends of the spectrum of poetic scale, the book's subtitle situates *The Children of Children* at a place of formal irony, forcing a rich frisson. At the levels of tone and temperament, however, irony yields to the celebratory—of heroes who ended slavery, who fought for civil rights, and who took seriously America's democratic ideals. The invocation of the griot, a West African bard and storyteller who is equal parts prophet, singer, and teacher, suggests both the book's pedagogical intent and its goals of cultural preservation and warning: "We channel impatience into creativity, / Where the beginning of an aesthetic is modest. / We blend the silence that / Death brings to the next moment with / Toms, drums, sticks, racks, / High-hats, rhythm, meter." Goings's list—and lists do much of this volume's work—links Black American music and verse to its African origins. The notion of a "modest" aesthetic in an epic context is a challenge to expectations, and not just in terms of genre. The challenge is spiritual and political, recalling the forbearance of Martin Luther King, Jr. and the quiet fortitude of Rosa Parks, the latter of whom is the book's central, yet humble, hero among many heroes.

The challenge of *The Children of Children* is also historical, for it urges the reader to attend to beginnings. In one of many moments of lyric ventriloquism, Goings has Prudence Crandall, a Connecticut Quaker who in the 1830's fell afoul of the law for educating African-American girls, speak to her students: "It's a time to encourage beginners, / Beginners I teach." This Whitmanian locution points to one of the book's major influences. Goings not only values Whitman's creative commitment to democracy, but like Whitman moves from the wide-frame of abstraction—"One nation, one people, one well, / One balanced scale of / Liberty, opportunity, equality"—to the intimacy of the close-up: "The gift to appreciate the inchworm[.]" Other poetic predecessors include Langston Hughes, whose translation of the blues onto the page is a touchstone, and Margaret Walker, whose use of folk mythology in her under-read *For My People* sat easily alongside the literary conventions of realism in a lyrical mode.

The characters Goings invents—Banjo Pete, Buddy Boy, Calli, Evalina, Running Boy, Maudell Sleet—are a manifestation of his claim that "We must create myths. / Myths fill the space between true and false." They are not characters in a novelistic sense, for though they have distinct characteristics, much of what they say blends together, creating a choral effect. The most crucial chorus in the book is the eponymous "children of children" themselves. Their voice is often introduced by a beautiful plain-style refrain: "Under sun high and moon low, / The children of children rise to sing." Such refrains as these that pepper the book point to Goings's assertion of the existence of two kinds of time. On the one hand, there is temporal (and social) progression, which is evident in the movement from Part One—"Taking the Train to Freedom," where the reader travels through the days of slavery to emancipation and the end of the Civil War—to Part Two, "Jubilee," which carries the reader through the Civil Rights era. (A third part, "Celebration of Survival," serves as a summary coda.) On the other hand, any given moment in time contains both the moments that precede it and those that might follow. Thus, even in sections that chronologically place us in the presence of Harriet Tubman, Frederick Douglass, or Colonel Shaw commanding the 54th Massachusetts Infantry, the voices of those who led the charge for change in the 1950s and 60s are heard.

"Power lives / In real and imaginary giants," writes Goings, but there is a counter-power in the venality of the "crows" who flap and caw their way through the book. They represent the a-temporality of evil, as well as the two kinds of time; for though they are named for the Jim Crow policies that arose during Reconstruction, they both precede and persist after the days when such policies were legally in place. Their methods can be subtle—they are "experts in ambiguous phrases." More often they are brutal, as in a passage that radically tempers the jubilation that follows the end of the war ("Murders increase, / Shallow, unmarked graves grow, / Horror settles[.]"), or one that charges Mississippi crows with the murders of James Chaney, Andrew Goodman, and Michael Schwerner. Less life-denying tropes threaded throughout include grass and lawns, respective figures for common humanity and a tended-to democracy, for natural rights and a stable place of rest. Also important are rivers and trains, which suggest the necessity of movement in avoiding danger, while pointing toward the goal of political and spiritual transport.

These latter two tropes come to formal fruition in the flow of *The Children of Children*, where verbal momentum is prodigious; you never step into the same poem twice, yet it is always of a moving piece. A similar correspondence occurs in Goings's turn around the figure of "notes." Whereas Wallace Stevens once wrote that money is a kind of poetry, for Goings, music is a kind of money. In the extensive glossary, itself an educational raison d'être for the book, among the broad but brisk biographical and historical sketches is an entry for "promissory notes": "An effective palliative used to seduce Black citizens' behavior and expectations by promising all those emancipated forty acres and a mule." This offer of compromised assistance was rescinded by a vindictive Andrew Johnson, but in Goings's poem, such deep disappointment and raw neglect yields positive resistance and artistic returns: "We ain't gonna / Carry no more broken / Promissory notes / We gonna cash notes, / Half notes, quarter notes, eighth notes, / Full notes, black and white notes." The giants of jazz are praised throughout, with such greats as Charlie "Bird" Parker flying higher and singing sweeter than the croaking crows who are heavy with hate.

If *The Children of Children* is a virtual hagiography of secular saints—of Abolitionists and Civil Rights leaders, soldiers and scholars, athletes and artists—it is also a capacious compendium of cultural forms. The African-American church is heard in its modes of prayer and exhortation, the latter especially evident in the insistence of anaphora; the "worried lines" of the blues embody repetition with a difference and prove the power of the Black vernacular; and the pre-history of hip-hop can be heard not only in the frequency of rhyme, but also through the open-ended, Scheherazadean, on-and-on-to-the-break-of-dawn flow that shows something of what rap was long before being fitted into the formal constraints of the four-minute song. (Indeed, in representing the sound of drums, or of the character Nexus's "tattered white pants, / Splattered with red mud, flap[ping] / In rhythm with his anxiety," Goings emphasizes this link with an onomatopoeic pun: "Rap-rap-rap-pat-rap.") Lyrics from a host of songs are sampled and sometimes refigured—"Down by the Riverside," "Go Down, Moses," "Nobody Knows the Trouble I've Seen," "Sometimes I Feel Like a Motherless Child," and "Strange Fruit" among them.

Like Romare Bearden, whose striking drawings taken from the author's personal collection illustrate the book, Goings turns the range, both troubled and triumphant, of African-American lives to aesthetic advantage. As a review of a recent Bearden exhibition put it, by "[w]orking and reworking his motifs and materials in ways at once extravagant and economic, Bearden synthesized not only his own visual and lived experience but also great chunks of 20th-century art and the cultures that fed it." This first book by the almost eighty-year-old Goings does much the same in the realm of words. Here is singing on a scale that transcends small-minded notions of time, yet down enough to earth to speak to a wide-ranging readership. *The Children of Children Keep Coming* is not merely a poem that includes history, but is importantly one that derives from and extends it.

\* \* \*

*Cultural Studies* by Kevin A. González, Carnegie Mellon University Press, 2009.

It is a paradox of language that as a word gains more traction, its meaning grows more slippery. The word "culture" is just such a case: laid on too thick or spread too thin, it morphs from airy abstraction into battering ram and back in the blink of an eye. In his volume of poems called *Cultural Studies*, Kevin González uses the word in its adjectival form in title after title: "Cultural Stud," "Cultural Slut," "Cultural Sellout," "Cultural Spar," "Cultural Strumpet," "Cultural Scheme," "Cultural Shock," "Cultural Schmooze," "Cultural Soliloquy," "Cultural Scope." The result is both a comic critique of a repetition compulsion and an ambivalent admission of the term's loose utility.

A native of Puerto Rico, González shows us how foundational that island and its culture are to him and his poems, as he reminisces about his youth (in one poem he movingly apostrophizes "Youth" itself) and tells stories about returning home after sojourns in Pittsburgh, Iowa, and Wisconsin. The poems prove that being peripatetic does not preclude being anchored: "Always, there has been a backpack / strapped to your heart, & asking Where are you from? / has not been unlike asking, What is this poem about?"

In addition to the many place names and the occasional easy shifting from English to Spanish, there is a sense of movement in the way González switches between the first and second person. Though the book begins with "I," it is "you" that predominates, as if some detachment is necessary to understand oneself in a life marked by dislocations. This grammatical device draws the reader into González's well-told stories, since we can't help but hear ourselves addressed ("Hey, you!"). To the poet's credit, he gives us over half the book to figure this out for ourselves, after which he admits to being self-conscious about hiding behind the deflecting pronoun: "it's Halloween, & you're disguised / in the second person"; "All I really want / is to be You for another twenty seconds / & maybe pull this off."

As these lines suggest, there is an underlying sense here that poetry is an elaborate form of lying, a con that one "pulls off" by being "disguised," or by overemphasizing the "cultural" because it is a hot poetic commodity. This comes through not only in subtle hints from the poet's father (who, himself capable of dissimulation, appears in several poems where he is wary of being represented), but also in the remarks of a fellow poet, who tells González "to be thankful / because at least you have a shtick." But the poet is so determined to reveal his methods—just another part of the con?—that he lets us in time and again to the institutional context of his craft:

> Back when I still believed in God
> is not a good way to start a poem
> & perhaps that is why Iowa passed
> & you wound up in an MFA Program

full of vegetarians who say
your poems are all about sex or poets
or having sex with poets
or not getting into Iowa.

Although we know that hardly any young poet gets published these days without the workshop imprimatur, it is annoying to have the facts pushed in our faces, as if the poet is pulling back a curtain or breaking a spell. The annoyance passes when one realizes that this is actually a starker form of realism than is usually encountered in books of poems, risky in its resistance to our fantasies of the untutored poet. (No worries, though, González got into Iowa after all.)

By the end of *Cultural Studies*, the "I" and the "you" at last share the page with a "Kevin A. González." In between these formal poems (matched elsewhere in the volume by two strong sestinas) is a suite of free verse couplets, impressionistic responses to three fights by the Puerto Rican legend Félix Trinidad, a ferocious boxer who won belts in three weight classes. The poet thus enters an august tradition, for the connection between pugilism and poetry goes back to Homer and has never since stopped yielding verse. Having read that González attended at least one of the eponymous fights in person ("The Night Tito Trinidad KO'ed Ricardo Mayorga"), this fight fan wished at first for a more ringside, sports-writerly approach. But the rightness of his response must be conceded. *Ring Magazine* and YouTube clips can convey the facts of the fight just fine. But only González can convey what Felix Trinidad might mean to a fellow native son:

> Our culture is a pair of Adidas
> dangling from telephone lines
>
> & a small child reaching up,
> fists gripping air,
>
> arms brief and contained
> like the two o's of colony.

\* \* \*

*Hoops* by Major Jackson, W.W. Norton, 2006.

The title of this impressive, enjoyable, readable book, Major Jackson's second, refers to the hotly contested games of basketball on the asphalt courts of the author's native North Philadelphia. After a prologue poem of well-paced three- and four-beat lines, in which Jackson and a friend, "off from a double at McDonald's," are stuck up at gunpoint while trying, despite "schoolboy jitters," to buy cocaine, we enter the macadam rectangle, a multi-ringed circus of which the game is only the central part. Around the edges of the chain-link fence, nicknamed figures throw craps and drink malt liquor to the soundtrack of a Boogie Down Productions tape pumping out of a boom box. On the court itself, urban art is being made: "At gate's entrance, my gaze / follows Radar & his half-cocked // jump shot. All morning I sang / hymns yet weighed his form: / his flashing the lane, quick / stop to become sky-born." The casual ballad stanzas of the title poem point to Jackson's greatest strength, which is his ability to marry without anxiety the traditional forms of the English poetic tradition with the poetic vernacular and the human concerns of an urban, Black population.

Jackson, of course, is not exactly a representative member of that population—he's a published and polished poet, after all; and no matter what population you're from, to be a poet is to be an odd man out. But this simply reinforces another meaning in the collection's title, namely, that American upward mobility, especially for a Black man, involves jumping through multiple hoops. The process is not necessarily hateful, although it can be dangerous, and not only psychologically. That the title poem is dedicated to Hank Gathers, the Loyola Marymount guard who once led the nation in scoring and rebounding but died of heart failure on the court during his conference tournament, suggests that even the most successful of the upwardly mobile are guaranteed nothing.

The poetic instinct was there early on in this author, if the poem "Metaphor" is any indication. Jackson recalls watching a thunderstorm with a cousin, the two trying to outdo each other in figurative invention. The eventual poet ultimately takes the prize, "likening the meteoric openings / to glowing keyholes into / an alien world," thereby describing not only electrical gashes but also the "openings" made by metaphor. Here is DuBois's famed "double-consciousness" oriented toward the particularities of the poet and operating at the most organic level.

But nobody rises alone and in this book Jackson pays homage to those who have buoyed him. In "Urban Renewal," a multi-part poem that constitutes the second part of this three-part book, Jackson honours in deft pentameter a man who showed him how to work in and beautify the world: "The backyard garden wall is mossy green / and flakes a craggy mound of chips. Nearby / my grandfather kneels between a row of beans / and stabs his shears into earth. I squint an eye, / —a comma grows at his feet." From close to the ground we rise (with hitches). Later on in the poem Jackson remembers the Kelly family of Philly, whose daughter Grace as actress and princess became a model of genteel beauty. But powerful locals could sniff out Irish blood: "No amount of Monacan / crowns or Hitchcock thrillers could propel the Kellys / up the Main Line. What W.A.S.P. would sign?" Jackson's own grandfather, meanwhile, "points at the skyline's glory / he once scaffolded," reminiscing, "'We gave the city light with those towers.'" Presumably, the Main-Liners refrained, if not from complaints about Irish bricklayers and Black construction workers, then from complaints about the light they provided.

"You might say," writes Jackson, that "my whole life led / to celebrating youth and how it snubs and rebuffs." And about two-thirds of the way through this book, one begins to wish for writing not so exclusively retrospective, something adult. The poet seems to have shared this wish, for the volume's final section is a masterful and multi-part epistolary poem to Gwendolyn Brooks. Although it is gently retrospective in being elegiac, its orientation is more toward the present, toward Jackson himself as a practicing poet, husband, father, and man. In 176 stanzas, a flexible rime royal, we are taken to places all over the world—vacations, writing retreats, academic conferences, family gatherings—without ever leaving the head of a man represented to us in a conversational prosody that is one of the best contemporary examples of the multi-tiered tradition of Wordsworth, Auden, Whitman, Frost, and Black vernacular poets. It has been some time since I have read such a successful poem of our time. "What age granted these lines material good? / Can the epistolary form contain our hoods?" The answer to the former is an ambivalent ours; the answer to the latter is a definite yes. Jackson's poem is the proof.

START TO FIGURE

\* \* \*

*Directed by Desire: The Collected Poems of June Jordan*, edited by Jan Heller Levi and Sara Miles, Copper Canyon Press, 2007.

*New and Collected Poems, 1964–2006* by Ishmael Reed, Carroll & Graf, 2007.

*Directed by Desire* is a handsome book, as one expects from Copper Canyon and as the late June Jordan deserves. Jordan, who died in 2002 after a life of creative and political activism, "went for human commonality," writes Adrienne Rich in the introduction, "without denying our cruel separations." From 1969's *Who Look At Me*, a long poem responding to images of African-Americans, to the fifty-one late poems collected here for the first time, among which one finds a glancing elegy to Princess Diana, a scathing reproach to Eminem, and a preference for sailing to chemotherapy, Jordan displays without fail her major strengths.

Those strengths—a propulsive way with the line and an emotional stance of intensity—are employed to wide-ranging effect. They can appear in sharp bursts as she remarks on aesthetics: "I have rejected propaganda teaching me / about the beautiful / the truly rare // the truly rare can stay out there." Or the rhythms can expand and the intensity turn mystic in a mode reminiscent of parable: "I was happy to think of the burial place and I asked my father to / tell me a word for my first dream / He held me on his lap as he gave me the word for my dream / Cemetery was what he whispered in my ear." Or they can be used to pacifist purpose in revising one of America's poetic chestnuts: "Something there is that sure must love a plane / No matter how many you kill with what kind / of bombs or how much blood you manage to spill / you never will hear the cries of pain." Jordan aims to inspire her readers, not merely fill them with rarefied air. Her mode is vernacular, as often as not, and fittingly for one who argued that Black English should be encouraged in schools, the Black vernacular: "we be wondering what they gone do / all them others left and right." As these excerpts also suggest, personal and political struggles are intertwined and are matters of life and death.

Especially death, it would seem. Poems describing in rage and sadness a Black boy beaten, a Black girl killed, a Black woman beaten, a Black man killed run high in numbers here. Those eulogized are not symbolic, but are real people, as the titles often emphasize: "On the Murder of Two Human Being Black Men, Denver A. Smith and His Unidentified Brother, at Southern University, Baton Rouge, Louisiana, 1972." What is as harrowing and disgusting as the contents of such poems is the knowledge that Jordan could have written thousands more. The ones she did write amount to a reimagining of the occasional poem in our problematic democracy, where gratefulness for having outlets for outrage is tempered by the fact that there is always a valid occasion for expressing it.

Jordan was one whose experience of suffering caused her not to contract but to expand. In "From Sea to Shining Sea," she moves from a description of a fruit stand to a series of vignettes about those who have it rough. There is enough pain and fear to go around and, by the end of the poem, we feel that these lives are balanced as precariously as the initial pyramid of pomegranates. Although the poem could hardly be more serious, there is humour in its juxtaposition. We also hear her wry laughter in "Notes on the Peanut," in which George Washington Carver brags about his peanut shoelaces, peanut calculator, and peanut painting by Renoir, before taking questions from an audience: "Please: / Speak right into the peanut!" Even the unpleasant scene of deciding who-gets-what after a marriage dissolves elicits a kind of joke: "OK. So she got back the baby / but what happened to the record player?"

The mixture of humour and anger is also a hallmark of Ishmael Reed, whose strength as an editor, essayist, and novelist (and whose reputation as provocateur) has overshadowed his achievement as a poet. That achievement, like Jordan's, is based in the vernacular, as well as in his use of folk materials, his fearlessness with form, and his "irrational" tendency toward the spiritual, which stands as an indictment of the impoverished soul of a bottom-line age. As he puts it in "The Neo-HooDoo Aesthetic," a recipe for gumbo, "The proportions of ingredients used depend upon the cook!"

Reed's *New and Collected Poems, 1964–2006* contains almost two hundred pages of work written since his *New and Collected* of 1988, including "Gethsemane Park," a "gospera" originally written as a libretto commissioned by the San Francisco Opera Company, and "Snake War," a prose piece based on D. O. Fagunwa's *Igbo Olodumare*. That these two works are hardly poems in a conventional sense says much about Reed's disregard of generic limitation.

In "America United," which gets by largely on the intensity of its reaction to hypocritical calls for unity after 9/11, the formal recklessness is frustrating but ultimately serves the poem's purpose. Indeed, the right indelicate balance is usually struck, as in the ever-relevant "In a War Such Things Happen," the title of which serves as a refrain to a series of lamentably predictable atrocities.

It casts no aspersions on the later work to say that the major achievement here remains those poems from *Conjure* (1972) and *Chattanooga* (1973) that first established Reed as a poet able to shift without anxiety between cultures and verbal registers and to do so with vitriol and wit. "I am a Cowboy in the Boat of Ra," "Catechism of d Neoamerican Hoodoo Church," and "Beware: Do Not Read This Poem" are ensconced in the postmodern canon, while "Neo-HooDoo Manifesto" is one of the best manifestos of an era that produced no shortage of them. There is also great pleasure in revisiting lesser-known poems from his early period, such as "Dualism," a compact parable about the inescapability of history, or "Railroad Bill, A Conjure Man," a stellar addition to the tradition of African-American balladry from which it is derived.

"This poem came at me / like a flash flood," Reed writes in an untitled poem of more recent vintage. "If I had paused to count meter / I would have drowned." Neither Reed nor Jordan is overly fastidious about form, but use it to their advantage as any good American would. Pragmatist poets of political intent, they remind us that the loosening of the line and the expansion of voice has continued into the twenty-first century. These two voluminous volumes suggest that future generations will have their own solid foundations on which to build, from which to speak their mind.

★   ★   ★

*Digressions on Some Poems by Frank O'Hara* by Joe LeSueur, Farrar Straus and Giroux, 2003.

If you lived with Frank O'Hara for a decade, as Joe LeSueur did from 1955, you could harvest a lot of gossip. The late poet's roommate and lover dishes it out in heavy helpings, a testament both to his memory and to his powers of observation. Typical is this account of what he calls a "gay bachelor party": "Several of the guests were chatting with a couple of hustlers, and, within a few minutes of our arrival, Tennessee [Williams] made his entrance from the other room, followed by another hustler. Dressed in a fancy brocaded robe—a djellaba?—and smoking an exotic brand of cigarette through a long, elegant holder, Tennessee parted the beaded curtains and stepped inside the room with all the grace and dignity of Anna May Wong."

Later, Truman Capote shows up, as does, improbably, Yukio Mishima. LeSueur remembers thinking that the Japanese writer "must be a size queen." Next comes that component, speculation (a supplement to facts), without which gossip hardly deserves the name: LeSueur "can't resist considering the possibility, admittedly far-out, that [Mishima's] apparent preoccupation with big cocks was so great that it might provide us with one of the keys to understanding [ ... ] his decision to commit hari-kari, wherein his young lieutenant, his lover, went with him to his death." Such informative leaps are sadly lacking from today's top critics, who could also learn from LeSueur's tales of prodigious drinking, along with his accounts of sex of such frequent variety that readers will be jealous and relieved never to have engaged in such exertions themselves. Yet everything in these *Digressions* is told with such tact that the whole affair is untacky. What a balancing act!

Alas, no one did exclamation points like Frank O'Hara. LeSueur's loving trip down memory lane glows with O'Hara's vibrancy, and yet it is heavy with sadness, for the true subject of these digressions died too young in a stupid accident. The poems, however, mitigate the sadness. In what amounts to an excellent anthology, LeSueur cites, to instigate digression, over forty of O'Hara's poems, which he then fills in for the reader with biography, history, and well-informed guesses. Who better to elaborate on O'Hara's list of stars in "To the Film Industry in Crisis" than LeSueur, with whom the poet watched so many of those stars on a secondhand TV? What better guide to the shenanigans in "John Button Birthday" than one who was there to help celebrate it?

The best service this book provides is showing us the poems again. They are, in the main, truly great: full of fresh air, original. LeSueur's critical memoir integrates the poems with the poet so flawlessly that the powerful source of originality, O'Hara, seems to be in the next room, sitting at his typewriter, pecking out another occasional piece with rapid jabs. Although he drank too much to be as happy-go-lucky as uninformed legend suggests, O'Hara had presence and was a man of incredible force. "[U]nacquisitive, generous-to-a-fault," and one to whom friends went "in times of travail, sadness, rejection," O'Hara was also capable of unleashing rejection if "he detected a flaw" in one he loved. Part of the melancholy that courses through this book comes from just such a rejection of LeSueur, whom O'Hara eventually decided was petty.

The memoirist gives us reason to think so, too. He can be snobbish, shallow, sex-obsessed. His wit seems dim by the light of his friends. Yet as the book progresses, one's respect for LeSueur grows, for in the name of truth he exposes his flaws, without expecting any credit for doing so. He also shows himself capable of learning from his great paramour not only how to write in such a way that the moment is conveyed, but also how to live. For a Mormon boy from nowhere like LeSueur, whose mother told him being gay was as bad as being a killer, O'Hara's sense, as a gay man, of his priority in the world must have been liberating:

> "There are other reasons for being homosexual"—that was Frank's way of expressing how relieved and content he was to be queer. What he meant was, going to bed with our own sex was just part of it, the great freedom we enjoyed assuming such importance that in his view it was more than sufficient compensation for being thought of as sexual pariahs and, in some quarters, as detested perverts. So we lived our lives the way we saw fit, and if it was our fancy to go gaga over a movie star, that was our business.

This passage, spun from a discussion of O'Hara's James Dean phase, shows how digression is a perfect way to open up the poems, and what reader of the poems would be surprised at that? Yet these gentle and smart digressions didn't happen by themselves. Their author should be commended. No other book so honours O'Hara; no other book (except O'Hara's *Collected Poems*) is such a complete and essential record of his oeuvre. Joe LeSueur, who died in 2001, has left a supple monument to the person he most loved and has, incidentally, memorialized himself.

★ ★ ★

SHORT REVIEWS

*Alpha Zulu* by Gary Copeland Lilley, Ausable Press, 2008.

This volume of poems by Gary Copeland Lilley—a poet described on the back of the book as an "outsider artist," who indeed turns out to be one but in unexpected ways—wears its cover well. The illustration, a painting called "Television" by Jacob Lawrence, depicts a group of people in black, brown, and beige peering through the window of an electronics store at night. They are on the outside looking in at the burst of colour, which turns out to be a TV broadcasting a boxing match. Both the image and the poems employ a subtle and consistent chromatic or tonal frame that at the same time contains the dynamic and dark. Central to both is the idea of aggression, but aggression transformed into artful battle, a contest of discipline, skill, and craft.

Lilley's title is apt. The dominant figure in many of these poems is an alpha male, or rather, a Black alpha male, or in Lilley's formulation, alpha zulu. The poems are rich in the iconography of Christian tradition, as asserted in the echoes of the "alpha and omega," while the African-American heritage of revising and deepening that tradition is heard. The military's alphabetic call signs are also there; Lilley is a veteran of the U.S. Navy Submarine Force, an experience he draws on in several of the poems. And in the stark trochees that encompass so much meaning in two totalizing bursts of rhythm, "alpha zulu" begins to suggest the poetic skill that characterizes this stellar volume.

*Alpha Zulu* is a book of archetypes fleshed out, so that there is something both immediate and timeless in its lines. An underworld aesthetic is pervasive, giving the poems a classical feel. Not contradicting this, its characters are often straight-up Southern Gothic with an African-American twist. A lot of whiskey is drunk in this book. Juke-joints are still called juke-joints. There is a black cat which, having been scarred by "boiling water / or a chemical cleaner," slinks "low and close to the fences" until its fur grows back. There is a grandfather who is an itinerant preacher, a grandfather who hauls wood to stills by mule and cart, a cross-dresser named Raven, a roadhouse owner named Sugar, a racehorse gambler named Zoot, a Boneman who smashes men's bones for money, an anonymous God-driven killer of whores, and a pack of ten poems in the guise of tarot cards.

Such a collection could veer with speed into the hackneyed. What happens instead is that we fully enter a world—of hidden Black history, of deprivation and desperation, of defensiveness and pride, of transience from rural towns to big cities and back—that in many contemporary volumes would be inadequately encapsulated by a pop cultural reference or an allusion to the blues. This book does not merely point to, but is an actual manifestation of the blues; it does not merely gesture toward, but actually manifests a milieu. Lilley is an "outsider artist" not in the way of elaborate and sometimes violent obsessions à la Henry Darger (although many of the poems are populated by obsessive and violent speakers), or of idiosyncratic religiosity à la Howard Finster (although there are apocalyptic and prophetic overtones throughout). He is an "outsider" because he writes with unsentimental sympathy of social outsiders; because, as someone who has left and then returned to a rural home, he stands slightly outside of his origins; and because his aesthetic is outside of the current poetic mainstream, more folk culture than pop culture, more reactionary-on-purpose than attempted avant-garde.

These are some reasons for reading Lilley, yet none of these accounts for why *Alpha Zulu* is so compulsively readable, or for why it gets better the more it is read. Lilley's formal craft, muted and sure of its way, provides the best answer. Just as his subject matter has an organic nature, so too do his formal choices. Variety here is not lack of focus or an attempt to show off, but a necessary range of response to different dilemmas of character, story, and mood. The eponymous "Ranter on the Corner of Babylon and Manhattan" rails appropriately in unpunctuated prose, just as the less propulsive language of "November 11: Veterans Day at Rite Liquor Store and Bar" represents the quotidian. "Boneman" smashes at us in a single long stanza of short lines with a blunt diction that is less simple than sinister. The sestina "Angels in the Geek Hour of the Morning" uses the form's repetitive structure to convey the closed-circuit lives of hookers and johns. Lilley's tercets are tight, his couplets contained, so long as the subject demands it, and when the demands are loosened, the form follows suit.

Best of all are the sonnets scattered throughout, as well as the poems that are near sonnet-length. (The Tarot Card poems are thirteen lines each and he also writes strong twelve-line stanzas.) Lilley demonstrates particular mastery of a compact and self-sufficient form, where every fine enjambment is a well-greased gear, every pause a cog, every right word another screw helping hold it all together. These poems allow us to see how tension is handled in an enclosed space—fittingly so, for a man who in a longer poem confesses: "I'm claustrophobic. I've made / eight submarine patrols / and this was a truth I knew / after the first four." The dark humour, self-knowledge, and depth signified here are characteristic of the book as a whole, one of the best to surface in a while.

★   ★   ★

*The Human Country: New and Collected Stories* by Harry Mathews, Dalkey Archive Press, 2002.

Oulipo (an abbreviation of words which in French mean "workshop of potential literature") is a European literary collective known primarily for producing difficult work under self-imposed formal duress. *La Disparition*, by the late Georges Perec, is perhaps the best-known example, a lipogrammatic novel written entirely without the letter *e*. Arcane and arbitrary stricture is almost everything in such experiments.

The result is not necessarily any less compelling than willfully "realist" writing, since it springs from a desire that is of psychological and aesthetic import. The motivation for such random devices as the Oulipists employ is their wish to make unconscious associative leaps and to generate sentences of unknown provenance. As even composers of doggerel know, form does have a way of forcing new things out of a writer. In *The Human Country*, Harry Mathews, a poet (*Armenian Papers*), novelist (*Cigarettes, The Conversions*), and the only American member of Oulipo, illuminates the importance of "potential" in this *littérature potentielle*. His new and collected stories are evidence of it both fulfilled and wasted. It is a frustrating collection in which every virtuosic success is countered by competence, which in turn is countered by failure. Since success and failure are interesting, and competence is respectable but boring, *The Human Country* is more interesting than boring. It is recommended on the basis of its verbal ingenuity and formal experimentation. Readers desiring a good plot and an emotional connection to fictional characters will likely prefer a different kind of collection.

Short story writers are usually invested in making sure the compositional tricks they use are secondary to the emotional effects their tricks produce. Mathews resists such hidden architecture, opting instead to lay bare his elaborate games. One story, for example, entitled "Clocking the World on Cue," begins with a note that will probably not inspire readers to keep a box of tissue handy as they read:

> The chronogram—a centuries-old literary form—follows a simple but demanding rule: when all letters corresponding to Roman numerals [...] are added together, they produce a sum equivalent to a specific year of the Christian calendar. The single words "memory" and "memento" are thus chronograms of the year 2000 (m × 2); so are "A moment for feasts & prayers" (m × 2) and "A year to pay homage to the dead" (m × 1 + d × 2). Both the title and text of this work are examples of chronograms of the current year.

You may, if you wish, find out whether the text indeed adds up to the "current year." (I won't say what year that is, only that I counted two thousand and six appearances of "i" alone in a tiring and apparently inaccurate process.) The true point of the story, however, seems to be the manufacture of semantically odd but grammatically pristine sentences (most of which include a food or beverage and an exotic place-name) out of any discernible context: "In Antibes, bingeing on pastis is getting Winnie higher than nine kites." Although sometimes funny, and including a banal and pulse-quickening pornographic sequence, "Clocking the World on Cue" finally belongs in a collection of sentences or equations rather than stories.

Several efforts here are predicated on professional or specialized discourses of the kind that often attend but rarely overtly determine more conventional character studies. Mathews knows the discourses even better than the characters that use them. "The Dialect of the Tribe," a response by a fictional linguist to a request for a festschrift contribution, purports to explain a language called Pagolak. Despite being largely nonsensical, the story's obviously crazy researcher-narrator is nicely abrasive when rubbed against the institutional forms of communication that define him. In the end, however, this ironic combination is asked to carry too much weight.

A different story, this one in the form of a recipe, is more successful, gaining in interest as its ingredients pile up. "Country Cooking from Central France: Roast Boned Rolled Stuffed Shoulder of Lamb (Farce Double)" shows how the construction of a good story is like the making of a good meal. The succulent sentences urge out wishes for a taste of the mysterious dish, even as some of them ("Your satisfaction will have been in the doing, not in the thing done") explain why other stories in the collection are undercooked.

An aesthetic of the kind displayed in these stories, in which process is valued as much as product, is problematic, since the reader is only a part of the artistic process after the fact. If the product is flawed, the most mind-tingling process in the world can't make it right. The author perhaps has the luxury of remembering fondly the past moment of creation. The reader has only in the present well-written stories marked often by over-ingenuity. Sometimes, though, Mathews shows his full power as an observer of human life in the world and the ways that we live it in language. "The Way Home" begins as a disquisition on objects before introducing Walt Maltmall and "his gift for noticing small, attractive anomalies in the course of his ordinary life. At lunch his place was set with a fork to the left of his plate, another fork to the right of his plate. On his way to the beach, a short clothesline sagged inexplicably with the weight of a single, fluffy diaper." Taking us into discursive and psychological realms of past, present, and future, Mathews condenses a Robbe-Grillet novel into the space of a story. Such a moving "real world of the imagination" excuses a lot of unfulfilled potential.

\* \* \*

*The Red Bird* by Joyelle McSweeney, Fence Books, 2002.

*The Real Moon of Poetry and Other Poems* by Tina Brown Celona, Fence Books, 2002.

Neither of these two first volumes, winners of prizes from the journal *Fence* and published in its book series, chooses the path of pre-fabricated competence. Instead, both poets, taking very different risks, go down potentially dangerous routes. The minor imperfections that result merely humanize their accomplishments.

McSweeney's collection will not seem strange to readers of modernist poetry. Its fragmentation can be a flaw, not because of the fragments themselves, which are appealing, but because there is sometimes no congealing mood or atmosphere to contain them. One is willing to forgive such lapses, for McSweeney has numerous talents, such as her rhythms, which are exquisite: "Ginned clean of seeds, packed into bales / through a season of ten-dollar hours... / who is it sleeps in these sheets? // Sleeps in the bale, sleeps in the parcel / of coveted land[.]" The dactylic waltz, which with the cotton conveys something of the South, is interrupted by "acres" sounding rightly as flat as a map "in the park's interior." McSweeney's internal anaphora reminds one of Whitman, and the spectre of Stevens shows in the appropriate ellipses, which most poets use as injudiciously as bullets on New Year's Eve. The motion from bolls to bales, to the sheets they make, to history is characteristic. Even greater than McSweeney's fine ear is her ability to leap from abstract to particular, between registers of diction, across referential levels. Like Dickinson, whom she is otherwise unlike, McSweeney uses small things to take us on great trips. From "little horses" to "miniplanets" and a "threadbare dachshund," we are often in a realm of minutiae. But, as her nine poems titled "The Voyage of the Beagle" suggest, what is small may symbolically evolve. Tracing unexpected trajectories of meaning, she finds detritus along the way, which she turns into poetry; she makes much out of things like old books and anonymous bands, and her sports allusions are among the best I have encountered in a contemporary poet.

She is also a heck of a naturalist. In "Toy Bed" we first see an "emperor penguin" whose crown "slips down halfway / over his eyes." Like the comical bird, the poet has her vision obscured by a hat, for her "black wool beret is sodden and itches / and pushes my wet bangs down into my eyes / in little points. The field is flooded, floodened." From the pressure of her artist's chapeau spring tears, changing what she sees. More magisterial than a penguin at the end, she is like the deer that appears in a final apparition, with "his too-huge stylized rack. It pulls his head back / black-lipped to the sky, or pulls his head down / and he must graze and brood. It pulls / his lips and makes him smile. It closes his eyes." Hers is a graceful summation of the gifts and demands that come with assuming the poet's role.

Tina Brown Celona's volume also considers such gifts and demands. Her summations, however, are sedate, with sudden eruptions into sorrowful anger that subside like stomach pains. *The Real Moon of Poetry and Other Poems* is, as its title suggests, bluntly concerned with poetry and reality. Although Celona's poems often remark on their own making, these metapoetic moments are not strategies for avoiding emotion, but organic and poignant reactions to the need to make something meaningful out of incoherent experience. Confessional poems of a sort, their honesty seems less a recollection than a direct recording of desire and despair. And because the recording mind is saturated with writing, we are given a rich textual simultaneity, as if life is happening and being remarked upon at the same instant. Wry and self-deprecating, such as when its "shrimp/Cry out for justice / From the seafloor, leaving tiny trails, / Traces of poetry," *The Real Moon* is also sweet, as when a recovered postcard says "i love you," and surprised, for "if even postcards love me i guess / i can do anything."

"My emotion was very small," writes Celona. "It was the emotion of a poem." One is moved by a poet who wants so much from the writing life, yet who won't efface its deficiencies by claiming false and grandiose things for it. This approach to the poem applies to her domestic life as well. Sitting inside, sheltered from a rainy day, Celona considers her partner, at whom she directs some harmless passive aggression, as her eyes take in a suddenly strange tableau: "i always say 'so should we go / swimming' doubtfully / looking at my jade rabbit / his humid color and placid posture / as he nibbles the orange ground / of a book by john ashbery, / rivers and mountains[.]"

Poetry here is a ground for the real, which itself, remaining real, becomes a poem. Once you truly see it grazing on the orange grass, Celona's green rabbit is as real as any object, as real as any rabbit, any poem. The poet as poet refuses to deny what makes things real for her. Such a refusal means asking some difficult questions. McSweeney, without a question mark, asks a hard one at the end of "The Premier": "Who am / I if I mean what I sometimes mean." Her answers are roundabout; she approaches the question in pieces and loops. Celona instead attacks the question like a pit bull fighting through tranquilizers. Different as these poets are, I intend, on the strength of their inaugural volumes, to read whatever both of them write from now on.

\* \* \*

*Poems the Size of Photographs* by Les Murray, Farrar, Straus and Giroux, 2003.

There are poems so loose in form, they might as well be bowls of spaghetti. Les Murray, burly Australian poet and farmer, caustic as acid, but with a decency often found among those who work the earth, has published a collection of poems instead reminiscent of stones. As poems go, they are small, as the book's title attests. Yet one feels, reading them, that Murray's poems can be picked up, handled, and hurled with force as a photo cannot, that these objects, smooth and hard, have been formed by applying intense pressure to the language.

*Poems the Size of Photographs* is the twelfth volume of poems by Murray (who received the Gold Medal for Poetry from Queen Elizabeth) and its contents suggest that age tends not to render a great writer less cantankerous. In *Subhuman Redneck Poems*, which won the 1996 T. S. Eliot Prize, Murray wrote, "Modernism's not modern: it's police and despair." The onslaught of a new millennium has apparently left this view unchanged. "The twentieth century," he claims in one snapshot, "grew such icy / ambition and scorn that it built marvels / or else crap." Mostly crap, one surmises, as the poem and the century draw to a close over "charm's mass grave," "a punitive mediocrity." Modernism's "police and despair" are even belatedly prophesied by Murray in the single quatrain of "Starry Night": "In the late Nineteenth century / one is out painting landscapes / with spiralling sky / and helicopter lights approaching."

A poet who can see the gyres and searchlights of our culture while continuing to paint landscapes is as timely as ever, even if, as in this case, such a poet (a less mad Van Gogh) sees himself as a mind outside the times. It is a necessary pose, for as an outsider, Murray puts distance between himself and the era's received ideas. Befitting the book's pictorial frame, he captures his complacent prey in a flash, and if, as in "The Poisons of Right and Left," the picture we get is developed in overly stark contrasts ("You are what you have got / and: to love, you have to hate."), deftness of composition makes up for missing greys. Usually what seems stark in Murray is merely poetry in the now unfamiliar plain style, with which this Thomas Wyatt of New South Wales steadies himself before investigating his materials and his world: "Identity oversimplifies humans. / It denies the hybrid, as trees can't. // Trees, which wrap height in pages / self-knitted from ground water and light // are stood scrolls best read unopened. / They lean to each other and away // in politics of sun-rivalry / or at knotted behests in the earth." His own hybrid, a mix of the natural world, human culture, and the craft of writing, is in its critical awareness appropriate to our age. It is also appropriately Australian, sometimes to the point of self-conscious parody. Murray plays at whim the local entertainer, or the dealer in postcards and broadside illustrations: Sydney's Opera House described, "An Australian Legend" retold, "The Aboriginal Cricketer" immortalized in verse.

Although Murray's accounting of his homeland suggests a man acquainted not only with his native soil, but also with his native self, that self is rarely exhibited in the open. With a reticence inspiring trust, Murray handles his own experience with masculine delicacy; so delicate, in fact, that one often wonders whose experience the experience is: "A man approaches the edge / of his life, which has miscarried." The man writing the poem, any man, anybody: Murray is not a sentimental, but a fatalistic, universalist. It is hard, however, to stay too dour in the midst of Murray's poems. One appreciates someone so obviously trying to communicate: "The effort is always to make the symbols obvious: / the bolt of *electricity*, winged stethoscope of course / for *flying doctor*. Pram under fire? *Soviet film industry*."

"The New Hieroglyphics," as the title reads, have a remarkable translator in Murray. He is remarkable in part for knowing what can go untranslated and still communicate, like the bare tableland he describes in "On the Borders": "I feel no need to interpret it / as if it were art." The poems in this excellent collection seem as inevitable as any natural landscape; yet they are finely crafted human things. Exploiting the tension between the world we inherit and the world we make, Murray's modern pastorals and portraits are classical in emphasizing our smallness, which we fight against, not always unheroically. The poems partake of that smallness, but their modest proportions belie the fact that these snapshots in few words are worth hundreds of thousands of pictures, clear speech amid the clutter.

* * *

START TO FIGURE

*The Vienna Paradox: A Memoir* by Marjorie Perloff, New Directions, 2004.

On the cover is the 1938 passport photo of beaming, pig-tailed Gabriele Mintz, the sweetest vision of European girlhood since Shirley Temple skipped as Heidi through the Alps. Inside the cover is the story of how Gabriele Mintz became Marjorie Perloff, one of our finest poetry critics and a tireless advocate for the so-called avant-garde. Perloff, in such books as *The Poetics of Indeterminacy* and *Wittgenstein's Ladder*, makes new stories out of literary history, using the tools of careful reading and fresh juxtaposition, woven in the clearest prose. These skills are put to compelling use as Perloff's attention is turned on herself.

It was not easily turned in that direction, as Perloff relates in her preface. She was hesitant to undertake a memoir: "For one thing, I am a critic not a biographer or memoirist, and the notion of personal confession or family anecdote has never appealed to me." So, to confession and anecdote she adds critical acumen. The memoir's foundational story is harrowing but not tragic, as so many similar stories were; for the author, then six-and-a-half, escaped Austria with her family in 1938, arriving eventually in America. Perloff translates from German an exercise ("The Departure") written at age seven in her New York City public school notebook: "It was on the twelfth of March in the morning when my mother came into our room and said now we are no longer Austrians. Hitler has taken Austria. I cried hard but there was nothing to be done." The memoirist remarks on her mother's words: "There is no mention of our having to leave as Jews, no doubt because despite our nominal Jewishness, we had been brought up as Austrians."

Such observations lead Perloff to explore the "Vienna Paradox" of her title. The crucial doubleness of Jewish Austrians, she argues, was set in the background until, too late, it was brought to the fore and used by others against them. Considering the case of her distant relative Robert Schüller—who worked for Göring and died at Auschwitz after a trial at which he still proclaimed himself a national socialist—Perloff shows "what terrible consequences passing could have in a society governed by such racial hatred." She concludes that in many cases, devotion to the strong artistic culture of the nation eased assimilation, the success of which was a trap. Thinking of themselves as patriots of the Kulturnation, the Jews of Perloff's Austria were still aliens in the Volksnation. The theory is tested by looking at the lives and work of such conflicted public figures as Theodor Adorno, Walter Benjamin, Ernst Gombrich, and Arnold Schoenberg. Adorno raises Perloff's ire for despising American culture while accepting the country as a refuge. She is more sympathetic in describing the young Benjamin's circle of friends, worshippers of Goethe and Kant. Alas, for these and other Jews who shared a faith in German culture, "their self-image as keepers of the cultural flame was not necessarily shared by the Aryan intellectuals and artists who were their counterparts."

These stories of well-known figures are arranged alongside tales of Perloff's family. We meet her elegant Aunt Susi, whose "eyes would glaze over" when "the word 'Jewish' came up," and her dashing maternal grandfather, the book's standard-bearer for moral ambivalence and personal strength. A high-ranking Austrian diplomat and master of Realpolitik, he, too, was forced to flee his homeland. The old man's escape through Italian mountain passes is cinematic in its telling. Yet Perloff also finds the story troubling. She describes a photograph of her grandfather surrounded by soldiers who were ordered to help him along by a telegram from Mussolini. In the photo, "everyone is smiling, but again, consider the ironies of the whole situation. At a time of hysterical nationalist frenzy, the Austrian Jewish diplomat is saved by *Il Duce*, the Italian Fascist dictator, because of their longstanding diplomatic friendship." There are moments like this throughout, when a telling scrap of evidence exposes the vicissitudes of history.

In the centre of the swirl of public and private, of paradox and irony, is Marjorie—a change of name she made at thirteen in an attempt to sound more American. The rest is education in fine institutions and in the heights of native kitsch, to which the transplanted Austrian feels no aversion. She marries, works briefly as a writer of subtitles at MGM (a funny episode), and navigates the treacherous waters of graduate school and an early professorship. We see, humbly handled, the development of Perloff's wide-ranging, life-loving mind, which has been on display for years in her critical work. To have this memoir now is a boon, a more personal critical fugue.

\* \* \*

*Dancing in the Dark* by Caryl Phillips, Knopf, 2005.

*leadbelly* by Tyehimba Jess, Verse Press, 2005.

Bert Williams (c. 1874–1922) was regarded by his peers and the generation of performers who followed him as one of the titans of the stage. Alas, he wasn't playing Shakespeare. Instead, Williams was blacking up his light brown face and playing a Jim Crow minstrel alongside his partner George Walker's urban dandy. And here—in the distance between Williams's dignified mien and his talent for low, racially disturbing humor—we have the tragic crux of the story told by Caryl Phillips in his new novel, *Dancing in the Dark*.

Perhaps Phillips—the Booker Prize short-listed, Commonwealth Prize winning writer from St. Kitts—identifies with the West Indian-born Williams. If so, that may explain why this novel is so staid in tone; no doubt Phillips does not wish to cheapen his subject. This decision is, on the one hand, appropriate, for the circumstances are serious indeed. Williams's internal battle was exacerbated by the criticism of his partner, the disappointment of his father, lectures from "his people," a peculiar marriage (not yet thirty, he called his wife "Mother"), unhealthy habits (he chain-smokes through the novel; we are unsurprised when he coughs blood), and white racism, the canvas on which this American story is painted.

On the other hand, the reader misses a sense of the electricity Williams discharged from the stage, as well as the joy he must have absorbed from the audience whose riotous laughter he provoked. This is a devitalizing absence, for it is precisely this electricity and joy that recommend Williams, among all the performers of the period, to our attention. Furthermore, because his personal battle is at the centre of the story, the absence of a fully felt sense of Williams as a performer makes the internal drama seem one-sided. The tension thus dissipated, the psychic damage already done, we are left without any sparks of friction as we move through a funereal tale.

Still, Phillips's novel is to be recommended. The prose is limpid, the chronological disruptions jar just enough at the proper moments, and the period detail, although from the beginning bathed by the light of nostalgia for a time that was no great shakes, is convincing and full of interest. And when you consider the subject matter, namely, Williams's navigation through the minefield of minstrelsy as it moved into the vaudeville era and then into more modern productions, it almost seems nit-picking to complain too much about issues of tone.

There has been a surge of interest in minstrelsy lately and no wonder, as the number of contradictions contained in the minstrel tradition, as well as its role in shaping and explaining popular culture, means that minstrelsy is as powerful and transporting as the Mississippi River, and like the murky Mississippi it cuts right through America. Williams and Walker are central figures in that tradition. Originally billed as "Two Real Coons," they began by playing boats, mining camps, and medicine shows and ended by orchestrating the first all-Black productions on Broadway. Going solo after Walker became ill with syphilis, and as the only African-American in a Ziegfeld Follies cast that also included Fanny Brice (who makes a cameo appearance in the book), Williams remained a major star. His life is certainly worthy of a good novelist such as Phillips. My only additional suggestion for readers of this carefully written book is that they supplement the novel with some of Bert Williams's recordings, such as "Elder Eatmore's Sermon on Generosity" or the immortal "Nobody," available on the Archeophone and Document labels.

Alongside the rise of minstrelsy we also find the birth of the blues, one of whose greatest figures is Hudson William Ledbetter (1885-1949). Better known as Leadbelly, this complex, often jailed, sometimes exploited, irrepressible, mountainous man is the eponymous subject of a debut collection of poems by Tyehimba Jess, who, unlike Phillips, has chosen a historical figure he knows how to make come alive. Mimicking the musical variety which Leadbelly embodied, Jess uses an impressive number of forms as a way to tell his story and to develop different characters. There are wonderful spare sonnets and a range of prose poems; there are letters and songs and good double-columned poems. Most of all there are the voices of the man himself, his lovers, his victims, jailers, and supporters, of Alan Lomax, of Cab Calloway—even Leadbelly's twelve-string guitar speaks out. A reasonably well-researched biography in verse, this first book, despite a prodigal use of alliteration and a purple passage or two, is a fine, fun-to-read example of how to bring back our past performers in all their essential vibrancy.

\* \* \*

*Stubborn Poetries: Poetic Facticity and the Avant-Garde* by Peter Quartermain, University of Alabama Press, 2013.

The title is apt, the subtitle less so; for while there is much here that can be called *avant-garde* (though this shorthand in taste is always on the verge of outliving its veracity), the term *poetic facticity*, placed where it is, implies that it is the central theme of the book—but it isn't, really; two essays address it directly, while elsewhere it appears glancingly. There is certainly no overarching argument made in this regard; after all, in the introduction the author admits the book's lack of one. It is no great deficiency.

Instead, the plurality and recalcitrance indicated in the primary title obtain as a through-line loosely connecting these twenty-one essays: plurality, because a number of poets are discussed, a variety of topics in poetics treated, habits of reading revealed; recalcitrance, because the critic comes up against something that cannot be explained right away. There are many admissions of, questions about, tentative explanations for the fact that there is something happening here, but what it is, is not quite clear: "But why? Why is he so opaque?" "[W]hat she writes does not 'make sense' in ordinary terms." "[It] refuses to stabilize finally into a settled meaning." "[I]t's a little more complicated than this, and not easily susceptible of explication." "[T]he difficulties are far more pervasive than he suggests." "[S]ome of [her] texts are impossible definitively to fix." "[It] *undoes* certainty." "It's a pretty weird poem, I guess." These are not merely self-reflexive tics. They accumulate to a point of advocacy for a number of "poetries" (and even poems), as if groping toward a response to someone who says, "I'm not reading that or anything like it again. It doesn't make any sense," and for whom the reply, "That's precisely how it *does* make 'sense,'" just won't quite do.

After the welcoming introductory essay and a cornerstone-setting piece on canonicity and Eliot and Pound, three poets are treated more than the others: Basil Bunting, Lorrine Niedecker, and Louis Zukofsky. "Basil Bunting: Poet of the North" features an opening historical tableau that indicates early on how Quartermain can use a good story to his advantage. His interest in matters of extremely local form is at the fore of "Parataxis in Basil Bunting and Louis Zukofsky" but not at the expense of either literary history or the epistemology of reading; remarking that parataxis "seems to be a medieval and modern form," the critic delightfully describes "paratactic structures" as "creat[ing] a field of apprehension." "Reading Niedecker" shows his ability to write to the general reader as well as to the specialist. There are three other essays on these writers, and as a group they mark a solid beginning to the collection and its concerns.

Essays follow on Robin Blaser, Richard Caddel, and Robert Creeley; "George Oppen and Some Women Writers" are considered; Bruce Andrews and Steve McCaffery pop up; the virtues of Mina Loy's *Love Songs* are sung, and sounds are of the essence in "Syllable as Music: Lyn Hejinian's *Writing Is an Aid to Memory*"—extremely local effects again. But so is the global here. The book closes with a quartet of essays—"Undoing the Book," "Poetic Fact," "Sound Reading," "Paradise of Letters"—that serve as a magnet for the general themes seen throughout. The strongest overall impression may be the book's versatility. Stylistically, Quartermain's voice sounds human, sometimes even talky, which reveals the origin of much of this work in lectures. He is a man who nuzzles up to the words yet finds much that is worthy in diversion; his juxtapositions in this regard are slightly bracing but cause no harm. He mixes moments of immediacy found in matters sonic with those of structure found in formal architecture, all the while asking foundational questions having to do with thinking and reading, reading and writing. This is a good book to approach piecemeal, essay by essay, in any order, as interest dictates and time allows.

\* \* \*

*Ceci n'est pas Keith/Ceci n'est pas Rosmarie* by Keith and Rosmarie Waldrop, Burning Deck, 2002.

In books like Keith Waldrop's *The Opposite of Letting the Mind Wander* or Rosmarie's *The Reproduction of Profiles* and *The Lawn of the Excluded Middle*, one finds work steeped in collage, fragmented inattention, historical inquiry, and formal variation. One finds, in short, two prime movers of the American poetic avant-garde. The challenge of that avant-garde, with its mix of ambition, art, and pretension, may send readers elsewhere for their simple memoir kicks. But in this double autobiography, the Waldrops (not their writing) are the heroes, and the heroes seem nice enough folks.

Keith, the goofier of the two, sports an ironic and corny sense of humour befitting "an unbeliever reared in the lunatic fringe of American Protestantism." (He also sports a long, white beard.) The liveliest passages are Keith's anecdotes about the stunts he pulled as a graduate student at the University of Michigan, like organizing a mock Beat happening which climaxed with the performance of a play called *The Quivering Aardvark and the Jelly of Love*. "'It's wonderful,' one spectator was reported saying. 'They give you the perfect work of art, and then—nothing, the void.'" Perhaps merely being a graduate student was a stunt for Keith, whose dissertation on the "aesthetics of obscenity" moved from the library into the bathroom, where the space-starved couple kept appropriately punning books: *The Golden Ass, Howard's End, Let It Come Down*. Keith, of course, does not miss the chance in this context to allude to the irony of his being hired by Brown University, surely a foregone conclusion.

Rosmarie, who grew up in Germany during World War II ("I burrowed under a heap of potatoes as the ground shook. People prayed.") seems more serious. Her part of the book consists of blocks of prose, solid paragraphs with portentous headings like "WAR, A SURFACE TO LIVE ON," "WE SWAPPED KNIVES TO PEEL OFF CHILDHOOD LIKE SO MANY SKINS," and "I CARRY YOUR NAME AWAY FROM OUR INTERSECTION." The tale of a smart young woman who came from a shattered Europe to the cultural wilds of America and became a respected writer is compelling. So is her love for Edmond Jabès, whose gnomic work she has translated with such tenacity, and for his wife Arlette. Rosmarie also conveys her love for her adopted language, and as the book (and her life as a writer) progresses, she gives us increasing access to her compositional methods.

As the title reminds us, however, this is not *really* Keith and Rosmarie, but a representation of them in writing. Although banal and fashionable truths pop up—Keith: "What is in my mind... well, in a sense, that is precisely what I'm not. In another sense, it is all in the world I am." Rosmarie: "No text has one single author in any case. The blank page is not blank. Whether we are conscious of it or not, we always write on top of a palimpsest"—what is remarkable are the stories: a unique cultural history of the American avant-garde, a double *kunstlerroman*, scattered shots of the post-war milieu. Most remarkable of all is the love story, in which Keith the American soldier meets Rosmarie the German schoolgirl and eventually sends her passage money to the States, where she arrives without incident, only to have her cargo checked with a Geiger counter after suspicious customs officials spot her bohemian-looking lover. Unlike most of the rest of the Waldrops's work, this book—put out to lovely effect by their own Burning Deck Press—makes hardly any demands on the reader, other than the sympathetic demands of human interest. What Keith calls "this partial experience of the total song" proves Rosmarie's quote of Blanchot, that "the glimpses amount to more than their sum, that the breaks allow possibility to enter." It is a slight, charming volume that will appeal to those with an interest in people and poetry. It is also easy to read, just the sort of book for the bathroom.

\* \* \*

*Borrowed Love Poems* by John Yau, Penguin, 2002.

Love poems in conventional guise are hard to find until the end of Yau's most recent collection, but there is borrowing from the beginning. In fact, the first six poems (all called "Russian Letter") seem to have been taken from a bin of Michael Palmer out-takes. The familiar Palmerian gestures are there: spare two-line stanzas, the flitting interjection of foreign phrases, and strategically dispersed anaphora that alludes to a mystic-prophetic past and a poststructuralist present ("It is said, the past / sticks to the present // like glue... / It is said, someone // cannot change / the clothes // in which / their soul // was born.")

Such obvious imitation arouses suspicion. Yet Yau forces us to take seriously poems that in many cases fail to offer the standard aesthetic rewards (originality, beauty, insight). He does this by making the procedures of other artists the conceptual scaffold of his volume. In "830 Fireplace Road (II)," Yau rearranges and repeats the words of a sentence uttered by Jackson Pollock: "No of the its of. Have the of have its /own have, Making have have. / No no because making changes / changes the making of the painting." In two Oulipo-like "Metabolic Isthmus Sestinas," the palette is equally restricted, as in this characteristic envoi: "Sack always taste slick hair seat / Taste hair sack mull why slick / Sack mull why mate taste false[.]" Except for the fact that the sestinas, when read out loud, begin to sound dirty in the mouth, this is linguistically boring stuff. Neither is the form compelling, made as it is to seem either random or over-determined. Yau is better in his more expansive, wackier mode, as in the four poems starring Peter Lorre or the three starring Boris Karloff. The best of these, "I Was a Poet in the House of Frankenstein," is a long, fascinating list of Karloff's roles that has the admirable virtues of a collection of arcane movie trivia.

Yau is an art critic as well as a prolific poet, and there are poems here about, inspired by, or referring to Eva Hesse, Philip Guston, Max Beckmann, Marcel Duchamp, and Joseph Cornell, as well as Poe and Whitman, George Trakl and Frank O'Hara. The book's epigraph by Osip Mandelstam—"What I am saying at this moment is not being said by me"—when read alongside these allusive poems, suggests that our "self" or "identity" is merely an articulation of our taste. Such a poetics is depressing, for though it posits a kind of freedom, and tends to be funny and philosophically quirky ("Princess Sitting Duck isn't my real name…Princess Sitting Duck isn't my nickname either"), it best shows itself in a series of negative definitions: "Okay. Okay. You want to know. Well, all right, / I am not an Egyptian napkin. I'm not even / a retired cosmonaut or guileless barber. / I am neither an escapee from the House of Grubb / nor an inmate from the Home of Hubbub." Sometimes, as in "Autobiography in Red and Yellow," some more or less straight talk seems to leak through the clowns-are-the-sad-ones static: "I was born in Shanghai / shortly after one cylinder of war ended // and another revolution / in barnyard fashion began." Yet the backpage biography reveals that while Yau's parents fled from Shanghai, Yau himself was born in Lynn, Massachusetts. Thus, we are left to ponder the veracity of autobiography, or the difference between conception and birth.

In *Borrowed Love Poems*, every shift in persona or subject is matched by a shift in form, tone or technique, and Yau's dominant modes of expression are dissociation, assimilation, and free association. In a way, this wilful inconsistency is the furthest thing from love. And yet the exhaustion such shifts produce, along with the plaintive simplicities of the "Borrowed Love Poems" which close and name the book, speak to the experience of love after all, which is exhausting, and requires a self in some relation to the supposed self of another.

## II.

# Poetry: Letters In Canada 2018

The most luminous little book of poems this year (and also a spiritual palliative) was *Years, Months, and Days* by Amanda Jernigan. It derives from a Mennonite hymnal, *Die Gemeinschaftliche Liedersammlung*, first printed in what is now Kitchener, Ontario, in 1836. As Jernigan notes in an afterword: "The *Liedersammlung* may not be the first book of poems published in Waterloo Region, but its continuous weekly, if not more frequent, use in Waterloo Mennonite homes and meeting houses for the last 180 years may well make it the most-read book of poems ever published in the region." Originally from that region herself, but having moved away, Jernigan returned as part of an artist residency along with other outsiders, including musicians, some of whom were religiously lapsed, and some, like Jernigan, who "were born and bred in the briar patch of secular skepticism." They collaborated on a project that reinterpreted the music and lyrics of the hymnal, from which the book's title takes its name; for therein is the admonition: *Lass mein Herz die Tage zählen*; and on the Mennonite graves in the area are marked the years, months, and days afforded the deceased by their God.

The dearth of ostentation demanded by the Mennonite sect is manifest too in their hymns; thus, the satchel of diction from which Jernigan selects her words is a sturdy grab-bag full of life-sustaining plain-speech. As she makes her miniature poems that fill her miniature book—scarcely bigger than a pack of cigarettes or playing cards and half as thick, a perfect pocket volume—one can ascertain with some uncertainty the ghost of a minimalist musical backing. The words are reworked in small moments of accumulative repetition and temporal advance, recalling the solid-structure-building notes of a Philip Glass or Terry Riley composition: "Summer to autumn, / how do we travel, / autumn to winter, / one to another, / winter to springtime, / how do we travel, / springtime to summer, / one to another." "Take note / did God // did God

/ your God // your God / from heaven // from heaven / itself // itself / call you // call you / to take note[.]" Something of the solidity of the vocabulary yields dividends in establishing the physicality of the body—that body "sewn with death," that "clay house / out worn," that "hand, / marrow-deep"—and the feeling of having a body is matched, nay, surpassed by the feeling of having a soul: "O, / my soul, / get thee / to higher / ground." In fact, although it is not formally arranged as such, the volume as a whole recalls those dialogues between Body and Soul that we associate with earlier eras; and just as Yeats (who in an interesting variation wrote his own such dialogue between the *Self* and the Soul) impressed upon us the dialectic of the dancer and the dance, so does Jernigan finally convince us that the dance of the soul and its ultimate rising is contingent on having been housed in the living dancer, yoked to the fallible, beautiful, mortal human body.

The sister arts, at least to me, in relation to poetry—and I read Jean Hagstrum twenty years ago, I promise—have always been the visual arts on the one hand and music on the other. Poems try to *look* a certain way (and some people feel they have actual objecthood) and they try to *sound* a certain way (the sibling link of poetry and music hardly needs elaboration). But what about the dance? It had never crossed my mind. Even in that famous line of Yeats, I merely took it for a figure of rhetoric. Some people delight in being value-capacious while yet pseudo-grudgingly "consenting" to "admitting" some great lacuna in appreciation, an exception meant to prove the rule of their ruling taste, but I find such performances unbecoming. So it is with no pride that I consent to admit my lack of appreciation for dance, especially for what is contemporary. I could count the modern dances I have seen on two hands. And yet that lack of appreciation, which is really a lack of knowledge, hardly hinders a power that is hard to predict. When these dances start, and as I shift in my seat and lean ever-so-slightly forward as if proximity helps revelation, scrunching my forehead and narrowing my eyes at the dancers on stage, I sit there frankly embarrassed: embarrassed *for* them, and embarrassed *by* them. The staging is often so corny, the weight of overwrought drama descends; and—but mainly—it is the bodies. Their bodies make me uncomfortable. They are so pretty, so young, so regal yet vulnerable; they are so gorgeous and handsome and sinewy and strong; they are so *present*, so committed and real. By the end of any given show, the skeptic in me has broken. I am inevitably in tears. It all seems now to have to do precisely with human being and living and dying. It is the most beautiful life-affirming thing I have ever seen.

So suffice it to say that my relationship to dance is manic and uninformed, but not without the capacity for emotional response. It is thus hard to assess Tim Lilburn's *The House of Charlemagne*. The brunt of the book comes out of a collaboration with the New Dance Horizons/Rouge-gorge dance troupe and a 2015 performance (of which there are two photographs of evidence); but if you were not told so, it seems unlikely that you would perceive anything particularly "dance-like" in Lilburn's text. In fact, there is a distance there that mitigates against the sort of uncontrolled response that strikes this reader most amidst the immediacy of purposeful bodies in motion. This is not a detriment to the book, merely a disjunctive conjunction that creates a space for musing on the "inherent" natures of various arts, if such "natures" really exist. Lilburn's hero is Honoré Jaxon, the last secretary of Louis Riel, and we begin after the former's trial, whereupon Jaxon is shuffled off to a psychiatric hospital, having expressed such beliefs as that Riel "had set fires in his clothes just by brushing by him" and that there were "multiple additional livable worlds" (not so crazy, that one). Jaxon is rendered in human form and there is a reality about him in Lilburn's conception. A second, more spectral "hero" here is a vanished book by Riel, called the *Massinahican*, which is the Cree word for "story" or "complete account." It sounds like the most astonishing conglomeration of prophecy, politics, and philosophy and Lilburn tells us that Riel probably had to leave it behind in Manitoba, where it was forgotten, literally lost, perhaps "burned by inattention" and then: "With rains, the document liquefied, yet kept for a moment a shape, then one drop attached to another and the whole drained into fissures in the ground." And that book is the solid-liquid ground for this one. *The House of Charlemagne*, though a slim volume, shares in the capacious polyglot discomfiting oddness that surrounds the lost *Massinahican*, for it dances between historical periods willy-nilly, switches from straight history to crooked fantasy, is a drama in dialogue for dance and a prosimetric lyrical hodge-podge, a documented story with a sinuous path, mixing portentousness and humour. For those with an interest in Louis Riel, the book is like an especially pregnant footnote that pulls you away from the primary text for a consternating, illuminating afternoon. As a prison guard says at one point, having apparently been inspired by the prophetic breath of Riel: "Behold the book. / Take its liquids into your mouth / and eat what it thinks."

A curious discombobulation, then, and a touch unnerving, but not unpleasant, in the end; still, this critic is more at ease with the sister art of the visual and as usual, there were ekphrastic endeavors to appreciate among the year's offerings. *The Eyelash and the Monochrome* by the poet-slash-visual-artist Tiziana La Melia is an oddball volume comprised of pictures and words that is greater than the sum of its parts. "Bricolage is suspicious to city officers," she writes, and perhaps the critic is a version of just such an officer, insofar as one is familiar with many a collection that throws so much at random at such speed that the reader is often led to suspect that the rapidity of the random is masking a lack of depth, or that novelty is a poor substitute for profundity. Then again, you can't spell "profundity" without "fun" and I ultimately took a liking to this book. The world has been surreal for so long that one longs to experience the freshness that must have attended the original Surrealists, where the physical world blends into the dream and vice versa: "I said to the Marseille Cat: 'The lock is a hole with a row of heavy teeth gating dislocated feelings barring contact inside that blur between us.' The Cat said, 'Sure, and the Border Guards require airy locks like names and sex and place of birth and then the passwords to the phone.' Undoubtedly the cat feels misunderstood. 'The locks support the house. Just built or just ancient fragments of brand new junk.' But there is this house that never locks its door." In its way it is a book *about* borders and whether or not it is devoid of Greater Meaning, its unpreachy energy is invigorating and positive: "But mostly the eyelash is nothing. / And out of this nothing came a kindness."

Similar energies are at play in Adeena Karasick's *Checking In*, yet I failed to glom on to her book in a similar way. Perhaps it was my mood. I think I read it at a time when what I really wanted to do was close my eyes, and all Karasick kept doing was winking, knowingly winking. Basically, apart from some visual shenanigans, the whole thing is a bunch of short pop culture jokes. The first half consists of 684 Tweet-looking lines that mix this-with-that, ha-ha, ha-ha: "Wu-Tang is in Wudang," "Fellini is drinking a Bellini," "Brion Gysin is Running With Scissors," "The Brothers Karamazov are watching O Brother, Where Art Thou?," "The Faerie Queen is listening to Prince," "T.S. Eliot is listening to Sometimes It Snows In April," "Anubis is smoking cannabis,"

"William Wordsworth is wandering lonely on iCloud." It ends with several "Titles for Poems Yet to be Written": "Hello Kittler," "Dr. Seussure," "Etta Jameson," "Rihanna of Green Gables," "Nicki Menagerie," "The Electric Koolhaas Acid Test," "Ai Weiwei Wu-Tang" (it always comes back to the Wu-Tang, natch). You know already that if you fail to "respond" to this congeries of verbiage that you are opening yourself up to being called both unsophisticated and a sourpuss—unsophisticated because this is in fact a critique of blah-blah-blah and a sourpuss because you can't take a joke, dude. Such is what happens when people who have devoted their lives to art and theory (especially theory) and the capitalist accumulation of status and stuff lose all sense of balance and also think that they are funny. *Mon semblable! Ma soeur!* Truly the joke is on me. The fact that I picked up *every single reference* and could easily see myself making all these very "jokes" and being satisfied in doing so almost, almost convinced me that I have totally wasted my life. *Hypocrite lecteur, c'est la vie!* So I suppose that amounts to a kind of achievement on Karasick's part, little glory as it reflects on her reader. It is certainly a *committed* collection, displaying the driving persistence of David Letterman at the Oscars repeating "Oprah" and "Uma" until mere names were transformed into an aria of cringe.

The best book that made use of the visual arts this year was *Visible Cities*, a collaboration between poet Kathleen Wall and photographer Veronica Geminder (who happen to be mother and daughter, one discovers deep in the terminal notes). The cities are Boston, Chicago, Montreal, New York, Ottawa, Paris, Regina, Saskatoon, and Venice. The photographs are (mostly) in colour and Geminder has a true talent for finding the rich abstract in what could hardly be more concrete. Out of these three-dimensional alleys and gardens and pedestrians and parks and towers and streets and public sculptures and objects for sale, she flattens them into rectangles of shade and structure, rendering architecture into composition and revealing the inherent variety of ways-of-seeing that materialize when stasis is brought to bear on the moving world, or when our own movement through the city-space is arrested by a moment of attention.

The poems by Wall that attend these pictorial moments of arrest are straightforward in their balance of sentence and line, comfortable in their unflashy diction; yet just as Geminder finds the abstract in the concrete, Wall finds the concrete-abstract in the abstract-concrete. This sort of looping re-transformation is accentuated in several poems early in the book, wherein Wall sees the work of actual abstract painters in pictures of scenes that could never have anticipated or intended such a connection. Thus a close-up of a wall of "rust and scratches" "behind a Chinese restaurant / in a back alley" in Saskatoon yields a poem titled "Rust à la Pollock," which transforms Geminder's photo into a piece of biographical and formalist art critical description (with metaphorical touches) convincing enough that one might think the object being described is a newly discovered painting by Pollock: "He pins the canvas to the floor, wrestling / with the hurricane gravity of black and white. / Rust and yellow thrum among black filaments. / Materiality spills from his paint stick / in a spare lichen of thought." A nondescript picture of a partly painted door becomes "Rothko's wooden door," and indeed by being so named, one sees it as a Rothko, the sun-blanched white of the plywood being the ground for the floating grey rectangle that is foregrounded against another similar but bigger space of ochre. In New York's Financial District we discover "De Chirico on Wall Street," one of those spectral receding inside-outside arcades, "the order of midafternoons that empty / like de Chirico's melancholy streets, / pursuing indifferent beauty." In an Ottawa alley, "discretion [is left] behind, like a Chagall goat." There is a photo of afternoon loungers on Boston Common that the poet rightly sees as a contemporary version of Seurat's pointillated park-goers enjoying La Grande Jatte. Actual (that is to say, intentional) works of art are described alongside their photos: "The Chicago Picasso" in Daley Plaza, that same city's "Cloud Gate" by Anish Kapoor, an anonymous spread of graffiti on a railroad car somewhere between Regina and Saskatoon—well, not anonymous, exactly; the art *is* the name or the tag of the artist, presumably, but it is in a sophisticated and arcane visual language hard for the layman to read. There are still lifes—"Red Truck," "Orchids in Grand Cerf Arcade." A windowful of "Convex travel mirror[s]" for sale in Venice lightly recalls the postmodern ekphrasis *par excellence*, Ashbery's "Self-Portrait in a Convex Mirror." Usually one goes to museums in cities, but here the cities are the museums; and the book itself is a compendium of ekphrastic strategies successfully staged.

Cities were central to other books this year. Michael Turner's *9×11* recalls the Manhattan of the World Trade Center attacks, given the two long rectangular columns on the cover and the numerical correspondence of 9/11 and the title. "Only in its shape did the poem anticipate the skyscraper," Turner writes, in language more akin to criticism than poetry, granting the permeability of the boundary. The book itself is attuned to architectural spaces and though its practical locus is New York City, its spiritual center is the Paris of Baudelaire's *Paris Spleen*. "I am interested in [Baudelaire's] thoughts on poetry, how he arrived at making poetry through prose. I am less interested in distinguishing between poetry and prose than I am in our perceptions of them." One of those common perceptions is that poetry is a "vertical" phenomenon while prose is a "horizontal" one, and in moving from the skyscrapers of *9x11* to Lucas Crawford's *The High Line Scavenger Hunt* we are still in lower Manhattan, but now on the ground instead of in the air. Well, sort of on the ground and kind of in the air—we are on the High Line, that elevated train track repurposed into a public park that is an incredibly pleasant place to stroll on a summer afternoon. Crawford has written academic work on architecture and culture and this book of poems brings that background to bear given its concern with the histories of the "old" New York and how those histories can be shadowed by city planning, public projects, gentrification. The poet manages to maintain his seriousness while also taking us on an amiable amble, where there is "stern"-ness at times but not "spleen"-ness and where the range of poems is various, like the lives of the pedestrians walking the High Line on any given day.

In Dominique Bernier-Cormier's debut, *Correspondent*, the crucial distance spanned is from Canada to Moscow, where the not-yet-poet relocates as a child when his father, a CBC/Radio-Canada correspondent, is sent there on the job. The book, which is primarily prose reportage of public events mixed with personal impressions and a scattering of lines from interviews and letters, focuses on three stories covered by the poet's father as they happened: the sinking of the Russian submarine *Kursk* in August 2000; the assassination of Ahmad Shah Massoud by al-Qaeda operatives posing as journalists in September 2001; and the tragic debacle of October 2002, when armed Chechen separatists took a play-going audience hostage and the Russian authorities not only shot the hostage-takers dead, but also killed the audience of over 130 souls, many of them children, with poison gas. It is a striking book, naturally, given the subject matter, and the manner in which Bernier-Cormier incorporates the impressions of a young boy in a foreign city learning a new language and registering events which he cannot fully understand gives it some aesthetic added-value over and above the stark reality of the events themselves. In his notes the poet is careful to point out that he tried not to be merely exploitative, and to my mind he succeeds. His brother's nine-year-old classmate is one of the few allowed to leave, and thus survive, the Moscow theatre hostage crisis, and later in their schoolyard his fellow classmates surround him—"Little journalists all wanting a piece"—a scene that strikes a delicate balance between recording the objective facts and acknowledging the voyeuristic energies of tragedy reportage.

* * *

Why did the critic cross the road? To get to escape, if only temporarily, from "the world [that] is too much with us," even from collections that are written out of a therapeutic purpose, or to expose historical wrongs, or to rectify the culture's ills, or to assuage the poet's guilt, sometimes by transferring it onto *me*; thus making such collections ethically or morally worthy, perhaps (depending), but essentially beyond critique in a civil, polite, reconciliatory—or at any rate in an impassioned, politicized, digitally vindictive society; thus annihilating the critic's existence *qua* critic. (The critic in this case is no disruptor and is temperamentally averse to arousing ire and hurting feelings, both his own and those of others—but especially his own.) What is found on the other side is David Alexander's *After the Hatching Oven*, which is a book about chickens. Now, the chicken is a bird with which the fleeing, road-crossing critic can identify. For the chicken begins as essentially yellow-bellied too, nascent in that gleaming orb of yolk; and as it clucks into the void it can strike us as myopic, erratic, annoying; but we grant some leeway to the humble if imperfect bird, who is merely pecking its way through life as best it can, laying an occasional fragile gift, or at any rate an egg, and awaiting an irrevocable fate. It cannot be easy to have such neutral, particular taste that almost everything is said to taste like you.

As its title attests in conjuring visions of an avian version of those horrific incubation factories from *The Matrix*, *After the Hatching Oven* is far from wholly ludic. Alexander is not averse to suggesting the darker side of the eggs and meat that most of us eat. An "Elegy" for a bird "unknown, at rest / on a bed of rue and rosemary" is not uncomic, but the former ingredient is finally more redolent than the rosemary. Indeed, the poem-meal ends ruefully with questions asked "above her unmarked grave: // *Who was she? Was she / yours?* A rooster cries." The pieced-together "Cento for a Chicken with His Head Cut Off" is another, harsher, elegy. "White Lies / White Meat" (said to be "*after*" a Ted Hughes poem but also a Velvet Underground allusion) hints at the little dissimulations that grease the path from cage to plate to gullet. "The Minimal Standing of Merely Conscious Entities" hints at how such dissimulations can hide behind ostensibly philosophical inquiry. "Animal Enterprise Terrorism Act" bespeaks the political pressure applied against even so much as advocating for these birds; and it all adds up to "Dead Chickens," or to "Erasure of 'The Hen'" (another poem "*after*" Ted Hughes).

Yet the book is far from predominantly somber, which is an unhypocritical approach. I gather that Alexander eats meat, not that it says so in his back-matter bio; and for those of us who do, and who also have at least a modicum of decency (though some abstainers would deny that we have it, and in this case perhaps rightly so), there is a consistent and largely subconscious toggling between acceptance, denial, and sympathy, between the obvious facts and oblivious self-willed ignorance, between humorous acknowledgement and deflective rationalization. A major way this toggling manifests itself is through uneasy jokes—uneasy and unfunny, really, though for some reason I got a big kick out of "Why I Am Not a Chicken," Alexander's rewriting of Frank O'Hara's "Why I Am Not a Painter." *After the Hatching Oven* is wry and sly and slight, which was all right by me, although if I have a serious criticism (and it sounds odd in the saying), it is that I never felt like we truly got inside the mind of a chicken, despite the promise implicit in a title such as "Chicken Cognition." "They Killed the Chickens" begins one poem, matched on the next page by its companion poem, "And It All Washed Out." You can cross the road as many times as you like, but it is an untenable miracle to escape this mortal cage alive, and to the victors go the bleach.

It was the ugly duckling, not the chicken, who turned into the swan, and I poach from that august transition in moving from *After the Hatching Oven* to *Tar Swan* by David Martin. Martin's debut falls under the generic designation of petro-poetry, the production of which has been increasingly prevalent of late (Stephen Collis's *Once in Blockadia* from last year comes to mind). Maybe because Martin is from Calgary, the politics are less stridently one-sided than might be expected. But then the book is too strange to be directly propagandistic and too shape-shifty to settle into a "position." *Tar Swan* is a four-voiced drama. The characters we hear from are Robert C. Fitzsimmons (the big-talking, paranoid first fellow to come up with an oil sands operation), Frank Badura (a plant mechanic whom the above boss suspects of subversive trickeration), Dr. Brian K. Wolsky (an archeologist examining the Fitzsimmons site), and the titular swan (who represents the oil itself). Martin notes that the book's "narrative" is "loosely based" on the work of Fitzsimmons and other early oil sands developers but that "the events depicted are fictitious," which I suppose could have been assumed given the primary role of a talking swan. But at least Fitzsimmons is real—Google him; there's a concise biography on the website of the Canadian Petroleum Hall of Fame, membership in which is rarefied, if polluted, air indeed—and he does come somewhat alive on the page. The other men don't really register.

The most compelling character is the Tar Swan itself. If Alexander never got me inside the head of a chicken, Martin somehow helped me inhabit this swan, this swan that is also many millennia's worth of glutinous gunk. It comes to us always in the form of what I like to call the "unlucky sonnet," which is to say, a thirteen-line poem with lines long enough to resemble by sight iambic pentameter lines; and there are thirteen of such "sonnets" here, although the final one in an act of conclusion consists of a proper fourteen-lines; so the whole sequence, although spread intermittently through the book, is a variation on the sonnet corona; which obviously, too, since the swan is the oil itself, is meant to make us experience the voices of the real-life men as the common sand from which the more valuable tar must be extracted. Formally interesting work, then, but it is the poignancy of the Tar Swan's voice that makes it stick. "I was born a single cygnet," starts the swan, "left fending / in quickening lichen" and then developing into a form of power: "My feathers and feces drive your cars[.]" The language can take on some vestige of the incredible geological torque necessary to make the oil, in a way that recalls the sonic pressures and prods of Hopkins ("Poor Karl's skull pitty-pat-slapped / sideways, spilling a terrible tantrum. / I did court him with plumes, yes, / busked us to saloons till dawn."). At other times, the tones are slicker ("I sashay as a winged-double, stalk / their brineboots, lope to Fitzy's gait, / and part feathers like greasy Frank, / but they're fire-blind to the fine time / I'm stewing."). By the end

Fitzsimmons is mad, and the swan dares to ask: "How was the fabricated flight?" Martin's debut is incoherent and not wholly convincing at the level of people, intriguing and complex at the level of its petroleum-poetry-bird.

In Randy Lundy's quietly striking and introspective *Blackbird Song*, the eponymous bird is part of an aviary chorus that includes sparrows, redpolls, golden finches, marsh wrens, warblers, "three pintails," "three flickers," a thrush, "seven white pelicans," a "dozen waxwings," "a passing gull," geese, crows, chickadees, "the low-winter-snowcloud great grey owl," "a single meadowlark," "a single kingbird," "that single eagle." A characteristic moment of self-correcting honesty occurs in "Octave: Asking Forgiveness":

> Last October, two birds in the bare-branched green elm
> with black caps, grey-blue backs and frost-white faces.
>
> *Downy woodpeckers*, I said, with all the confidence of middle age.
> I don't know how to tell you this, but I was wrong.
>
> The birds with chestnut under tail and nasal plaintive voices.
> Yesterday I filled the feeders. The nuthatches are back.
>
> I don't know how I could have made such a mistake.
> Although this comes late, I have to ask.

In the poem that follows, "Surrender," Lundy, speaking of himself in the second person, admits, "You think you may have been mistaken / every moment of your life until now." Such caesuras splitting into the rock of certainty stimulate the reader's trust. Even the poetic practice of finding a metaphorical objective correlative for one's feelings is gently interrogated, at one moment rejected: "Do not call it *lonely star* [ ... ] / Mind of Indirection, / will you get to the point? // The star is not— / It is you who are lonely, / motherless, fatherless orphan-child." He is mindful of family ties, careful to maintain them in feeling them lost. He offers "A Prayer" to his Cree grandmother, this "Woman Who Taught Her Grandson To Love": "[Y]ou lit a candle in front of the black and white / photo of that woman / holding a small, brown boy on her knees." Recalling Stevens's "The Plain Sense of Things," it is a book of leafless trees, but also of the birds therein, which inspire by being creatures of *being*, unencumbered by doubt or regret, whose "Sleek, bright wings glisten in the sun. / They have no shame." The muted nature of the book is nonetheless conveyed in a tightly-woven tapestry of sound. If this were not a mere part of a review, but instead were an article on poetics, I think I would title it "Randy Lundy's *ee's*," and my thesis would be that because his name itself is a couplet of trochees ending in rhyming long-e's, and because he and his heritage are Cree, that that sound is especially embedded in his mind's ear and his poetry's body (all italics mine):

> I cannot *be* sure, though I know you might *need*
> something more certain. *Please* understand that certain*ty*
> won't *ease* your *grief.* If *she* were to arrive today
> on my back step, *she*'d smile to *see me.*
>
> Sitting here, drinking *tea,* looking out the kitchen window
> into the backyard, I *see* a *deep*ening *green* in the *leaves* [ ... ]

"You are here, now, with a *sleep*ing dog. The maple *trees*. The moon's re*treat*. The frogs in the flooded ditches along the tracks sing their gelatinous *breed*ing." "Two miles *east* of where you sit with co*ffee* and cigarette, / in the cou*lees lead*ing down to Cottonwood *Creek,* / a pair of Great Pyre*nees* guard *sheep*." Or maybe it is not the sound of his name and his people that provoke his sonic returns, but rather the aforementioned "dozen waxwings," hearing them in his sleep alongside his lover, "those voices—*tsee, tsee, tsee*" (italics his).

Hopefully it is not too kooky to imagine that a poet could see (or hear) himself and his heritage in the vowels he chooses to use and those he picks up from the songs of birds. We find ourselves in all kinds of such small ways. Helen Vendler once noted, in an essay on John Ashbery, Fairfield Porter, and Saul Steinberg, "the degree to which our own initial[s] ('S' for ['Saul'] 'Steinberg') loom much larger for us than the other letters of the alphabet (as do, *mutatis mutandis*, all such mental representations of our own interests)." I see a version of this in *Rouge*, Adrian De Leon's intriguing, engaging debut. By that I don't primarily mean that the TTC system (Toronto's public transit system)—and specifically the subway and its chain of stops—is a "mental representation" of the poet's "interests"—although that is indeed the case; instead I mean something much more minor. In the poem on the "Old Mill" stop, De Leon gets out and the first sign he sees reads "66 Prince Edward," to which he responds:

> Prince—it contains six letters, of course—
> leads to this fun formation:
>
> 666 Edward
>
> Not wanting to be outdone,
> a Satan-phobic
> churchman might notice, too,
> the six letters of the next word.
>
> 6666
>
> it reads.
>
> The allure of this clever numerology
> tickles and stimulates my gooey cortex.
> Then a most disappointing
> guest arrives at the curb:
>
> 66D.
>
> Oh, what to do?
> Two groups of six quarters
> peek from my wallet.
> Two groups of six, six groups of two,
> *don't you see the madness—*
>
> Yes sir, I'll get on the bus now.
> I'd like a transfer, please.

If you'll begrudge my indulging in what Susan Howe once called "poetry telepathy," I'd submit that the poet, Adrian De Leon, notices these numbers especially because his first and last names both have six letters each, for a total pair of 6's; and that carrying around a pair of 6's makes those your lucky numbers; but that you also can't help but consider the proximity of those two 6's to the evil number 666; so you think of how one less or one more 6 changes the nature of the number of the beast, how a pair doesn't quite reach it and how two pairs negate it or bracket its negativity, and thus surpass it. As a person who shares Adrian De Leon's initials—and you can intuit what having the initials A.D. means to those that have them, if Vendler is right in speculating that our initials loom larger for us than other letters: those era-beginning, date-defining initials—and as one whose first and last names also contain six letters each—and by the way, and I kid you not, my birthday is June 6, so I really get the *two pairs* of 6's—well, the feeling here is: we're onto something.

De Leon is onto the subway, then off, then on, then off, but mostly on, because we feel that that is when he is writing his poems (a nice creation of the sense of immediacy), until we've run the whole route. I would advocate for a readership of this book among any audience, but it is only honest to say that for TTC riders, *Rouge* must have exponentially more impact. That said, it is an enjoyable and various book all around. Every car on the subway is virtually the same, but every stop is different, as every poem in a collection is the same in its being a *poem*, but different in each poem's actual execution. De Leon makes every poem almost *deliberately* different, thereby making this not only a serial poem but a kind of anthology of poetic genres and forms. It is also a documentary poem, an elegy and a reclamation-celebration, given that we are told on the back of the book that the project was inspired by the 2012 mass shooting at a block party in Scarborough, which the last two poems, titled "Rouge" for the Rouge Valley and for the colour of the blood that was spilled at the scene, most directly address by being scattered like a scared crowd over the closing pages. It is a book that reaches for several registers and by doing so successfully shows a grasp of a city and of the human needs of its inhabitants, especially of its subway-riding poets. *Rouge* also reminds one of last year's commuter-train book (Emily Izsak's *Whistle Stops: A Locomotive Serial Poem*) and is itself a sort of the aforementioned petro-poem (or given the subway's reduced carbon footprint, an anti-petro-poem). In short, a super start from a writer who has produced something to take everybody somewhere worth going.

In a sonnet at "Bessarion," De Leon stops and looks up, moving from the TTC to another trio of Torontonian letters: "Above I see airplanes / Tossed hard from YYZ." It is a shift of vantage that Nasser Hussain could appreciate. Hussain's book SKY WRI TEI NGS is premised on a gimmick that you know is a good one because when you consider it, you say to yourself instinctively: I can't believe nobody has thought of this before! The idea is to take all the available three-letter airport codes and only write the poems using conglomerations of those codes—an Oulipian-level stricture with lots of global implications. What it yields up, of course, is dependent upon the talent of the poet and Hussain makes the most of his concept. Since we are in the air, let's start with a poem about a fellow high-flier, titled "FLY HIE" (the codes for airports in Finley, Australia and Whitefield, New Hampshire, respectively):

IZT BRD?

PLN?

KNO!

SPR MAN!

(LEX LUT HOR: RUN!)

The inherent limitation set by the parameters perhaps leads the poems to tend toward the comic and gnomic. Suggestive things can be done within the self-chosen confines of concision—two lines that contain a whole Modernist history, for instance: "POE TRY ISS NUS THA TST AYS NEW / PET ALS ONA WET BLA ACK BOW[.]" Along the same line is a diptych called "DEP END," the second part of which reads

SUM OCH DEP END
SUP ONA

RED WEL ELB
ARR OGG

LAZ EDW ITH RAI
NWA TER

BES IDE THE WIT
CHI KEN.

It is right that a book such as this should pay homage not just to Modernist experimenters, but also to more recent ones ("EUN OIA (FOR BOK)"), or to pre-Modern yawpers ("FOR WAL TER WHT MAN"), and indeed these codes are good for sheer sounds ("SOU NDS")—"AGH AHH ACH / AIE OHH HOO"—and can also accommodate in truncated form "STO RIS" ("THE ASP BIT / CLE OPA TRA [...] EVE ATE THE APP LES / AND SAW THE LIE") and even "HST ORY" itself. There are twenty-four illustrations, maps that show the flight trajectories of movement between the airports whose codes appear in a given poem. Hussain follows his project (PRO JCT?) through to the end—END? these codes are contagious—as even the "THA NKS" that close the book are rendered in the secret language of our baggage tags.

Among the possible modes of transportation, one that most readers of this review likely no longer take is the river. We don't take it, perhaps; but what do we take from it, and from whom do we take it? These are questions streaming through Rita Wong and Fred Wah's *beholden: a poem as long as the river*. This is the most visually *moving* of the books this year so it comes as no surprise that it was first exhibited in a gallery, as part of a project called *River Relations: A Beholder's Share of the Columbia River*. The original piece consisted of a 114-foot banner depicting the whole of the Columbia River in scaled-down form, along the banks of which Wong and Wah wrote two connected and often intertwining long poems related to the river itself. Certain precedents come to mind: Gary Geddes's *Swimming Ginger*, which reproduced and remarked on the Qingming Shanghe Tu scroll; Jack Kerouac's original manuscript scroll for *On the Road*; A.R. Ammons's *Tape for the Turn of the Year*, which was written on a roll of adding machine tape; or something less literally river-like but still in perpetual movement and full of personal, political, and historical flotsam and jetsam such as Allen Ginsberg's "Witchita Vortex Sutra," which Wah mentions in a conversation with Wong that closes the book.

There is a moment in that conversation—which is honest and pleasant and serious and full of the requisite "grateful acknowledgements" and "listening to the rivers"—that is telling; namely, when Wah asks Wong, "Were you consciously avoiding being didactic with the language you ended up using in your poem?," to which Wong answers, "No, I wasn't thinking about it. The words that came were the words that came." The idea that this book, with its admittedly gentle preaching, *avoids* didacticism just shows you how totally saturated contemporary Canadian poetry is with didacts. This might seem rich coming from a critic and professor, but it seems that we have reached a tipping point here of poets always overtly teaching people things, telling them how to talk, explaining what they should attend to, correcting their misconceptions, urging them into action, asserting their own selfhood as a model for others to attempt to achieve or at the very least to be chastened by: so many *shoulds*, so much *you must*, such self-aggrandizement under cover of helping others, such paucity of humility, such compromised poetry. Not every ostensible authority figure holds the authority they think that they do. In the cases of Wah and Wong one listens, for they are hardly Johnny-come-latelys to advancing an environmentalist ethos in art and because their temperaments are unhectoring. They are not just elders, but poetry elders who have earned a certain latitude in turning our attitude toward listening and, following from the listening, on to the potential for action. What is more, the undeniable beauty of *beholden* makes the message more digestible, like putting pills in ice cream.

Then again, even though the ice cream is fine, what you really need are the pills, depending on what you've got and how bad of a sickness it is. Let us agree that we have got a climate crisis on our hands as we turn to Alice Major's *Welcome to the Anthropocene*. In "Climate change debate" there is not much talk of climate change or of debate at first, though it does progress briskly to the assertion that "It will require / spring's clearest signs of warming / to liquefy positions, offer mild rebuttal. // But then, too quickly, ice will pass / and the creek bed will be fired / to cracked, crazed mud, a fringe / of desiccated willow, gasping grass." I don't know what she's telling me to *do*, but I kind of know what I think, and these lines somehow accommodate a space for that knowledge at the same time as they put a touch of pressure on it. It is funny that the poem on the facing page is titled "Badger," because this is not a badgering book. (The badger of that title is not a verb, anyway, but the character in *The Wind in the Willows*.) Major is another person who has been around the poetic block for a long time and warrants listening to. *Intersecting Sets: A Poet Looks at Science*, a prose work of hers, came out a few years ago and I was excited to read it, but slightly disappointed after doing so; it was too amorphous for me, not devoid of interesting parts but unformed and a tad overplumped with air. *Welcome to the Anthropocene* is airy but tight. The long title poem, a verse essay in the manner and close to the metric of Pope, does a strong version of what the earlier book had attempted to do. Elsewhere are shorter lyrics that contain a sharp stab. "Draft of a poem on 'inclusion'" is a case in point:

> There's a helium balloon up there.
> A puffy silver star
> pressing its cheek against the glass-peaked ceiling
> over City Hall's grand stair.
>
> It wants to be included in the larger air beyond.
> That's what inclusion is — not letting in
> but letting out.
>
> We're tired of being kept inside
> our glass-paned containers,
> tired of hardness masquerading
> as transparency.

It is important that the poem is figured as a draft (since what constitutes "inclusion" is always in the process of being "drafted" and the final, clean copy is always a dream) and even its most overt pedagogical statement ("That's what inclusion is — not letting in / but letting out") is rendered less overbearing than it might be by being slightly against the grain. "[H]ardness masquerading / as transparency" is a phrase that might have appeared in one of Marianne Moore's harsher character studies, such as "To a Steamroller," "Those Various Scalpels," or "To Be Liked by You Would Be a Calamity." There is after all something of the eccentric Moore in Major, someone who is unimpressed by the conforming type of self-satisfied "nonconformist" but who values the truly different, those who take an oblique angle on things.

There is a funny moment in George Plimpton's account of taking Moore to a World Series game that is relevant here. It starts to rain and some boisterous banker types, realizing they have a celebrity seated in front of them, offer Moore one of their parkas to cover her head. She is wearing her tricorn hat and she accepts the parka from them, but instead of covering her hatted head, she takes off the hat, puts it on her lap, and places the parka over the hat, leaving her head uncovered and growing wet and the banker boys nonplussed. I thought of that scene when reading Major's "The hat," about an older, "squat, lace-collared" woman in a chain coffee shop, wearing the eponymous object, lushly described: "an explosion of crochet — / wooly loops of rust and pumpkin / puffing upwards like the crust of a soufflé[,]" a hat which "conforms / to no known pattern." Nearby stand a gaggle of slack-jawed jerks, and Major reminds us that, generosity aside, there are indeed some people who just weren't raised right: "The sullen young / snicker nearby, a tattooed chorus / of conventional rebellion with stapled lips / and earlobes. They'd never wear That Hat. / They wouldn't be caught dead. / They crave to set themselves apart, / unequivocally unique. But not / with that thing on their head." Major is a moralist, yes, but a quirky one, which we will call in this context a Moore-alist.

Suzanne Zelazo's *Lances All Alike* has an elaborate hat on its cover, begins with an excerpt from Moore's "Those Various Scalpels," and takes on and from the work of two women Modernist poets, Mina Loy and Baroness Elsa von Freytag-Loringhoven. Loy will have been heard of, probably more heard of than read, by many of the readers of this review, whereas I doubt the Baroness is known by more than a scattered few. I had only heard of von Freytag-Loringhoven randomly, by coming across selections of her work in the first volume of the anthology *Poems for the Millennium* (a multi-volume anthology edited by Pierre Joris and Jerome Rothenberg that is highly recommended). I never followed up on that initial exposure, but seeing that Zelazo has co-edited *Body Sweats: The Uncensored Writings of Elsa von Freytag-Loringhoven*, published by MIT Press, and finding the poetry book here to be itself compelling, I plan to rectify that and read more of her work; which, incidentally, is what I always think when I read Mina Loy: you know, I should read more Mina Loy. (I once used as an epigraph to a think-piece on "Partners" an amazing sentence from a memoir of Loy that she wrote about her lover Arthur Craven, a mysterious figure with whom she was besotted (and he with her), regarding the first time they met: "The putrefaction of unspoken obscenities issuing from that tomb of flesh, devoid of any magnetism, chilled my powdered skin." Disgust at first sight! Vampire erotics!) Zelazo's are really good collage poems, bringing her two predecessor poets together with shards of other stuff. Aphorisms flash forth, aphorisms about aphorisms: "Aphorisms of plenty / where his hands were." Brief sibilant and sharp chunks ("Deciduous trees leave / cracks in crystal canopies. / Splash pool, lucid / semiotic darkroom." "Ribald tonnage / radium swoon"), with lots of this-and-that balance, a logic of twos ("honeysuckle fists," "shadow bodies," "red spoon," "patient howl," "nuclear wind," "inflated crest"—a hundred examples are possible), structured by the forebearing poetic duo, but often recalling artistic others: Duchamp, Stein, Pound: see Zelazo's "Sutures on a wet blank continuum" as a further reduction of "petals on a wet, black bough." This is almost scholarly poetry, literary-critical-historical refiguring, if you can see what you are looking at, but funner than that sounds. (Kudos to Lizzie Gill for *Crown Jewels*, the striking collage on the book's cover, a collage cover for a collage book, where the aforementioned hat appears.)

\* \* \*

"You can't judge a book by its cover." Well, supposedly, but a book's back cover is part of the cover too and it is chock full of judgments already, always very positive ones, it turns out. The language there is often hardly to be believed. Somebody should write a yearly omnibus review of blurbs, of their hyperbolic amorphousness, of their most tendentious claims, of the intricate networks of influence and fealty they suggest or reveal. Less dyspeptically, one might turn from the words on the back and remark instead on the overall quality of book design across Canadian poetry publishers. It is very high by my estimation— money has been spent and talent has been employed. In that sense it is true that you can't always judge a book by its cover, because the overall quality of the poetry inside the books is closer to crop-duster altitude—higher than just off the ground, but definitely sub-stratospheric (although a few rockets are successfully launched every season); but the generally high level of design insures that you don't just read the prettiest looking books, because they are all pretty much pretty, and so it is strangely democratic, judging these books by the sight of their covers—the democracy of quality *of a kind*—the way all the contestants in a beauty pageant look better than your average person, even if some of them flub a question such as, "If you were to win the crown, what will you do to help the world?".

Among many luminous and eye-catching covers, then, I was especially drawn to the image on the front of *Trauma Head* by Elee Kraljii Gardiner, a plouffy plume of crimson red, from a photo by Alberto Seveso. I was also drawn to the title *Trauma Head*, which would make a great name for a Black Flag album. I was drawn too to the first two parts of the poet's name—I couldn't place their provenance with any certainty. Whatever the reasons I zoned in on it were serendipitous. Here we have an interesting, successful book. For one thing, it has a compelling story behind it, which helps locate you somewhere specific by giving you a "narrative" that precedes less tangible matters of form, tone, and style. In 2012 the author had a small stroke and then shortly thereafter, the lining of an artery in her brain tore and she could barely use language anymore. This book is about learning to use language again. Just because this *really happened* and that it is terribly scary stuff, stuff that has a closer, more organic connection to the writing of poetry itself than do most real stories, that does not mean that it should necessarily turn out to be a good book of poetry. *Trauma Head* turns out that way, though. The existence of the object is like a worked-for and earned happy ending, as is the actual story itself—the fact that Gardiner recovered to write the book in our hands is the proof.

"I feel like a letter printed backward in the line," we begin, a quote from Kierkegaard. The words tend to be printed all over the pages in an Olson-ian kind of "composition by field," an oft-employed strategy in this year's books, but rarely one that yields *Maximus* results. *Trauma Head* is an exception, given that Gardiner uses the unfilled spaces to insinuate cognitive negations and linguistic absences, with a backslash often suggesting the definitive moment when a break occurred:

/ stroke presents
/ fear aphasia — what will I w / out words —

/ yet I am think / placing yllables correct / am I not

catalogue simulacra: >ffwd
/ rehab / adaptive / / wheels
cyclical caregiving, drone

We "enter the disruption" (a repeated phrase) and find not just blanks but attempts at recombination ("mudhoneycalm," "braincomicstrip," "fearritated," "janglecrimping," "mindelectrical," "ownlanguage") as well as words breaking apart ("ill lumen," "formulate form," "pupils di / late," "flipping d / ang / er to ang / le," "re / known to myself"). By the end of the long process of treatment and rehabilitation, we have graduated into health and into prose: "Strange how fast we turn corners," writes Gardiner, whose previous 130 pages are a testament to how un-fast it took to reach that corner, and "start feeling better and forget what we were [....] Spoonful by spoonful each day I taste the river, the salt, clouds, all the recipes of blood." And then it dawns on you—that beautiful red plume that arrested you on the cover of the book is blood, and all those arteries carrying that beauty through your body are like life-sustaining lines of poetry that you take for granted daily.

The every-dailiness of life and the little snippets of verbiage one finds therein prove to be important in Shazia Hafiz Ramji's *Port of Being*. Such snippets, in fact, proved to be sorts of such ports for Ramji, who writes in an afterword that in order to ward off a creeping depression, she would go down along the waterfront in Vancouver and listen in on semi-public conversations. The poems in the first section of the book ("Container") record these and, as in Gardiner's book, the words are scattershot across the page, representing the scattershot way one would hear them; they are also printed in various shades of ink, where moving from grey to black and back seems to signify changes in volume due to the audio-voyeur's proximity, the movement from what you overhear to the thoughts generated by the sounds of others, all the while taking fleeting note of your physical surroundings. The second and fourth sections (titled "Surveiller" and "Spooky Actors at a Distance," respectively) contain short-lined poems with spaces in between lines, marching down the page like lists, while the third section ("Flags of Convenience") combines the two styles; the fifth and final section ("Port of Being") consists of roughly conventional free verse poems that are more obviously autobiographical—at least, so it seems, for their markers of "reality" are high. Perhaps because there is no single "port" but there are actually various "ports" (both in the sense of places to settle in and ship out from, and of places to dock your devices), we find an absence of a sense of coherence of being: "likening / the fish in the pond to movements // of the self. Being me, I sit on the bench, // stroke my thumb against the upper / part of my other self." Yet there is a through-line of verbal and attentional intensity and a wary, weary registering of the high-speed ways we watch and are watched in our world: "I didn't tell you of the hands / that led the Internet cable / into the sea, / that they were brown / or that I was thinking / of rows of royal blue binders / in a hospital in Afghanistan: / records of amputations / from drone strikes. / I saw all this on TV, / as in, my laptop: torrents, Netflix."

In a "Poem Beginning With Falsehood," Ramji writes, "I imagine you jerking off to parts / from *The Society of Spectacle* [ ....] you cry and watch me / make the mistake of thinking // I can out-think everything. Now I want to say / I've got Marcuse! I've got Deleuze!" If something about this scene appeals to you, or at least if the names ring a bell, you might also like Julie McIsaac's *We Like Feelings. We Are Serious.* Therein: We are dry. We are ironic. We write in prose with muted sonic effect. We have been in the vicinity of the academy. We include screenshots from our computer and illustrations from what looks like some sort of Dick-and-Jane primer on puberty. It is an amusing book but it also sometimes cuts too close to the bone, which is good because that is just another way of saying it cuts through the distancing fog of proximity: "Big Dan's Presentation on the Female Poet," "Notes on Big Dan's Presentation on the Female Poet," or as another series of poems has it, "No Theory," "No Theory," "No Theory," "No Theory." There are some sonnets of interest, but mostly the reader encounters sentences adeptly rendered in plain speech but usually also with panache. This erstwhile indie rocker appreciated a whole page being devoted to the following facts: "Thurston Moore and Kim Gordon split. Sonic Youth to follow." And indeed it proved to be true.

If McIsaac's approach to academic mores and certain tendencies toward the "cool" is ironic and oblique, Janet Rogers jettisons the cool for the hot and approaches the academy with a fiery tongue. *As Long As The Sun Shines* traffics in invective and, as ever, as long as you are not the one being invected against, the results can be hatefully humorous. Pity the "White Indian Academic Wannabe Expert" who gives one poem its title: "you fucking career-almost-Indian / just stop playing / with this culture / outsider anthropologist / pimping pain and struggles / as award winning novels / penned from the deluxe comfort / of your convention / writing about my realities / speaking with authority / for me and mine / the more you rise / the more we morph / warped academic rewards / with built in audience / posturing is posing / you goddamn Grey Owl[.]" This is performance poetry that pops off the page as if being declaimed from a stage and one imagines Rogers's own "built in audience," a portion of which is doubtless white academic-activist "allies," shifting nervously on their seats during the recitation of such a screed, wondering if they have ever inadvertently drifted too far into putative expert territory—a straight-forward enough warning to practitioners of what I call *O.P.P. Criticism* (Other People's Problems Criticism) which, let's face it, is pervasive and grants you a good deal of cultural capital with a dash of righteousness on the side, until it doesn't. "Title Me This" is a three-page-long list poem of book titles (invented?—but they seem so real) pertaining to indigeneity, clustered into categories: "Generous Book Titles" (these all include the word "People"), "Plain Ol' Indian Book Titles" (these all include the word "Indian"), "'Man'-'Woman'-'American'-'Red' Book Titles," and the most capacious category of all, "Poetic Book Titles"—a remark on the incredible proliferation of books on the subject, and also a mirroring remark, since *As Long As The Sun Shines* is an example of one. This is a species of stand-up comedy poetry, which is akin to performance-based poetry, whereby the need to corral the audience's enthusiasm and provoke an immediate response leads the poet to try to make 'em laugh, make 'em mad, or make 'em say "amen!" There is also a natural impulse to preach to the choir-that-is-present over and against some other choir-that-isn't-in-attendance. "[K]now your conscientiousness / be aware of what you are aware of / keep it alive in timelessness / this is not an instructional"—oh, you bet it is. In the book's final section Rogers is "Singing The Peace Hymn," but here the more convincing (because dominant) mode is found in "Revenge is Honest," because, yes, after all, perhaps "revenge is honest / while its ugly cousin regret / sits silent / and the thing / you promised / was broken / before it even / left your mouth"—very "instructional" indeed.

Self-instruction is the order of the day in Christine Stewart's *Treaty 6 Deixis* and Sonja Ruth Greckol's *No Line in Time*, which also means that the reader is meant to get taught. "Deixis" is actually an ingenious way to frame a consideration of "the author's obligations as a settler," as the copy on the back of Stewart's book has it, but, with all due respect, despite being a pretty-looking book, and a book that uses its spaces well, it is not very educational in any specific way, at least if one has done one's own thinking about the aforementioned obligations. Still, criticism aside, the orientation on *here-ness* is a kind of conceptual coup. Greckol's book is another work of self-education, as the author acknowledges "writ[ing] from settler privilege of education and opportunity conferred by occupying institutions," and I cannot lie and say that such language inspires much confidence in the *art* (as opposed to the pedagogy) that one is about to encounter. But Greckol is self-aware, mature enough to have had a range of experience in the world, and is bold in trying out a wide variety of poetic tricks, in wearing a series of historical masks: "however driven this quest is still summary betrayal in hindsight as each feint and parry inverts to death thousand cuts by rally cry data slice wedge tweet enflames them;us[.]" Her previous books were ones to cherish (especially her stellar debut, *Gravity Matters*) and although I found this one less compelling, I did appreciate the way that real work was being done in trying to integrate the growth of herself as a political person with the growth of herself as a poet. It overstates things, perhaps, to think of a book such as this as a profitable-failure, for failure is too strong a word; but it often seems to be the case that when one looks back over the career of a poet one likes, it is often for such oddities of stalling and simultaneous growth that a reader feels the most fondness. It reminds us that sometimes it is admirable simply to try.

# Poetry: Letters in Canada 2017

It was a struggle of a year—did you feel it too? And frankly, the stress of this always-on, 24-hour world is unallayed by a bunch of poetry books; but if you choose one book (and you can really only read one at a time) and settle in on the sofa... Outside, it is cold and the wind is outrageous; inside the book, lord knows what you'll find... in here, you're simply reading; just being here still proves a pleasant challenge and sometimes, after all, an alleviation, albeit not always an easy one.

Not everything needs to be hard, though. You can make Nelson Ball's poems as hard as you want them to be, but I for one wouldn't. It *is* hard, perhaps, to accept them. They are so *there*. If you know Ball's work you probably know it in chapbook form, small and sparsely-printed-upon homemade books with small and sparely-dictioned poems of sensory observation, of thought. Ball is your most minimal minimalist. In selecting and collecting these poems in a Laurier Poetry Series anthology, *Certain Details: The Poetry of Nelson Ball*, Ball and the volume's editor, Stuart Ross—one of the more generous and industrious figures in the Canadian poetry world—know that the process takes the poems out of their original context, but I enjoyed reading them together all the same. Some physical and mental space was lost and that is significant given how important space is to these poems, how space is palpably *in* them (from "Fragment of Poetics": "A tree—the spaces / between its parts"); but it is also a pleasure to read a string of them in a row, easier to see links, to ascertain a path. The essay on himself that Ball pens at book's end finds him to be like his poems: succinct, attuned.

In his introduction to the book, Ross recounts how he often gives a Ball poem to readers unfamiliar with contemporary poetry and how it serves as a good first opening. Another sort of opening in that regard might be first books by new writers. Talk about being so very *there*—copious blurbs aside, there is less reputation to hide behind; and the serious flaws to be found, if any, are mostly yet ahead—but are they nascent? And the successes—who is unfamiliar with the slow-growing thrill of hearing an original voice, of inhabiting a fresh presence, or even of learning new words in which to say old things? Although there were too many debuts this year to read them all (that is, while also reading anything else), the haul encountered was promising and one hopes it is relatively representative, though I regret that due to considerations of space, energy, inclination, and timing, there are some worthy books that had to go unincluded (and that doesn't just go for debuts). Poetry-wise it was a pretty good year all around, more than enough for any single reader.

\* \* \*

One Ball-like first book was Emily Nilsen's *Otolith*, in part due to its approaching (though not matching) the poetic equation "less is more" as exemplified by Ball, in part because its "points of attention" (a phrase that turns up thrice in *Certain Details*) are often turned to the natural world. In *Otolith* ("ear stone"), however, we discover a beginning that resists the clarity we often assume we'll find outside ourselves. Isn't balance meant to be found somewhere in there, in here, the inner ear? Hers is a world of fog, and a world of work on the West Coast in which fog is so pervasive as to take on many forms and figures: "Before a storm, its stench / was as though a wet mammoth / had shaken itself at the door"; "like an eclipse / of hungry moths." I read it in winter on the most opposite side of the country and it translated well. Nilsen works best incrementally, by returning to certain evocative questions—"And What of the Fog?," "*have you seen the ghost?*"—and by listing things ("Meanwhile" this, "Meanwhile" that), or many versions of a single thing: "Fragile Morning of the Landlady," "Fragile Mornings of the Couple Moored to the Dock Next Door," "Fragile Mornings of the Farmhand Who Longs to Leave," "Fragile Evenings of the Man in His Trawler," "Fragile Night of the Hitchhiker from Up Island." Characters, stories appear, then fade; some figures (the grandfather) are more persistent; it has mystery to it at the same time as a sense of place.

This year, due to the vicissitudes of which box was opened when, I began with four first books from Signature Editions, a press I hadn't perused a lot.

They were all good though quite different. It is nice when a press comes out bold with lots of debuts—you get the anticipatory excitement of watching a draft class form, a cohort you can follow. These four are strange bedfellows—and speaking of that, there are lots and lots of bedfellows (or fellows bedded) in Tenille K. Campbell's *#IndianLovePoems*, my starting point of the four. Every poem has a number for a title and is about a different nameless guy—well, some have nicknames—that the poet has known—you know, "known" in the old-fashioned sense. This was my first encounter with a hashtag-titled book and it was invigorating and somewhat scary to cross such forbidden boundaries. It felt a little like becoming the *môniyas* numbered "#782," the one with "white guilt and privilege / narrow in your eyes[.]" It would be better to be like "#438," "my first / *môniyas* / [who] was everything a / *môniyas* should be[.]" There are plenty of men from the rainbow of flavours to be had here, all numbered, some loved, none spared. There is "#92," whose post-coital presence leads Campbell to "[ponder] / the age old question // how the fuck / do i get him out of here?" There is "#2001," "my gifted Cree man [ ... ] // make me / speak pleasure / once again[.]" There is "#32," "warrior to my maiden / the one who makes me victory cry / as we ride to freedom // he speaks low and rough / *nêhiyawêwin* / run down my spine // my dene tongue licks / my thick lips kiss / a body that once / would have been / banned from mine[.]" One hesitates to quote the juiciest parts out of regard for the propriety of the *UTQ* readership, but there are lots of juicy parts. Having been tepidly if briefly promiscuous in my youth, and being a good moralist in public today, one is obliged to remark that such behavior doesn't always spring from the happiest of places or result in the most propitious of outcomes; and then there are the problems of voyeurism, objectification, stereotyping that might arise: "judge me / i dare you[,]" Campbell warns at one point, a dare this critic is not brave enough to take. Noting at another moment that "this is dating / in 2017[,]" she paces the selection, so that the reader is all the more pleased at the pleasant (or mind-altering) encounters precisely because not all of them are. Are there, after all, sad or troubling or troublingly charged aspects of an honest book about sex, how one person (a very specific person, with an *identity* of interest) does it and imagines it and describes it? Yes, which is why it is good, because it is honest and unafraid; there is also its tactility, its debauchery, its wistfulness, and its sense of humour to recommend it.

With that, *Cityscapes in Mating Season* by Lise Gaston, *Midway Radicals & Archi-Poems* by Ted Landrum, and *Whistle Stops: A Locomotive Serial Poem* by Emily Izsak (the rest of the quartet) cannot compete. As they say on draft night, their "skill set" is different—but not totally incompatible. One thing that caught my eye (or ear) in Gaston's book was the diction. You could feel her rolling words around, especially in a section called "bonescapes," where some of the freshness of the vocabulary is because it is fresh to the poet, although the occasion is a clinical one: "This doctor gives me sickness, pronounces its / polysyllabic name. I offer him glances, // teeth bared in a grin. He says *chronic, / progressive*. My blouse is open / just enough. He prescribes. Vocabularies slip / from his    parted    lips    to mine." The poet has something badly wrong with her back, her spine, and much of the book is dedicated to trying to find out what is causing pain and how to name it. The final series of poems titled "Silence" uses the relative blankness of the whole page nicely; but then *Cityscapes in Mating Season* is stably architectured and ably textured throughout. Ted Landrum's book, on the other hand, is less textured but more memorably architectured. The *Archi-Poems* of his title are short for "architecture poems" (among other things) and the author himself is an architect (among other things). The use of erasure and negative space is indicative of talent. His Eiffel Tower poem (or his Roland Barthes poems) is (are) exquisite (superb). His Fly-Trap Poem is a concrete chuckle.

Izsak's *Whistle Stops* is what its subtitle says it is, namely, a serial poem on the move, on a commuter train back and forth between Toronto and London, Ontario. It is not all a waste of time, commuting: "Weather bastes our / latest interval with / sky lard and / crystal regimens of three / secret Kegels / per round trip[.]" The titles are the times and train numbers of each day's trips, which are stultifyingly similar and sensorially and meditatively different. (This aspect of *Whistle Stops* recalls #IndianLovePoems, with its numbered lovers, and which is, in its own way, also a serial poem.) "Oh train / it is strange for your shape / that I / am inside you[,]" she writes, flipping the phallic script, but also acknowledging a phenomenology of trains that has always made them good figures for simultaneous movement (what passes outside) and stasis (as you sit in your seat). "Everything has a schedule if you can find out what it is," ends the first poem in John Ashbery's first book, spoken from a train station. The schedule here is the waiting, the hustle, the bustle, the sitting, the moving....

"MAR 29th 74 TO UNION STATION 07:32" ("Transient culture / baked in / syntactic alignment"), "DEC 10th 76 TO LONDON 16:42" ("There is a lamppost deep / in each and every / one of us / who screams reductive / dogma to the skin"), "FEB 4th 83 TO LONDON 20:09" ("sediment sexts / with the new matriarchy // Lick my silt // Maybe next year"), and on and on and on, another dollar, another day.

Sometimes these things take time. You are perpetually overscheduled. You are the dean of a small college, trying to keep it afloat. You are going to write those poems one of these days, right after this meeting, and that thing next week, and the big review next month, and you need to fundraise and propitiate and network and decide... Nobody said it was easy being a Dean, a maligned and oft-mocked figure, from *Animal House* to *Old School* (no "from *Beowulf* to Virginia Woolf," but still). Even the writer before you has been wary of deans on occasion. All joshing aside, Roger Epp's first book of poems, called *Only Leave a Trace*, is by a retired dean of a small college, who had worked prodigiously to keep it afloat. It has a reserved warmth to it, a careful reflectiveness. It is measured but emotional. There is an elegy for a beloved dog, titled "On Sunday They Will Walk," that is almost the equal of Pratt's "A Reverie on a Dog." That Epp takes a potentially bathetic subject and turns it lovely and considerate is characteristic. He does a similar thing with academia, which is now almost inseparable from satire, generically speaking (it is certainly no longer pastoral), whereby he allows it some follies while also asserting its humanity. The book is illustrated throughout with paintings by Rhonda Harder Epp, his partner, which are beautiful.

Perhaps even more stunning—at any rate, as the fellas in the shed say, it left me "stunn'd as me arse"—was the cover to Joshua Whitehead's *Full-Metal Indigiqueer*, a painting by Kent Monkman called *The Chase*. It depicts a long-haired, brown-skinned person of indeterminate gender and tribe in thigh-high patent-leather high-heeled boots with a bow and arrow and a six-pack (the stomach muscles, not the beer) riding a badass red motorcycle (white handprint on its side) down a residential street alongside some strangely rendered buffalo. A striking image and a striking title for a book. Based on them both, one anticipated an experience brazen, excessive, combative, wry, indigenous, and queer and beyond that one had no expectations. It met those and then raised them; indeed, in poker parlance, this book is all-in. It is *far-out*. It is a total experience—the zero degree of something. The perfect reader for this book would be someone who prefers William Blake's epics to his lyrics, who loves Jordan Abel but finds his work too formally conservative, and who secretly thinks Vivek Shraya is overly reserved. There is a shape-shifting Zoa figure talking to the reader, for the reader, at the reader (depending on the reader) and the typography is constantly breaking apart, disintegrating and destabilizing. By the time we have moved from our first sighting of the *Full Metal Indigiqueer* of the cover to the "Full-Metal Oji-Cree" of the final poem the brainpan circuit board is a little fried: "this is the hive / mind, you, i am calling you— / i am calling all freaks like me who like freaks like me / robotics have always been poc / : : :: ::kaneta tetsuo: :: :nice2meetU: ::: i am kanada post-conciliation[.]"

Another first book that I admired for its excess this year was *Table Manners* by Catriona Wright. If you read Wright's book, you'll laugh at that, because it is exquisitely controlled. The "manners" of the title speak to the fact that decorum is an agreed-upon barrier holding back an anarchic pressure of multiple desires. Here the figure for desire is food: "I would cut off my own thumb for the perfect thimbleful / of wood-ear mushroom and bamboo shoot soup. // My paychecks all go to heirloom parsnips and pickled lamb tongues." The excess of desire, only partly contained by the measured prose of the lines, can sometimes be embarrassing: "I ditch the waffles and swirl pudding cups / when I see her standing at the cash." At other times there is a voyeurism to the plenitude, watching someone shovel in "three steaks, a bucket of kimchi, ten carp pastries / filled with custard and red bean paste." Food is also a figure for our constant consumption, consumption is tied to production, production is tied to waste, and the whole big buffet is a figure for the simultaneity of too much and not enough: "Om nom nom, a life organized // around feedings & groomings." To take the most meditative of syllables and follow it with sounds that conjure up the poet and reader as Cookie Monster is also a class-oriented, generational remark, as in, though things are hard, they are easy compared to other and prior lives; and there are all the things one could want, which strangely produces psychic malaise, which can be somewhat assuaged by consuming more, a vicious circle, say, a lemon tart or sprinkle-covered doughnut. But there is nothing *saving* about this: "I've never rationed anything in my life." *Table Manners* could have devolved into some cutesy kind of "project," but the layering of meanings through the food conceit is so rich that the book is admirably organic. Wright is tricky and constant and with all the *amuse-bouches* coming at you, it is like you are Lucy Ricardo trying to eat every single chocolate coming off the conveyor belt; but Wright controls the pace of the belt so you get just full enough in one of the stronger debuts of the year.

There is also a sense of control in Leanne Dunic's *To Love the Coming End*, at times to the point of seeming anhedonic, as if a reservoir of feeling had been purposefully drained, as if something has been evacuated. The book consists of short prose blocks (sometimes single sentences) and feels like a cross between a travel journal ("MRT to the last stop, switch to the monorail to Sentosa Island.") and a book of meditations ("Does anyone else wonder what happens to an eleven that loses a one? Is it still eleven?"). We are finally in Japan, and the cross-generic and fragmentary nature of Dunic's dealings with the subject recalled Roland Barthes's *Empire of Signs*, faintly. The careful description of objects and feelings sits at odds with the sense of dissociation. But then this care mixed with quietude is a figure for eventual eruptions—emotional, volcanic, atomic: "Mishima believed that Japan's brutality was a result of emotion—a sudden explosion to free the Japanese from constant consideration of manner and elegance. That it still existed, concealed, perhaps awaiting its next eruption." "To be in Japan after the quake. To witness the complex endurance of lives ripped by sharp seismic spasms and aqueous assault." "There are some that survived both Nagasaki and Hiroshima bombings, and another who survived nuclear bombing and 3/11. Niju hibakusha. Blessed or cursed?" This book can't answer the questions it poses, but it does track a pattern of convergences with a consistency of tone.

Several other debuts were books concerning journeys, which makes sense insofar as a first book itself is the first step on a journey. Carolyne Van Der Meer's *Journeywoman* considers such abstract usages of "journey" as well as ones more concrete. Her preface quotes Emerson on life as a journey, then reminds us that the journeyman was one who had finished his apprenticeship but was not yet a master. She also digs into the word's etymology, where it originally meant something like a day, a day's work, a day's travel. Van Der Meer's own journey starts from the start: "I can be no one else / when my mother is with me[.]" This is another way of saying that your journey keeps restarting, as if there's a hitch in it. Many of the journeys are trips and the poems are about the pleasure and tedium of travel. (My favorite poem in the book was "Puppy Fat at the Rijksmuseum.") The section titled "The Cancer Journey" is naturally sobering, almost mercifully short, as some journeys should be. A short suite of poems on "Fellow Travellers" closes the book in a communal spirit.

The journey in Emily Ursuliak's *Throwing the Diamond Hitch* is a happy trip and based on a true story. In the summer of 1951, the poet's grandmother and a friend traveled by old car (a 1927 MG Roadster) and horses (who are substantial characters, especially the packhorse Pedro) through the Rockies, starting in Victoria, BC. This book proved a satisfactory Sunday read in front of a space heater and a sun-filled window, having a tomato juice and beer in their honor. (They quaff a couple of concoctions on their journey, but their favorite form of sustenance is the bacon sandwich, which they make the night before so as to get going early in the morning.) Remember lazy weekend afternoons watching random westerns? *Diamond Hitch* is a similarly lazy jaunt, but not lazy in its craft; the "diamond hitch" is a knot on which the journey may depend and is also a conceit for the book itself. There are times when the malicious, modern world seems to have caught up with them: "The howl of gravel, / spat by tires, / that crow-hop / off the road. // Phyl and Anne / ride the horses / in the cradle / of the ditch, / their distance / from the road / measured / for safety. // While passing, / the car swerves at them, / the horn cackles, / flash of the driver's face, / in echo, / a man laughing." For the most part, though, the two adventurous women encounter a host of nice folks, kind and curious and ready to help these intrepid travelers shoe a horse or bend an elbow or ear.

Fenn Stewart's *Better Nature* takes on Walt Whitman as the latter records himself trekking through Canada, as found in Whitman's journals of that journey. Stewart's approach is a fairly gentle iconoclasm, pulling the bard's beard for saying the wrong thing. (Apparently a pretty good guy all around, though, Walt Whitman, and a hell of a poet.) She imagines him in different guises: "If Walt Whitman, hired as a Don Cherry replacement, were asked to whip up some patriotic fervor before the big game, & took the opportunity to wax poetic re: his summer cabins"; "If Walt Whitman were a Canadian journalist, celebrating in her column the end of a 'ruinous native occupation' of land (the judge sided with the developers)." There were a number of books this year that made effective use of preexisting ("real") documents (Eng's *Prison Industrial*

*Complex Explodes*, Connelly's "redaction" of "Song of Myself" in *Xiphoid Process*, Queyras's *My Ariel*, Mac's *Human Misunderstanding*, all to be considered later). Stewart shows some talent for this; her list of sources—and her sources are not only Whitman—is in and of itself worth reading. (Probably half the books this year had lists of sources; and the acknowledgement pages! They put academics to shame.)

A humbler sort of journey is found in E. Martin Nolan's *Still Point*, a triangular one between Detroit (where he grew up), New Orleans (where he went to college), and Toronto (where he lives now). The "still point" is a hockey puck, or the eye of a hurricane, or the biggest city in a country: it is Eliot's "Still point of the turning world." This is in large part a book about city planning and demographics (the section on Toronto is called "Boom"), which the poet makes interesting by giving it narrative force, by having genuine insights, and by being, as they say, "detail-oriented." It is also about people with the freedom to move and about people who are forced to. Nolan admits and accepts his status as the former. ("To leave is a privilege that I have, just as it was / to come here to study and be a drunken fool / who was never given any trouble.") Yet however we get where we are, we often form strong attachments, and his poems about Hurricane Katrina are a quiet weaponization of empathy (to steal a phrase from Superchunk): "*It looks like Detroit now,*" a friend says, after the water is gone. A little later, throw in an oil spill for good measure. This book illustrates two old saws: when it rains it pours, and you can't go home again. It is a muted, stern indictment of planning to fail, to fail *certain people.*

Some of the people who are failed in Canisia Lubrin's *Voodoo Hypothesis* are also felled, mortally, by those who have sworn to serve and protect them. In a trio of poems at the center of her impressive book, she uses the resources of elegy to memorialize the needlessly dead: "And If I Die Today" is for Tamir Rice, "Sons of Orion" is for Alton Sterling, Andrew Loku, Philando Castile, et al., and "At the End of the World" is for Sandra Bland, Charleena Lyles, Darnisha Harris, et al. (The "et al." in both cases is Lubrin's own and it is powerfully employed, as it seems to conjure an almost endless spirit parade of "others.") These are preceded by "Up the Lighthouse," in which the poet reminds the reader (and the lighthouse): "black isn't always a void." Lubrin is talented at animating objects and calling natural forces to life, as in "Unofficial Biography of the Sea." In the title poem, we are a rover on Mars, which is the furthest we go in this book to get away from this wicked world: "And while waters still vaporize before us / Curiosity will keep on until the organic secrets / of that Martian puzzle become as household to us / as carbon. Oxygen wasn't the only disaster to befall Earth, / to bless her with life." A mixed-blessing in a book that knows from blessings, that uses prayers ("Final Prayer in the Cathedral of the Immaculate Conception") and insists in one poem that we "Let the Gods Do Their Work." I began by framing *Voodoo Hypothesis* as an elegiac experience, but one aspect of that experience is mostly missing, on purpose: consolation. There is not a lot of it here: "oh crypt / of man / all along // extinct:"

Although Rebecca Păpucaru's *The Panic Room* has a wicked side, or perhaps because it does, it made me laugh out loud a few times: "My teeth were an affront to evil[.]" "Whatever wonder it is, we could use it // in Edmonton." "[D]o I deserve you telling me / that the Dairy Queen is behind me?" "Is it just my imagination, / or do I really need to put on / my bra in order to write?" From where such dry wit originates, mixed as it is throughout with a sometimes-vicious surrealism, might best be ascertained in the wonderful poem called "On Watching an Eastern Bloc Comedy," which Păpucaru describes as the slapstick of deprivation: "It's hard to pull off, a getaway in a Lada. / Mud road. Sudden appearance of a goat." She is from the next generation, and remembers her father, saving old vegetables for soup stock. That shift from funny to (a bit shamefacedly) elegiac, the journey from film stock to soup stock, is characteristic. Hers is a lived-in voice, a skeptical-of-cant voice, but something about its way of noticing, of still being surprised enough to make an image of that surprise, of surprise's confusion (that is, to *imagine* it) is youthful. "Dismal, yes. But how much more without us?" An enjoyable book for this reader.

In "Vernal Aspects," a poem dedicated to Nelson Ball in Jack Davis's *Faunics*, it really does matter how you lay it out. Here is the whole poem this way: "Small frogs // stipulating // rain." These words are much nicer taking up a whole, creamy page in the sumptuous Pedlar Press production. *Faunics* brought me closer to the natural world than any of the year's books. It is various, quiet, careful, watchful—quite a beautiful debut.

* * *

"Much of your time has been occupied by creative games / Until now, but we have all-inclusive plans for you." A sentence from Ashbery's "These Lacustrine Cities" that stuck in my craw as I read Aaron Tucker's *Irresponsible Mediums: the chess games of Marcel Duchamp*, a Book*hug book, from a press that has published lots of "game" books in its day. In this one, Tucker takes Duchamp's chess games and, using a program called ChessBard, translates them into poems: certain words equal certain pieces and they get moved around on the page the way they did on the board. Now, I consider myself as knowledgeable about Duchamp as any rank amateur, but with one shameful caveat: I don't play chess. So the fineries of the moves don't register for me. I can say that the poems don't amount to anything too earth-shaking—here is one representing a game in Paris in 1929 in which Duchamp played black against George Alan Thomas's white:

> each centre, each hooded diagonal
> memorably paves darkness or
> stains into ill-formed ownership
>
> molecule clogs or clumsily
> reproduces proud drug and
> this forever steeply assures noise

As the old kid's book says, could be worse. When you read the poems in sequence they deepen just through the gentle force of repetition. There are interesting implications for digital poetics aficionados here. There is a full introduction by chess champion and writer Jennifer Shahade which was informative—this is not a coy book, to its credit; it is very clear about its procedures. Shahade says, "Humans still write better sonnets than robots." It is only fair to the robots to say that humans also write worse ones. Ultimately, they'll figure out how to get robots to write pretty good ones every time, eliminating the need for human mediocrity, but I predict that the very best ones will always be written by people.

"*such plans are sheer folly*" "*going nowhere in particular*"—epigraphs to poems in Catriona Strang's *Reveries of a Solitary Biker*, presumably from Rousseau, from whose *Reveries of a Solitary Walker* she takes her title and other aspects besides. It's no chess, granted, but there is some sort of playing card logic to the thing that is explained in an afterword, which also explains how it results from notes from a grad school class. I also took a class in grad school in which we read that concise curiosity. It is a deep and delightful book, the Rousseau. The Strang is less so—it is too slight to be both—but it is still worth a go. I ended up reading it a couple more times after reading it straight through, just by picking it up when I was eating, or in a car, or during commercials. So in that sense it is successful, in being effective in a perambulatory or ambulatory or faux-*flâneur* context. (A flitting attentiveness.) It consists of daily bits and pieces: "in our mutuality / might we finally / impede our monstrosities" (April 9, 2014). A nice idea. A diverting book. A decent homage.

In *The Girls with Stone Faces*, Arleen Paré pays her respects to the sculptors Florence Wyle and Frances Loring. I tend to enjoy poetry books about artists and my genre preferences trend ekphrastic anyway, so this book was especially interesting. Normally there is more *sturm und drang* in such books, but Wyle and Loring seem dedicated to their art and to each other and that's about that. Paré seems dedicated not to sensationalize their story. They are artists; this is their art; deal with it. There is a solidity of approach appropriate to the sculpture so often under display. She begins the book with an epigraph from Michael Redhill beginning, *"And poetry can also be sculpture,"* and that idea, which has had its many proponents, is treated with craft and intelligence here. Murray Krieger most expanded on this virtual yearning of the poem to achieve sculptural plasticity and in doing so to announce its own poetic. This book is a gallery full of case studies chipping away at the notion, or remoulding it into various forms. My favorites are the frequent returns to Wyle's Torso ["*Mother of the Race*"] (c. 1930): "There is, midway, the navel / where once you were hinged / and unhinged[ ... ]"; "what I love about you / is the way you / shift your left leg to the fore / as though making a point / though you have no left leg / nor a right   only / a fierce suggestion / of leg [ ... ]"; "You could rise on a thought[.]"

You would have to have a stone face indeed not to wince while reading Beth Goobie's *breathing at dusk*. It can even make you cry. It was the most horrifying of books, chronicling mental, physical, and sexual abuse perpetrated on Goobie by her father, a religious-zealot-sicko. You wouldn't believe me if I told you, it is so terrible (or you would, which is also terrible). The whole first two thirds of the book is macabre, too, in its generic conventions. There is a gothic element, not least in the way she makes the house a character, full of fears and secrets and treacherous corners: "these are the preparations the house makes, changing into night." "with this, the child sees / how this house has fooled her[.]" But like the cicadas that title one poem, "all that dark wisdom [is] translated into sound[.]" The poems "moon illusion" and "what i learned at bible college" mark a turning point and a relief. The poet experiences relative freedom; but the self-struggles, the grappling with her mother's ignorance or complicity, the dawning clarity of her unrepentant father's monstrosity continue until book's end. This is a strong and sad portrait of a survivor, a survivor of one who takes all the most important things, of "thieves [who] invade, smash what they do not take[.]"

Thank goodness there are *Other Houses*, as Kate Cayley's title has it, with fewer moral horrors but nevertheless a little sinister. The book is thoughtfully sequenced. The first part begins with "The Pied Piper Enchants the Rats," and that story sort of nests there for a handful of poems; then the second part begins with "Pied Piper: The Children, Leaving, Sing to Their Parents," and whatever was nesting there is activated: "Our eyes are brighter than the rats. We, too, / are built of curiosity and appetite, we vibrate / what we touch," with a final warning: "Don't look for us, though. We don't look for you." There are several strong poems scattered throughout on real-life persons who thought themselves to be Christ; they take the people's claims seriously. In the final section, Cayley conjures a "Library of the Missing," with its own history, curatorial strategy, and set of objects. For instance, part of "Map" reads: "There are toothmarks in the map, which may have come from an animal, or, possibly, indicate the cartographer's foolish wish to eat the world. The attempt was unsuccessful." At times it gets flat and mordant and at those moments it reminded me of Bartleby's dead letter office.

Catherine Graham uses a dark-fantasy-land, we've-entered-another-world frame of reference in picturing *The Celery Forest*, which is the thicket she passes into after learning she has cancer and moves through while being treated. Its effective balance is a stark (stalk?) obliquity, a quizzical distance interrupted by weird creatures. The emotional violence and physical pain she experiences spasm out on occasion in bursts of torqued verse (*"This. Hello. Hat. Honey. Fool."*) or in an apostrophe like a prayer:

> Owl, you never asked to be wise
> or a companion to the witch.
>
> Fly in for the scurry—vole, field mouse,
> creatures with eyes scuttling through grass.
>
> Then pluck the tumour out of my breast
> with your sharp, curved talons—
>
> let the only thing that spreads be your wings.

Graham is good at coming up with images that help you see her plight as though through a shadowbox, as in "Deciduous," where you can make out the limbs of the trees and superimpose them on the tendrils in the body, the leaves fallen off, with the nests in the naked trees being the tumours, the nests in the naked trees the fear-filled thoughts in the tendrils of the brain. The staging of this intense book-long meditation on the dread of death in the mysterious Celery Forest yields shifts in scale that disorient the reader in a way meant to show how scary it feels.

The most consoling title to a book this year was Aisha Sasha John's *I Want to Live*. One reads it and repeats it to oneself and says, yes, I want to live. Exactly! John also says inside the book, insistently, that "I have to live." That also resonated. Yes, I have to live—one of the most useful things to be found in a book this year. Now even though these are straightforward statements, they are also very twisty and turny, being about a) an "I" and b) a life. A friend who had also read and liked the book and I were talking and I said, off-hand, "This book is really egocentric." At first, I was a little confused by it. She took that as a put-down and, being a poet herself, replied, "Isn't most poetry egocentric?" Anyway, I didn't mean it as a put-down. Its egocentrism was clarifying. It is as if Emerson's transparent eyeball had a definite body attached and was sending uninhibited transmissions. It has *presence*. The voice of the book conjures up a person, Aisha Sasha John, who is also the one inventing the voice. There is a not unpleasant kind of gamesmanship going on in tying and loosening knots of willful directness: "I am eating someone else's cashews. // I think it was smart of whoever's idea I am / To be me." "If I'm wrong / If I'm wrong—who gives a fuck?" But there is also, not just a personal rhetoric, but a personal *mythology* dispersed throughout the book by the presence of the voice ("the allegory of the $50 high-tops") and there are surrealistic swerves that displace you, in case you were getting too comfortable. Is it a dream journal, a travel diary, an autobiography, a first-person narrative serial poem? The above-mentioned friend came back the next day and reminded me that the kind of egocentrism John was employing as a device was usually in the past reserved for men, usually certain kind of men, so there was something manifestic, terrific, and defiant about the book's persona and voice. "Would you call it political?" I asked. She said, "Isn't most poetry political?," but I couldn't tell if she was kidding.

\* \* \*

It seems almost redundant to call a book of poetry "political" now. Everything is political; the personal is political; the subject position of the writer is political, the subject of the writer is political, the press is political, the project is political, the line breaks are political, the semi-colon is political; the period is political (more's the pity). (The parenthesis is political.) The presses and the writers (dependent on grants) are encouraged to be political ("political"), in the way the liberal arts are encouraged to be "relevant" (accredit people, get people jobs, generate publicity, monetize research), in the ways one might have been encouraged in the past to be "national" or "regional" or "confessional." So people send signals. It is not that such signals are insincere, exactly, but depending on their context they might seem more or less convenient or transactional; most of us do it, by my estimation; when it comes to poetry and politics the most common miscalculation is not, I think, the propagandistic urge (which can be a problem, but is an obvious one), or overt cynicism, but rather to expect the politics to carry weight that the poetry can't. The one is incompetently grafted onto the other, and it is hard to know which is the graft, the graftee, or who is the grafter or what gets grafted in the final result. It is not a new confusion.

But there are some books that are political in an almost Platonic sense, and these one must attend to. There were a few of them this year, as aforementioned: Whitehead's and Lubrin's books come to mind; and George

Elliott Clarke's *Canticles* will be discussed shortly. One of the most successful was *Prison Industrial Complex Explodes* by Mercedes Eng. The title itself hammers home its intention, or its prophecy. Part of its power is personal, as Eng uses documents from and stories of her father: "a settler / a husband / a father / a property owner / a taxpayer / a no-good recidivist chink[.]" He is in and out of prison and, though starting in close to the bone, Eng broadens out in a condemnation of the structures of incarceration more generally. Here you don't encounter the problem of strong politics and weak poetry, because there is not much poetry, per se. The raw documents and very raw facts are placed in juxtapositions that are also meant to illustrate how Canadian prisons run in the direction of discrimination and privatization not substantially different than in the United States; but Eng shows that at least the Canadians are more *polite* (or at any rate, maddeningly bureaucratic) about it, as evidenced by a ruefully dark-humoured exchange with a number of prison and government officials whereby Eng's father tries to get paid back for a $150 gold chain that was snatched during one of his arrests.

In *Human Misunderstanding*, Kathy Mac also uses a variety of documents to political ends. The book is made of three long-ish poems, the middle of which is the weakest, as it pulls from Hume's "Enquiries Concerning Human Understanding" in a way that was too amorphous for me to hold onto. The final poem, though, uses a Lai of Marie de France to strong effect, as Mac positions the 12th-century text "Bisclavret" against the story of two recent sexual assault cases that involved men who were refugees and women who were sex workers. She doesn't tell you what to think and yet the poems have opinions. The first of the three is the most powerful and fully developed. Called "Omar Khadr is Not Harry Potter," its quirky title belies its dark and troubling core. Through comparisons to the bespectacled child hero and the denizens of his world, Mac humanizes young Khadr, so often reduced to a political punching bag. It is not a poem of excuses, but of exposures, showing through documentation what was done to him on a number of fronts, from physical and mental torture to byzantine legal manipulations.

Cecily Nicholson's *Wayside Sang* was, to my mind, the best book of the year, or my favourite, or however one frames it. Though the language of political critique is employed purposefully throughout, you couldn't necessarily say it was "dominant." In fact, "the language of political critique" is too vague to explain the various methods whereby Nicholson takes little nuggets of verbiage from one realm and melds them into a greater concentrate. It has points of view, but I certainly wouldn't claim that the book was impressive for any ostensible "position" it held. The simplest way to put it for me is that *Wayside Sang* uses language so that it yields up the optimal amount of implication. Everything means something and everything sounds good. The fact that the individual poems (as opposed to the book's sections) are not titled, and that the lines are not long and the stanzas are short and there is a good deal of space on the page and a dearth of punctuation and capitalization are all factors that make for a modest experience, though it is not the kind of modesty that is "humble"; it is more a matter of clearing away what is unnecessary so that what remains has a stronger impact. It takes effort, though it must not seem effortful (and doesn't). Here, in the section called "Waystations," is a compact mix of travel poem, monument poem, pastoral poem, and ecocritical poem: "at a rest-stop monument / to sacred erratics // a storm came through / mustard flowers // in green brassica oil seed // genetics grown / wild along roadsides // escaped fields to ditches / through schoolyards and parks // plants plowed back into soil[.]" The reader notices how the seemingly innocuous scene in fact contains a "storm" that is also the specter of genetic manipulation being reincorporated into the natural world, into ourselves (or in this case, our children's "schoolyards and parks"). The juxtaposition of the easily-blown seeds and the monumental rest-stop boulders is ironic since the "erratics" themselves were moved to their final resting place by glaciers; just as the "escaped" roadside seeds are juxtaposed to an absence, the prison work gang, whose members might help tend to those mustard flowers, depending on where we are: "crises of carceral logics[,]" begins one poem in the section called "Road Shoulders." Elsewhere a poem ends in arrest as protest: "refuse erasure / in defence of land—precious bodies // going to sleep, a light sleep / listening for the phone // arrest intake forms on the bedside table[.]" This last comes from a section called "Port of Entry," and you cannot spell "port of entry" without "poetry," and here poetry is the port of entry that allows for ports of entry in general to be considered. It seems like the proper arrangement. There is much "music for the eco-elegiac[,]" as one poem puts it, as in the first poem in the first section, a section called "Fossil Fuel Psyche":

fossil fuel psyche

pressed for			time

means for
transformation
means

will travel or			drift

\*   \*   \*

A great teacher once said there was a kernel to every poem. George Murray says that every poem is potentially an aphorism, that every aphorism could become a poem. *Quick* is his second collection of aphorisms, after *Glimpse*. This one has 489 of them. A small number of them are distillations of prior poems. His version of Atwood's "This Is a Photograph of Me" reads: "In a world made of surfaces the only place to hide is in depths." My only complaint is that there aren't enough different sentence structures, sentences being engines of thought, or playful jungle gyms of design. That being said, a fun and frequently pointed book to dip in and out of.

"A stickup is not a cash advance any more / than a spaghetti strap is a footbridge." "It's not the height of the fall, but the cut of the prat." In *Xiphoid Process*, Kevin Connolly comes up with some aphorisms that might just have jumped down from *Quick* up above. But since these poems have more than one line, the follow-up to the off-kilter saying is likely to be a slant or a swerve. (An exception is the poem to the hipster on his hipster bike, which is hipster-focused with laser intensity.) I would put much of the poetry in *Process* on a continuum of what might be called non-sequitur verse, where the very structuring of the object is based around verbal movement, on ping-ponging from discourse to discourse, reference to reference, tone to tone, mood to mood. Some people do this overly manically, but I would put Connolly on the James Tate side of the ledger, which is my kind of side. Some poets who try it come off as too jocular, but he leavens it with the occasional scatter of ashes.

There is a section (the best section) of his book that Connolly calls a "redaction" of Whitman's "Song of Myself"—a nice way to say it. He turns that loping, expansive, ecstatic predecessor poem into 52 sort-of haiku, and they have a wonderful life to them. Along similar lines, I thought Sina Queyras's *My Ariel* was one of the year's exceptional books. They take Plath's *Ariel* and rather than redacting it, they prod it, expand it, wonder at it, argue with it. They add to it and honor it. For a while I was scared to read Queyras, and then when I did read them, I was wary of writing about them. They are the "Lemon Hound," remember. We have all got our attackable subject positions and fears and superstitions and my first impulse regarding anybody who is an *Internet Presence* is to RUN! Still, you find yourself indulging, but I could never get past my perception of the persona. Last year, though, I was reading around in *Barking and Biting: The Poetry of Sina Queyras*, a Laurier selection chosen and introduced by Erin Wunker. As its title circumstantially indicates, the book hardly relieved my fears that Queyras was somewhat querulous; but I could appreciate the way they went about their business; it was smart, it had an ear, it had range. So, late to the party, I dove into *My Ariel* and found it full of verve and meaningful connections. Any reader of Plath will appreciate the echoes in Queyras. Poems by writers who in clumsy homage are too *close* to the prior poet, or that apostrophize that closeness, can be cringe-worthy—I'm thinking of Pound's to Whitman, for instance—but Queyras here is deft in measuring their relative distance from their subject, how close to get, what corners to peek into or perspectives to raise one's chin to, in the face of, to get a better view. In an essay on how Stevens constantly returned to Keats's ode "To Autumn," Helen Vendler sees Stevens as "the best reader of the ode, the most subtle interpreter of its rich meanings" and goes on to list "various paths" an author may take in "commenting on a received aesthetic form": she "may make certain implicit 'meanings' explicit; [ ... ] extrapolate certain possibilities to greater lengths; [ ... ] choose a detail, center on it, and turn it into an entire composition; [ ... ] alter the perspective from which the form is viewed; or [ ... ] view the phenomenon at a different moment in time." Queyras takes all these paths, but most frequently treads the last, as they make comparisons or distinctions between themselves and Plath (and between Plath's relationship to her own mother and Queyras's to theirs) that account for differences in the times in which they lived, the experiences they experienced. "I don't mean to animate my library, I just do." This line from "The Sturdiness" is followed by an interesting tall-tale of ownership: "The first book I owned I stole from the Hudson's Bay on Portage Avenue. I walked home across the river with it under my parka. I want to say it was *Ariel*, Sylvia, but the truth is it wasn't until the babies came that I could really turn to you." ("The babies are becoming more stylish[,]" they write on "September 25, 2011.") Queyras begins their *Ariel* with their version of my favorite Plath poem, "Morning Song," which could have stopped me in my tracks if it was a travesty, but it isn't. They pick up the language of their predecessor poems, manipulates it a little without roaming too far from its original intent, as in their "Edge": "Death perfects nada." The long section titled "Years" does a good job mixing Plath's biography with their own. A book of brio, able to laugh at itself and its pretentions and worries, able to critique and to love its motivating subject, and a wonderful exhibit of how writing is a form of reading and reading is a spur to writing.

★ ★ ★

*Quick connections.*... The title of Douglas Barbour's *Listen. If* comes from Phyllis Webb: "Listen. If I have known beauty / let's say I came to it / asking[.]" A nice tinge of defiance in the tone. Barbour has known beauty and writes a section of his book in homage to those who created it: Cezanne, Monet, Tom Thomson, Roy Kiyooka. The range of his poems in this full collection is wide and one is in sure hands, as there are no particular missteps, as there often are when a poet is doing a lot of different things. The reader here is happy to move along wherever the poet wants to go. About midway through the book comes "The Gap," which begins with an epigraph from Sharon Thesen: "the gap, from which all things emerge." Sharon Thesen's *The Receiver* shows her own beginning as a beauty-maker, in "My Education as a Poet": "At least they were being / responsible by not getting behind the wheel in a condition / Mom referred to as 'tight'. This was poetry: terms like / getting tight. // Both Bill and Dad were good joke-tellers but Dad / a big fan of Bob Hope, had a more technical approach. / He'd study Hope's routine on the *Ed Sullivan Show*. / 'Listen to this,' he'd say, as we scrutinized the timing. / Dad could even imitate Bob Hope's little smile. / Poetry: timing, a little smile." There are some funny student apercus from a creative writing class, prose portraits of an aunt and uncle, some off-beat book reviews, and a long section to end the collection with an essay on Charles Olson and Frances Boldereff and Thesen's work in editing their correspondence (an essay that first appeared on the website *dispatches from the poetry wars*), which in turn is followed by some poems made of conversations with Boldereff, transcribed, Thesen says, verbatim, which were stimulating.... *The Receiver* has a picture of a rotary phone on its cover. So does *send* by Domenico Capilongo. On Capilongo's cover, however, the rotary phone is inside a cell phone, on a screen. There are cross-generational comedies of errors: "christopher marlowe pocket calls william shakespeare," for example, which contains an abc's of arcane insults; "57 ways to sign off an email according to forbes," in which something simple is needlessly complicated; "middle age morse code," in which every ache registers. I especially liked "marconi talks to himself as a child" and "man @ urinal with cellphone" (a phenomenon that, when seen—and yes, I have peed next to a peeing stranger who was using a cellphone—is creepy and baffling and admirably dexterous). It is a silly book, really. That was okay with me for an evening. A lot of times when one is dealing with such matters of modern technology and mores, one is, after all, made to feel silly, or simply does.... "We Woke To a New Century," Karen Enns titles a poem in *Cloud Physics*. This aubade offers a vision of the future—that is, now—that is not horrified or even frustrated. There is some amazement, some looking around, a couple of new questions, an observation: "The way we slept was different." The book is clear-eyed and classical. She notices where things are at and whether they are meant to be there, usually something organic: "Weeds grow through cracks in the floor / in a small frenzy of revolt." "These days of asphalt and old sunflowers. / And time?" "Grass never did grow over the cisterns, / and gangly trees from which the jays and grackles have scattered / still reach for the gray-brown fields." "Today I found a clump of shoots / behind the piano leg, green / and shining, apparently unfazed / by my arpeggios"....

\*   \*   \*

There weren't many anthologies this year, but the two that caught my eye are exemplary. They are also unique. *Refugium: Poems for the Pacific*, edited by Yvonne Blomer, is deep and wide and contains wonderful work written about, or while living by, or in defense of, or in awe of the ocean, as an ecosystem, as a resource, as an idea, as a magisterial thing of beauty and pain. Its contents really do run from Abel to Zwicky (an ad-copyist's dream) and there are lots of good poets in between. You could safely assign this as part of a class on contemporary Canadian poetry, such is its range of writers. An anthology around a conceit or a theme doesn't always work, but this one feels focused and taut, even though there is plenty of it: 83 poems, many fairly long. It makes a political and poetical and commonsense case for not exploiting the natural world, a case made through accretion and good editing, that is to say, lightly but strongly.

The other anthology of note was *In Your Words: Translations from the Yiddish and the Hebrew*, a slim book that contains the work of eight poets, most of whom are represented by a substantial number of selections. They were all born between the 1890s and the 1930s and they almost all ended up in Israel or Montreal. None of them had I ever read or heard of, though of their translator I couldn't say the same. Seymour Mayne has been writing poetry for a long time and I had encountered his work in journals and in a couple of enticing books from the seventies and eighties. How much of the strength here is due to Mayne is not something I could say, but either way, these poems are so powerful, they stare you so straight in the face, that it is hard not to blanch. An incredible work of reclamation and consolidation, not so pointlessly grandiose as to diminish from the poems themselves.

The two most important (or certainly biggest) books of the year both came by way of Atlantic Canada (in an originary sense, at any rate, due to the provenance of their authors) and are both by major Canadian poets, one living, one dead. Alden Nowlan is the latter and his *Collected Poems*, edited by Brian Bartlett and published by icehouse poetry (a Goose Lane imprint), is a monument and beautifully done. From early poems that imitate Edwin Arlington Robinson and at other times have a bit of the bellow of Dylan Thomas in them, to poems that turn a dry eye to a dark world in stark diction and a hurt persistence—if his was not an especially long life, then he at least had a long period of poetic maturity—this 700-page *Collected* is easy to read and a pleasure to hold. Bartlett's rich introduction is a perfect specimen of its kind. One anticipates that this volume will kickstart the critical engine and that Nowlan will be rediscovered as the crucial figure that he is, as crucial figures must always be being discovered again and again.

This year brought the completion of George Elliott Clarke's *Canticles I*, the first part of which came out last year. The beginning of a triptych (or a sextet: 3 volumes in 6 books), the 900 pages printed so far in this epic are full with Clarke's presence. This is his *Cantos* and this is his version of History. These initial books are focused on the history of the slave trade, the depredations of slavery, and the connections between slavery and imperialism. The primary method is to "voice" certain predecessors or to act as amanuensis for important figures from the past. There is never just "one" Clarke anyway; he writes with such variety that you can love one thing he does and the next one just isn't for you, so the variety you find in this voluminous compendium is almost the quintessence of Clarke. As this epic develops toward Nova Scotia it will doubtless include many horrors and wonders. As was the *Cantos* for Pound, so is *Canticles* for Clarke: an anthology of the mind, a commonplace book for historical voices, a ground to air grievances, a court to indict criminals, a museum of curiosities, and an opera house or cabaret or church or juke joint from which to sing. This is a difficult history that has to be dealt with. It isn't easy, though. Sometimes things have to be hard, because they are.

# Poetry: Letters in Canada 2016

*Mañana* is another day and every tomorrow brings a new book of poems. Perhaps spurred by the (not always blindingly enlightening) public discourse around poetry during the year, one felt as if the language in many of these books—and this is meant as the complete opposite of opprobrium—was especially ("culturally") appropriative and appropriable, that English could taketh and giveth wheresoever it listeth, depending upon whosoever steereth… okay, well, let's abandon the suffix and whatever remains of the meandering metaphor, while nonetheless maintaining the line of thought, such as it is.

*Dashuria* is the message in Albanian that gives Majlinda Bashllari the title to her second collection (but first in English), *Love Is a Very Long Word*. Not that the opening lines are that loving: "You never know the difference between / a human and a pig, till you decide to buy a house." A funny and representative start, in the way that there is a blurring, a vacillation between two states: here, human and animal; overall, the waking and the dream. Bashllari makes you feel these states of in-betweenness, of temporary stasis, then movement, a de Chirico canvas with a sirocco blowing through it. Nothing stays the same: "I think of myself as a boat, / or a house on a shore / that likes to sail / a little toward the sea." Elsewhere: "our houses cannot sleep." It is a world where everything is alive, even the houses, even the dead. Although less formal than Charles Simic's work, these free-verse poems remind me of the former's archetypal-fairy-tale-transformations, these just-off planes of being: "Before I learned to fly, / I was a young pretty lizard." One poem is titled "My Spell Fails," but most of them don't.

*Neds' maest mingin'* is a little bit of Glaswegian from a sonnet in Alexandra Oliver's *Let the Empire Down*. That's the "hooligans' nastiest" to you and me although, title aside, the book is not about rounding up soccer rabble, nor even about decolonizing or recolonizing Canadian poetry, either. It is not political in that way, though the "empire" of the title is not an empty figure. Oliver does something interesting through formal acuity and dictional rigor mixed with an almost aristocratic tone—not one of those dim in-bred aristocrats, or the petty merely pretty mean ones, but rather one of the witty ones who doesn't lose her lightness even while being dark and incisive (for all I know it's an act), so that the formality of the poems and the now-alas-anachronistic tone seem to speak to questions of demeanor and decorum, and thus necessarily of loss. I don't know how many *new's* we're on when it comes to New Formalisms, but I gather that Oliver is part of one of them. Good—somebody needs to write them, these poem-type poems, and if the person wears pearls, so much the better. A brief bit of wit like "Diagnosis" rings of Dorothy Parker, while other longer (though never overlong) poems recall Philip Larkin. In addition to old verse verities such as rhyming or composing lines that scan and also resolve themselves into regular stanzas, Oliver has a talent for out-takes on genre: "Achievers' Cradle Song" is a curious lullaby, the final suite on "Movies" another few shots at the moving-picture ekphrastic poem.

*Solo fantasma* describes in the form of a refrain the subject of Daphne Marlatt's *Reading Sveva*, the Italian-Canadian artist Sveva Caetani, for Caetani seems to have been very *solo* (fundamentally alone both while being smothered by her reclusive mother and after her mother's death), but also a fantastical person who in her painting could tap into fantasy in a way whereby, even in the reproductions here—good ones they are and several—you can catch more than a glimpse of what must be an overwhelming experience in a gallery or a museum, standing in front of the thing itself. An artist suppressed, an artist reborn: Marlatt's opening prose biography tells how she herself came across this fascinating figure, but always keeps Caetani at the forefront; it would of course be galling to have Caetani suppressed again by another mother figure in an attempt at poetic revivification. I had wondered if the strong opening in prose would overdetermine the poem, or whether I would simply prefer the prose, being as informative as it was. (Sveva Caetani was entirely new to me so it was all fresh learning.) Instead they worked in tandem: the poetry and the prose, the poet and the painter. The book has that intriguing Marlatt spaciousness on the page and the interspersion of several voices works like a cracked chorus that still coheres. It is also valuable in that its artistic subject actually made wonderful art, rather than just living an interesting life.

*Las Caras Lindas de Mi Gente Negra*, lines from a song by Ismael Rivera, give the title to a section of Michael Fraser's *To Greet Yourself Arriving* that is dedicated to Black heroes outside of Canada or the United States (but not by far.) Other sections are dedicated to figures closer to home. There and elsewhere almost every poem is named after honorable writers, musicians, scientists, athletes, activists, and others. Fraser constructs a multi-roomed portrait gallery. Whether you are African-Canadian or not, I suspect you will share some of the same heroes as the poet. One of mine shares the poet's last name (almost), Joe Frasier, who warrants a poem here, as does the great Louis Armstrong. Although I will never not flinch at the rote, scapegoating denigration of Elvis in almost any discussion of Black music, which inevitably happens here, this is nevertheless my kind of book. On the one hand, it is fulfilling to hear a good writer's version of the story of these figures you admire and know well, but who are only known from your limited perspective; on the other hand, there are figures you never thought of in this context before, or figures and facts that are new to you. (Fraser is a teacher, and he taught me. Did you know there was an all-Black Maritimes hockey league between 1895 and 1930?) Although many of the people he memorializes here are musicians, Fraser is not a particularly musical poet, or at least he doesn't go for flashy sonic effects. His musicality is in his measured quality, his pacing, as well as in an affinity for sensing the proper shape and size of the thing.

*Comme un rossignol qui aurait mal aux dents*—so goes one of the composer Satie's instructions for performance—"like a nightingale with a toothache," in direct contravention of Keats. In *Après Satie—For Two and Four Hands*, Dean Steadman notes that such a simile "demonstrate[s] Satie's attachment to the Paris Dada movement." Since Steadman himself repeats some of Satie's instructions, we can infer that he too is Dada-attached. The book is less about Satie than *Reading Sveva* is about Caetani, but it is more about his work than *Reading Sveva* is about hers. "After" Satie, Steadman writes for four hands, two of them on a prose-poem side, two of them on a poetry-poem side. This makes for the kinds of prosimetric fluctuation that are *frisson*-rich. I listened along to some Satie whenever I could match a song with a title, given my limited music collection. Even though it never made much difference in how I read a given poem, it was at least a nice exercise in having a distracting soundtrack to read to on purpose, as opposed to the basketball game, the ambulance, the neighbors' argument, and the internal interlocutor all mixed up in a ear-brain-blender.

*Dzsúsz* is what they called it back in Tupac's time when you had that special status, a rolling vibe; likewise in Hungarian, it is what you call "juice," though in that case it means a sweet liquid that comes from fruit, which you'll be familiar with from childhood, much like the alphabet. Helen Hajnoczky in her collection's title demands *Magyarázni*—"Make it Hungarian"—as if in alterna-Modern mode, a Pound that went further east. In fact, she is nothing like Pound, at least temperamentally. Because I have a friend by the last name of Szabo, I once tried to learn some Hungarian, as what's more I had read that Edmund Wilson was doing so at the end of his life. (You can already see this comparison ending badly.) As with Cherokee ("Look! A bullfrog!") and Finnish ("I love you"—works mostly with Finns), my Hungarian studies faltered, but for a long while I could remember how to say "raisin"—kind of the opposite of *dzsúsz*, now that I think about it. Hajnoczky's is a charming alphabet book, progressing through a series of words you won't know (though a few look familiar) which begin with letters of the Hungarian alphabet, in order, which is very like our own but more so. Just as I was listening to see if I could hear Satie in Steadman, so was I attuned to broken-telephone (or are they intended?) sonic correspondences between the word and the poem that follows the word in Hajnoczky. The poems are perfectly fine and felt, translational objects between first and second generation immigrants to Canada, but the thing I liked best about the book is the nonrepresentational depiction of each letter drawn on the verso side—these illustrations, done by the poet, are especially lovely.

*Studenetz*, which is to say, not some weird new self-referential digi-word the millenials came up with, but rather "pig's feet," are munched on in *Ukrainian Daughter's Dance*, Marion Mutala's debut collection. In the pages prior to that we are given the recipe for "Baba's Borscht," and a while after that shown "Baba's Apron." Food and family are inextricable and, as also happens in *Magyarázni*, their fusion provides the occasion for meditation on what one generation and the one before that gives (and gives up) to the next. As she notes in her acknowledgements, Mutala had intrepid grandparents who immigrated to the Prairies in 1912. (2016, incidentally, was declared the year of "Ukrainians in Saskatchewan" by Premier Brad Wall, as also noted by the poet.) Responding to a recantation from her daughter Natasha, in the title poem Mutala disavows nothing and lives an untroubled doubleness: "'I am what I am' I say / I bleed green for the Saskatchewan Roughriders[ ... ] // I'll always be a prairie girl / and daughter of a Ukrainian matya[.]" The book is dedicated "To Ukrainians in Ukraine that are struggling for independence, and to all people of good will around the world supporting them." And if and when good will isn't enough?

قملة *OPERACIÓN OPÉRATION OPERATION* 行动 *ОПЕРАЦИЯ* takes us from one kind of list (the alphabet) and one kind of conflict (a fight for independence against an empire) to another kind of list and other kinds of conflict altogether. The six versions of the same word that serve as the title of Moez Surani's book come from the six official languages of the United Nations, though the words therein come from 193 countries, which the author correctly counts as his collaborators. "It is a collection," writes Surani, in a stern, measured, and personal introduction, "of the names of military operations conducted by member states of the United Nations from the UN's inception in October 1945, to the incorporation of the Responsibility to Protect (R2P) document in 2006." Usually when we talk about list poems, we are talking about poems in which there is a good deal of verbiage containing the listed items, the latter like glacé cherries and pineapple chunks in a Jello mold of words. Here, the names of the military operations are everything and all, cherries and chunks only, arranged vertically and chronologically. Rather than leading one to conclude that this is thus actually *just* a list, rather than a list *poem*—true or false enough, depending on your definitions, but in the current case a wanly academic concern—what Surani accentuates by having the names speak only themselves, is that the names themselves are creative acts already, but creative acts meant to pinpoint or obfuscate violent ones, a creativity of destruction. (Unless one is a devout pacifist, it is impossible, given the range of these operations in place and time, that the reader, had he more knowledge of each of them, wouldn't find some of them warranted and worthy, unless he was a hypocrite; nevertheless, this book is, as Surani says in different words, a compendium of violence.) Having read his debut *Reticent Bodies* but having run up against a deadline in wanting to write about it, one welcomes the chance to make up for it, albeit too briefly. This, his third one, is a powerful, Power-filled book.

*Acel aryo adek aŋwen* means "one, two, three, four" in the Acholi language and in Juliane Okot Bitek's *100 Days*—another, even more powerful list poem—counting is horrifying. A century of poems for a century of days, one day after the next, one hundred days of genocide in Rwanda in 1994, not even a third of a year, not even a third of a century ago. When read alongside Surani's book, one can't help but wonder what intervention might have meant. *100 Days* is among the two or three best books of the year, and to me the single most affecting, *not only* because it is about a tragedy written from close proximity (there were lots of poems about tragedies this year, plenty of them deeply felt), *but also* because: 1) the repetitions in the poems mimic the repetitions in the days; 2) the poet disavows official sanctimony or a needy aestheticizing of trauma ("machete hangs in a museum in Ottawa / a machete hangs perpetually / in a museum / in Ottawa"); 3) the diction is spiritual and visceral; 4) there is not a single wasted word in a world in which there is not a day to waste. Did this book get the attention it deserved? I doubt it. It stands there, ready to be attended to, a book of singing pain and terse, terse fire.

*Flankers* are sparks from out what Torontonians consider the East, although I haven't verified that use of the word in the *Dictionary of Newfoundland English* published by the University of Toronto Press. (Pedants gonna pedant, as they say.) I'll trust Newfoundland-born and Halifax-residing Genevieve Lehr, whose *Stomata* is excellent. I mentioned before the spaciousness one feels in Marlatt's book and one feels it here too; but it is more constricted, or controlled, it is hard to say which, and saying which might not matter, as it is oxymoronic anyway. Suffice to say, there is an open economy to it but not a profligate one. You see from Lehr's biography that she has been publishing for a long time in a variety of ways but sparingly; here, as in Bitek's book, there is a distaste for wasted words. The long opening poem "Arcana" is rare in being a long poem that needs to be long. It develops, or grows, one layer on top of another—mostly layers of sorrow, cut with creative defiance (that is to say, the existence of the poem itself.) The "crow picking at entrails on the roadside" may be an omen, or it may be a hungry crow. "Was thought conceived by the dog // gazing into the fire, patiently waiting for meat?" We enter a world of outports, places in Newfoundland where hunger is not an omen, but a scarcity; places where all is not well, blustery coves of ill-health: "My new breast is the shape of an Egyptian moon;" "Sometimes the children we love go mad[.]" Still, "Myth is a way to frame grief," and the extended family stories here touch on the gently mythical.

*Kitul-l'-miey* ("I want to go home") are the heart-rending words in Mi'kmaw that even the "boiler hisses" in a poem at the center of *Stomata* called "Residential." The experience of the Residential Schools as well as the aftermath of them are the subjects of two other books this year, *The Red Files* by Lisa Bird-Wilson and *Burning in This Midnight Dream* by Louise Bernice Halfe. The "files" of the former come from archival work, recovering and recording Bird-Wilson's family stories. Drawing on her Cree-Métis background, the poet begins the first third of her book in ekphrastic mode, trying to divine information from a set of silent photographs of children at a school. Later we travel back to the signing of Treaty Four in 1874, see a "Scrip Buyer" at work in 1905, and forward to the revelation in the early '90's of systematic sexual abuse of hundreds of boys. Bird-Wilson has a difficulty on her hands, which is maintaining the reality of the fundamental anonymity of these poor, stolen, maltreated children, while also giving them specificity and life. It is a balance she manages well, though it is an awfully sad one, and it is hard not to choke up when faced with "dormitory room 204 / on the second floor / twelve-year-old Charles or Charley / or Bobby or fourteen-year-old Hector / and Donald and Mike / one boy / who is many in a repeating shell game" and the resulting refrain: "he hangs / himself… / he hangs himself… / he hangs himself… / he hangs[.]"

*Wīsakan* remains in one's mouth after mouthing along to the English and Cree words that make up Halfe's *Burning the Midnight Dream*. It means "a bitter taste" and although this is an angry book, it is not embittered. It is certainly not "reconciled," though. A dispassionate response to the forced relocation of children—call it kidnapping—and the excision of their native language from their throats is not a rational response nor a proper one. Thus, the matter and the tone here are a match, because Halfe fights ashes with fire. She is especially powerful in drawing lines through generations, in showing how dysfunction gets reproduced. *Pōni-āhkosi*, she titles one poem: "quit the sickness," but unlike a job or even a cigarette habit, the sickness is harder to quit. But whatever happened before in her life and the lives of those before her is precisely what leads her to where she is: "This marrow is packed with the litter / of that wayward path." The past, both recent and distant and somewhere in between, is ever inside and ever surrounding: "I found myself released from residential school yet / the four walls slithered everywhere I went." At the end of the book, Halfe testifies before the Truth and Reconciliation Committee and one feels a faltering of confidence, ever so flittering, in the face of being finally asked to speak after so long an enforcement of silence. These two books, along with Rosanna Deerchild's of last year, make for a strong and various trio of responses to the Residential Schools.

*Nindizhinikaaz*, Anishnabeg for "I am," is in any language the fundamental statement of human being, and it plays a role in the story of David Groulx's *The Windigo Chronicles*. (It is also crucial in Gregory Scofield's *Witness, I Am*, which begins with a stunning *âtayôhkêwina*, or Cree Sacred Story, adapted to some of the horrors of current times, which I will leave undisclosed. "If I am not banging the drum / I am no one. No one, I am[.]" Scofield was the first indigenous poet I read that made a particular impact on me as a *Canadian* indigenous poet. His poems always feel tight and like they were written with nostrils flared. A book to be recommended, as well as is its author.) The child of an Ojibwa mother and French-Canadian father, Groulx has made a serial poem that is fertile with the kind of linguistic intermixing we've been tracking throughout this review, as indicated by a glossary of 86 entries and, without which, these would be some hard *Chronicles* to follow. It is a story not of a single people, but of aboriginal *peoples*, if I am understanding it correctly; and not knowing all of the traditional stories of the various native traditions, it was not easy to know what was, on the one hand, a kind of transcription of tales the poet has heard, and on the other, what was his creative embellishment of them. This concerned me as a reviewer—how would I know what to *say*?—but it didn't bother me in the least as a reader. One knows enough to know that there is a proud and tragic history out of which come these tales of a spirit world that are nonetheless material. As in Bashllari's book with which this review began, *The Windigo Chronicles* often felt like a shape-shifter or a plane-changer, when the mythical gets physical real fast (as in the "tender rotting faces" that come upon the people) and in meditative moments of memorialization that are shot through with action sequences that suggest the drive of an oral tradition.

*Injun* is a piece of American slang, or so I'm supposing (the American in me refuses to look it up), just as "Indian" was a piece of American slang before that; indeed, American slang before there even was America, such as it was called. Now, a Canadian of Aboriginal background, Jordan Abel, has made it the title of his third collection. It won the Griffin Prize and it seemed as if most poetry readers I spoke with had read or were reading it (this was not an extensive survey, mind you), but I was a little suspicious of all the attention. Instead, the book is still growing on me, which is one of the best things you can say about a book. It is not so much that I re-read it often, but I'll just find myself thinking about it, out of the blue. *Injun* is based on a procedural pun, as it were; the poet takes some texts and types "injun" into a search *engine* and a bunch of stuff comes out of the injun-engine. The book looks quite compelling because those results are manipulated in all kinds of ways—columns in two colors (well, grey and black), a whole lot of words and letters printed upside-down, some things that look like sonnets that got dispersed by a shotgun blast. So, what's the big deal? Well, the big deal is that *Injun* is about (and is an example of) the production, reproduction, and representation of indigeneity, past and present, and is thus a kind of theoretical excursus-in-practice on both a certain old sort of silence and a certain contemporary proliferation of voices, as evidenced by the books above and by others I read but haven't the space to review. (These include Garry Gottfriedson's *Deaf Heaven*, of which I thought very highly, and Gwen Benaway's *Passage*, about which I had mixed feelings, but which I appreciated for its hurt yet often erotic directness; it is certainly not an *evasive* book.) Because there is synergy—forgive me the word—between, on the one hand, a government-sponsored (or re–enforced) initiative such as the Truth and Reconciliation process and, on the other, book publication in Canada, such production-of-representation will increase; that is, because 99% of the poetry books in Canada are contingent on federal and provincial funding for their existence, and there are certain initiatives or drives at certain times that command more funding, and the potential for funding itself drives which books publishers publish, one awaits with interest the impact this will have on the balance of Canadian writing, such as it is—the balance, not the writing.

*Keimēlion* ("something laid away or treasured up") is a good word for what ought to become of a copy of Anne Carson's *Float*, should you acquire one; like her *Nox*, it is a beautiful object, this one in a plastic slipcase, not a paper box. One part of Jordan Abel's "Process" as described at the end of *Injun* is: "Sometimes I would just write down how the pieces fell together." The instructions for this cluster of 22 chapbooks by Carson are, I kid you not, to drop them on the floor and read them randomly after that. They don't actually float when you drop them, though. What's more, the last thing I needed to do for domestic bliss was to drop any more books on the floor, but I get the drift. These are occasional pieces, just the kind of mix of poetic-philosophic-scholastic-fragmentated-variegated-aggregated-ephemeral-specificity that, as I read recently in one think-piece essay, was starting to get annoying to some people. But I'm not jumping off the battleship to join the bandwagon. It took a long time for folks around here to recognize her talent so let's not embark on any takedown reevaluations just yet. Carson is consistently compelling, simple as that; the worst that you can say about her is that some of her tendencies are mildly cloying. But somebody has to wear the felt Amelia Earhart hat-helmet to the honorary doctorate ceremony, just as someone has to put, on the cover of her case full of 22 little books (or pamphlets), one of those floaters often found, found, found in the middle distance when you wake up in the morning and are staring at the wall. She's one of a handful of the finest writers going and I still treasure the chance to read anything she writes.

*Et In Blockadia Ego*, goes one poem in Stephen Collis's *Once in Blockadia*, and was he ever. If his *On the Material* was a really good book and if *Decomp*, his collaboration with Jordan Scott (who published a worthy book of his own in a single column called *night & ox* this year), was a really interesting book, *Once in Blockadia* is somewhere between those two books, which I guess makes it good and interesting. What happened was, Collis got involved in writing about and resisting the Trans Mountain pipeline expansion, and then those fellas that wanted that oil didn't like that, see, so they took him to court for a lot of dough. That'll shut a lot of people's yaps, but not his. Speaking of languages, this book has lots of legalese, which is sort of humorous, but scary, and then there are pictures and variations in type and other aspects to make it more than merely a book with just regular words in it. But why not put it all out there when you get the chance? There *is* some ego involved, after all, in a project like this (and the projects that led to this project) and you would need a strong ego indeed to make it through such legal harassment as Collis endured, or at least I would. One thing I noticed about *Decomp* was that it had a ton of *implications*. This book, a fall from the garden, is the same kind of thing, implication-wise. I bet it would be a good book to teach.

*Naah, m-gek-thlai nee-ga meng* ("Ahh, I can't remember all your names") is sometimes how I feel not only when I'm teaching, but also in the face of the abundance of books that come down the pike—so many poets, so little time, as much as I try to recall them. But I can't forget Weyman Chan and his *Human Tissue*. Last year I admitted to having lost Liz Worth's book before acquiring another copy. This year it was even worse. Chan's was the first book from the first batch of books I read. I spent a lazy day in a Muskoka chair out on the back porch dutifully going through it with pleasure, making notes with a golf pencil. (Note: I don't play golf.) Finally, I went inside, but without the book. Next, it rained, heavily, one of those flash storms. Now the book, which I thought could be trimmed a bit in length, is in actual fact bloated, physically, which is not so great for the book, but is kind of ironic, since there's something in a petri dish growing on the cover. (Human tissue?) Nothing grew on this book, though; the pages dried to a wavy crisp. I liked Chan's voice, which felt familiar to me: "Figuring out who you are by what you won't tolerate is like looking / anywhere else but your own mad speech in a vat[.]" It (dis)integrates its references ("Cell prep on a fish hook, who made thee?") and vocabulary ("globbed and inspissated") and with its reference to Donna Haraway, and its sort of robot-hummus nature, it makes sense to read it alongside Larissa Lai's *Automaton Biographies* and Rachel Daley's *Plasmos*. There is something *searching* about it, someone trying to figure out how to be good in the world. Nice bit, this: "One last clarion: consideration." A good start in the figuring.

# Poetry: Letters in Canada 2015

Perhaps let us start with some good old stalwarts. Brick Books published six handsome and functional reprints of "classic-contemporary" Canadian writing—some of it poetry—and they are recommended for their utility and to help with the filling of gaps in one's reading. It is the start of a series, so it will be curious to see what books make the cut as it continues. The initial sextet is Anne Carson's *Short Talks*, Michael Crummey's *Hard Light*, Marilyn Dumont's *A Really Good Brown Girl*, Dennis Lee's *Riffs*, John Steffler's *The Grey Islands*, and Jan Zwicky's *Wittgenstein Elegies*. To each there is added value, in the form of new introductions by Margaret Christakos, Adrian Fowler, Lee Maracle, Lisa Moore, Sue Sinclair, and Paul Vermeersch (listed alphabetically, not respectively). Some of these books I had read, and some I had not, but the format was inviting enough that I reread one I had already read and started reading the ones I hadn't yet. It marks a promising inaugural of a purpose-serving solid series from Brick.

The only "Collected" of note was also the only other notable reprint, namely, John Thompson's *Collected Poems & Translations*, edited by Peter Sanger and originally appearing twenty years ago. If you've got that one, you don't need this one; if you don't have that one, you might want this one. Everyone writing ghazals these days should read Thompson, for instance; of course, some people (like myself) may have *only* read the ghazals before. (His collection of them, *Stilt Jack*, is in this Goose Lane *Collected*—with a few new things, according to Sanger, but not many.) Sanger's introduction is very fine and straightforward, without dispelling a certain mythology that envelops its subject (and that makes the poems better). As Jeffrey Donaldson has said, Thompson is "like a bear you can't quite make out in the depths of the forest, going about doing its thing, shy, independent, unpredictable: you have to watch it from a distance." It is not quite full-on bear season yet, but I'm looking forward to reading more Thompson.

The significant "Selected" volumes that came to the *University of Toronto Quarterly* (*UTQ*) headquarters from 2015 were three more entries in the Laurier Poetry series, one treating Paul Dutton, one Phil Hall, and one Jan Zwicky. The Laurier series is my favourite, just nipping the Porcupine's Quill "Essential." If you read the annual offerings of both, you cut a decent-sized swathe through the poetic dell by the time all is said and done. Edited by Darren Bifford and Warren Heiti, *Chamber Music: The Poetry of Jan Zwicky* (which is the first anthology of her poetry) would be a good book for the classroom. But I bet fans of her work already have most of these poems in individual volumes, and since it is not the most copious oeuvre in the world, a selection is not a pressing necessity. Still, there is an erudite introduction, a bibliography, and a condensed conversation between the author and the editors, so the volume makes its own case.

The Dutton and Hall books are more interesting than selections usually are, and for related reasons. The types of poems the two write are unconducive to discrete picking and choosing. This is due in Dutton's case to the fact that he is so sonic, a "sound poet," a performer—you do best to hear him out loud. In Hall's case it is because he writes not-so-much-single-poems as more-like-some-kind-of-continuous-flow. Dutton's compilation is called *Sonosyntactics*, which Gary Barwin in his introduction explains thus: "*sono* as in sound, *syntac* as in syntax, *tactics* as in tactics, *syn* as in 'united; acting or considered together' [ ... ] and also *syn* as in synthesis: to combine a number of elements to create a new thing." Whew. A lot of this work is contingent on setting up straw-man binaries that one burns up in the flame of interdisciplinary liminality. So, if that's your bag, you'll dig this book: eye against ear, sound against sense, mind against body, idea against experience.

When I first moved to Toronto, the Small Press Fair was on my way home from work, and Paul Dutton was there selling chapbooks. It made an impression on me—and was also an introduction to the do-it-yourself ethos of Dutton's generation of Canadian poets—that this famed member of The Four Horsemen was still on the shill, putting in an honest day on the job, with a not-totally-unpleasing unpleasantness, selling good art for a fair price. Since then I have heard him in various venues and ways, and all of these ways are the best ways to hear him. But of course you "hear" him when you *read* him, just in a different way; what's more, you *see* him in a different way, as a series of marks on a page—and some strange marks they are—while in another sense you don't see him at all, physically, with the eyes, and in person, or on a screen. This Laurier selection of Dutton is a *fun* book, it turns out, although it is not always so obvious what to *do* with it, which can be irritating, but in a good way. I suppose one could perform it like a score. Since *UTQ*, for its many merits, is devoid of the spirit of a freaky poetry journal and is typographically Tory, there's no point in trying to reproduce any of the good stuff.

The Phil Hall book, *Guthrie Clothing*, described as a *Selected Collage*, was revealing for this reader and has been superbly edited by rob mclennan. (So as not to have to say "sic," say instead that the latter is of the e.e. cummings school of populist uncapitalizers. Perhaps a touch over-prolific with his own poetry, he is nevertheless capable of smart concision; he gives a lot of true support to his fellow writers; he is capacious; and he has good taste.) *Guthrie Clothing* starts with an excellent epigraph from Hall: "The failure of order is the work / disorder is not the work[.]" Although I had read Hall's *The Last Seamstress* a few years ago and liked it, as well as a recent chapbook of his, I didn't get how good he is until this collection, arranged like a self-cento in chunks. That's a coup for mclennan, who pulls parts from poems and puts them together into a visual current that enlightens the reader and enriches the poetry. It is a nice collaboration between poet and editor in which the division of labour is not the main point. Hall is shown in his best light by mclennan, whose introduction is dry, insightful, and short.

Short story long, then, these two short but full collections are delightful and educational garlands, blurby as that sounds. Overall, however, there was a dearth of compilations and a paucity of anthologies. Yet there were two more to catch the eye. The first, edited by Wayde Compton and Renée Sarojini Saklikar, is *The Revolving City: 51 Poems and the Stories behind Them*—the city spinning in the title being Vancouver. As a man of the world, I've of course heard of Vancouver and, having now been told of Vancouver on several occasions, have been led to understand that Vancouver has a certain Vancouverness to it and that poets from Vancouver necessarily honour, reflect, manifest, recritique, and all the rest what makes Vancouver the Vancouverest Vancouver in all of Canada. Would *The Revolving City* prove this to be the case? Sort of, but not exactly, and to its credit. Turns out you don't have to be from Vancouver or even want to read poetry from Vancouver to get something from *The Revolving City*. You do get a positive sense of the place, though.

These fifty-one poems are occasional poems, the occasion being a "Lunch Poem" public reading series at Simon Fraser University—closer to a kind of Frank O'Hara occasion, say, than to a coronation of the Queen of England kind. The poems are written by people you might have heard of and by people you haven't, by people you've heard of but haven't read, and by people you've read. There is no consistent theme, not even Vancouver itself. Because of the writing of poems there is no end, as says the wise but tired Ecclesiast, the best part of the book—the *breather*, if you will—is that each author talks for a page or so about his or her poem, or deliberately talks about something else instead. This fills in a lot of local lore, zooms in on aesthetic details, and personalizes the whole endeavour. It is my belief that as a reader of a book like this, you are entitled to ask whether or not you would want to be among such a self-selecting group of people. I was surprised to find out from my Ontarian perch that I could practically almost imagine it.

My experience when preparing omnibus reviews is that there's not really enough time to read anthologies closely, but this one, so nicely done by Compton and Saklikar—to say nothing of everyone managing to get together consistently and writing what is a good batch of poems—is a book that I want to come back to. I know for a fact that it will spur me to read, more deeply, a handful of poets I might not have known about otherwise, which in and of itself makes for a successful anthology. Furthermore, it is also a fact that the trees here are easier to spot than whatever forest they are a part of, so, over time, perhaps this group of individuals will clarify itself in my mind as more of a collective, poetry-wise. Either way, it's a user-friendly book with enough rough edges to keep it interesting. (One minor cavil, though: Vancouver may be the revolving city, but as anyone who has ever been to that restaurant on top of the CN Tower can attest, the whole world revolves around Toronto.)

If we were making a commercial instead of writing a review—not unrelated activities—we would cut here with a rotating fade to a basketball spinning on an upright finger. (But which one?) *Erratic Fire, Erratic Passion: The Poetry of Sportstalk*, put together by Pasha Malla and Jeff Parker, is not an anthology of poems about sports, that is to say, poems that are usually interesting in theory but actually awfully disappointing, for never being remotely as fun as the sports they attempt to describe. Instead, this anthology is a bunch of real talk from true athletes, repurposed into poems. You're probably thinking the same thing I did, that is, of how it could all go horribly wrong: condescending, exploitative, formally lame, lamely formal, over-sincere, under-astute, and who knows what all other flaws. It turns out that this well-crafted and just-long-enough collection is none of these. Given what it is and intends to be, the book approaches an insouciant perfection.

Sports fans who also like all the little quirks of language will watch a sport they know nothing about just so they can overhear the goings-on. They then find themselves parroting such trenchant observations as "Randy Ferbey's corn-husk brushes beat the new synthetics any day" or "I don't think she can hit herself out of that lie." And for the sports that such people *do* understand and devour, the verbiage is half the fun. This applies not just to the terminology particular to any sport, but especially to the words of athletes, who are also actors delivering lines, many of which they write extempore, often when they hit the high pitch of competitive inspiration. *Erratic Fire, Erratic Passion* is a stocking-stuffer book, a subway distractor, a washroom reader, a when's-the-last-time-you-senta-buddy-who-doesn't-read-poetry-a-poetry-book book: you get the idea. Every time I've opened it, it has given me pleasure and, as often as not, some wisdom amidst the play. As Charles Oakley puts it in his poem: "You want to rob the bank / But you better not be complaining when you get caught." Sound advice, so let's say it's a keeper.

\* \* \*

Liz Howard's *Infinite Citizen of the Shaking Tent* got an unusual amount of attention for a debut. For instance, it won the Griffin Poetry Prize. Since almost all Canadian poets eventually end up as "award-winning Canadian poet[s]," at least on the back of their books, it is just as well to get that over with early on by taking home the big one. As for the book itself, it is very good, not just very-first-book-good, or very-good-supposedly-because-it-won-a-prize. (My wife, who read it before me, told me it was the best book of Canadian poetry she had read that year (along with Sue Goyette's *The Brief Reincarnation of a Girl*), and you cannot beat word of mouth.)

Another of the best first books this time around was Madhur Anand's *A New Index for Predicting Catastrophes*. Its austere diction is troubling—as bad as things are, what is it that is still coming down the pike that will warrant from the poet a shout or a shriek? What is being held in reserve? What is being, or will be, destroyed? Dr. Anand is a professor of environmental science, and unlike in most poems that cite academic papers, Anand cites her own—which being genuine scientific papers are collaborations—thus introducing at least two different notions of authorship. I like how she resists certain effects and plays down certain affects. The title "Normality Assumption" gives you a sense of it, or the way that there are two experiments going on at the same time in *Cantharellus*: "We were boring jack pines, storing their cores in plastic / drinking straws. It had been raining. I'm no naturalist / but understand the association of fungi / and forests, their partiality for recent rain [ ... ] [W]hen I saw them—creamy orange / against first brown, then grey, then green—I was 95 / per cent sure." Professor, poet; classroom, mushroom; outside, ingest: if it weren't so lowly in wit to do so, you could say that the way Anand combines aspects of herself is especially organic. (By the way, McClelland & Stewart, which sometimes seems staid, knocked it out of the park this year. Along with the debuts of Anand and Howard was Cassidy McFadzean's first, *Hacker Packer*, which is also strong.)

So far is it from being a "radical" collection that it may seem silly to compare Anand's *Catastrophes* to another science-central book released this year, Christian Bök's *The Xenotext: Book 1*. Still, despite their totally different aesthetics, one might imagine that there are readers with interests that would allow them to appreciate both. As far as that goes, one can hardly help *appreciating* Bök's book: it is more complex, more experimental, more technically assured, more far-reaching than Anand's, in just the measure of difference you might expect in comparing the debut collection of an academic with another book from a mid-career poet who is currently Canada's most famous avant-garde conceptualist. The Oulipists that Bök calls to mind have nothing on him for exoticness of stricture, and if another predecessor, Marcel Duchamp, had found not bicycle wheels, urinals, and Paris air to repurpose, but rather our very own genetic junk, then he could perhaps approach *The Xenotext*. Since I wasn't quite sure how to approach it myself, let me quote the poet himself in the "Vita Explicata" that brings to an end this first of what will be a two-volume set:

*The Xenotext* is an experiment that explores the aesthetic potential of genetics, making literal the renowned aphorism of William S. Burroughs, who claims that "the word is now a virus." Such an experiment strives to create a beautiful, anomalous poem, whose "alien words" might subsist, like a harmless parasite, inside the cell of another life form. Many scientists have already encoded textual information into genetic nucleotides, thereby creating "messages" made from DNA—messages implanted, like genes, inside cells, where such data might persist, undamaged and unaltered, through myriad cycles of mitosis, all the while saved for recovery and decoding. The study of genetics has thus granted these geneticists the power to become poets in the medium of life.

This "power" is not contingent on "the study of genetics," of course, nor is it limited to geneticists. A couple of horny teenagers with a back seat at their disposal and physics (friction) as an ally have also been granted the glory of becoming "poets in the medium of life." That is, unless *poets* is being used literally—which it is not; or is it? That may mean that when Bök says he is writing a poem, that, too, is figurative, at a literal level, just as Burroughs in his awesome aphorism was literally being figurative. But all this poetry stuff about metaphoricity and meaning that we're bringing up is way less interesting than the nitty-gritty details of the experiment at hand:

> *The Xenotext* consists of a single sonnet (called "Orpheus"), which, when translated into a gene and then integrated into a cell, causes the cell to "read" this poem, interpreting it as an instruction for building a viable, benign protein—one whose sequence of amino acids encodes yet another sonnet (called "Eurydice"). The cell becomes not only an archive for storing a poem, but also a machine for writing a poem. The gene has, to date, worked properly in *E. coli*, but the intended symbiote is *D. radiodurans* (a germ able to survive, unchanged, even in the deadliest of environments). A poem stored in the genome of such a resilient bacterium might outlive every civilization,

persisting on the planet until the very last dawn, when our star finally explodes.

Talk about "A New Index for Predicting Catastrophes." The old notion, always pejorative, of playing God comes to mind, but opinions regarding God and God-ness notwithstanding, let a poet play as he will; and yet I don't think we, as a culture, should allow this one poet, no matter how smart, to write and encode the one poem that will be mutating and replicating and reading itself and being read for all eternity. Who the hell does this guy think he is? A twenty-first-century "Orpheus"? You know what happens to Orpheus, right? That's a hell of a thing to launch into the temporal end-all-be-all, this...this...

It's the kind of thing that can get you all heated up. But *The Xenotext* is a cool book—apparently too cool for this reader, though this reader is truly trying to get it, or catch it, or however one does it. Bök is not devoid of a sense of humour about his own grandiosity, as in the poem "The Xenogogue," and he is an exceedingly lyrical writer who knows how to manipulate sound into virtual song. The coverage of genre, from pastoral to primer, is impressive. If constant intertextual tickles turn you on, here's a book of virtual feathers for your sensitive parts. Sonneteers will find variations on the form that will impress and amuse them. The book as a physical object is beautiful and usable, even more than Coach House books usually are. Nevertheless, in a hundred-million-billion-trillion years, when those benign beings of whatever sort—which will doubtless best us terrible, no-good, very bad humans by every measure (so proud we seem to be these days of our own awfulness)—finally get around to "reading" the "poems" resulting from this *project*, my prediction is that their first question will be either "Wonder how much SSHRC and Canada Council money went to fund this lark?" or "Where do you think we could get a copy of the *Dazzle Ships* LP by Orchestral Manoeuvres in the Dark to which this virus refers?"

After being exposed, rest a bit, drink plenty of fluids and read Joanne Epp's *Eigenheim* and Kevin Spenst's *Jabbering with Bing Bong*. Like Anand's *Catastrophes*, they are books that hold something in reserve, the former on purpose and the latter I'm not so sure. Epp and Spenst have in common a Mennonite upbringing, though take it from a person who lives in an Ontario town founded by and still well-stocked with many of Mennonite stock, a common theological heritage does not mean they are all the same. Who knew? They do have in common a pacific demeanour and a will of resistance to deliberate sophistication, although one could take the titles of their books and trick someone into thinking hipsters had written them. Yet that's not the case. No one would confuse Epp for such a figure of fun and studied frivolity. She writes with an appealing stolidity from an older woman's perspective. She is cautious because she is good. I think she would like Spenst, based on their poems. His Mennonite upbringing was different, suburban rather than rural. He is of a generation in which those ways of life that eschewed ostentatious consumption—of necessity, of course, but also on purpose—were overcome by popular cultural stuff, plastic junk. Both Spenst and Epp can see this as a *spiritual* crisis, and there is something in the formality of their poems that emphasizes this.

*Calling Down the Sky*, Rosanna Deerchild's second book, comes as part of a Canadian Aboriginal Voices series, although you wouldn't need me to tell you that if you looked at the cover or read the book itself, which I recommend. Deerchild's voice is strong, and she is direct in depicting her own, but primarily her mother's, experiences—in some ways similar, in telling ways not—as Aboriginal people in Canada, in this case, Cree of Manitoba. Deerchild writes in an unpunctuated, lower case, free-verse, stark-dictioned, visually vertical manner that may remind you of William Carlos Williams. It is nice to be able to settle in with a style; often in debuts, but even more so in sophomore *efforts* (pun intended), the poet is trying everything out at once, as if there's not ever going to be another chance to show off, as well there may not. There is none of that here; the book is mature, second book though it may be.

There is lots of pain and sadness, as one would or could only imagine when it comes to residential schools; there is stoic humour, invective insight, and the sharp stab of attention as well. It will come off like a claim reinforcing a stereotype, alas, but there is a sense of a silent, watchful being (amplified, as it were, by the blank space on each page and the non-rococo syntax and sound) whose observational process we access less through elaborate rhetoric or overt argument than through ostensibly simple stories. This silence is even more interesting if you know that Deerchild is a respected CBC radio host, not the quietest of professions, which is merely to accentuate what a conscious *choice* she is making with her minimalism. (It is always easier to ascribe intention to adding, stacking, putting things on than to taking things off, or knowing better than to put them there in the first place.) In "rosary," for instance, we see a scene of destructive instruction, when prayers are being said under a nun's unsympathetic command ("she has no grace to spare"), and having been beaten for speaking Cree she has "no words // just this prayer // hail mary / full of grace / [ ... ] a testament / of my stubborn will // that not even / the mother of God // would scrape the Cree / from my bones[.]" That final verb, *scrape*, is vicious, especially in how its tactility, if applied to itself, would result, physically, in the vowel sounds of *Cree* being scraped from it; furthermore, both existentially and sonically, it is the denial of "grace to spare" that leads to this "scrape." *Pray, grace, spare,* and *scrape* are spoken; *race, scare, rape,* and *escape* are heard. *Calling Down the Sky* is a "testament" to the "stubborn will" of silences and sounds to tell the truth.

Sometimes the sky is not called down; the sky calls down on you. From the luminous stained-glass cover of Pamela Mordecai's *de Book of Mary* glows the "mother of God" to whom Deerchild refers above. Mordecai, from Jamaica, retells Mary's story in the diction and rhythms of the Islands. This wasn't an approach I had high expectations for, being wary of written-down dialect poetry, on the one hand, and figuring the story had been fairly exhaustively told, on the other. Still, I took it along to an ophthalmology appointment, knowing I would have three hours to kill. The other patients were constantly looking up over the tops of their waiting-room-worn and germ-marinated magazines to see me chuckling at some new turn of phrase or appropriately comic response from the protagonist and her kin. Upon realizing that you are pregnant with the Messiah, in the middle of a desert, already engaged, and that the absentee father-to-be was God, what are you gonna do, cry? Better to laugh till you cry.

\* \* \*

From the eponymous suburb of Regina, Saskatchewan, comes Gerald Hill's *Hillsdale Book*. Since it is also about the author and since there is a man inside the town (even inside its name), it has something in common with *Paterson*. Like that earlier city-person-poem, *Hillsdale Book* also contains a bunch of different stuff: Hillsdale history proper, Hill's history, his telling of other people's stories, other people's stories told by themselves, maps, lists, drawings, documents, poetry, prose, and photographs. This reader really enjoyed Hill's *14*

*Tractors* (2010), but, as one might expect, it was somewhat narrower in its focus. That was great, because my theory is that if you're going to read about one tractor, you might as well go ahead and read about fourteen of them. But it's not hard to imagine that this book might have wider appeal.

According to my curriculum vitae, the first conference I ever regretted was the one about manifestos. A lot of people had very strong opinions at that conference. But then conferences have often proved disappointing. So even if it's my problem and not the poet's, I couldn't manage much enthusiasm for the second section of Shane Neilson's *On Shaving Off His Face*, titled "Able Physiologists Discuss Grief Musculatures." It consists of a made-up conference on Fervourism beginning with a preamble and an "unfinished prayer and a moment of silence," after which Able Physiologists 1 through 14 give talks on such disturbed and disturbing subjects as dying, mass murder, mass murderers, mafiosi, Edvard Munch, Jacques Lacan and on and on; the pain don't stop until the break of dawn, or at least until the "Afterword to Conference Proceedings" and, always my favourite part of any academic or scientific writing, the notes. Too close to the personal and professional bone are these poems, for this reader, anyway, alas. Aficionados of mental illness, the macabre, and the machinations of doctors should, without question, attend to them, though. *On Shaving Off His Face* is angry, hurt, and horrifying. The formal range and the range of reference are both wide—the latter too wide for me, who prefers to avoid poems discussing angry young men who also happened to murder a slew of innocent people. The formal range, though, is impressive—not the range itself, so much, but that in ranging Neilson remains in control.

Carolyn Smart was sharp in *Hooked* (2009), which consisted of seven portraits of seven women of some renown or some infamy. I appreciated it when I read it; and it stayed with me, deepening the more I considered it. It is a scary book in a lot of ways, and, like Neilson's, it took up a space in my mind. Smart's new book, *Careen*, is about Bonnie and Clyde and shares some of her prior book's virtues. There are worse things to read than a poetry book about Bonnie and Clyde, by a poet who writes well about recent historical figures, especially in their own voices, and who is competent in a variety of forms. But after *Hooked* and the way it started to fester in the best sense, *Careen* was a bit of a disappointment.

The fact that the ground is so well trod—please, anybody, everybody, no more Bonnie and Clyde, Billy the Kid, Marilyn Monroe, Jack and Jackie, or Second World War, and, for God's sake, no more O.J. Simpson—can be compensated for. Yet revivification is not set in motion by epigrams that aren't true ("Nothing lies more than a photograph") or by stepping over one's own best lines: "damn you Henry Ford, you and your knack for slick design." That's a good line, and it's a last line, sort of a Dos Passos line, quite like the regular pulse of the assembly line, with those monosyllables and those dinging and knocking and singing sounds. But the line before it is this: "the car they lived and died in like a shrine[.]" The only thing added is the rhyme, if that is an addition (which it isn't, here); everything else takes away—the martyrdom, the car-culture-as-religion cliché. Perhaps this is too harsh, as maybe someone as innocent of Bonnie and Clyde as I was of some of Smart's earlier subjects will be grabbed by *Careen* the way that I was hooked by *Hooked*.

Not every poem in Sheryda Warrener's *Floating Is Everything* comes off, such as the early-on prose paragraph "We Bought a City," which is okay enough; but by calling to mind Donald Barthelme's "So I Bought a Little City," an ever more prophetic classic story, it undermines itself. At the same time, Warrener's strength is to reflect the right amount of light on other people's images: "I'm looking at pictures / of Morrissey in a beige / corduroy shirt unbuttoned[;]" "in this photograph, / the bend of the tree is a replica of the bend // of the river[;]" "[l]ook how / the rectangles of paper become sky!" My favourite is "*Oh, Yoko*":

> Imagine [ ... ]
> Front cover, a polaroid [ ... ]
> Back cover, a photograph [ ... ]
> [ ... ] famous picture [ ... ]
> [ ... ]
> [ ... ] he's shot, and still [ ... ]
> [ ... ], a red rotary telephone
> [ ... ]
> [ ... ], *At any moment, Ms. Ono / might call.*

First off, the spaces between the lines are crucial, not superfluous. I had to type them in when writing this, obviously, and if you format them without the space, a good deal of the power is gone. Now notice how "Imagine" is both a noun and a command. See the album inside spinning like the red rotary phone that shows itself later. See the image in your mind's eye (that is, *imagine*), a series of interrelated images, photographic images. Hear how the call that might be anticipated from Ms. Ono appears in the title that is both the name of a song and a call to Ms. Ono. It is layered and recursive, palimpsestic and elegiac, and it is characteristic of the collection. The proliferation of ellipses is not the poet's but mine and occurs because somebody trustworthy mentioned that I might need to get permission to quote anything about music, the way Sarah Blake couldn't use any Kanye West lyrics in her book; so I erred on the side of caution and just cut a bunch of stuff out, which would have been a very Yoko Ono thing to do if I had done it on purpose.

On the back of *Merz Structure No. 2 Burnt by Children at Play*, we learn that as a child, its author, Jake Kennedy, "accidentally burnt down an abandoned house. Years later as an adult, he read a story about how Kurt Schwitters's 'interior house-sculpture' ('Merz Structure No. 2') was destroyed in 1951 after some children playing with matches accidentally burnt the building down." The adverb is curious. Be that as it may—and one would know only from the blurb, not the poems, that their author was a precocious but inadvertent arsonist—the book purposefully plays with mismatches on two levels. The first, less interesting, albeit inoffensive one is an incongruous bifurcated word hoard consisting of both quite austere and what-the-fuck-dude diction: "Even Eurydice is dullsville in truth"; "residue of / time travel at light-speed / hokey-ass sci-fi elongations of beings"; "the yippee-ki-yay of the wordless."

That last word leads to the other, richer level relying on a mismatch, which is Kennedy's book-long prodding of Bhartrhari's paradox: namely, to name the unnameable gives it a name; or perhaps it would be better to describe *Merz Structure* as apophatically ekphrastic; or, since the book is "framed" around an absent (because destroyed) aesthetic "structure," perhaps it can be seen as the assertion of a poetics of negative space, a Bachelard vacated of real lyrical romanticism. If you have spent significant time mulling over Wallace Stevens's observation in "The Snow Man" of "the nothing that is not there and the nothing that is," then this may be a book for you.

Kennedy's prior collection, *Apollinaire's Speech to the War Medic* (2011), would provide a field day for the object-oriented ontologists out there, with its studies of a claw hammer, salt-shaker, steel wool, town dump, subdivision sidewalk, nail-polished toes, butterflies, and an iron frying pan. Even there, though, what made a thing a thing was not just what was there, but what was going, going, gone: "Study of Dog Print in Snow," "Study of Rotted Canoe," "Study of Vacant Lot." In *Merz Structure* the absences are all, which makes them entirely present: "The best thing is to watch the will of the wind distribute your papers out over the water—but not name it. Do not name it!" This poetic self-prohibition brings the book into the realm of mystic theology, whether kabbalistic or Zen, but it is still a *self*-prohibition, and thus is rooted in an everyday world: "A person can be told: try to lose to try to be true. But that sounds stupid in real life."

Liz Worth's *No Work Finished Here* is derived from "stupid in real life," or at least one of the earliest versions of what became reality TV, which became real-life stupid, which makes life more stupid. Like Kennedy's book, it has something to do with visual art—and like his, not directly. Worth has taken Andy Warhol's *a: A Novel* (1968) and whacked lots of it away (*erasing* or *editing* or *rearranging*). What you're left with is 400 pages of short, free-verse poems that are vague and tired and sad and cumulatively moving. That might not sound too exciting, except for the moving part, but I for one really enjoyed this book. I was reading it around and about so much that I *lost* it, which is about as likely as ... well, who loses *books*? Not me, and probably not you, either, if I had to guess. There's something infectiously distracted about Worth, or the focus had to pass through massive distraction to be achieved.

*No Work Finished Here*, it turns out, is about work: authorship, appropriation, the work of mourning. One remembers "The Factory" from which art constantly flowed, and that Warhol, of course, was an ultimately self-debilitating workaholic; he was dehydrated and nearly starved when he finally went to the hospital for the last time. *The Warhol Diaries*, which I found to be fascinating at the level of detail, of style ("fashion"), of prose style, prove that he was always at work, which needs no proof. Soon after reading the *Diaries*, hoping for something as great at the level of the writing (or "writing"—they were transcribed tapes), I got *a*. I maybe trudged and sludged through forty pages of it. Boy, was it ever boring, and not in a so-boring-that-it's-interesting way.

Unedited conversations with Warhol personages and factotums and prophetic so-called stars: that could go all kinds of ways, and perhaps I should have kept at it. Still, given all that, Worth's version is very much an improvement on the original. It spares us all a lot of stupid. It's hard to see what she's done, though, unless you had already concluded that the thing she's done it *with* was not worth actually doing it *to*, or not worth doing, but only of conceiving of doing, until from the very conceiving of it, something productive got done. That's worth the work. The concept works.

Speaking of which, I've got to be honest. I did something stupid or bad or both, for although I am reviewing it, I *did not read* Gustave Morin's *Clean Sails*. Don't put that on my tombstone and especially not in my file for full professor. The truth is—this is not a rationalization—you don't read it; nobody does. You *look* at it; maybe, as in Elizabeth Bishop's "The Monument," you watch it; or do both or neither, and either you do or don't argue about and/or discuss the difference, if there is one. *Clean Sails* is a collection of concrete poems, typography poems, visual-art-on-the-page poems: call them what you will. I might as well admit to something else, since we're unburdening ourselves: I don't tend to like these kinds of poems, and I care less and less about their implications—though one does go through stages. But *Clean Sails* was delightful. You can certainly look at it. It has the right amount of verbiage: almost none. I'm never sure whether to call it witty or funny, but it's witty-funny. I wish I could call them "generous," but that's played out. Morin himself calls them "typewriter poems," and they are the prettiest typewriter poems I've ever seen. I'm telling you, these things are really good. If only you could see them.

# Poetry: Letters in Canada 2010

Among the year's most successful books were Dionne Brand's *Ossuaries* and Anne Carson's *Nox*, quite different on the one hand yet on the other with aspects in common. Brand's book-length sequence has as harrowing a start as any work in recent memory, initiating the reader into a world in which "so many dreams of course were full of prisons," in which "my every waking was incarcerated," in which "at night, especially at night, it is always at night, / a wall of concrete enclosed me[.]" That bracketed period misrepresents the book's overwhelming momentum, as these poems are devoid of end-stops—not merely a matter of punctuation. The sections, fifteen in all, alternate between the first-person and the third, in the latter case manifest in the character of Yasmine, a member of a revolutionary political group—think Weathermen, Baader-Meinhof, Black Panthers. Tracking the movement between the "I" ("the slippery pronoun, the ambivalent, glistening, / long sheath of the alphabet flares beyond her reach") and the "she" is part of what makes the book unnerving; the reader is in a disadvantageous position as far as being solidly situated, which is a way to instantiate as felt experience the violence and vicissitudes of Yasmine's life, as well as the "harassment and provocations" that follow the "I" even into sleep.

In this world of bourgeois illusions and bad dreams, a line such as "she flew like shrapnel off the bed" is diagnostic and prophetic. "Yasmine knows in her hardest heart, / that truth is worked and organized by some, / and she's on the wrong side always[.]" Brand's verse is worked as a counterweight, organized in terms of counter-truths: "the presumptive cruelties, / the villages that nursed these since time, / it's always in the lyric // the harsh fast threatening gobble, / the clipped sharp knifing, it's always / in the lyric[.]" Such staccato phrasing and repetition are found throughout, at one moment being used for the depiction of states of mental and moral urgency, at another for the purposes of invective, at another for an insistence on basic human needs. Certain rhetorical figures are returned to with great effect, especially "no time, no time, this epistrophe, no time, / wind's coming, no time," where the epistrophic ending is as much an oxymoron as "lived and loved" ("if I have lived, I have not loved, / and if I have loved, I cannot have lived"), since this terminal repeating undoes the temporal terminus:

> it may be useless now, to say
> the awkward life, the hovering life, the
> knowing life, born so early in me
>
> [ .... ]
>
> leathered skin, gelatinous skin,
> threnodic skin, shrugged hands, you see,
> I've sat here all this time being reasonable
>
> like this, in the eye-filled years, the wall-filled years,
> the returning years, the formaldehyde years,
> the taxidermy years, the dishevelled years

Less easy to demonstrate in this space than such cases of sonic assertiveness are those in which the momentum slows and emphatic sounds are replaced by something closer to "replete silence" or "her stillness," or how the narrative sweep of the book is sustained, as a kind of psychological and political thriller, while all the while it includes constant interruptions of the plot, as if to imply that an unbroken story—"events happening in their order // [with] a certain regularity" —amounts to just another illusion.

Brand's protagonist Yasmine, on the run and gone underground, has at least that in common with the mysterious figure at the hurt heart of Carson's *Nox*: "My brother ran away in 1978, rather than go to jail. He wandered in Europe and India, seeking something, and sent us postcards or a Christmas gift, no return address. He was travelling on a false passport and living under other people's names." This accordion book in a box, both concrete art object and elegy for Carson's brother, contains reproduced scraps of letter, pieces of envelope, stamps, family photos, drawings, staples, crumpled pieces of paper, and deliberately unlovely collages. One goal of elegy is to remember the dead by putting the pieces of their lives together after the fact. *Nox* achieves this goal as best as possible with the limited materials at the elegist's disposal and emphasizes, through both exposition and its physical hodgepodge form, how the goal is next to impossible to achieve. As Carson says on the back of the box, "When my brother died I made an epitaph for him in the form of a book. This is a replica of it, *as close as we could get*" (my emphasis). Even the book's accordion folds suggest the difficulties of re-membering, of re-presentation: on the one hand, there is an organic wholeness here, as the work is printed on one long piece of paper; on the other hand, the book is in essence a diptych, inherently divided, with the left side being an elaborate word-by-word translation of Catullus's poem 101 ("poor prayers for the dead, / brother, to say / to give you the last gifts of death" [from Frank O. Copley's version]) and the right side being everything else (biography, memoir, mini-essays on elegy, history, translation). Yet sometimes a scrap from the right side will be folded over onto the left, crossing the gutter, yoking them together in poignantly piecemeal fashion.

"I never arrived at the translation I would have liked to do of poem 101," Carson writes. "But over the years of working at it, I came to think of translating as a room, not exactly an unknown room, where one gropes for the light switch. I guess it never ends. A brother never ends." It is a unique and sad book. At the very start, in contemplating elegy but being stymied ("There is nothing more to be expended on that, we think, he's dead. Love cannot alter it. Words cannot add to it."), Carson "began to think about history." She reaches Herodotus, whom she describes as "an historian who trains you as you read." It struck me that both Carson and Brand also train us as we read. Even more than the fugitive figures they create, their books have in common fractured stories that are embodied in their books *qua* book. The physically impressive nature of *Nox* makes it obvious that under consideration is precisely how to collect and, in a way, to sanctify what must be imprecise and what is not, after all, saintly. What else are *Ossuaries*, finally, than concrete manifestations of the urge to retrieve and collect and sanctify, artistic re-presentations of the body and, through the body, the soul? If it is less obvious than *Nox* as an object, *Ossuaries* in its title and formal fracturing should at least suggest a clue.

The year saw a host of volumes *Selected* and *Collected*. Patrick Lane's *Witness: Selected Poems 1962–2010* begins with winter and the sound of weeping "for a crying bird. In the morning / you found him dead on the window sill. / His beak was a crust of ice / that melted as you breathed. / When I threw him away, he didn't fly." Even if, a few pages later, we are told that "Only words / can fly for you like birds" and that "A bird is a poem / that talks of the end of cages[,]" the relationship between the poet's song and the natural world is hardly conceived as one that is wholly free. These poems can be tough going, as in "Because I Never Learned":

> Because I never learned how
> to be gentle and the country
> I lived in was hard with dead
> animals and men, I didn't question
> my father when he told me
> to step on the kitten's head
> after the bus had run over
> its hind quarters.

"It isn't just violence I told them," Lane tells us in "Just Living," and for him it really is just life, in which people tend to fare no better than a cat put out of its misery. One story "is about a man who walks out into the storm / and is never seen again. We all know that one." In "The Happy Little Towns," with its curdled title, there is a kind of pain to be found, even if it isn't terminal: "That was the year my wife slept with my best friend." Characteristically, "The wreckage of that world stayed wreckage, though / we tried to build it back." Without that trying, wreckage itself could turn from catastrophe to affectation; but then the poems are manifestations of an admirable, albeit often-thwarted resistance. The selections range from 1969's *Separations* to five poems appearing for the first time. Many of the newer poems settle into the page with lines as long as they can be without being broken to accommodate the constrictions of space, which strikes one not as a mere expansion of form but as the further staking out of a position toward life.

Having published some 800 poems, Lane is restrained in choosing only sixty-three of them. A selection probably *should* lean toward being lean, and

Lane helps the reader focus through his curatorial economy. Not that one is bound to complain in the converse case, if the results turn out all right. Running to over two-and-a-half times the size of Lane's book, *Kaleidoscope: Selected Poems of P.K. Page* gives no reason for wishes of excision. In his introduction, editor Zailig Pollock (pulling from essays by Brian Trehearne and Dean Irvine) describes Page's poetry of the forties and fifties in terms of "personality and impersonality, interiority and exteriority, subjectivity and objectivity, multiplicity and wholeness." He also remarks that seeing her early career "in terms of a conflict of opposites will only take us so far." An inability to synthesize these conflicts into a "Triclopian view" brought on an impasse, but after a period of silence Page was able to continue writing, this time bringing a third term— "the spiritual"—to the previous logic of conflict. His description of these poems from the mid-sixties onward (with "simple diction, free of the verbal knots and intricacies" of the earlier work, "more visionary poems" notable for "vividness of imagery and lyric intensity") is to the point, but what most caught my eye was his citation of the opening of "Could I Write a Poem Now?," which he says is "probably the last poem she wrote before lapsing into her long mid-career silence," a period marking "the pivot around which Page's career turns" and one which the poem "portends." Turning to "Could I Write a Poem Now?," I was grabbed by its finale: "But how do you write a Chagall? / It boils down to that." Following Pollock's narrative, one might say that Page's creative silence is precipitated by the fact that a poem cannot do what a painting can. So it was striking to come across the sestina "After Reading *Albino Pheasants* by Patrick Lane" (written in 1978), in part because of having just read the title poem of that collection of Lane's in *Witness*, but also because of the sestina's reversal of Page's painterly, interrogative poem of portent: "What is there about the irrepressible imagination / that the adjective *pale* modifying *beak, eye* and *flesh* / can set my sensibilities awash? // If with my thickest brush I were to lay a wash / of thinnest watercolour I could make a world / as unlike my own dense flesh / as the high-noon midsummer sky; / but it would not catch at my imagination / or change the waves or particles of light // yet *pale* can tip the scales, make light / this heavy planet." This is merely one thing to notice, of course; but then in a book of some 250 pages, stretching from "Ecce Homo" of 1941 to "Cullen in the Afterlife" of 2009, readers will not be bereft of noticeable things.

In addition to *Kaleidoscope*, The Porcupine's Quill continues its *Essential* series, one entry of which also celebrates a poet recently deceased. In introducing her selection of the poems of Margaret Avison, Robyn Sarah tells a story not so far removed from one we read earlier: "Avison herself felt that if her early poetry was difficult, this was a shortcoming: she spoke of her process as one of growing simpler... Avison's later work did become simpler—less virtuosic in its associative leaps, less intricate in vocabulary, more conversational in tone... Avison's became more and more a poetry of inquiry, an inner pondering of her daily givens, to which we are made party. Her question mark is a straw to the wind, testing premises, language, commonly held beliefs or interpretations, familiar texts, the evidence of her own senses." Sarah's straw question mark is a nice touch and this is a nice selection. Although her work has its mysteries and its moral weight to contend with and appreciate, Avison is not a poet best described as intimidating (and more's the credit); but *Always Now: The Collected Poems*, in its thick separate volumes, *is* a bit intimidating, imposing itself on the bookshelf in a way that is no doubt necessary but which also feels a touch disjunctive given a certain modesty in the poems. So this paring down is welcome. Sarah's claim that Avison "seems a natural descendant of Marianne Moore and Elizabeth Bishop" is partly validated by a stanza from "Poetry Is":

> At a ballgame when
> the hit most matters
> and the crowd is half-standing
> already hoarse, then poetry's
> eye is astray to a
> quiet area to find out
> who picks up the bat the runner
> flung out of his runway.

If you ever come across George Plimpton's account of accompanying Moore to a baseball game, you will see that the latter's way of looking at the contest includes moments similar to Avison's oblique attention. Seeing the thing that most people might miss or seeing anew what one didn't know one had missed: these are appealing talents in a poet. Although by most standards it is not the finest poem here, "Cement Worker on a Hot Day" may be the poem I like best. When the title character "(why of course!) / wrenches the hydrant till / it yields a gush / for him to gulp and wash in[,]" the poet can no longer see the oft-seen yellow hydrant as "just a knob / shape." It comes to life and adds to life.

The other entry in the series this year is *The Essential Kenneth Leslie*, a curious case. I had never heard of Leslie but do not expect that either the press or the selection's editor, Zachariah Wells, will hold it against me. "Leslie's all-but-disappearance," "his slide into obscurity," "[t]hough barely remembered today," "little notice has been paid to Leslie and his work"—all these descriptions appear on or in the book. In short, this is a reclamation project. As projects go, it is valuable, a fine use to find for *The Essential* series. You learn something that you did not know before; get to ponder whether the verdicts of literary history are sensible or arbitrary; and, one would hope, come away with some poems worth having read and worth rereading. From the foreword and the biographical sketch at the back of the book, it is clear that Leslie was a fascinating figure. Born in Nova Scotia, widely and well educated (he studied with Josiah Royce, for instance), Leslie published four books between 1934 and 1938, picking up a Governor General's Award for the last of them. An edited collection (not edited by him) appeared in 1971, but "angered" by what he saw as its expurgations, he self-published *O'Malley to the Reds and Other Poems* the following year in response. Leslie was involved in politics, the threads of which wove through him in atypical patterns. He was "an indefatigable anti-Fascist activist" (one of the results of which was his founding of *The Challenger*, an "anti-Fascist comic book"), and "his socialism was inextricably intertwined with his Baptist upbringing. He founded and edited *The Protestant Digest* (later renamed *The Protestant*), which reached a circulation of 50,000 at its peak," and made *Life* magazine's infamous cut of fifty Communist "dupes and fellow-travellers" in 1949. His "tumultuous" personal life is enclosed in a pregnant paragraph, around which bounce several marriages, estrangement from his children, an affair with his secretary, and his being left for his own nephew by a much younger paramour.

A compelling life, but how about the poetry? The first poem, "Open Lading," begins with a "barge of dreams" and ends with a stanza that can be read in light of the decades of obscurity for which the present selection means to make amends: "I have a sheaf of words, have I, / but never a soul to show it to. / I'll let it roam... it will find a home." The fact of the book makes of these airy lines a prophecy. The next poem, "New Song," represents what Wells calls the poet's awareness "that the verse he wrote was out of step with Modernism." It also suggests another side of him as wordsmith (one mentioned in an essay on Leslie by Burris Devanney, first published in 1979)—that is, as composer of "a few dozen songs which did not sell in Tin Pan Alley"; his "Cape Breton Lullaby," however, has not gone un-recorded and is included here. "New Song" turns a wary eye toward time and argues against compulsory originality: "I cannot sing a new song, / I fear to sing the old, / and I would sing a love song / to melt a heart of gold." One cannot rightly be "blamed" for not being "new" given that "for their ancient madrigals / thrushes are not ashamed," though the introduction of "thirsty buttercups" as further evidence, "filled / with oft-repeated showers," is unconvincing, if unobjectionable. The book picks up and begins to make its best case for recuperation in the very fine sequence of twenty-eight sonnets, "By Stubborn Stars." The capacity to move from archaism to contemporaneity, the approach to love that is both idealized and clear-eyed, and the overall facility with the form remind me of Edna St. Vincent Millay, an exceptional sonneteer whose reputation likewise took a precipitous fall (though of late it has made some recovery). The sequence also calls to mind the genteel versifier George Henry Boker, who wrote sonnets that touched on the thematically profane but did so under the cover of formal convention. It may seem incompatible, the move from the kind of (admittedly knowing) "romance" suggested here—

> Seldom are words as empty as that king's
> who taught his vassals how what was to be
> must come to be in the deep tide of things[.]

—to the starker version below—

> The cold resistance of your lips was here
> upon my lips, and on my hand your hand
> dropped down and trembled in a frost of fear;
> your eyes were wet and red with reprimand
> against the sharp decree of circumstance
> we had allowed to rob us of our right.

—but the excerpts represent two sides of the same coin. Idealism and frustration work in productive concert throughout. Leslie thrived on conflict, as indicated by the title of "The Word Had Need of Flesh," as well as by a stanza such as this: "Aestheticize, anaesthetize, / one is mist, the other fog. / Propriety, licentiousness, / two names, but the same old dog!" There is something of both propriety and licentiousness in the sonnet sequence, though the latter aspect is muted and the former paradoxically compromised by being out of step with its time—an aesthetically improper propriety, as it were. Reactionary though his critique is, it is also partly self-directed, which endows such conflict in Leslie with psychological significance and frees one's sympathy for the poetry's unstable stances.

Much of Leslie's energy went into resolving what the book calls his "deeply ambivalent relationship with institutional education"—namely universities, several of which he attended and "saw as breeding grounds for dullness and conformity[.]" Wells picks up the theme in his introduction, even bringing it up to date: "It's not hard to imagine what Leslie would think of today's Creative Writing industry, snugly ensconced in the folds of academe, star pupils destined to become tomorrow's teachers, poets acting more as bureaucrats than as legislators,"—Leslie and Shelley are favourably compared— "safe in a hermetic world of their own." Such moments of provocation in the foreword are befitting given the man it introduces. "Tea With the Professor," another sonnet, is tense with a desire to reconcile "this 'now,' that, narrowed to a name / for what is not, was never, nor can be," with the "eternal brew of the world[.]" Leslie begins by exclaiming, "Hang history and its seven thousand years," but what is really causing his reaction is not centuries and centuries of history but the symbolic representation of history, the professor himself, with his "wisdom, heavy and old[.]" At the very end, reactions and abstractions are replaced by a winning human moment, with the speaker reminding the professor, "your tea is getting cold!" More fascinating still is the long satire "Cobweb College," intriguingly subtitled *An Antinomian Parable written for Robert Frost*." Beginning in heroic quatrains, varied throughout by blank verse and lines of three and four beats, it is an attention-grabber, and, apart from the sonnet sequence, the most interesting work in the book.

There are more sonnets, such as "Harlem Preacher" (dedicated to Martin Luther King, Jr.), "To My Father Drowned at Sea," and "Beauty Is Something

You Can Weigh in Scales," which in typical fashion for Leslie finds a way to concretize the abstract: "I found it first and best in father's store, / measuring yards of calico, weighing out nails, / sprawled among nets and cod-lines on the floor, / venturing cut-brier, rifling candy-pails." The tableau is well-arranged, convincing, a treat of composition and nostalgia. Unrelated to those candy-pails, "The Candy Maker" is a curiosity dedicated to his first wife's father, a chocolate magnate. Oddly prescient is "The Computer," with its ambivalence toward this figure for the future: "And this machine, this habit chilled to steel, / this stealthy anaesthesia of the hand, / this row of rigid numbers that can feel / no shade of yielding in their stark command, / yes, even with this our will may weave a cage / wherein protected we may sing our rage!" Be it the future, the present, or the past, matters of time are of the essence for Leslie. Wells writes of him "stubbornly ignoring the fashions of modernism" and ventures that one explanation for his current obscurity "is his old-fashionedness." This seems plausible, of course, even likely, but then there are forgotten poets galore who did not ignore but who cultivated "the fashions of modernism" and must be obsolete now, in part, not for being old back then but for trying too hard to be new. Does Leslie, regardless of what ostensible fashion he is ignoring or adopting, create a personal idiom, or take a memorable approach to his materials? The more you consider the selections here, with their heady mix of conflict, romance, and reaction, as well as their facility for their chosen forms, the more you incline to say yes, while acknowledging that Leslie is also being recuperated for symbolic purposes, for what he can represent in relation to a particular version of the modernist past and the MFA present.

In *Why Are You So Long and Sweet? Collected Long Poems of David W. McFadden*, the poet is kind enough to show his hand: "A long poem begins when a poet accepts his ignorance / and moves out into all the magic space he can afford / with longing for the capture of a moment so perfect / all moments will submit forever to his will." A few lines later, that desire to capture a perfect moment is shown to be, in the words of another long poem of note, one of those decisions and revisions which a minute will reverse: "For it does not befit a man / to worry overmuch about his verse. // And that which is studied starts to stink / and the ultimate stink is the stench / of one who strives for perfection[.]" The contents are roughly chronological and have a roughly recognizable arc. ("Roughly" because, again, nothing here is "perfect" nor is it meant to be. Stuart Ross, who edited the book—as he did its "selected" companion and predecessor *Why Are You So Sad?*—admits that "this isn't strictly the *collected* long poems of David W. McFadden.") The early poems are fragmented; the next ones, which make up most of the volume, have a meditative expansiveness and are pleasant to get lost in; then, there is a turn into shaggy-cow stories that conclude with outright doggerel.

In "The Poem Poem" where the book begins, the poet is pregnant and the pregnant poet is also a radio receiver. Picking up bits and pieces of sonic info is a good conceit for justifying formal fracturing; being big with verse-child is another way to say that creativity is a virtue. The attitude toward perfection is early in evidence ("I wish only for a perfect baby, / it means the end of me / from my point of view"), and relying on the muse of radio waves sometimes yields little ("after eight hours spent / listening to radio static / it's nice to get up / stretch your limbs") and sometimes pays off ("Different poets write from different parts of the body. // For instance, I listened to the radio all day and feel like a new man"). The deadpan congeries of raw information, oblique confession, and vatic statement ("the human race is going places") is a winning mixture. "The Ova Yogas" keeps the fragmentation and mostly forgoes the rest, placing an emphasis on sound in and of itself. The book ends with poems that are also winning and digestible, if you value the simple and goofy. The beginning of 1983's "The Cow That Swam Lake Ontario" may give you a taste— "A curious story is mine to tell / and I must tell thee of it" —and the newer version of the poem published as a chapbook twenty years later, "Cow Swims Lake Ontario Or, The Case of the Waterlogged Quadruped," is even more ludicrous: "Cows are nice but they don't catch mice." Truer words were never spoken; and while "Danny Quebec" and "Nevada Standstill" can't match the cow poems in silliness, they too have their simple pleasures, as when McFadden in the latter admits cheerily (then less so), "I'm happy with my little radio / which I turn on at random intervals / (decaying molecules of plain old dreams)." This randomness is of a piece with the spontaneity found in the first version of the swimming cow's saga: "And so I went home and wrote this poem / without even bothering to wash my hands / or change my clothes." In the poems in the big middle of the book— "The Poet's Progress," "I Don't Know," "Night of Endless Radiance," "A New Romance," "Country of the Open Heart" —the reader overhears McFadden's most engaging voice.

One could cull many passages worthy of a commonplace book devoted to the writing of poetry; here's a nice one: "And the rules for writing are precisely / the same as the rules for love: Be natural, be affectionate, / and keep your heart just a fraction / below the point of absolute explosion."

From a few of the more tightly formal poems early on in D.G. Jones's collected poems, *The Stream Exposed with All its Stones*, one might have predicted, given the shift into a lower-case line of prosaic speech, as well as an interest in Chinese and Japanese models (along with the French and the classical Greek), that the poet would settle into a minimalism of gnomic utterance. Though such moments do abound— "half a bird's egg is sufficient / proof of violence"; "for something to happen, something's / got to stop happening"—these poems are not really minimal, for while they may well be taken as discrete units, they are just as much parts of a moving whole. In this sense, naming the collection after a Jones poem that isolates the stones in the bed of the moving stream is apt. In addition to the link between Jones and those models from other climes and times, and the way in which the literary arts are so frequently seen as sister to the visual arts (part of an aesthetic continuum), the poet also locates himself in a Canadian context marked by poems either dedicated or referring to contemporaries and immediate predecessors such as Atwood, Duncan, Frye, Gustafson, Kiyooka, Lampman, Lane, Marlatt, Pratt, Scott, and Thompson. The poems from *Under the Thunder the Flowers Light up the Earth* (1977) that are titled by date only make clear a journal-like quality that is consistent throughout, insofar as the sense of day-to-day attentiveness persists. In some of the long poems, especially "Christmas / Going On" and "How to Paint in the Recession" from *The Floating Garden* (1995), we get a sustained run of "blanks and bits" that make these among my favourites in the book. In the latter poem, Jones writes that "your lawyer / may not buy it, but I put it to you / seriously, a life is a collage[,]" and as these poems are a kind of collage, by aesthetic logic they represent life—compellingly, all told. Also worth noting is the unflashy introduction by W.J. Keith.

There were two books among the year's selected and collected, both of them posthumously honouring the poets between their covers, that made a bigger impact on me than the others: *The Collected Works of Pat Lowther*, edited by Christine Wiesenthal, and *The Collected Books of Artie Gold*, edited by Ken Norris and Endre Farkas. Of the former, the first remark one is tempted to make is *what took so long?* It is a necessary and overdue book. Wiesenthal's introduction is a helpful start, and her informative notes are unpedantic. The design inside is a model of attractive utilitarianism (or as Lowther writes of the octopus, "beautifully functional"). The fonts are inviting and the layout is tight but still open enough to give the reader some breathing room; the generous margins pull one's pencil toward them like a magnet. And what might it note when it gets there? Perhaps the equilibrium Lowther achieves of expansiveness and parsimony, or the economy of her images: "The tamed killer whale / leaps for his fish / and falls back in a huge / angel of spray"; "birds' egg speckled hands"; "even the black [anemones] / have an aura / like an afterimage of light"; "we animate our city, / abacus of lights"; "his eyes blue / as watered milk[.]" There is warmth in her directness of expression but also at times an aggression, a sharp humanity in revealing not only the easiest things.

Wiesenthal describes Lowther's "concerns with evolutionary time and prehistorical origins," concerns which on the one hand seem paradoxically forward thinking and on the other hand make for a link backward not only to the prehistoric past but to the poetic past of Pratt's *The Great Feud (A Dream of a Pleiocene Armageddon)*. "It's only belief," she writes in "Levitation," that "sets us up in contradiction / to the universe"; this belief is rejected in "Random Interview" not because it is false but because such rejection is a pragmatic response to fear and exhaustion and the fulfilment of a desire: "i am tired of pain / i am tired of my own pain / i am tired of / the pain of others [ ... ] // i go out to the cliff pours / of stars, the tall / volume of stars // i go down / to the grains of soil / to bacteria / to viruses / to the neat mechanics of molecules // to escape the pain / to escape the pain"; "what i want is to be / aware of the spaces / between atoms, to breathe / continuously the sources of sky, / a veined sail moving, / my love never setting / foot to the dark / anvil of earth[.]" Looking back—"I am always aware of / the origin of birds, he said, / their scaly reptilian claws / Yet I grew doting fond / of a little creature / in a cage chirping" —and looking up— "For a star to be born / There must be mutual attraction. / There must be intimate relations / between excited particles." —are gestures commensurate with love in the latter case ("Is it love love love / that makes the universe go round?") and a complex affection in the former. What is on earth is always liminal, as in a poem whose title comes from a line by Atwood, "'At the Last Judgement We Shall All Be Trees'": "Trees are / in their roots and branches, / their intricacies, / what we are // ambassadors between the land / and high air / setting a breathing shape / against the sky / as you and I do[.]" The book includes everything found in the original first editions of *This Difficult Flowering*, *The Age of the Bird*, *Milk Stone*, and *A Stone Diary* (and restores a poem from the typescript of the latter dropped by Oxford University Press on first publication), as well as around seventy unpublished or uncollected poems from both early and later in Lowther's career; also appearing for the first time is the text from *Infinite Mirror Trip: A Multi-Media Experience of the Universe*, which was staged at the MacMillan planetarium in Vancouver in the summer of 1974.

"Little Gold books came out just about every year in the seventies," writes George Bowering in his introduction to *The Collected Books of Artie Gold*, "and in their unique bindings and designs they illustrated Artie's penchant for curios." That uniqueness of physical bookmaking is not in evidence in the present collection, but poetry-making is here in surplus. As Bowering also wrote, this time in the fall of 1974 in a preface to Gold's first book, *cityflowers*, Gold was one of "the first 21-year-olds I ever saw getting turned over by the great dead poet of SF, Jack Spicer, and the great dead poet of NY, Frank O'Hara." Certainly O'Hara is there in the emphasis on spontaneous everydayness, in the mock apostrophes and in the campily genuine exclamations ("Oh Jesus / how hot the sun has gotten / even in an hour!"). Spicer appears not just in the commitment to serial production but also in a certain insistent repetition ("The sea is not / exotic / the sea / is mediterranean / middle / of the earth the sea / is birth / the sea is the floating gestures"). Both are echoed in the movement between a sharp-eyed postmodern knowingness and an often-elegiac wistfulness, as well as in a tricky straight-faced naïveté that can shade fast into an eroticism or dourness that snaps you to attention.

But perhaps I am getting ahead of myself (and reading ahead in the volume), for the most obvious sign in the earliest of the work collected here that O'Hara and Spicer are influences is the fact that their names pop up a lot. A poem beginning "'The trouble with comparing' yr life to a ballgame" is written "*after Spicer*," while another brings in "the finger-nails of O'hara [*sic*]" and imagines him as a kind of topographical feature: "nothing stood between O'hara & the sea / but a handful of impossible footprints // across a shoulder of the shrinking world of land, / land which lay like O'hara[.]" Another poem takes his name as a title, while still another considers with liberty the untimely death of "this crushed gentle poet." The directness with which Gold admits his poetic affections is fitting given the men who provoked them and dampens one's enthusiasm for diagnosing the aesthetic influenza of anxiety. The most intriguing among these early poems is a six-page dialogue between the ghosts of O'Hara and Spicer that begins by recalling the "I am little Eva" section of the latter's "Imaginary Elegies" and like those "Elegies" introduces God as a major character; nor can one forget while reading this dialogue O'Hara's "A True Account of Talking to the Sun on Fire Island."

(Incidentally, Spicer also shows up as a significant presence in one of the year's new books from a familiar name and as the entire *raison d'être* of another. The middle section of rob mclennan's *wild horses*, titled "After Spicer," begins "a seriality, then" and goes on to say that "the serial function takes / a map / a perpetual pattern // sustain a rhythm & then[.]" Last year in this space, I reviewed mclennan's *gifts* and felt drawn to refer to O'Hara; now it is Spicer in play, and after having read Gold and encountered his poem "sex at thirty-one" (a phrase mclennan has turned to his use), I wonder about mclennan's place on a particular poetic quadrangle. This could be way off; suffice it only to say that *wild horses* has the same stimulating ellipticism that characterized *gifts* but that its increased compactness and geographical focus may make it a more inviting read, depending on whether you prefer your volumes capacious or controlled. The other case is Garry Thomas Morse's *After Jack*, which ought to be read alongside the Robin Blaser-edited *The Collected Books of Jack Spicer* to be best appreciated. Morse's is a deep book-by-book engagement. I suppose he is so close to the voice he is "translating," ventriloquizing, and responding to that a certain kind of Spicer aficionado will feel that he is both *too* close and can never *truly* get close enough; but this is finally just a conjuring of possible objections that I do not personally share. If you admire Spicer, you will want to read *After Jack*.)

The direct references of Gold's first book fall away but not the first-person addresses, nor the humour. Among the first few poems of *Even yr photograph looks afraid of me* (1975), Gold considers himself in relation to his nation and finds several jokes in the meeting of poetry and patriotism. "Don't Stop Clapping Till I'm Famous..." is set at "the greatest poetry reading Canada ever heard[,]" attended by A.J.M. Smith, Earle Birney, the governor general, and

Robert Service's ghost: "Everyone was related to everybody else." Passive-aggressive listening leads in the end to more forceful demands and a dropping of facades: the poem's pointed politeness in two languages is a nice touch and one can see that the cultural nationalism of the seventies wasn't winning over every potential participant. "Canada First" and "The Pumpkin Eaters" advance the theme: "Deep are your ways, Oh Canada, long are your days / and you deign to let me sit on your lap!" In "Ultra Modern Times," "the Americans are coming" and Gold ties nationalism to marketing, noticing how quick is the slip from cultural R&D to national PR: "in ultra modern times / you've got to plan a product / to seem suddenly wonderful tomorrow / to seem as though it might last forever / you have to be ultra sneaky / and give them different reasons / when you come across the border." Gold himself feels a need to excuse his crossing of it: "if people ask us why we really / drove our bodies so far southwards / because, we will tell them in Atlanta / the magnolias are more beautiful in winter." There are other scandals, as in "Folk Poem": "My cats have ruined my life / It's as simple as that[.]" As Endre Farkas writes in an afterword, Gold "prowled the night like his many cats; the cats he loved but who in return gave him not affection but allergies." The small book titled *some of the cat poems* (1978) is ambivalent and loving and ends with a sketch by the poet suggesting that these feline creatures are finally an alien species.

The smallest of Gold's books is *5Jockeypoems* (1977), the first of which looks exactly like a jockey and the third of which works with negative space expertly, words surrounding an emptiness that is crouching down on an unseen steed. *Mixed Doubles* (1976; written with Geoff Young) was first printed to look like a tennis court; it even came with a net. Here you get just the poems, not the package, but imagining the miniature court makes the poems better. In *before Romantic Words* (1979), the speech and the forms retain their freedom, but the making of poetry feels less free for Gold, if his apologies to the muse ("I am sorry, muse, for the difficulty / with which I am drawn") and his self-diagnoses ("my life seems full of holes / that come together only in sadness") are any indication. Not all is despair, however: "More things interrupt my work / than carry it on, yet / some things do carry it on." One of those things is this *Collected*, which ends with *The Beautiful Chemical Waltz* (1992) and *The Hotel Victoria Poems*, the latter first published in 2003 but containing poems from the late 1970s. Like the Pat Lowther collection, this bringing together of Gold's books took a while: "[S]o much damage done by the waiting," Gold writes in "'A-12,'" "but it all serves like commas / finally to have been valuable not merely annoying[.]" Those like myself who are new to his work will find this to be more than a fair assessment, given the surfeit of value in this book, while those who have read him since the days of *cityflowers* will surely be happy that he is getting his due.

The crisp and colloquial, playfully serious prose of Bowering scattered throughout Gold's *Collected Books* is also our gateway into Bowering's own *My Darling Nellie Grey*, another example of the year's abundance. In this case, it is also an example of *a* year's abundance: "Here it was, the last week in December of 2005 [ ... ] It struck me that a new year was going to start in a day or two, and I had never really made a New Year's resolution, ever [ ... ] What if I were to write a page of poetry every day, winding up with a 365-page poem? There aren't many of those around. Then I had an attack of the sensible(s). Okay, what if I were to write a page every day, but make a dozen poems, or maybe a dozen monthly parts of a long poem? What if, thinking ahead, I aimed at getting a chapbook published for each month, and then a 365-page book made from those twelve chapbooks of thirty, or thirty-one, or twenty-eight pages?" And that is what Bowering did, resulting in this calendar book or book of days.

January opens in the elegiac mode, what with "the death of Irving Layton," "another USAmerican war," the seventy-year-old poet's own sense of mortality, and that "other mortality called the news" all finding their way into each day's dose of discipline. The chapbook that resulted is titled *Crows in the Wind*, and that bird flies often there: "A crow in the wind / seems to know / as much as you do." "Old crow, / inherit the wind." The wind that blows is Solomonic in its wisdom, diction, and form, either in agreement with Ecclesiastes ("Of making books there is no end, / and you have always known / you will die with pages to go, / you will go / out of print, / out of fashion, / out of mind, / into the wind."), or in rebuttal to that great king's Song ("A weak January sun shows me / your breasts are / nothing like roes, / lovely as they might be."), or in its Proverbial balance and moral clarity: "He giveth to the beast his food, / and to the young ravens which cry." "Rise at noon, / and the hours speed before you." "A fool's voice is known / by amplitude of words." In February, as Bowering puts it, "[t]he crows in the previous poem are joined ... by a lot of other birds, all of them vocalizing," and those birds are joined by Bowering and his lover, whose "comic acts in the kitchen" motivate the series of two-stanza poems that turn the tone of the year.

March finds the act of remembering manifest in the lightest of formal strictures, the "I Remember" prose poems invented by Joe Brainard, then followed by Bowering himself in 1993's *The Moustache*. This series is less somber than January's, though no less revealing:

> I REMEMBER the bottle of rye whiskey that was on the top shelf to the left of the sink. It was there for years. I don't remember my parents having a drink, though they went through coffee or vice versa like a teenager through sugar or vice versa. I don't remember them swearing, though my father the preacher's son did say "Judas Priest!" when he banged his thumb. I don't remember them dancing, though they played cards under the smoky air. I don't remember them fighting or arguing or shouting at each other, ever. In my lonely self I vowed never to do any of those things, and then I did them all.

April's "*U.S. Sonnets*" flash anger or shake their head in disgust at those overbearing neighbours to the south. This is like shooting fish in a barrel, and one needn't wade into the deepest waters of irony to fish out the guy wearing "a St. Louis Cardinals tee shirt" and "the stars and stripes around his head" who carries one sign reading "GO USA" and another one that misspells "morons." September's "*Fulgencio*," which indicts the same neighbour for criminal imperialism in various places south of *its* border but which is mostly concerned with Cuba, has the narrative thrust of well-told history. If you like misspelled signs, you will like the ludicrous headlines of "*Tocking Heads*," October's offering that takes a range of newspapers at their ambiguous word: the title "Parents Furious After Schools Are Forced to Cut Teachers" leads to a report that "Blood on the classroom floor / is bad education, says mom, / poor pedagogy, adds dad."

May and December's chapbooks find Bowering on the go. The former, "*Montenegro 1966*," mines its lines from a diary he kept on his first trip to Europe, an event he commemorates forty years later, "[j]ust in case no one else was going to do so[.]" The latter, "*There Then*," is arranged alphabetically, from

"Aarhus 1995" to "Zürich 1995." "If you want to give up control of your materials," Bowering writes, "go for the alphabet." From letters and places we travel to people: June's *"Some Answers"* all begin with a different writer's question, with each poem being Bowering's answer. August's *"According to Brueghel"* is made of six-stanza ekphrases, in each of which we learn to see "according to" a given artist: "According to Chagall / it was twenty after seven / when the blue-legged bird man // flew or was it / hopped into view"; "According to Rivera / the children / do not smile[.]"

November's *"Valley"* is Bowering's "humble offering to Lorine Niedecker," a "friend's response" to some of her five-line poems. And then there is *"Shall I Compare,"* written in the lusty month of July, a mathematical serial blazon: "Each has three step-down stanzas, and each step is made of three words. 3 3 3 = 27." In the attempt "to write with some airy music and lay myself bare as a courtier of the early twenty-first century," Bowering has succeeded, all the more so given that the poem's subject/object was won: "Oh, and the lady and I got married two-thirds of the way through the writing of the poem."

Victor Coleman and the late Roy Kiyooka are the dedicatees of Bowering's book, where in the introduction, the former's *America* (1972) is singled out for its use of acrostics, an early attempt to bring into Canadian letters the kind of "baffles" (Bowering's word) that are perhaps best associated with the collective of playful and serious formal rigorists known as Oulipo. In Coleman's *The Occasional Troubadour*, the form at work is the mesostic, which is like an acrostic except that the spelled-out phrase, rather than being flush with the left, runs through the centre of the lines. John Cage's mesostics may be the most familiar to some readers, poems made by "writing through" texts such as *Finnegans Wake*, *The Cantos*, and *Howl* and selecting lines from them, arranged in such a way as to find the names of their respective authors there. The text being read through in *The Occasional Troubador* is a book from 1898 or so, called *The Troubadours at Home; Their lives and personalities, their songs and their world*, written by Justin Harvey Smith, a decidedly un-Cagean choice in not being a classic but cagier in emphasizing musicality, for the impressive sonority of Coleman is on display here, as ever in his work.

Recommendation can also be made for its humour and humanity, which belie any belief, if any such persists, that arcane stricture is likely to result in a mere clinical procedure of verse; the case is quite the contrary in Coleman's work. Conceptually, the running of names of friends and cultural figures vertically down and through the horizontal lines of the poem is interesting in thinking about the different spatial aspects of both poetry and the reading of it, as well as in considering how a living person can be "found" in lines the existence of which preceded the existence of that person. Of course, more crucial than any such conceptual interest is how there is an otherworldliness to these *Troubadour* poems, one which is remarkably consistent throughout and puts the reader in a strange frame of mind as he moves through their courtly passages. "Laughing long at his keen jests, reflecting his glory, and anticipating his wishes / His figure gained an appearance of height from its thinness / And in the nearer distance the peak towers above the baths / As if drinking of their inexhaustible freshness." Each poem touches on what one of them calls "Beauty of form, of attitude, and of expression[,]" which are "combined / To make an exquisite picture[.]" Mesostics tend to have a quality of randomness surrounding the vertical phrase, but not here. A spectral balance obtains, another example of the skills of sound, form, and feeling owned by Coleman, whom the reader can take as the troubadour of the title without disrupting the spell.

Another of the year's books composed under peculiar stricture is Priscila Uppal's *Winter Sports: Poems*. Under the aegis of the Canadian Athletes Now Fund, Uppal served as poet-in-residence during the 2010 Vancouver Olympic and Paralympic Games. In a preface, the poet describes the initial resistance she encountered regarding the mixing of sports and poetry, not a divide she finds unfordable. She also describes the kind of training necessary for the eventual production of two poems per day during the Games; namely, Uppal familiarized herself with the "rules, histories, judging criteria and terminology" of all the relevant sports, as well as with the stories of various athletes, and also prepared ahead of time a wide range of poetic strategies. The book begins with a parade of countries, just as do the Games themselves; into the alphabetical list Uppal adds athletic jargon: "Finland four-point lands in France / France faces off with Germany / Germany Gundersons to Ghana / Ghana glide waxes to Great Britain / Great Britain goofyfoots to Greece[.]" The alphabet-as-limitation returns in her "Winter Sport Abecedarian":

Amazing bodies congregate:
daredevils emancipating future
glory, hearts intensely juggling
kamikaze leanings, miraculous
notions of perfection, quasi religious
superstitions towards
ultimate velocity, weathered
x-rays yielding zen.

There are a good number of lists, love poems, and haiku. In two poems called "Canada Is the Hockey Ward," one for the men's team and one for the women's (and with parenthetical "nods to Ron MacLean"), puns on the names of the players assert the crazy importance of winning at this sport in particular: "Crosby your fingers. / [ ... ] We Neidermeyer top prize. / Bragging rights must remain here, / No crossing Brodeurs." There is an "Ode to Sliding Sports" that is also an elegy for Nodar Kumaritashvili, whose death in the luge event was a reminder that "games" can be a misnomer, as well as a poem in admiration of Joannie Rochette, to whom "[n]o one had to say, *Get out on that ice*" after her mother died.

The book ends with a double-coda in prose. "Play Like a Paralympian" pays respect to the elite athletes of the Paralympic Games while also claiming a personal connection through the figure of Uppal's father, who was struck quadriplegic in a boating accident in the 1970s. "The Arctic Games Experience" details an amazing array of aboriginal sports competed in by athletes from territories above the fifty-fifth parallel. Take the Kneel Jump, for instance, where "competitors begin on their knees, feet behind them. They can swing their arms, but cannot rock their legs, and then must propel themselves forward, landing on two feet and holding their landing. Scoring is determined by distance. This sport is derived from a survival skill needed for ice fishing. As most would fish on their knees on ice floes, if a floe began to break away, or ice crack, the fisherman would need to jump quickly—in a single action—to a safer spot." This exploration of the esoteric reminds us that not only the Arctic or the Paralympic but also the Olympic Games in general are worthwhile in large part for introducing us to forms of excellence that we would otherwise never notice, as well as for stoking our imaginations in ways that watching out of habit one's hundred-thousandth irrelevant mid-season baseball, basketball, football, or hockey game cannot.

The year was a big one for Uppal. In addition to *Winter Sports*, she also published her sixth major collection, *Traumatology*, as well as *Successful Tragedies: Poems 1998–2010*. The latter, a selection from Bloodaxe Books, is likely meant to introduce her work to a European audience. It is a handsome volume, as well as a generous one, especially for a relatively young poet, with just under 200 pages and just over a gross of poems. In fact, it contains among its selection almost half of *Traumatology*. Not bad value for the money, but what is gained by reading *Traumatology* on its own, in addition to the additional poems, is the sensible division of its parts between sections labeled "Body," "Mind," and "Spirit." Uppal appears before the reader in a variety of guises, but it would be fair to describe her as a confessional humorist, a tendency which may be hereditary. On her mind in the "Mind" section is her family, a compelling and sardonic bunch. In "The Old Debate of Don Quixote vs Sancho Panza," a "large-armed uncle" declares, "The men in this family / are much stupider than the women [ … ] But the women all go crazy." The sentiment is accentuated in "My Mother is One Crazy Bitch." "I Know My Uncle is Dead, But Why Isn't He Taking Out the Garbage" shuffles off this mortal coil a number of relatives, plus a husband and a child for good measure, in creepy-funny fashion. "My Father's South-Asian Canadian Dictionary" dispenses with laughs in favour of devotion. Uppal is good at achieving a flat affect that usually rests in ironic relation to the intensity of her look at self or social mores. Stylistically this flatness is manifest in a mode that can pan as close to prose as to lyric; sonic density is not absent but is less the point than a persistent curiosity and a commitment to deploying common locutions with critical intent. She anthropomorphizes abstractions, turning them into characters: the tired "Soul" gets "dragged onto the elliptical machine"; "Death" is a she who "rang the doorbell twice, / kicked her heels against the concrete / steps and, considerately, brought in" the poet's mail. "Suffering" is not a person but instead is an object, sat on like an exercise ball.

That final image is as good as any in returning us to the link between art and athletics. I await with interest *Summer Sport: Poems*, a companion to her winter book that Uppal promises as poet-in-residence at the 2012 Summer Games in London. In the meantime, we turn to Kerry Ryan and a book about her experience with boxing titled *Vs*. It begins with a quote from A.J. Liebling's *The Sweet Science*: "A boxer, like a writer, must stand alone." It is not an uncommon analogy. Pugilism has an august connection not just to writing in general but to poetry in particular. Liebling himself laid down links to that history in referring to the up-and-comer Cassius Clay as "the poet" (among Liebling's essays on the sport are "Poet and Pedagogue" and "Anti-Poetry Night") and by frequent reference to Pierce Egan, who in his early nineteenth-century *Boxiana* not only noted the verses of "the Lancashire Giant" Bob Gregson but penned some himself for good measure. (The 2003 anthology *Perfect in Their Art: Poems on Boxing from Homer to Ali* paints a picture of the tradition.) Ryan thus enters two rings at once, one in the literary arena and the other as a participant in a "white collar boxing match." She won the latter, which victory culminates the collection; she puts up a solid fight with the poetry, too.

The book is in five sections, each one beginning with a poem named for a kind of punch ("Jab," "Cross," "One-two," "Hook," "Uppercut"). The "Why" section tells us something about the neophyte's personality in the titles "careful" and "tentative," traits that will have to be modified. The theme of how surprising to herself Ryan's burgeoning interest is, how outside her prior sense of literary personhood, is persistent: "This is not the library / not a coffee shop or movie theatre / not any place I belong"; "Never imagined / my name on a fight card / the way I did / a book cover"; "Because you've read too many books [ ... ] // You can't see the punch[.]" She finally owns it, as they say: "But gloved fists say *fighter* / just like words / stacked flush left mean *poem* / no matter how clumsily / they've been placed[.]" In "heavy bag" she approximates the rhythm of punching, while in "gloved" she finds her "hands dumb, / useless except for hammering / a nose flush with a cheekbone," noting how when "[t]ied and taped, you can't pat / sweat from your face, / flick hair from eyes"—a small moment speaking big about the difference between the hard work of boxing and merely working out. There are several such moments, which Ryan does a fine job of distributing along a measured arc of a story, one that sees her being hurt, suppressing fear, gaining skills, noticing a sparring partner's pedagogical control, a trainer's tricks for pricking one's pride. As an account of the education of an amateur boxer, *Vs.* is neither as extended nor as explicit and visceral as Robert Anasi's prose memoir *The Gloves* (which, since we are on the subject, is worth recommending). But for moving from the tendency toward stand-alone pugilist poems to a more dedicated narrative commitment (related to her commitment in the gym and in the ring), Ryan has made a modest place for herself on the boxiana bookshelf.

This brings us back to stricture. In the training Ryan describes, days do not get taken off without setback; when days in the gym lead to months, then you have got something. Bowering's *Nellie Grey* is the year's most extreme and literal example of this idea applied to poetry, but another publication takes the movement of the calendar as a looser model—one might say loosier-goosier, as the book in question is the attractive rerelease of James Reaney's *A Suit of Nettles*, which won the Governor General's Award in 1958. Reaney, who died in 2008, takes Spenser's *Shepheardes Calender*, relocates it to Ontario, and populates it not with shepherds but with geese. After an abecedarian intro abandoned at the letter *n*, an explanatory address to the reader, and an "Invocation to the Muse of Satire," the year begins. We find ourselves "within the goosehouse" where "lived, I know not how, various kinds / of geese[.]" As many kinds of geese as there are, there are more kinds of verse. A January eclogue opens with two geese, Branwell and Mopsus, discussing different kinds of love. (Variety itself is being explored in a variety of ways.) Branwell wears the prickly suit of the title, and we can find reasons for his self-abnegation in February when his fiancée, Dorcas, is found to have double-crossed him.

There follows *"a bardic contest in honour of Spring,"* wry take-downs of "propagandists" and education reformers, and an allegory in which Branwell battles the owl, of whom Mopsus remarks, "To fight that bird were downright folly / For her name is Melancholy." At the funeral of one Scrutumnus (who stands for F.R. Leavis), a ghost appears, having *"been raised after a bout of its favourite activity—putting poems into order of merit."* As the contestant Blot recommends to the mourners in an attempt to honour the deceased critic, "Ladies and gentlemen, after I've sung / These three songs from my leather lung / Establish a preference among the three, / But evaluate judiciously." By any evaluation, John Dong and Edmund Goose are execrable allusive puns, but they fail to detract from what is after all a deliberately ridiculous scene. In September, a wedding takes place and there are carnival rides, but these turn grim: one is "Dante's Inferno & Funhouse," while the merry-go-round has horses modelled on philosophers; to ride one is to hear its philosophy. By October Branwell's *"nettle suit has turned brown & dry with age."* By December—well, not to spoil the ending, but most of the cast await the fate of any Christmas goose: cooked. It is a silly, charming book, set off perfectly by Jim Westergard's sensitive woodcuts.

Also smart and charming, but decidedly less silly, is Tim Bowling's *The Annotated Bee & Me*. This little book responds to an even littler one, as Bowling describes in a preface: "One oyster-coloured winter afternoon not so many years ago, I found in a box of assorted family keep-sakes a thin chapbook written by my Great-Aunt Gladys Muttart and privately printed in 1961. Fifteen faintly-yellowed stapled pages, the back cover coffee-stained, the front cover rather cleverly replicating a cluster of honeycomb, with a hole in one comb revealing a not unskilled pen-and-ink drawing of a little girl sitting on the ground and looking up at the sky [ ... ] The chapbook, whose production remains shrouded in mystery, is a lighthearted, whimsical, though occasionally dark, memoir of my family's beekeeping adventures in Edmonton between 1906 and 1929." Bowling's "annotations" of his great-aunt's book not only speak to the highly specialized occupation of apiculture, they are also meditations on work, on family, on the past. Not devoid of humour, there is still less to laugh about than one might have expected given the premise. In this book based on a book, the smell of old books—the essays of Hazlitt, Maeterlink's *The Life of the Bee*—has a mnemonic effect; memory leads back to meditation: "Days lived are chains / and wings, there is drag and there is flight / gathering the lost self, the old mood. We / labour, sullen and joyous, for the Queen, Time, / and kill her, and choose her, and kill her again." It registers fears, as in "The Worry Poem" and its litany of what will keep you up at night, or in the "Mystery Ailment" that is killing all the bees. In the face of these, the poet does not overstate his control: "I follow / as far as I can, which isn't far—/ in middle life, the range of an ordinary man / is more than the bee's two miles, less / than the salmon's ten thousand." That limited physical distance is countered by one that is temporal, for the past seems far away; yet in a moment it flashes forward in time to sting the present: "From a boy's hand, a bee falls / like a breadcrumb. // My childhood is old now / and I brush it off, but O / the pain in the palm is young." The richness of feeling is matched by the exquisite Gaspereau Press production, where two old and arcane practices, beekeeping and bookmaking, meet.

In Barry Dempster's *Blue Wherever*, we also encounter bees, in this case a swarm of them "buzzing *Pomp and Circumstance*" around the "pink flutters" of some magnolias. The bees in the trees are just a small stinging part of the book's menagerie. They are among the flying things, siblings of the mosquito from "Relentless." These are joined by moths "leaving / dusty streaks on the kitchen floor" as a fatal result of having been invited to Ariel the cat's "private paw-swatting party[.]" Rusty, a second cat who makes an appearance, may also have been invited but was otherwise engaged in messing about with unfortunate robins, caught "with his mouthful / of beak and fluff." Elsewhere another, unmolested "robin pacing across / the frozen grass" agrees with Dempster that the persistence of winter in April is conducive to despair, and the "ladybug echoes her impatience[.]" Mosquito, bee, moth, cat, robin, and ladybug are met by a "beige-bodied / daddy-long-legs," a warbler, a deer, a cedar waxwing, a gull, and a woodpecker whose percussive tenacity "even the grubs can't resist." Dempster's deepest feelings are reserved for Sprout, the gelded hero of "Blindness,"

> one of the castrati, whose head-bends
> beg a bold friendliness. From the left,
> he's suede and apple butter, with
> an emperor's snout, a profile
> fit for a coin. But seen from the right,
> he becomes a missing eye, a long ago
> accident, as if a cage
> had lost its golden bird, or a shrine
> its simple saint.

The poet remarks in "Pastoral" that in "idealizing the beasts again" he is "disowning my humanness[,]" but I'm not so sure; it is rather as if he disowns his idealism regarding animals by idealizing his own human beastliness. "Is it narcissistic to want a / personal relationship with everything?"

The turn from the zoologically-curious, but also self-concerned first section of *Blue Wherever* to its second section is instructive. The poem titled "Tacky" is a tip-off. Its "four-foot plastic Santa tied / to a front yard pine by yellow twine" leads to the eponymous "Office Party" with its "Naked Santa screen savers." The "poet in the corner, probably / a temp" observes all this, just as the poet in the passenger seat of a new Mercedes-Benz observes his friend's "Mid-Life Crisis": "Did I mention the car is the same shade / as cherries soaked in vodka?" As a result of "opening up the way a poet / should" on a bus ride down Yonge Street, the "kinds of conversations / that were once whispered in stairwells or closets" are, thanks to the advent of cell phones, overheard: "*All he wants to do is fuck me.*" These behavioural wastelands are matched by their concrete manifestations in "Wastelands" via "chronic / vistas of strip malls and construction sites, / wind-drummed parking lots and townhouse / jungles." Even something as lovely as a hydrangea "enters the house / in a bubble of cellophane, / blue-mauve hairdo intact." Thus is tackiness shown to be catching. The turn toward the tacky activates an aspect of the book that was there all along but dormant, which is the aesthetic and ethical "tackiness" of all that prior anthropomorphizing and pathetic fallacizing. By the third section, Dempster has picked up too much antithetical energy to settle for synthesis or sweet epiphanies. "There's a Moment in The Restaurant" might lead you to look for the latter, but—take that, Rilke— "You didn't change your life[.]"

The first section of Eve Joseph's *The Secret Signature of Things* is actually named "Menagerie," and so it is: carp, spider, turtle, dog, frog, and birds, birds, birds of different sorts are the subjects of, and give the titles to, the opening poems, and birds, birds, birds wing their way through the book. (They are there at rest as images, too, from the wraparound cover photo of birds on a wire, to those same birds in silhouette inside, to the pictograph from Santee Cave.) It is not, however, a book that approaches, on a lyric continuum, the "pure sound" of birdsong that some poets cherish but can never achieve; despite being a kind of aviary, the collection is not most notable for its sonic effects. Indeed, one of its best poems is called "The Language of Birds" —language, mind you, not song—which has a marvellous beginning: "If one were to interpret the language of birds / one might begin by confessing a fear / of heights[.]" What a notion, that the bird would be afraid of the skill that helps define it. Joseph is good at making you see an animal in a new way, without over-elaborating the encounter and thus draining its charm.

Such transformations occur throughout. In one poem the speaker is reincarnated as a "Violet-Green Swallow." Being that the speaker is a poet, it is not unusual that she sees the swallow's flight in terms of writing: "above the trees // I return // as // script." In a series of prose "Questions" addressed to a personified "poetry," the figure of that return returns: "I want to ask poetry where the birds went when they disappeared and how it was they reappeared in cursive loops like a new language above the daffodil fields one afternoon in late March." This recalls Elizabeth Bishop's "Large Bad Picture," in which "are scribbled hundreds of fine black birds / hanging in *n*'s in banks." Echoes are everywhere in *The Secret Signature of Things*. Although the prose poems are on the whole weaker than the others, insofar as Joseph is at her strongest when sparse diction is accentuated through lineation and there is typographical space in which a tense and muted waitfulness obtains, they nevertheless have the merit of telling us what we are looking at. I was prepared to be critical of the long poem "Tracking," about missing and murdered aboriginal women, given that the possibility for exploitation runs high when poets turn to what in the world is an abyss of suffering but in words may be merely macabre. But the terrible story is decent in the telling, marked less by plot points than by legitimate questions. "Tracking" is foreshadowed by "Halfway World," a sort of diptych or mirror-poem in which two 21-line halves are exact reversals of each other and in which the phrase constituting the hinge or mirror asks, "How will the dead speak?"

That question is just as relevant in relation to Lorri Neilsen Glenn's *Lost Gospels*. The spiritual centerpiece of Neilsen Glenn's book is "Songs for Simone," which attempts to fathom the mysteries of Simone Weil's life and death. "Tell me," the poet requests, "how to speak of you or for you without offering the food of your creed, bread for the bellies of pilgrim spirits wandering alone and far behind? How far can I travel with you?" The answer is only so far, but the poet can be credited with naming the impossibility of the task she has set herself: "I want to offer you something. This is difficult. My words seem inadequate[.]" "I read you and read you, but cannot understand the ferocity of your will." Discomfiting is the direct address to the dead mystic and philosopher, as is the attempt to bring Weil into a context not her own: "Simone, are we fools to hope when snow still flies?" "Travel to Winnipeg with me, Simone[.]" The poem took me back to Anne Carson's "Decreation (An Opera in Three Parts)," where a certain level of familiarity left me unbothered, which led me to wonder if I was being unfair or inconsistent; but the dramatic structure of Carson's approach to Weil provided distance enough that doubts about an assumed intimacy were assuaged. The documentary passages in "Songs for Simone" — "It is August, 1943. The Allied forces are embarrassed to find that the Japanese have slipped away from Kiska before they arrived. Duke Ellington plays Carnegie Hall for the first time. Northwest of Winnipeg, in the town of Neepawa on the Canadian prairies, Peggy Wemyss lands a job as a reporter and applies to United College, her novel about the costs of unflinching conviction still years ahead."—are one way to frame the existence of Weil, but they feel like a diversion from the search for answers. The best parts of the poem are those in which Neilsen Glenn crystallizes aspects of Weil's thought ("The virtue of humility, you say, is nothing more or less than the power of attention."), or quotes her subject ("I find direction in your words: *attention, to its highest degree, is prayer. We must empty ourselves in order to be filled.*"), or expresses her own desires vis-à-vis Weil ("And I realize I am reading you because I am blind, feeling for the walls of belief. I too want belief so deep it will swallow me.").

It would be disingenuous to claim that the book benefits from the fact that its central poem doesn't come off, but then the inability of "Songs for Simone" to achieve an organic wholeness or to reach a satisfying conclusion is not inappropriate given the subject with which it is grappling. The spiritual and intellectual searching, the powerful role of desire, and the honouring of dead and living saints and of others who undergo suffering are maintained throughout *Lost Gospels*. In the title poem, Neilsen Glenn commands and inquires: "So ask yourself: when desire strums you like a fingerboard, what else can you // feel but faith, how it resonates[.]" These words are echoed in a later poem which is in the voice of Marilynne Robinson's *Gilead* protagonist Reverend Ames: "But here, now, I am ready as a tuned string / to witness what is ravenous, mythic." That readiness, that attunement is evident not only in the desire to be spiritually ravished but also in the many moments of empathetic connection, be it with a figure as far away as "Lucy, / in the silt and ash of the ravines / of Ethiopia: hominid, woman[,]" or one as close as the poet's mother, "the hospital bracelet orbiting her wrist" as her daughter dances with her to imagined music.

Steven Heighton's *Patient Frame* is not concerned with saints per se but does see in the world two categories of people: there are the just, then there are the monsters. The book begins with "Another of the Just: Warrant Officer Hugh Thompson, My Lai, 1968" and tells how the title character kept the massacre from being even worse: "down you banked your recon / chopper to light between [Calley] and the enemy // women, toddlers, crones. Ordered your door-gunners / to fire on any comrades who'd resume that riot / of infanticide, mob rape[.]" It is a shocking start to the book, a moral *deus ex machina* that comes *in medias res*. After that the reader's sensitivity is heightened, already jolted into taking seriously questions about what makes us human or what being human might mean. "Breathe Like This" shows "peopled scenes" and notes that "even our quarrels / or stalemate silences are coupling of a kind / and parole from the hellself: cellblock walls / are balsa compared." That evocative "hellself" is matched by other kennings in "Collision" ("eyefar," "heat-feel," "hardpan," "snowlast," "flankflat"), but in "Breathe Like This" it is matched by "that other hour, when my love revives[.]" It makes formal sense that a poem beginning with the line "Each day an hour in heaven, an hour in hell" would be in two distinct parts that also cannot be un-twined. This drawing of a binary that is then synthesized occurs even in dealing with a subject as prosaic as "Jet-lag," which well limns that state: "It's night in your bones though noon." "Some Other Just Ones" closes out the first section, and, among its list of possibilities, none are as heroic as the example of Hugh Thompson with which we began, but which suggests that the reader too could manage to be just.

If such a conclusion is drawn, however, it is only right that the reader ask after reading the next section, "Selected Monsters," if he might be monstrous too. You may not feel implicated by the horrific, maddening self-certainty of "'Thar He,'" a deathbed monologue from one of the unremorseful killers of Emmett Till, nor by "Not the Kind to Die," about the man who murdered a guard at the Holocaust Memorial Museum in Washington, DC. But is there not an off-chance that some part of ourselves exists that is not wholly unlike the Chief Inquisitor Torquemada who starts off "Prayer for Heather," or unlike Cosimo de' Medici in the poem that gives the section its title, looking to pull off a spectacle to thrill Pope Pius II? Certainly none of us have corralled together a lion, a bull, a bloodhound, a gorilla, and a giraffe (a giraffe!) in the hopes of determining which would win a battle to the death—the beasts were wiser than the humans, as none would consent to fight—but have we never been party to a dubious spectacle? The moral calibrations may be finer than they appear at first glance. Poems such as "Herself, Revised" and "Memo to a Self" suggest as much, with the latter recognizing that unfulfillable desire creates an existential dilemma: "Nothing fills the famished chasm." Even an "Election Night Dream, November 2008," which one might expect to be celebratory, concludes that "Really we're a rotten tribe." *Patient Frame* is a worldly book, in terms both of its outlook and of the places the poet has been ("Reading *The Saxon Chronicles* in a Field Hospital, Kandahar"), and in "World Enough" the reader reaches a loaded inquiry: "We own so little / of ourselves, how / did we think to own // anything of the world?" Perhaps the answer to this rhetorical question provokes the council of one of the "Fourteen Approximations" that closes the book— "Learn to live in the self's retreat"—or perhaps it provokes the "Remorse" (a version of a poem by Borges) in which the poet "stand[s] guilty of the worst sin any man / can commit. I've failed to be happy." Yet in the end, "this shadow of having been a man of sighs" is a dark absolution.

That last section of *Patient Frame* is set off with an epigraph from Robert Kroetsch that reads *"Every poem is a failed translation."* In Kroetsch's *Too Bad: Sketches Toward a Self-Portrait*, the last book of his published before his death in June 2011, the poem may not be a translation but a transmission. The book begins with the author "On Tour" and in the studio: "When the radio host said, Now tell us again / who you are, I knew I was in trouble." Fittingly for a book that Kroetsch says is "not an autobiography" but "a gesture toward a self-portrait, which I take to be quite a different kettle of fish," matters of verisimilitude are taken up throughout. "I am not (quite) a convert to truth," he writes in a poem titled after Williams's dictum "no ideas but in things." *Too Bad* at times approaches the nursery rhyme or fable, which in their ostensible simplicity almost deflect the reader's attention from how revelatory these poems can be. ("It was the improvements in mirrors that improved / the portraits of self.") Examples of childhood are matched on the timeline by poems of old age, with the movement between them instantiating the poignancy of maturation: "How do you write a poem about forgetting?" "He tries growing old. His face maps / his terror in delicate lines, a path / to his secret longing. No one takes note." And in this book made exclusively of three-line stanzas, "Time is a kind of poet, writing three-line stanzas / on the blank above our eyes. We read the lines / with our fingers. We rush to the pharmacy. // It's always too late." Lines as wrinkles, lines as time: "I offer these lines to poetic death." One regrets that more time was not granted him and regrets the loss of more lines. There is great pathos and humour here; like the "Country Boy" who gives the title to one of the poems, "His humour is so sad." Yet his "sadness is so funny. Hurtin' / makes him sing, and flirtin' / is his way of putting up a curtain." This last book is a model of plain-spoken storytelling and self-investigation, shot through with wit and delight.

In one of *Too Bad*'s poems, "Terracotta Army," Kroetsch draws on a formal tour taken by himself and six other Canadian writers to China in the summer of 1981. Gary Geddes was also on that trip and in 1984 published *The Terracotta Army*, a sequence of twenty-five poems, nine couplets each, that Geddes calls "Chinese sonnets." Each poem speaks in the voice of one of the 8,000 figures accidentally discovered in Xianyang, a virtual standing army of the afterlife commissioned by Qin Shi Huang, the first emperor of China. An illustrated reprint of the book was released in 2010 to coincide with the Canadian tour of some of those warriors in clay. Geddes's poems take a time-honoured twist on the etymology of ekphrasis, allowing these long-buried statues to "speak out" from their respective positions in the military hierarchy. A "Minister of War" has the historical drop on Machiavelli, seeing "to the depths of [the Emperor's] and all men's hearts, / where artist lies down, at last, with bureaucrat." He "scorned the golden mean of men like Mencius / and learned [his] politics from rats in the latrine[.]" A "Lieutenant" is inordinately proud of his manifold talents in the arts, including the writing of epics and lyrics; he brags while he is modelling. The artist overseeing the enterprise, Lao Bi, is not pleased when a "Regimental Drummer" notes the similarity of Bi to one of his terracotta soldiers; after a night of dancing, drinking, and poetry reciting, the drummer finds himself "winking at the copy instead of the original."

The relation of copy to original is part of the backdrop to *Swimming Ginger*, a new work by Geddes that serves as a companion to *The Terracotta Army*. The book is based on the Qingming Shanghe Tu scroll, said (though this is disputed) to have been painted before 1127 by Zhang Zeduan. Geddes got a copy of the scroll, which is reproduced in the book, on a 2001 trip to China and, impressed by what he calls "its detailed, urban realism," found that "the figures in the painting, and some hidden in the shadows, began to speak to me." As in the earlier book, the characters speak for themselves. There is "The Perfect Son," whose "love-interest...went south" as a result of a "blessed father / insinuating himself into the mix, / beard trimmed in competition." There is "The Storyteller," for whom "Bad taste proved invigorating; / vernacular was music to my ears." There is the "seller of knick-knacks," "chock-a-block / with bric-a brac," who is "at a loss for words," which the poet steps in to provide. Rejecting the hermit's life ("Miserable, / cold, wind blowing up my kazoo"), the bureaucrat's life ("Within six months / I had ulcers, enemies"), and the bucolic life ("up to my nuts in pig shit or bent low / behind an ox's ass and plough"), one character turns *artiste*, which consists not of making art but of getting "[h]igh on the grape[.]" In addition to these narrative annotations of the scroll, the book ends by addressing the poet Qu Yuan (332–296 B.C.) in what Geddes calls "nine swan songs of disengagement," a sardonic finale for a wry sequence.

There is a moment early in Don Coles's *Where We Might Have Been* that fans of the ekphrastic will also appreciate: "A naked body spied under a lifted sheet in the early morning—/ mine, in a Lucian Freud moment." Coles sees the past and the present, but especially *himself*, through art: no apologies, no slick distancing. Other examples abound: there is the moment right upon waking from a dream in which he is "gazing back through gold / like an old king[,]" wearing Schliemann's mask of Agamemnon; or the "WWII photo of a roomful of Lyon's / Corner House waitresses—nippies, they / were called[,]" the detailed description of which leads him to reminisce about the only such restaurant he ever visited. "*Liebespaar von* Dresden" depicts the scene of young lovers in a painting by Conrad Felixmueller, looking behind to the 1928 of its making and ahead from there to the 1944 Allied bombing of the eponymous city: "It's all / very far off from this late afternoon which is / the only glimpse we'll ever have of them. Did they / outlive that distant, thousand-engined, droning / hetacomb?" "Memory, Camus, Beaches" begins with an admission of diminished memory from Camus's *Carnets*, "Which is interesting," Coles writes, "but not blown-away / interesting." As Camus is here, so is Coles—interesting, but not in the way of shock-and-awe monumentality; but you circle back (a form of literary travel the poet facilitates) and find more and more revealed. The sophisticated but unpretentious leisure of the poems allows the reader to settle in and, before she knows how it happened, to find herself deep in some significant mentation, some memorably rendered scene. This is a strangely fearless poetry—brazen even in the piling on of adverbs, flouting a shopworn editorial prohibition—made of what one poem full of epitaphs titles "True Words." Despite being his first new book in a decade, *Where We Might Have Been* is short; but like the title character of the long poem that ends the book, "'Too Tall' Jones," as well as the six-foot-four-inch poet himself, there is much of a muchness here. Coles has a fullness of voice and an ease of intelligence that is remarkable, and as a result, many of his poems are masterpieces of memory and personality.

Like Coles's book, *Memory's Daughter* by Alice Major and *On the Material* by Stephen Collis are also elegiac, working the genre in differing ways. Major's book is an elegy for her parents which makes several relevant shifts in time. Her father and mother are first figured as "Baucis and Philemon," and she writes less as daughter than as one of many observers (it ends with "we remembered"): "Transformations started first with him, / the husband. / Tangles and thickets grew inside his brain," which the wife "could only watch // in sorrow, unaware of what was growing / in herself—burl / and wormhole in her lungs, their smooth sponge gnarled / by knot and whorl, / canker and gall." The section *"Eve learns endearments"* takes us back further, as Major is symbolically the first woman on earth, looking for accurate words. It also takes us forward, to a contemporary moment of temptation: *"You could put him in a home. / The serpent makes a sibilant / kind of sense."* In this unfortunate Eden, her father, unlike his poet-daughter, cannot find accurate words. The next section takes us back again just slightly, to the beginnings of her father's diminished capacities, to moments as specific as a doctor's prognosis and as general as a changing rhythm of the mind. The longest (and central) section imagines the difficult youth of her parents, exemplified in "My Mother As History" by the response to a too-easy turn to nostalgia, a transformation to which her mother will not yield: *"That's not history,* she says, on edge / with insult. *I remember when they brought / power to the orphanage."* A few poems later we now see pictures of her mother, among them a "Chest X-Ray" and a "CT Scan of Lungs," images of incipient death and sadness, an emotion quietly plumbed in the "Lullaby for My Mother" that follows them. The sonnets, *"Metamorphoses,"* and alchemically-oriented ghazals that close the book give a sense of the formal facility found throughout.

The sequence with which Stephen Collis closes *On the Material* is titled "Gail's Books" and it, too, is terribly sad. The title refers to Collis's sister, who died young of cancer, and to her books, those that her brother had borrowed over the years or squirreled away right after her death as well as those that burned when Gail's house caught fire a month after her passing: "Her study and books destroyed the firemen having cast the burning volumes through broken windows into a yard of rain and darkness. Many land in a small fish pond where I find them blackened soaked and crumbling the next morning. Only one book is recoverable." It seems a final cosmic indignity, but Collis's attempt to "recover" not only these material objects but his sister's material presence has the dignity of classical elegy. He takes an epigraph from Michael Palmer and shares the spare, haunted seriousness of that poet, but the ultimate voice is his own; a line such as "To catch hummingbirds hand and an ossuary of sorts" suggests the difficult task set before him of catching in words the moving memories of a beloved sibling, collecting those parts of her still extant that are sanctified through secular grief and love. The task is one Collis is fit for, for it is Collis's structural strength to take parts and put them together, as in the four-quatrain poems that make up most of "4x4," the book's first section. Sometimes, in fact, those poems are *about* how things are put together: "Parataxis is as simple as / McDonald's / Subway / Mac's / What narratives do we need / If all we are doing is eating?" In the battle between "The poison in my body in the globe" and "the mindset that thinks / If it can be done it should be done," the poet asks, "Is this poem helping at all?" The pressure he puts on *poiesis* is not hectoring, self-sanctifying, or an elaborate dodge of the responsibility to make viable poems. "Limits are what we are combined of / But where there is a boundary / There is also a beyondery / Like *I-fought-the-lyric-and-the-lyric-won*[.]" That italicized appropriation of song may suggest that the lyric is law; but here, as we are told, the law of lyric is just a limit to be pushed beyond. The phrase gives its name to the book's central section where the problems raised earlier are delved into most deeply: "Is making itself / the problem?" If so, let us absolve Collis, who has written one of the finest books of 2010.

 The same thing can be said about Margaret Christakos's *Welling*. In last year's well-chosen anthology *Regreen: New Canadian Ecological Poetry*, Christakos's long poem "Wellington" was my favourite among many. It now reappears in the present volume as the (almost) title poem. Wellington is Sudbury's Wellington Heights, where the poet was raised; it is both topographical place and lingered-over place name: "Like in its name there are three suckable bends / en route to the summit." "A mountain of three notes, // ascending serious redundant turns, and packing a blown, / unlovable view of its whole self: Wellington." Williams's *Paterson* comes to mind, as this poem too invests in a place a range of figurative energies. The synecdochic understanding of the place as its high point increases not distance but proximity, and in the travelling up, down, from, to, and around it, two things are achieved: first, the autobiographical aspect is accentuated, and the changes in a life are given an ambulatory objective correlative; second, the poem embodies motion in a way that shades into emotion, and the "tenacity" that the place "encourages" is also felt in the recourse to considerations of love and hate and work throughout. (In an insightful online review of *Welling* in *The Puritan*, E. Martin Nolan at one point focuses on such movement and does a better job than I can do of considering it in terms of the volume as a whole.) This second aspect is already figured in the title of another of the book's sections, "Motional," and there is a registering of kinds of difficulty elsewhere, such as in "Beach," in which Christakos finds herself "starting // to know how to parent can be torturous / like the most jealous love affair, or // the drawn-out celibate winter after love / or dissolve of a love altogether." Another hardship is the fact that "Too much happens of anything // to report or order[,]" but here the ordering is so devoid of stasis that we feel we can trust it. At any rate, "It's not just nostalgia," she writes, "& poor driving. Some of life // is time deciding at which stop // to get off." In "The problem of confessionality," my favourite section of the book, Christakos creates a meta-poem of high order; its insights into the difference between pure sounds and coded words (as well as its sexuality) are handled with humour and the intelligence, both formal and existential, that characterizes her work. One senses that this poet will suffer codes, sounds, and even cities—but not fools—gladly, or if not gladly, then smartly, sharply, tenaciously, lyrically.

At one point in Christakos's "problem," a character—human siren or figuratively full robin?—maybe "just / dropped by to check your / facebook status, chortle / for a moment, tweet at you." The "confessionality" of the computer speaks in manifold ways. In *Bardy Google*, Frank Davey turns to the dominant Internet search engine to power a series of prose poems. Well, he doesn't call them prose poems. They are "texts," and because "search engine priorities [...] change continuously, these texts are unrepeatable." Unrepeatable but determined by repetition, insofar as each is marked by the same word or words popping up over and over. Also significant is that they pop up amid sentences rather than fragments, which Davey explains as "part of my ongoing work to use the sentence as the basic structural unit of poetry—to create poetic texts, as they have always been created, out of the materials of prose. They also constitute another of my forays into cultural commentary." I may be predisposed to see the fruits of that commentary as an indictment when it could well be intended as otherwise. It doesn't seem like a celebration, at any rate. With some distance one might say that an overt judgment on our current culture is not the point, or that the book's readers have to do the judging for themselves: "Nothing gold can stay. That is why you should make every effort to stay legitimate and include only materials you have the rights to use. Renault's chief executive Carlos Ghosen says the French manufacturer is planning to stay in Formula One for many years despite their slump in form. How do you stay teen? Even though the magnitude of the disaster will be enormous, people just can't stay alert for 200 years. It goes against human nature." So "stay" is the spindle around which the thread of this text is spun. You could manage a reading of this passage that has to do with modernism as post-romanticism, a rejection of which is an unnatural disaster or is necessary for staying young or for growing (or a disaster which leads to new growth through death); or a comment on the vicissitudes of form; or even, in the confluence of the Frost quote and the "teen" question, some reconsideration of the movie version of *The Outsiders*.

Okay, that last one is a stretch. But maybe any reading of this sort would be a stretch. First of all, I cherry-picked the excerpt; there is plenty of other verbiage to be accounted for around the search term. Second of all, here is Davey in a text titled "Surviving the Paraphrase": "If the sense of the poem's resonance surviving its paraphrase holds, then one might just start on a road leading to the naif's conclusion that the poem just is, just rings in our hearts, and that most exegesis is spurious." But of course this is not really Davey—the Internet wrote it; or did it? He and a search engine collaborated to generate that sentence; they both "chose" it. Either way, we might come to the above-named naif's conclusion that exegesis is spurious; but then what would that tell us about the preconditions we impose on the poem that are necessary to produce a viable exegesis or about what we mean by a paraphrase? These texts, for instance, cannot be adequately paraphrased, if to paraphrase is to re-narrate the poem as prose—they are prose already.

Whereas Davey's poems end up being less random than you would expect, in *The Little Seamstress* Phil Hall makes you feel as if you have stepped into an even weirder, arbitrarier Internet of words: "To stage *The World*—cast the audience / reduce its role to one word—in English of course // *rhubarb rhubarb rhubarb rhubarb rhubarb* // so it sounds like the extras are talking to each other / in the crowded streets & arenas—but they aren't // to get real— then—might mean to heckle reruns of *The World* / through the frayed weave of an antique Alphabet Sampler[.]" In "The Alphabet" the poet comes clean: "I tried to be that funny friend / who always has something interesting to say / & makes a lot of sense—but is also a bit of a wing-nut[.]" Although he is funny, interesting, and a wing-nut, in a way this is not wholly about him, perhaps, insofar as he may make sense (he often does) but not "a lot" of it: "beak-regal," "guck," "blizzard memo pom-pom," and *"gup guff hum flummery"* are eruptions of words or sounds that swerve away from denotation. What is happening, though, is that sound is being taken too far in an attempt to find sense in sound itself, a poetry of reaching and pushing past limits: "tongue-creature in mouth-cave grunting *unh-unh*[,]" "this roar / oar / ar / r's inner platelets and folio-shades[,]" *"my great story / migratory*[.]" We are not meant merely to hear but "To Listen": "they lean forward—kids do / when you read to them— they *list* / they know how to listen // but adults think of things they have to do / they lean back—tick off items on a list / while you read[.]" In "Folding-Fork" we find a figure for what we are reading ("It has become a metaphor of the kind of poem that turns on itself to make emptiness sing"), and in "Tinguely" the poet gives us an apt image to settle on amid the strangeness and sonic sensuality: "I—we—why // want my tiny word-machines to / falter burn & self-destruct / like Jean Tinguely sculpture-devices—wonky / enough to deserve to be treated as if / they are alive / & dying[.]" This is fair and self-explanatory in its successfully faltering, afire, and self-destructive way; you leave each poem with a crease in your brow but smiling, prepared to wind up the word-machine and try again.

The do-over, the change, the fresh start: all of these fuel dreams in *The Philosophy of As If* by Fraser Sutherland. In a section titled "If Wishes Were Horses," he wants on certain days "to begin again / in some stranger-city, to drift into a bar / secretive and self-contained, my whole past / packed inside me like a bomb." His desire is to be an unknown man in an "unknown / city, free of personal associations[,]" but he carries his personal history in a way that makes him a home-grown suicide bomber of memory. In "Texture," Sutherland imagines instead being on the other side of the law: "I would like to become a cop. / It would give my life some meaning." He would like to be a lot of things, "would like to have a dozen lives, each one different." The "as if" or what might have been can seep into a poem to the extent that what actually *is* becomes confused, as in "Punch": "The other day on the sidewalk / a stranger punched me in the mouth. / I never found out why—/ I wasn't talking on a cellphone. / Maybe it was an *acte gratuit* / or a rage against the universe / or he didn't like the way I looked / or he got up on the wrong side of the bed / or he didn't have a bed / or from undifferentiated malignity." So many options, so little certainty; a good deal of sympathy, even if the whole scenario is imaginary: "Many times I wanted to punch a stranger / and couldn't have said why. / No stranger punched me. / None of this happened." The demeanor of the speaker in many of these poems is not personable; there is gruffness on occasion and, in a poem such as "Replies to a Little Girl in the Back Seat of a Car That Draws Up Beside Me At a Bus Stop on a Chilly Night in March Whose Smiling Mother Calls Out, 'She Thinks You're Santa Claus!,'" a smart aleck lurks behind every imagined response.

Ultimately, though, the reader is almost drawn to Sutherland's personality, divining the insecurity beneath the armour. "Yet it's true I am fishing for a compliment," he writes in "Explanation," "though I fail to specify what it is that I require." Speaking "From a Hospital Bed," the poet in his frailty gives a gentle gift of apology: "Since, in my hurting, I hurt you, / forgive me." When up and at 'em, this is a man you might well want to talk to, and much conviviality is on display. The book begins with "A Party," and there is time spent talking in bars; and "at 3 a.m. in the Kam Kuk Yuen," the poet and two friends "talk and talk and talk" over barbecue, rice, and tea; and "sitting in a busy deli north on Bathurst Street" with a pal, the poet sees in a family of fellow diners a tale begin to unfold, a story which "could have several outcomes"; and in "Patience" the poet notices a bundled-up girl "sitting near / the door of the Wok & Noodle, which admits icy drafts." These moments of friendly conversation and voyeuristic vision prepare the way for the long, final poem "And All Shall Be Redeemed," consisting of around 220 anaphorically arranged statements of prophetic possibility: "and first attraction shall be final attention, and elective affinities arrange marriages"; "and we shall escape being self-lessly dedicated to the discomfort of others"; "and the lump of fear in the throat, the waiting for news bad or belligerent, shall dissolve[.]" Each "and" introduces yet another manifestation of the desire for things to change, each one a speech act that in a perfect world would conjure a beginning again.

Beginnings of another sort are treated by Paul Vermeersch in his fourth volume, *The Reinvention of the Human Hand*. The book begins with "The Painted Beasts of Lascaux," the discovery of which "has been a kind of homecoming, too." The poem "Ape" takes us back further, imagining even more distant origins. But the connection drawn is neither simple nor comforting. The coexistence of us and our predecessors is troubling, maybe impossible; so too the existence of those aspects of our predecessors still found within ourselves. The former is demonstrated when the eponymous "Ape" (based on a real gorilla named Michael) recalls the poaching of his mother; the latter is symbolized in "Twenty-One Days With a Baboon Heart" by its dedicatee, Baby Fae: "When one of their hearts was fixed inside / an infant girl, in Orwell's year, how long / do you suppose she survived with their terror?"

Vermeersch is a measured poet, both in tone and in diction—there is nary a word out of place—so such moments of terror are particularly disturbing. One comes to him in "Hands" against his conscious will:

> But my bed was soft and my back
> ached from the excess of comfort.
> Each night, the dreams grew worse.
> I saw, severed from their body,
> the heavy, black hands
> of a mountain silverback.
> It felt like wires tightening
> around my wrists as I slept.

In "Beautiful and Swift," those animals under threat of death and those cave-painters the collection began with meet: "The business of killing things, / the hunter knows, is difficult / because of beauty and swiftness, / because his quarry astounds him / with its grace, and then it's gone." The cave-painters, in both their hunting and their painting, are a version of the poet: "In preparation, he makes an image / on the wall and speaks the word." More recent images are also treated, from Jan Asselyn's *The Threatened Swan* to those of Bosch and Van Gogh, from "A Photograph of the Human Retina" to Bugs Bunny, Daffy Duck, and Wile E. Coyote. Monologues from this latter trio of characters make up "Three Anthropomorphic Studies," which, in addition to being entertaining, are interesting on the one hand for anthropomorphizing not an animal but a cartoon (itself already an anthropomorphizing) and on the other for asserting the relation of animation to matters of the hand. This organicism in terms of parts relating to the whole is a strength, and as a group of poems the book makes sense. The distance travelled between "Ode to *Amoeba Proteus*" and "This Is Where Your Life Begins" (a close-up of hands manipulating a video-game controller) is both vast and minute; so too the distance between the historical sweep of biological life and the personal obsessions of the poet. This is a finely wrought collection marked by its balance of emotions and backstories, which is really a balance of stanzas, lines, words.

At the risk of contradiction, perhaps the most notable quality of Tammy Armstrong's *The Scare in the Crow* (also her fourth volume) is its sense of imbalance. This partly results from the fact that the poems are always in motion, travelling from one place to the next in unpredictable patterns. The trip to the Eaton Centre to see Michael Snow's installation is just as much a journey as to a lagoon in Iceland, but of course they could hardly be equal, could they? They are equal in the poems, an equality strangely slanted toward de-emphasizing difference. One can travel far away and find that one has hardly left home, a situation overheard as "the pub here, at the Arctic Circle, / plays *Sweet Home Alabama*"– whose creators, incidentally, came not from Alabama but from Florida, site of the book's longest poem, "Beauty to the Alligator's Beast," which takes the reader back into a past of feather-trading but makes it seem like the present through a mostly believable first-person voice in prose: "I'll admit we weren't sent to kill the pelicans at first, but did it in the off hours, fashioned their satchels into tobacco purses, before returning to cull the plume quarries... Still I make time to watch the geese fletch a chorus outside of the mean, toward rigour pointed south—my Florida." Or imagine, as in "Speak Softly, Low One," a "swing-shift living room / with only the equalizer lights shifting frequency, // a guitar's thumb-picking about elsewhere: / something left standing in Tecumseh valley or Tuscaloosa. / All that stateside mapping where things are apt to happen." The shift from the "swing-shift" room with its "shifting" lights to an "elsewhere" conjured by sound is a shift also made by that last sentence and its "mapping/apt/happen" mellifluence. It is finally less the movement from place to place than it is between levels of diction and sound that gives *The Scare in the Crow* its off-kilter interest.

It is a ubiquitous bird. In her debut, *The Crow's Vow*, Susan Briscoe moves us through the changing of the seasons as she also moves us through the ending of a marriage. This latter change is dampened, manifest in descriptions of the natural world. It is a temperate volume, both in its treatment of love's dissolution and in its form. Just as the changing of the seasons is an immutable fact, the changing of the relationship is rendered in a way that stays consistent. The unrhymed couplets, five per poem, sixteen poems per seasonal shift, bring a visual stability and a balance of sequence to the emotional upheaval. We begin with "Winter into Spring," when the cold seems unliveable but isn't. The tension of change meeting constancy is figured in a conceit of sound and silence. One poem begins with "Satie's black lines on white, / songs like winter forms[,]" and the composer seems a good choice given the quiet and solemn repetitions of Briscoe. (Satie's playfulness is not what is valued here.) But there is something quieter even than this, quiet but not uncommunicative: "What is left unsaid // becomes an affirmation." "We have learned nothing / from the songbirds. // You have brought me shiny bits / and baubles [ … ] // But not once have you danced, / and I have yet to hear you sing." The move from "Spring into Summer" is hardly less so, for although "You / resist, want this to be easier[,]" it is not: "There is no echo / of slammed door. No, you slip out so quietly[.]" By "Summer into Fall," Briscoe has suffered an emotional amputation, though the phantom limb that haunts her is not her own, nor would she have it reattached if she could: "All night I've held to my side, wished // a forgetful arm around my waist, / if only to shrug it off." Passing each other on a bridge, the couple are finished: "It's already over," she says, but still has to hear, "'You're smart; this shouldn't be hard.'" (As if "smart" had a thing to do with it.) Over time, the old "you" is replaced by a new "you," one not overdetermined by disquieting quietude. A shoveled driveway—we have entered "Fall into Winter"— "clear[s] a space for your arrival." Now, that which indeed is quiet is calm, no longer a figure for lack: "Still night in the morning, you / still beside me." And we are back in a world of snow, the same world and different, having come to the end of a volume effective in its reticence and tracing of cycles.

Another kind of cycle is the reason for Ariel Gordon's *Hump*, which is a book big with child in its middle section. Come to think of it, that is the sort of pun of which Gordon might approve; she does not object to them in general: "I hafta admit, Baby, this is a stretch"; "two-stepping down the hall in the dark of this body / to empty a bladder hardly big enough for a princess' pea"; "mum's drunk with the spirit of moving on"; "he uses the sharp blade / of his shoulder to get by her" (this last describing a robbery at knifepoint in a laundromat). I was eager to get to the poems that take the reader from "Two months: moving day" to "Three months: morning sickness" to "Five months: all knocked up" to "Six months: in the bath" and on through the rest of gestation. The fifteen poems preceding the depiction of a pregnancy's progress do, however, have their place. For one thing, they are often romantic. Gordon's frequent invocation of "my love" is just tongue-in-cheek enough to make it consistent with her demeanour elsewhere. Sweet is the way in which she attends to her partner in bed: "My love invents new languages in his sleep," she writes in "Somniloquy," while in "Pre-conception" (the last poem before the pregnancy) the twitching and jerking and easing and stretching of the lovers' limbs under covers, the search for heat or for cold beneath or outside of them is cute and recognizable, made easier to imagine by the inelegant turning of the syntax and the cluster of similar sounds. It ends in a vision both scary and heartening, but surely just a dream of which only the good parts will prove prophetic. Once conceived, the baby initiates a journey for the mother from the "ba da bump" to "ultrasound introductions" to "what to expect when you're expecting" to "swelling & swollen" to "what you may be concerned about," which provokes a strong response: "Concerned? I'm ham-hocked, fat-ankled / & groggy."

Once the child is born, there is a good deal of noise. In "Chorus" (aptly named), three stanzas begin, "You squawk," "You squawk," "You squawk." A "heavy tit" and a "giant tit" bring temporary silence. (Gordon puts to good use a number of blunt monosyllables: conk, suck, tit, squawk, hump.) There is a "wet howl," and "shrieking" during car rides, when "Syllables batter against the rear-view, cling / to the meat of my earlobes / still half-a-city from home." There are moments of change well-noted, such as when "you move from sound asleep / to salty anguish // in one breath." The poem "A year in: mash note" once again carries a pun in its title and is directed from mother to child with an aggressive kind of love: "You are my savviest lover, crawling into my lap &

mashing me with gummy smiles while you weigh your options." Baby as savvy lover and weigher of options, a degenerate and desperate addict; as an adult in having "had" its mother, a teenager in its selfish and painful overscoring of flaws that the mother gained only on behalf of the child; as a child making its mother into nothing but a pump: not just the subject but the sounds in which all this is depicted have a barely restrained violence to them. There is not a deficit of love, perhaps, but rather a disinclination to misrepresent frustration and exhaustion. Characteristically, though, as we saw under the covers earlier, Gordon can represent sleep; the book ends with a mother less shaken, a baby un-stirred.

 A mother and her child are also at the centre of Ian Williams's debut *You Know Who You Are*, but in this case the child is a teenage son who, having a pregnant girlfriend, is about to take on adult duties. The teenage son's name is Dre and the speaker is his mother, in a series called "Emergency Codes." Codes lead to a "Coda" with an ending I won't spoil, but in between Williams develops a persona, speaks in a voice belonging to a woman who is convincing in her refusal to give in to nonsense and poignant in her protection, not suffocation, of her child. "Don't be stupid. He wasn't born in jail." So warned are any grown-ups who take at face value Dre's bragging of fights, solitary confinement, and time tallied behind bars. His mother reworks the conceit; preceding Dre's time "at Spruce Lake K-8," which is whence his stories came, "he spent nine months locked up / in me." Just thereafter she asks, "What of the fatherless?" The answer says much about her stance toward the world in relation to her son: *"After all you only mine."* In "Code Purple: Child Abduction," an ungenerous teacher with an overactive eye for critique, which settles on Dre's dark skin and his cornrows, is critiqued herself: "She best stick // to teaching and leave off hairdressing / and psychotherapy: *Would you prefer / to sit quietly there or join us and sing? / /* and *We don't use words like that here* and / *Inside voice* finger to her lip. She wrong / to make him think he got a choice."

 Dre finds work but gets fired, sometimes for "nothing much. Sometimes for nothing." This makes it no easier keeping him straight: *"Not in my house*, I said when he lost / his job again and took up hunting // weed." When Williams writes (or when his persona speaks) that Dre "spits a language that only grows (explosive) and grows (extinct)[,]" he is not only referring to the slang Dre uses but is seeing in that language a figure for the son himself. He, too, "grows...and grows," and his own subconscious tricks him toward potential extinction: "He dreams of it / many times / being shot [ ... ] // That's what he wants—/ that and his name like an ice cube in everyone's cheek[.]" The most moving moment is one near the end of the sequence when Dre's mother mixes resignation and calculation, before referring to her own turn of phrase: "I get sixteen years on and off with him / before someone else gets him. By *gets him* / you know what I mean." Maybe, maybe not—as it turns out, she implies a lot in those two italicized words, and the ambiguous gulfs between peaks of possible meaning range in their nature from pits of despondency to plains of contentment. One of the strengths of the series is how Williams sets the stage for moments that speak loudly but efficiently. What is not there is not elliptical, exactly, because what *is* there renders extremely full whatever goes only suggested or unspoken.

One of the "Codes," subtitled "Medical Emergency (Pediatric)," begins bemusedly and lovingly with a story registering childhood's serious silliness: "When Dre was about nine he and a friend / tried to pierce their ears with a thumbtack / and a stapler. Quick. Where Dr. Huxtable at? / *Boys.* I tell you." The ending begins with a turn (the poem is a slightly disguised sonnet): "It's time to blame someone. / Not Dre or his friend or the school system, / the government, sitcoms, hip hop videos, / the streets, whatever. I don't blame myself either. // That leaves you. Maybe I blame you a little. / Because. You. Should have." Those final two lines lead us outside the story of Dre and his mother and into an overarching concern of the book, which is defining the union and disjunction of the first- and second-person. (This is indicated even on the cover, where the letters *I* and *U* are as orangey-red as the single ice cube falling among a cascade of bluish brethren.) A great flexibility is thus available to the poems, insofar as the "I" and "you" can suggest a conversation between the poet and himself, or suggest the poet addressing the reader; matters of racial and social identity are raised; and relationships between people, and between people and the words that describe and delimit them, are thought upon.

Often these concerns are filtered through contemporary communication technologies, which have the interesting effect of both increasing and diminishing intimacy. After a series of opening epigraphs that establish the volume's location at the crossroads where pronouns meet identities, a preliminary poem finds us eavesdropping on a recorded phone call that has been left unheard to the point of overripening: "Now you understand / why I got back to you so late. I ignored the call for days, / the voicemail icon at the top of the display, / ignored the options *Listen Dismiss*, the area code, / the last four digits I miss. And why, when I finally could, I couldn't / listen to the last part *Anybody could love you* of your message, / *look at you* the part you whispered *look at your face* without hearing / something like a newspaper shake. // You could be anybody." The broken-up nature of these lines, with the speaker's thoughts cut through with parts of the message from "you," marks a strong start to the book; it is not a loud beginning, but it asserts that the emotional stakes are high. The power of the last sentence lies in the contrast between its sparse diction and the ambiguities contained therein.

There is a funny scene shortly thereafter when *The Terminator* is alluded to and "you rode 20 km along the Don Valley Parkway to tell me / in person *I've decided to make myself into a machine.*" The sense persists throughout that it is rather the machines that are remaking us. "Recalculating, Recalculating" is another comic turn, in which the speaker, who is driving, gently argues with his "churchlady" passenger, in her "sixties," about the directions they are being given: "You should listen to the GPS man, / she says *Turn right* and dropping her voice, / He sounds irritated." She looks toward the sky but knows the voice does not derive from there; she guesses that it is coming to them live from Delhi. Williams is good at using syntax to his advantage, forcing it from its normal purpose of logic-through-composition and into a mode whereby logics are competing. He also reconfigures the ellipsis in both typographical and existential terms in "Buffering, A Sonnet," where instead of that quaint little trio of periods, we are constantly interrupted by a circle of polka dots moving in Ferris Wheel motion. If the conventional ellipsis is a poetic place for meditative pause, the ellipsis of buffering is a place impatiently to wait, where the only thing being "thought" is whatever comes next. Williams has written a book well worth coming back to, multivalent less in its answers than in the fecundity of its questioning: "You? / I mean I." "You? / No, you." The reader will find himself trying to map his relationship with the author, as well as reaching for an understanding of himself, which never settles down into singularity.

If the status of the "I" in relation to itself and to others is at stake in Williams, it is perhaps even more central to Ray Hsu's *Cold Sleep Permanent Afternoon.*

Hsu's experiments take as their materials the vicissitudes of grammar—the book's two sections are divided into "Plural" and "Singular"—and, like Auden's crack in the teacup, the difference between the "I" and the "we" can move from a minuscule space to a widening gulf in a split second. The poems have titles (which tend to be repeated) such as "Angel," "Atrium," "Border," "Chorus," "Citizen," "King," "Narrator," "[Offstage]," "[Onstage]," and "Ventricle," which suggest that this sequence of poems is at essence a drama. They also suggest that in the treatment of grammatical borders, in the mapping of kinds of personhood through language, we will encounter versions of power both sublunary and transcendental, variations of self, individual and collective, structures of spirit, internal and external. We begin the drama with "a gravedigger" in a "deep hole in the middle of nowhere," speaking to us of scraps, a figure serving as one half of a pair of comic bookends, the other half to which we will return.

Despite this beginning, humorous notes are rare. If we cannot be certain, we can certainly be serious, and there is an effective solemnity here. Considering personhood and power, Hsu is also considering suffering in its many guises. In an effort to "gain Tamil Eelam," and in anticipation of losses of "over 8,000" in "this next round" of fighting (which is what "we expect"), a mother is coldly terrorized by "our recruitment / drive," which "we have pushed" to her city. The pronouns do awful work: "You must have already / received the letter with our request. // His studies are important, / but our war is urgent. Education // comes later. If we knock / and you do not come // we will use / the roof. A month from now, // grown ill, finally broken, / he will lose his mother as you lost him. Somehow // he will escape custody and reach / Vavuniya. Or Colombo. His sister will be taken // as your married son was. In any event, / for now, we ask for two // unmarried ones. Perhaps you / will fear for your son, so grown, // if you don't hand over those two." Collective power speaks here in the split-tongued hiss of intimidation and foregone conclusions. Not every such exercise occurs in a literal war zone, as the "Chorus" explains in a poem for which the epigraph (*"beauty for ashes"*) comes from the "master builder" Robert Moses: "We saw the expressway express / your power concretely. One G.I. Bill later / homebuyers found homes / where ours were [ ... ] / We mind./ Never mind / they said."

Such moments of political valence provide ballast for the book and remind the reader (if he needed reminding) that what is at stake is not "merely" language. Thusly saturated with real-world relevance, certain turns of phrase become more than metalinguistic riddles: "We are unique. Aren't I?" "This us is our art, is us and isn't." "I you / he she it: who knows." "That isn't they." "More than anyone you refuse / to be yourself." One of the "Citizen" poems begins with Frost's "*on a day we meet to walk*" from "Mending Wall" and runs in its entirety:

> between you and me does not allow us
> to be us. You demand to be you. To be useful,
> be yourself. We are you and me
> all day. We take care of each other.
> We are worried about you and me.

As a concise gloss on the Frost poem, it has a certain strength. In addition to how it divides (or reduces) the two wall-menders into "you," "me," "us," and "we," it also, when read alongside some of the book's other poems, asserts as central to the Frost poem that the exchange is taking place in a (misguidedly) divided field. The notion of "field" is crucial to Hsu's understanding not only of the way we compartmentalize experience and meaning but also of the way we situate ourselves or find ourselves situated. Personhood is radically contingent, an existential composition-by-field that was at the very least (among Hsu's potential progenitors) implicit in Olson (in this sense, the latter's "Projective Verse" and "A Plan for a Curriculum of the Soul" are of a piece) and is also argued for most recently by, among others, the L=A=N=G=U=A=G=E poets, spurred in part by poststructuralist insights, echoes of which one can hear in lines by Hsu such as "One morning language thought me" and "Carry within yourself secret police." Perhaps even to try to locate the origins of such concerns and the standard ways of expressing them is redundant at this point. For any young poet with an avant-garde, academic, political sensibility, this is the *lingua franca* at his disposal, like a waterfowl winging toward God was for Bryant.

The real question regarding such language is what gets done with it. It is impressive how Hsu worries his terms. Returning to "field," for instance: "Enough can remind you you exist. / Listen. / In your mind you draw a field // where the suffering go." "This is how I picture it. There / is a field that // I would have drawn [ ... ] // This field / walks through me. It / weighs barely anything. // I thought I had gotten rid of everything. // But the field." "Whoever finds me in a field / I will envy like the balance of a cold sleep or a permanent afternoon." Just as the language in which we think that we think in fact thinks us, we think that we walk through the field, but the field plows us. Befitting a book that turns several times to the "Border," one crucial "field" is the categorical kind one must fit into on documents. We encounter these latter objects of delimitation more than once, sometimes making imperious demands, sometimes in redacted form. There are signs of a liveable life, perhaps—Is the bird flitting through the book a sign of freedom, a creature that might mirror the lyric qualities of which the book is not absent? Are the scenes in the kitchen and other domestic moments meant to bring some warmth to the "cold sleep" of the title? I am wary of saying so, not wanting to seem like a sucker in the face of a very knowing volume. Yet the volume, which itself provokes my hesitancy ("Are you fooling me? What kind of openness am I looking for?"), also validates my desire to find some point of recuperation. For every deflation of some commonly held value ("What others / mistake for my integrity / they know now is just a body / we bring under control." "I am divided as to what / I think you'll sacrifice for me. / I say it takes patience and hysterical / discipline. Within earshot I've lied / about chastity[.]"), there is a tacit admission that we want to be human and want to be so together: "How others carry on this task / of being human shouldn't be beyond me." Elsewhere: "*Hurry home,* / we say from our sincere directions / so we can escape / being alone." A gentle and welcome finale, but there is still that other bookend; in this case, a return to documents but not the over-deterministic sort from before. No, this is an extremely rational, unpushy, and well-spoken discourse on the nature of the archive—the purpose of it, the principles of its selection and ordering, the role of donors in its maintenance. The stage direction reads: "[*A dumpster. Someone stands inside.*]" I laughed out loud when I read it.

From considerations of pronominal identities straight-faced but framed by comic scenes, we turn to a book that treats the past and the present in the solemnest of ways. To describe poetry as "the spontaneous overflow of powerful emotions recollected in tranquility" is to foreground the twofold temporality of a poem without necessarily making a problem of it. Johanna Skibsrud finds the matter far from settled. In her second collection, *I Do Not Think That*

*I Could Love a Human Being*, one might at first mistake the writer's present as a position of tranquility, so low-wattage is the figurative energy, metaphor unnervingly muted. On further consideration, the tone conveys something more like traumatization, a kind of existential shell shock. To open, the speaker sits on a boat with Ed, among other friends, hearing stories and getting ready to row. But a set of indented verses calls us to a different preparedness: "Remember, // I write this poem with nearly / five months retrospect, and so // I know that Ed is dead now [ ... ] / Which begs the question: / Why write this poem in present tense, / knowing what I know?" Next, through the conjuring of a verb, Ed is resurrected: "Leaning again into his oar, Ed says: / *It felt too good to go out there to turn back home.*" Elsewhere he mimics the cartoon character Wimpy: "*I'll pay you Tuesday, for a hamburger today,* / he says, bowing." In both cases, Ed's reported speech is related to Skibsrud's dilemma. In the first, the magnetic draw of the past pulls one into dangerous waters; in the second, the pleasures of the present are asserted over the price that pays for them, which can so easily be put off, for a future that promises nothing.

In fact, *now* and *then* are the book's most important words; they recur too frequently to be a mere tic. There is a darkness around them, best represented by the dominance of the negative: "It is not // terrifying as I had once believed it to be." "*No bottom!* Ed has said." "It was not gentle, no. In the end, / it was an accident [ ... ] / No—it was not *gentle*. It was, / instead, original and whole." "...where we // never now will go." Skibsrud takes *then* and *now* as two points in time and spatializes the temporal distance between them. It is a case of a ruling metaphor, varied in its details but set in its figurative goal—to *show* you time, as well as the fulfilments and failures of desire along the way. For the way in which a consideration of the travails of passing time accommodates both general unease and concrete moments of intense focus; for the fugal quality of elements being repeated to purpose through the length of the book; and for the starkness of diction equating not to an absence of feeling but to an abundance of it, *I Do Not Think That I Could Love a Human Being* is recommended.

Leanne Averbach's *Come Closer* also treats time passing, though the tone in which its poems do so is not as flatly tortured as Skibsrud's. Averbach begins her volume with "A Thing Past," which (poem picking up where title leaves off) "may be plucked of a sudden from the well, its memory / cavity. No query is necessary, nor forwarding address. // It may arrive dull, meaningless, slathered in vague clutter, / or rise pristine to quake us, better // than ever from nowhere. It will peel us raw / in a flash—that muted ransom." Her picture of being young in such poems as "My Youth Machine-Rolled, Smoked to Its Stub," with its unevasive first line ("Tales of my youth are a big hit at parties"), is entertaining but can also, as in "Beached," carry a sharp critique suggesting that the adulthood which replaces it isn't any great shakes: "Youth has the wingspan of pterodactyls—/ a bony useless confidence. / And I grow old in places I watched being born." In an apostrophe to a "Pigeon," she ends with advice— "In short, be trashy / but be choosey"—that is only an indirect kind of advice for herself; for though these poems cannot be considered "trashy," they do avail themselves of a range of cultural figures and objects, most of them "popular" in some way, and are "choosey" in adding up to a general sense of taste: billboards, posters of Mao, Yves Montand, a "nasty piece of obit" of Derrida, her Mom's Benson & Hedges, a McDonald's waste basket, Viennese quartets in Venice playing Bach and Broadway for tourists in San Marco Square—not trashy, exactly, but not wracked with classiness either.

Although a garbage man in "Taste of City" "swings from machine to curb like Gene Kelly," music more than dance is Averbach's art of choice. In a subway tunnel, a busker captures her ear and her thoughts: "It's fun / to think about the sad secrecies of others while a musician fondles her cello / into the rotten underground air, and an empty train screams past us, hopefully / fast, / towards repair." Chet Baker staring moodily from a picture is her silent partner as she sits "being bloosy" in a New York City café, the troubled musician also providing the title: "Let's Get Lost." "Waiting" in another bar, jazz is heard— "its fast nothing." "A Brief History of the Blues" is no more nor less interesting than the names of the bluesmen and -women the mere listing of which is the real reason for the poem. That is a good deal of interest, to be sure, though the poetic solution containing the names does not have over-much of what they nowadays call "value added." Preferable in its use of pre-existing art is a condensation of the three parts of Woolf's *To the Lighthouse*. Apropos of that novel, there is much journeying through time but also between places. Trips to other places may be purgatorial, as when one waits at "Baggage Claim," with its comic ending—the crowd cheers the speaker's retrieval of her bag from the carousel; or the opposite of purgative, as in "Cuba, Por Fin!," where there is much to obtain, only some of it stuff to be purchased: "The roads from Havana

/ scrawl into unscripted / distance. Frond / paradise, and no ideas / on what to buy, oh my."

The book's most important journey is the one undertaken by Averbach's family from Siberia to Romania to Canada. The sequence of twenty-three poems called "Teacups & Mink" (which also serves as the basis for a short film directed by Averbach) covers a lot of ground. Concision works in favour of both narrative momentum and emotional investment, keeping us moving and feeling without the soggy effect of excess sentiment. The sentiment is embedded in the recounting of the story; the poet is wise to let well enough alone. An immigrant story and a love story, "Teacups & Mink" gestures us close enough to Averbach's parents to make the first poem after the sequence—"Dusk, If That," an elegy for her mother—that much more felt. "Vigil" and "Hand Me Down" are also elegiac, the latter ending with "motherless hands" and beginning with a periodic sentence of some force: "After the funeral, after the worn wall of faces confused to be grieving / next to the Original Cast of characters, and the children / clear-eyed and mound-leaping among the headstones, / after the rhythmic hands of the *Kaddish* deftly picking / at my secular lock, the seagulls following the procession / away like a boat, expecting like us to be fed; after all / this we return to living." The ability to "return to living" is remarked on as a necessity or inevitability rather than as some proof of human will and its supposedly admirable tenacity. The "return" finds the same problems extant as before, the same makeshift ways of handling them, seen from the vantage of the death of a parent to a world in which Predator drones kill innocent people from above: "Yesterday's hit: / a funeral procession. // And fear just rolls / another cigarette."

Journeys are even more central to Elizabeth Greene's *Moving*, though here they are primarily journeys of self-discovery. The phrase sounds more trite than the book warrants, and one appreciates that Greene does not obfuscate what keeps her mobile: "Makes my mind spin. I'm still searching. / After sixty years, a little less lonely." In "Epidauros" and its "guest house for / pilgrims who came to heal," one can imagine the poet settling; a stay "At the Chelsea Hotel" finds her learning "a language I don't speak." These are real places, in addition to being places only of figurative value, and there is some credible travel writing scattered throughout. From a distance, having just left the Sphinx, "a plain of camels" chew cud and seem cute; but those camels are also real, as the traveller is forced to recognize: "We're supposed to RIDE / these creatures? Closer up / they look bad tempered, / have green mouths, unpleasant teeth, / bad breath." A comparative insight speaks with epigrammatic balance: "We have snow that melts. / In Egypt they have sand that lasts." On a "Poets' Walk in Chile," we see that Greene's journeys are not escapes but approaches to a renewed attentiveness: "Most of it is looking and listening—/ the rabbit scat, the spiny little trees / on the bleached hillside, astringent eucalyptus—/ small doors into the mysteries, into the poem." Those final moves, from nature to mystery to poem, more a circuit than a discrete series of steps, are similar to what is discovered in "Neruda's Houses—Valparaiso," "a space / where everything's reshuffled // so it's hard to tell where nature ends / and art begins, // where motion stops / and stillness / creeps in." Greene does not oversell her travels in terms of travails ("Inanna lost her seven veils / descending to the underworld. / I've only lost a suitcase."), nor does her personal search preclude a concern for others or for the earth itself. "Dreaming the Land" is a multi-part poem about Greene's participation in environmentalist protest, which also shows her sympathy for Bob Lovelace, a former chief of the Ardoch Algonquin Nation jailed for leading the way. Her son plays a role in the poem, and in some of the poems that help to make the title of the book not only about travel but also emotion, the poet plays a role as a daughter, remembering her parents, especially her mother.

Motherhood is the motivating force for Merle Nudelman in her third book, *The He We Knew*, which situates its poems in a context heavy with the past. On an airplane above the Atlantic, she "imagine[s] again" the "layered ocean journey" of her mother, seeing the latter's "uncertain head" on "a pillow / marked with your tears for the years / of the calendars of loss: / the grey pages and grey numerals." Other numbers tell even more of the past, of how history's atrocity shapes the present: "two new Old World boys // lucky to live" flirt and play at a ballroom dance as "Polish Valentinos" who would "forsake" steak dinners "in a blink / for a dreamless sleep, forearms / blank of blue numbers." In "Razing Sorrow's House," "when she heard the wailing / Yiddish songs her parents sang, / pondered the tattoos on their forearms, / the empty places at the table, / the house grew." The book's most frequent source of sorrow, however, is a mother's estrangement from one of her two sons. We first see the potential for a problem when we are introduced to "my two / indulged boys, one starting to stew the bitterness, / the other trying to fix it." Just like that, in the next poem, "Family Secrets," "[w]hen the clocks / tock / the he we knew / disappears." A majority of the poems thereafter are touched by maternal sadness. The mother enters a bistro and sees the son. His response is cold ("Cold as a cocktail," in fact), even as she "toast[s]" her words in an attempt to warm him. She wonders "did I ever know the son within, / acerbic from over-feasting / on sugary memories spiced // into ordeals." If the food-and-drink-in-the-bistro conceit seems a bit much, the reader must nevertheless recognize that its very excess leads to the diagnostic high point of the book, insofar as Nudelman's guessing assessment regarding how one turns "acerbic" is insightful.

Because we never know exactly *why* the estrangement from the son has happened, it is possible to wonder if we are encountering a lyric version of empty nest syndrome, a notion from which the poem "Emptiness" does not dissuade us: "That, I believe, is / what emptiness is: // the spirit a nest / where the broken blue eggs // of the flown / keep rattling." But quantity affects quality, and the frequency of intense feelings on the matter makes us register its seriousness, even if there is something about it that is still obscured for the poet and thus for the reader. This resistance to clarity is thematized in "Suddenly the Old Photograph," where the "Father's smile flickers / at his obscured son, the one / gone, gone in the foreground, behind / the candle, burning." The candle is a figure for the intensity, illuminating but debilitating. The poems, sad as they are, try to keep a space ready for the wandering son to return. Thus we have the sonnet "These are the days when birds come back" (after a line by Dickinson), where a garden full of birds recalls not an imposing and empty nest but a hospitable one, "of string and twig woven into home." About three-quarters through the book, in a poem asking "Is it safe," we read, "I hear you, / and my heart's door / lets you in. / Deep breath now—/ my son is home." We wish this to be a final moment of reconciliation, but old hurts die hard. The penultimate poem remembers that "[s]he had two thriving sons until / one's festering cyst burst: rank / stench of the broken Old Country." But with the arrival of a granddaughter, "She began the work: / dismantling walls plank by plank." The book ends with "The Wanderer," where, in an interesting reversal, it is not the brooded-over son who is the eponymous figure but presumably his mother: "I carry home on my shoulders—/ a nomad toting a sack[.]" In the book's last couplet, "enduring loves" abut "travail," reminding the reader of the earlier poem "Where I Place Love"—"More precious when near-lost," it claims, speaking to what is elsewhere described as "maternal love, / my withered need." The language of the poetry is not always as compelling as the themes it houses, but all in all Nudelman moves the reader in her descriptions of love, loss, and the necessity of having a home.

The title of Triny Finlay's *Histories Haunt Us* would apply just as well to Nudelman's book, but whereas the latter is relatively concrete about what histories are doing the haunting (even if specific details are sometimes left unlimned), the former begins with five poems called "Abstract Loss"—not the sort of loss conventionally called forth in verse in a post-confessional world but relevant just the same. There is also a scattered series of five self-portraits: "Self-Portrait as Cannonball," "Self-Portrait as the Spanish Civil War," "Self-Portrait as Someone You Might Like to Meet," "Self-Portrait as Rubenesque Figure," and "Self-Portrait as the Long Way." If loss can be abstract, then self-portraiture can be oblique. Even when she is direct in these sideways ekphrases, Finlay confronts the reader who may put his desire for simplicity over hers for truth: "I was broken—I'll say it plain / and that's what you'll like, / the plainness, smooth / face, pop of blue in the eye." Finally, however, "[t]he words weren't enough / and neither is this." The words, in fact, expose the poet to examination, force upon her a violent stasis: "Freeze me, frame me, hang me in the air / like the horse in Picasso's painting. // Suspended in space and time, lyric / as a moth, loved by the lepidopterist." Lyric as a moth is poetry as a death.

Although she is too subtle to have intended a pun where the unnamed pin we can imagine pricking the moth in place for study meets the poet's pen with which it is rendered stuck, Finlay does give us a figure for how poetic "voice" ceases to be a set of freeing strategies when it settles into being a reified thing. "Of Any Chorus" is a triptych in which the centre panel tells how to "make it," surrounded at left and right by the oddest of disembodiments: "Took my own tongue, stuffed in a jar, / and carried it home to find you. // Took my own tongue for a ferry ride / and watched you trail behind." "Took my own tongue to the river's edge / while the rain set up its trespass. // Took my own tongue to the baker's house / and sat by the open oven." This is like a meeting of Gogol and the Grimms. Finlay is good at being slyly gruesome ("Exhume me. I've fermented.") and dryly unnerving. Another three-part poem, "What Is Cut or Negative," begins unpropitiously for a nativity scene: "After the bliss of the baby came the flies." A striking, maybe morbid first line; but don't worry, although for a minute there you can hardly help it—the baby is fine, alive and well. Those flies aren't there for him but likely result from a summer sanitation strike: "The city, the garbage ripe, / in heat beneath our kitchen window. // They cruised through a hole / in the screen and gathered, / a buzz of watchful parishioners." By the third part of the poem they have left, while the baby, who slept through the poem's centre, remains presumably safe and sound.

For whatever reason, children poems—about, not by or for, them—are appealing as a genre. Perhaps such poems clear a pathway for exploring human creativity, one leading by analogy back to the creation of poetry itself but forcing upon us hard distinctions between poems and persons that are easy to elide. Perhaps in the right hands they provoke both sentimentality and a hard-won reaction against it, a mixture rich in ironic possibility. Perhaps, like Coleridge in front of the fire, they allow for moments of quiet all the more to be cherished for being fleeting. In "What Passes Between," Finlay does not quite make it to midnight and the fire-place grate is replaced by central heating: "In our living room, nothing / as trite as tension. // Bluegrass on the stereo / and warm air shooting up from / the floor; the baby tired but rolling / toward Etobicoke." Another couple is over for a visit, trailing behind them some pre-existing problem ("that quiver between / them, that cruel elephant"), but through mutual will it is not allowed to mar the evening's pleasant tedium. "We were going to order in," she writes, from "muted menus [ … ] But eight-thirty came and went, the baby / fell asleep on my shoulder, and we ate nothing." In a poem called "Falling," we return to the directive *to make* in a way that reflects not only on the poem but on the newborn: "Make this a study of gravity. // Make it move / like the plates in the soft, tiny skull." My favourite of Finlay's depictions of motherhood, an account of the actual birth, where cliché at times is wisely unavoided because it tells the truth, ends on a touching note: "*Comerado, I give you my hand*, my breast / to share your bliss, slick from the passage." Whitman would appreciate the appropriation of his loving lines in celebration of nascent life.

The previous excerpt comes from the second and last part of *Histories Haunt Us* (the first part is called "New Astronomers"), a series of twenty-six poems of six couplets that shares its name with the book. Each but the last uses somewhere among its lines someone else's words. The poaching is varied. Any poem that annexes both Anna Akhmatova and Ulysses S. Grant, to give a choice example, is likely to be of interest. The series is notable too for its depiction of fear and anxiety and for distinguishing between them. "[P]regnancy" and being "under the knife" are linked through "causality" to the rules of the safari: "If we move suddenly in the open-air jeep / the feasting lions might lose sight // of their humbled impala. This is a line," Finlay writes, and that line is drawn by a sensible fear of being attacked by a pride of lions. "Before I knew to think critically I was only a judge // of pleasure." But now, she and her partner, returning from Toronto to Fredericton, "won't drive in the dark / this time, we're older, more afraid." Critical thinking has substituted for pleasure the spectre of pain and of death as determinants of judgment. Preceding this is a plane trip, where the poet is "[r]estless" and "pumped full / of Ativan." Here is anxiety rather than abject or sensible fear. Four poems later and it seems she is back on a plane, having "been stashing pills for a week, some / from everyone. No trust in myself," and the poem that begins "Vaguely, just vaguely, from my point of view" ends "just vaguely, beginning with this, my confession, / *to calm, to calm, to calm an impetuous tide.*" The italicized words are Mary Wollstonecraft's; such "ghosts" are listed in the back. If these changes commensurate with adulthood are unpleasant, they are not the end of the world: "There was a time when sunlight // was enough, when oceans sustained us. Ours / was a fair landscape, an equal field. But this // is a myth too, the myth of progress reversed. / We suffer, but we are not land to be elegized." You get with Finlay both the elegy and its undercutting. "I wanted to write a short talk on beauty, / wanted to hide and sound like somebody else." But she is not somebody else; and when her son ends up back at the hospital with "seizures, swollen joints, vasculitis[,]" she declares to the somebody she is: "These things encroach, they devastate, so that / you must decide: you are an anchor or you are not." Finlay in these poems is like the anchor *and* the chain—the former stays put, the latter sways a little, and there is a good deal of honest unsteadiness here.

Although she does not name them as such, Finlay, in the series of twenty-six poems in couplets that round out her book, is working in the tradition of Canadian variations on the ghazal that can be traced back to Phyllis Webb and John Thompson, especially the latter's *Stilt Jack*. Indeed, the epigraph to her series is from that book's "Ghazal XXVII," as if closing out her own group of XXVI in a circular fashion. In his introduction to *Stilt Jack* (published posthumously in 1978), Thompson remarks on the ghazal as it is "practiced in America (divested of formal and conventional obligations) —he mentions Adrienne Rich—and notes that his "interest in the 'form' lies in the freedom it allows—the escape, even, from brief lyric 'unity.'" Two collections from 2010, Sheniz Janmohamed's *Bleeding Light* and Rob Winger's *The Chimney Stone*, are books of ghazals, though their relationships to the form differ. Janmohamed is far less "divested of formal and conventional obligations" than Winger—not that the latter has lost all sense of constraint; in addition to the necessity of generating couplets (loose enough shackles, really, when not incorporating the ghazal's traditional rhyme and refrain), Winger, like Finlay, has assimilated into his own lines the words of other artists. The section epigraphs are by Rich, Thompson, Webb, and Emmylou Harris. The trio of poets points to the recent history of the form, the musician to Winger's recourse to popular song. A jukebox worth of wordsmiths pop up: Johnny and June Carter Cash, the Clash, Bob Dylan, Joni Mitchell, the Pogues, Paul Simon, Talking Heads, and U2 among them. (That's just for the musicians; page-based poets are also recurrent.) This makes the beginning of "Ghazal for Empty Nets" amusing: "I'm tired of lyrics; / what else is there?" On occasion the sampling from outside sources seems too bare— "Don't think twice, Bob; / there's blood on the tracks, all right" —but for the most part it is a pleasure to see old friends in new places; and at least these quoted lines follow the rule of putting the poet's name in the final couplet.

But *The Chimney Stone* is not about following formal rules. Winger mentions as much when he notes that "Ghazal for Gazelles" and "Ghazal for Once in a Lifetime II" "are what Agha Shahid Ali calls 'real' ghazals." That leaves thirty-seven some-other-kind-of ghazals, if not "real" ghazals then at least "real" poems. One feature the poet follows is how the ghazal couplet is both closed in form and freestanding in content. Enjambment between couplets is nearly nonexistent; poems may have a story, but their narratives are fractured, insinuated more than foregrounded; most of all, Winger follows form in the making of gnomic statements, which quality is emphasized when a couplet has neither a before nor an after. These statements are rendered as command or report first, universalism or question second: "Unfold your glasses; / between nightstand and vision is the meaning of distance." The sense of mystery is appealing, as is the quick expansion from local instance to existential generality, from "glasses" to the "meaning of distance." The allusive reliance on the past is a topic taken up in interesting ways. In a poem dedicated to Webb, he begins, "In your book, they've underlined, in pen, / all your lost allusions" (a service his notes provide for his readers). Elsewhere he makes a Dylan-rich, self-referential prophecy: *"When your rooster crows at the break of dawn, look out your window,* love: / the future of nostalgia is utopia." By making his allusions "found" rather than "lost," Winger is somehow revealing but resisting his nostalgia, or rather resisting nostalgia's turn to utopia, which is bound to turn dystopic. But how to drink from the streams of influence without becoming overhydrated or slurping them down to their beds? Both possibilities are present in the finale to "Ghazal For MacGowan's Molars," which names the notoriously tippling frontman of the Pogues (as well as his notoriously unfortunate teeth): "And *if the rivers all run dry,* Shane, / what about the currents?" One can take that last word as a double entendre that wonders how the contemporary artist would fare without the art that precedes him.

In Janmohamed's *Bleeding Light*, the ghazals are more strictly configured. Though she begins by remarking that hers "are not 'anti-ghazals' or traditional ghazals" but "simply an attempt at maintaining the essence of the tradition and form[,]" they are steeped in the tradition and approach the form's essence as both musical setting and communal event. (That "simply" must be modest or ironic or both.) A brief introductory prose disquisition on the ghazal, called "The Last Cry" (*"Ghazal: The cry of a gazelle when it is cornered by a hunter and knows it will die."*), is interesting in its emphasis on pain and suffering and their relation to the form: "To write a ghazal without knowing pain reduces the writing to an academic exercise." "The ghazal must be exquisite in its suffering. A last beautiful whimper, as it were." The easeful musicality is belied by the distress that often underpins it. At the start she introduces the figure "Israh," the "Pen name" that becomes the personage who appears in every last line. Sometimes Israh and Sheniz seem just maybe to meet ("Israh fears your death more than her own. / Do not die for her. Live for her, Noble Soul."). Sometimes they certainly do: "When Israh encounters Sheniz, they exhume each other—coughing words cut like jewels. / We adorn this page with gems. Will he bear the weight and lift this lettered palanquin?" As in Winger's book, there are diagnostic statements followed by mysterious questions: "They drill oil from oceans, drag seals to slaughter, unsalt seas. / But whose hands will control the boat when there is no boat to steer?"

That last line is characteristic of the kind of mystical anti-logical logic in which the book abounds. Its sections are set off by definitions of spiritual terms of Arabic and Urdu origin, terms featured in their respective sections. For instance, the section marked *HU* ("Allah is. God is, just He! He Himself. / A declaration. A celebration. / A recitation.") and *RUH* ("Spirit. / One of the six subtleties / that must be illuminated.") includes the poem "Light Is Bloodless," which, in addition to sitting in contradiction of the title-concept of bleeding light, draws from the deep well where mysticism meets sexuality: "He lays her down to make love to himself. She digs up rotting soil—the muck of deceit. / She must abandon him now. If she does not, she will only thirst at the shores of his ruh. // You have twisted your veins into shackles, Israh. Stop running, allow your self to sit. / Light is bloodless. Do not puncture your heart to pour light—simply drink from your ruh." There is that "simply" again, which in this case speaks of the spiritual paradox whereby the most complex searches for meaning are most successful when reduced to what is simplest. Although there are turns of phrase that have the flatness of commonplace—as in a metaphor from the same section: "He is closer to me than my jugular vein. My blood circulates Allah-Hu."—this is not terminally detrimental to the overall tone Janmohamed means to achieve. At times it accentuates the poetry's religiosity and colours it with a patina of antiquity: "When everything we create has already been created, what is innovation? / Israh's words were penned before, with ink that leaked Allah-Hu." These ghazals work within an ancient tradition more than within a recent one. There is less an attempt to revise than to reinforce the paradoxical freedom of stricture. This pays off in something as seemingly small as the repeated name, as the one-word refrain, both of which *Bleeding Light* uses well. "If Israh does not squeeze the valves of your heart, how can we claim to be a ghazal?" Not every practitioner of this fecund form would take that question to be rhetorical, but it is interesting, even a touch chastening, to encounter one who does.

From the ghazal, which despite its great antiquity is really just getting to its feet in English-language poetry, we turn to a form that might well by now be exhausted but somehow never is. Reading Camille Martin's *Sonnets* reminded me of a house we lived in when I was a kid that had a little upstairs room replete with odd angles thanks to a dormer window and a low slanting ceiling. I had a bunch of Super Balls—small, hard, incredibly bouncy—which when hurled against the wall all at once produced percussive results. In short time they would all roll or bob to a stop, after which they would be gathered up to repeat the procedure. Now, if you can imagine the sonnet as the garret space of lyric, and take my word for it that the approach of Martin to its fourteen lines is often odd of angle, then the way that she uses repetition and rhyme accounts for many verbal swerves and a surfeit of springy sound. Every word is always lowercase, though that is not meant to suggest moderation: "however you endeavour to sever the found / ground or ring of things too soon to be a boon / to a tablespoon of sable moon, or whenever / you forget to fret over being so uncool as to drool" and so it unspools until it is stilled by an end-stopped last line. A poem called "citizen" has a similar, if more compacted flow: "in the meagre theatre / of my unfuelled labour, / in the dishonourable parlour / of my moulded behaviour, / marvelling neighbours humour / the rancour and clamour / of my sulphurous demeanour as i," etc.

More direct repetition is also prevalent. There is a kind whereby the end of one sentence determines the start of the next: "so many melodies are lost in the time it takes / to sing. to sing is to quote a slice of lore's / flashy headlights[.]" A nursery rhyme mode ("if all the sea were one big sea, / then cats would marry poodles. // if baby and i were baked in a pie, / the dog would eat the mop") sometimes obtains in its repetitiveness and plain-style surrealism. The series "glasshouse chimes" begins as a repurposed "House That Jack Built": "this is the tune that paper sang...this is the fly that fanned the flame / that burned the loom that wove the words / that graced the tune that paper sang." The starkest use of repetition is in a series of five box-shaped poems titled "reft link." Each consists of a single word—crown, frame, brink, flee, prow—repeated several dozen times, with only one variation per poem, a substitution of "l" for "r" or "r" for "l." The resulting words—clown, flame, blink, free, plow—are printed in fainter ink, a ghostlier demarcation amid the minimal block. One might compare this series to Carl Andre's "one hundred sonnets (I...flower)" of 1963, with quantity being the biggest difference. Speaking of visual artists, one might also mention Martin's cover art, a suitably strange collage of her own making depicting a child riding a sheep which leaps across a waterfall's plunge basin as a mottled and sheep-coloured moon floats in the upper-left foreground.

Although not as formally single-minded as Martin, other poets in 2010 availed themselves of the cozy dimensions found in fourteen lines. Jane Munro's *Active Pass* is at its strongest in a series of twenty-one sonnets based on the work of the painter Mary Pratt. These so-called "Illuminations" are aptly designated. Taking their titles from Pratt's paintings, they shed light on their subject by trying out a range of ekphrastic approaches. Four poems on "Eggs in Egg Crate" demonstrate Munro's deftness of constricted scope: there is objective description, art historical contextualization, biography-as-frame, and a rendering of what is seen by a naming of what is not. "Reflections of the Florentine in the Salmonier" adds to this repertoire the immediacy of memory, the testimony of personal association. These latter aspects are features found elsewhere in the book, as in "Delight in Solitude" and its picture of the poet's mother, whose "real shrine / was the bathroom" where "[e]ach morning / she'd carry in a little red book / and a cigarette, then sit / for twelve minutes behind a locked door." In the book's title sequence, closer to the present, her mother is in intensive care, "fighting the respirator." Her father too is found here, exiting this life: "'Well, dear—/ goodbye for now.' My father's last words to me. // The man interred not only in my DNA / but in my turn of phrase, my taste." She had "thought his death would be easier than hers." The silence that follows that line says that it was not. Now, "All my wise ones, my contradictors, have died." Such lines add to a poem such as "How sweet to be free" another taste than that found in the title, so that the sweetness of freedom is bittersweet, a characteristic kind of emotion in this unostentatious but moving volume.

Not every poet, of course, is inclined to hold back. Perhaps the best compliment that could be paid to R.D. Patrick's *The Stonehaven Poems* would be to say that at times it is pretty unpleasant to read, plus it quickens the pulse on occasion, given the contagion of rage. Patrick voices his belief that civilization is done for, which is naturally an angry voice. When "apocalypse, it seems, becomes us[,]" there is no reason to temper the tone of one's poetic temper; true, the book is not all tantrum, but, unpleasant or not, the bristly, gristly parts abound: "you've made a monster out of me / I want to pound your stupid face / into paste and feed it to my dogs." Sometimes these lines are spoken from behind a mask. Sometimes they are spoken from another era, as in the suspected-witch-killing poem "possessed." Sometimes they seem to derive directly from the poet, a representation of him and his values alone, but it is not always easy to tell whether or not the heightening of emotion has made you mistake the immediacy of what you are reading for an unimpeded conduit gushing from the author's heart. Sometimes a passage becomes engorged enough to reach a (sort of) comic pitch, which strikes us as intended: "and while I was firing blanks / at class after class of infinitely / incorrigible, elliptical oxymorons[.]" This engorgement cannot be maintained, though Patrick gives it a good try, and sometimes the objects of anger, disgust, or even mere disapproval are not equal to the energy expended on them, "a fat man dies for his country" being a case in point.

At other times the energy, as in "tillman," feels blocked in the story it tells. (It begins by rhetorically asking "what more is there to say" about the case of Pat Tillman, but what is said seems incomplete.) The bigger the historical conceit is not always the better—"I'll be your adolf hitler / if you'll be my ghetto jew" is a terrible start to a poem—and indeed, some of the stronger moments are those that are most self-reflective, as in the poem "jackie," which looks back on the "childish cruelty" that Patrick and his friends visited on the disabled title character. Because there is much that is unpalatable to Patrick, however, being palatable is hardly his goal; but even outrage can be personable. Furthermore, there are tonalities in *The Stonehaven Poems* in addition to those of anger. (It is just that anger is so emotionally disruptive that it will create an imbalance even in the midst of calmer poems.) The responses to the maltreatment of animals encountered early in the book, which are unhinged even though they are understandable, are given a personal context in late poems about dogs, Leo and Teddy, that the author has known. These are sweet and gentle poems (although one of them still allows itself a sour consideration of "the entire modern-day middle class," to say nothing of "eternal evil"), as are several in the collection as it draws to a close.

The latter part of Patrick's book is marked by several poems about his late father. Such poems of a parent now gone are at the heart of Larissa Andrusyshyn's *Mammoth*, which treats grief in unexpected ways, sometimes by apostrophizing the death itself ("In Which My Father's Death is Registered to Vote"), at other times by scientizing it ("The Mammoth Sequences the Ivan Andrusyshyn Genome"). The vast spans of time from the days of the woolly mammoth to the days of the author's father are frequently collapsed. In "Where the Dead Things Are," she sees him in a diorama of Cro-Magnon man in the American Museum of Natural History: "This is where I find my father, / hiding oranges in early man's fire pit. / Living, like an imposter, a dead man / among glassy-eyed mannequins." What to say to this father on display, this resurrected exhibit? "I tell him that I haven't celebrated anything since he died. / That the Habs refuse to win another Stanley Cup. / That the Hubble telescope recently took pictures / of an empty corner of space and found it to be full of galaxies, / millions of them, each with a black hole at the center / sucking everything in like a drain." These junctures at which the daughter attempts to communicate directly are countered by those in which the death is depersonalized: "We are a sum of parts, my father / is a code, a genome, in a language of four letters: / adenine, guanine, cytosine, thymine." "In Which the Mammoth Goes to School" finds that prehistoric creature hard at work in the lab, trying to "sequence the genome of a man named Ivan / in order to complete his research in the field / of bringing things back."

The "event" that constitutes the life and death of her father is to be "interpreted in two ways": either through the frame of "intelligent design" or through "astronomical accident," both of which she figures at "4:1 odds." The interpretation is important, for "[t]o apply meaning to the creation of a man is to write his elegy." In the collection's first poem, the speaker remarks, "I have a collection of dead things," and this tendency leads to a kind of autopsy logic, with particular body parts endowed with the living *dinglichkeit* with which so many collectors endow their *dinge*: "Portrait of the Heart as Blood Donor," "Stomach Prepares for Dinner," "Your Kidneys" ("dressed for the winter with sweaters and wool socks"), and "Portrait of the Liver at the Open Mic." Grief is handled here through humour, through science and history writ large, and through local bursts of memory: "In a hospital room in Montreal in the fall of 1990, / a girl named Lara touches her dead father / and is transported to the lobby of a casino in Jackpot, Nevada, / in the year 1986 where a child named Lara is touching a taxidermied / grizzly bear whose right paw was recently hacked off and stolen. / Her father lifts her up, to look the bear in the eye." Andrusyshyn distributes these approaches throughout *Mammoth* in a way that pulls together what could easily have spun off into disparate parts. It is a book about "Extinctions" (as one poem has it) but just as much about various modes of preservation.

Science and death meet differently in Michael Lista's *Bloom*, with large amounts of love gone awry and literary history thrown in the mix. Compelling in its narrative and impressive in its technique, *Bloom* takes us to Los Alamos and inside the Manhattan Project. The grand story that one might expect is instead rendered at the most human of levels. The protagonist is the Canadian physicist Louis Slotin, who jerry-rigs a nuclear experiment with a screwdriver which slips, causing the plutonium to go critical—this is the primary meaning in the book of "bloom"—and leading to Slotin's death. The physicist is also being cuckolded by another member of the team, and in this sense Slotin is a version of Leopold Bloom. Because almost all of the poems are written in the manner of other writers ("*after John Crowe Ransom,*" "*after Frederick Seidel,*" "*after James Joyce,*" and so on) and thus call to mind the matter of influence, Harold Bloom may also be recalled by the title. As in *Ulysses*, the links to prior works help devise a structure of interest, a set of correspondences worth meditating on, but as also in that work, the major claim of *Bloom* is less literary resemblance than the double strength of stylistic facility and insight into character. When early on we read that "It is we / Whom we ache to destroy // Us[,]" it is clear that Slotin's complicity in his own death will be a theme; from there the reader embarks on many extrapolations. These may be as overarching as a consideration of the sublimity of scientific creativity and the nuclear-driven death drive or as local as the bar in "Louis Slotin as Pigeon Feeder," where seedy actions suggest complicity in his own cuckolding. When Lista writes in Slotin's voice that "it took every suicidal atom in me / Not to see fidelity as resignation / To extinction[,]" or in "Louis Slotin and the White Lie" that "we are the source, not what the source illuminates[,]" we think of the poet's own fidelity to his sources or lack thereof and ponder the meanings of his literary and existential illuminations. Like the light of the moon found late in the book ("the moon hangs thanatonic on its hook"; "the moon is wearing its own face as a mask") or the variety of blooms that serve as a light-motif leitmotif, these poems cast a good deal of glow, as well as attendant shadows.

"*Oh Lord, don't let them drop that atomic bomb on me.*" These words of Charles Mingus grace a canto near the end of Michael Boughn's *Cosmogra-*

*phia: A Post-Lucretian Faux Micro-Epic*. As in Lista's book, the dangerous nature of sex and the potentially world-ending threat of war and its products commingle, though Boughn has no intention of giving it to us even as straight as does *Bloom*. The post-Lucretian aspect of *Cosmographia* is manifest in an Epicurean atomism in which sounds are in a constant state of motion and the rubbing together of phrases and discourses in an often agrammatical arrangement creates a frenetic and extremely weird onslaught of frissons that are practically pornographic, but not in a way so explicit as to shame you if you are reading the book on a train with a straphanger looking you over. The twisted language of sex found here—with its "fantasies" and "assignations" and "penetrations" and "unnatural pairings" and "licentious / seductive promise of damp paradaisal // intimations" and "lowdown lascivious / mediations" and "overdone // erections trussed up for the holidays"—is inextricable from the persistent recourse to scraps of a post-9/11 thesaurus of war: "derived linguistic sleeper cell intent / stripped naked and subjected to various / cavity searches while the pursuit of happiness / looks on in august and judicious disinterest[.]" The distance from "Democratic" to "Demonic" vistas is mapped in satirically vicious fashion and the Demotic is in there somewhere too for good measure. The political message is that the way the "war on terror" (I think Boughn would insist on quotation marks) is being waged is obscene, whether insofar as the "marriage of justice and payback in popular / determinations of repeated rolling heads // garners huge ratings and deep satisfactions" or how you "never know what gawdawful combination / of unintentional retorts will find their way / into stories of carnal anxieties' wars / of dubious intent," to say nothing of the innocent dead. The epigraphs and footnotes featuring musicians, novelists, philosophers, and poets provide a running chorus of aesthetic and moral rectitude (as opposed to the "Moral Rectumtudes" that give one of the book's twelve "Books" its name) and assert a humanity meant to counter the warmongers. This dark comedy of "when the cows come home / and the hot lead whizzes" is finally not a fake epic but is indeed "faux micro-," as the subtitle says, for there is really nothing small about it. It only plays at being minor to make its major claims.

# Poetry: Letters in Canada 2009

Because the "Letters in Canada" number of *UTQ* is not just an issue of a journal but a kind of critical anthology that comes around every year, the thoughts turn first to such books. In Canadian letters there are the big ones, the ones that remind us that anthologies are often less well-described as books than as tomes. From the collections of Dewart up to Smith, from Geddes up to Bennett and Brown, such tomes have had an impact on the national literature, not only when considered at home, but also as it has come to be considered elsewhere. In "tome" the skeptic may also hear the echo of the tomb, as an anthology these days is often felt to entomb as canonical what before was part of a living and breathing tradition. Arguments on this score have always struck me as wanting; truly living writing cannot be made moribund by being placed in new contexts, and the "canon" is more chimerical than convention would have it. Instead, in "tome," one may rather hear the echo of time. The anthologies mentioned above took much of it in their making, while their making of an impact, though in some cases partially immediate, took still more of it to be better known.

Yet there is another way in which time may operate with respect to anthologies. Rather than biding one's time and producing a tome, an editor may be compelled to respond to events that are more immediate. In these cases, although collecting and sifting and evaluating remain of the essence as always, so too is the conviction that there is no time to spare, that the right time is now, that time stands still for no one, editors of anthologies included. Several such collections appeared in 2009. One of them, *Gulch*, edited by Sarah Beaudin, Karen Correia Da Silva, and Curran Folkers, gathers not only poetry but also prose, continuing both to accentuate the differences of these two modes of writing by placing them in close proximity (as have centuries of prosimetrists), but also to resist the perception of differences by blurring them (as have prose poets for the last hundred years or so). It calls itself an "assemblage" rather than an anthology, the latter word doubtless too stodgy for this bright and youthful volume.

The collection counts among its opening epigraphs a Wikipedia entry and this statement by Deleuze and Guattari: "The book imitates the world, as art imitates nature: by procedures specific to it that accomplish what nature cannot or can no longer do." At first I took this as a heartening defence of the book as book, which it may well be. But a likelier interpretation is that the editors are asserting that in a digital age, the printed book, to retain its relevance, must more effectively imitate the world, a digital world now dominant—the only world, I suspect, ever known by some of the volume's contributors. From its opening statement, "This Book Is a Rhizome," to Adebe D.A.'s "Poemagogy," to John Unrau's "New Age Muskie Considers a Change of Lifestyle," *Gulch* privileges the rhetoric of (and itself exists as an example of) that ever-regenerative genre, the manifesto. Indeed, there is an assaultive claim being made in the very layout of the book, with Alice-in-Wonderland font sizes that shrink and shoot up willy-nilly; with poems and prose and pictures printed in passages every which way, be they upside down or crooked or shaped like a pyramid or nestled among one another like Russian dolls; with chunks of words in one column, two columns, three columns, four. It is all a little busy for me, but then the book, its texts and its layout included, is meant to be—must be—provocative to remain true to its intentions. In Shannon Webb Campbell's transparently titled "A Fragmented Manifesto," she writes, "Because we live in a time beyond distinction. / Because we are characteristically uncharacteristic. / Because we've boomed, busted and echoed our way into a state of numbness. / Because video games and instant messaging have bastardized our language. / Because we value quantity over quality." Campbell is against these trends. Less certain is whether the editors also mean to critique them or instead intend to exacerbate them. Probably even trying to make the distinction makes one hopelessly square.

Another anthology published by Tightrope Books is more staid, perhaps, but for most readers will be more useful. *The Best Canadian Poetry in English* continues the series begun last year. Given the abundance of poems published in Canada these days, a yearly sifting is helpful. The series editor is Molly Peacock and the poems in this year's volume were chosen by A.F. Moritz, both of whom provide prefaces. They are short and to the point, reasonable and enthusiastic, and give way briskly to the poems themselves. Moritz chose fifty of them by fifty different poets after trawling through and culling from magazines and journals. There is also a list of the fifty poems that were runners-up, a list of print and online sources considered during the choosing process, and brief biographies of the chosen poets. I suppose someone could quibble with the selection, but it won't happen here; the choices strike me as unobjectionable. If you like good poems, you will find much to like. This series provides a needed service for readers of Canadian poetry, and so far the results are just right—sharp, elegant, neither over nor underwhelming in scale and scope. There may be a moment down the line to reassess what the current culture variously means by "the best" of any given thing, but this is definitely the best *The Best Canadian Poetry in English* in English. It marks an efficient use of one's time as a reader.

One valuable anthology released in 2009 that is firmly on the tome side of the spectrum was *Open Wide a Wilderness: Canadian Nature Poems*, edited by Nancy Holmes, who obviously expended much time in collecting its roughly three hundred poems written by nearly two hundred poets and spanning 150 years of the nation's writing on nature. A smaller volume, *Regreen: New Canadian Ecological Poetry*, edited by Madhur Anand and Adam Dickinson, purports in an introductory essay by Anand to be responding to a call urged by the larger volume's editor:

> On April 14, 2009, the first-ever historical anthology of Canadian nature poems was launched in Guelph, Ontario. The volume's editor, Nancy Holmes, remarked that what we need now is an anthology of new nature poems. We feel *Regreen* answers that need, but not in any premeditated manner. Unfilled niches in the poetic world are not leftover space, but new space created in the understory of towering legacies.

This last sentence is somewhat confusing, but it can be sorted out. In addition to its appropriate forest metaphor, it contains by implication a compliment of Holmes, as well as of the poets she collects—a likeable gesture. At the same time, it justifies the later volume's existence, which every editor of an anthology must do, even if the justification is redundant, given the obvious value of the anthology. The close proximity in time of the two volumes raises interesting questions about the inherent difference, if any, between the "nature poem" and the "ecological poem." The latter obviously has more political and activist overtones, but given that the political efficacy of poetry is itself a matter of perpetual questioning, a clear-cut and final distinction is unlikely to emerge. At any rate, *Regreen* contains a slew of some of Canada's best poets working at the top of their game and is thus a book worth acquiring, if one is concerned with the theme and wants to see it handled well.

My favourite anthology of the year—*Rogue Stimulus: The Stephen Harper Holiday Anthology for a Prorogued Parliament*, edited by Stephen Brockwell and Stuart Ross—wasn't published in 2009, but early in the year that followed. However, because the event that inspired this quirky, quickie collection—the prime minister's "despicable" (as the editors have it) second proroguing of Parliament—occurred on 30 December 2009, let's consider it to have crept in just under the wire. The dispatch with which the book came together makes it the ultimate anti-tome. Brockwell, angered by Harper's manoeuvring, called Ross and pitched an idea. Ross pitched it to a publisher, Denis De Klerck, who agreed to it. As Ross describes the scene in a funny introduction, the agreement was not enthusiastic, though the response from poets was:

> Denis rolled his eyes, smiling faintly, and maybe a little resignedly, as I suppose all publishers do when they agree to that big moneymaker—a poetry book. So later that day we sent out the call: we approached writers we admired; we alerted listservs; we sent out press releases. Our deadline was five days from Denis's nod. Over the first four days we received about 200 submissions. Then just before our Tuesday-midnight deadline, Stephen Brockwell appeared on CBC radio. The segment was kicked off with an awful limerick, but the interview went well otherwise. In the few pre-deadline hours after the show, another 100 or so poems flooded in.

If Mount Parnassus has a library, *Rogue Stimulus* won't be sitting on its shelves. However, because such directly political poems can be portentous, it is pleasing (albeit revealing) to read a book that represents how we often actually talk about political events around the time that they occur. We rant and we rave; we make demeaning remarks about the decision-making fools in high places; we make jokes and sigh about our own inability to influence events; we commiserate with one another; we offer redundant suggestions to like-minded people; we castigate those morons who won't hear us anyway; we talk about history, precedent, outcomes, and alternatives, suddenly scholars and theorists; we rant and we rave; we try to palliate disgust, to evade our exhaustion with the political process; we move on to the next event in a gerbil's wheel of response. Although the moment may have passed—remember the prorogue? Just checking—it's still worth getting your hands on this book. It is not a rounding up of the usual suspects, which is part of its interest. There are a few known names (George Elliott Clarke's poem is terrific, a striking piece of invective that has a mirroring ambiguity in its title), several soon-to-be-better-known newcomers, and doubtless some first-and-last-timers who were spurred to good verse just this once. Who knew that Harper could so inspire? The charming cartoon cover of him skating and whistling Dixie in front of an emptied Parliament, drawn by Gary Clement, is also a part of the volume's pleasant but pointed roguery.

Calling off in a unilateral move the truce between the frivolous and the serious declared by Brockwell and Ross's collection, we turn now with a straight face to a cluster of edited volumes that (in a nod to the etymology of *anthology*) gather together flowers from the gardens of single authors. The Laurier Poetry Series continues apace, producing in 2009 three more additions to its helpful catalogue of ever-growing significance. This year's offerings include *Fierce Departures: The Poetry of Dionne Brand*, selected by Leslie C. Sanders; *Mobility of Light: The Poetry of Nicole Brossard*, selected by Louise H. Forsyth; and *The False Laws of Narrative: The Poetry of Fred Wah*, selected by Louis Cabri. In this case the persons doing the selecting also speak through a detailed introduction; luckily there is compatibility between the commentators and the ones being commented on. (Cabri's introductory essay is especially apt as a stylistic fit.) The authors themselves also appear in afterwords. These Laurier volumes are inviting, being both comprehensive and without bloat, an impressive balancing act. They are easy to inhabit in terms of their size and design, even if the poems they contain may be difficult. A great tool for teachers, students, autodidacts, or dyed-in-the-wool poetry lovers who want a movable feast of their favourite poet to take on a trip or on the subway, the books in this series should become indispensable.

As far as selection goes in the various volumes, the slimmest by page count but boldest by conception and execution is Sanders's of the work of Dionne Brand. Moving from *No Language Is Neutral* through *Inventory*, Sanders creates a new poetic sequence in the name of a poet who has shown herself to be a master of the form. Such congenial meetings as this between poet and professional reader are serendipitous. Perhaps the same can be said of Robyn Sarah's selection in *The Essential Don Coles*. Not being familiar with most of the volumes from which its poems were taken, perhaps there was a preferable selection that could have been made, but it seems doubtful, given that the one found in the book makes such a strong impact. Sarah's introduction is a gem of concision, and the controlled gems of Coles have a sharp-edged capaciousness. There is much responding to a range of art, which is also a way of responding to the times and places where particular works were made and still are stored, to the things that art represents, or to the desires that it fulfils and provokes. For someone so good at looking, there is no dearth of hearing in Coles—the dramatic monologue of "The Prinzhorn Collection" recalls but modernizes Browning's voluble voice, the "Sampling from a Dialogue" with its overheard conversation reminds us that the responsive poet is often an overhearer, not only of others but primarily of himself. This is the third volume in *The Essential* series, put out by the Porcupine's Quill, inexpensive and delectable collections recommended not only for their contents but for the qualities of their objecthood.

Does an author's own *Selected Poems* count as an anthology? It is, after all, a kind of gathering of flowers, even if the one doing the gathering is also the one who grew the garden. When I was just a schoolboy in short pants (or at least a fourth-year undergraduate), I had the chance to talk at some length to my poetry hero at the time (and one of them still), John Ashbery. I mentioned how surprised I was that "These Lacustrine Cities," a favourite of mine, hadn't made it into his *Selected* and asked him how he had felt about its omission. "Well, I *was* the one doing the selecting," he said, and left it at that. The notion had never occurred to me. I guess I assumed that God or some editor did it. As for Robert Bringhurst's *Selected Poems*, even a silly schoolboy might figure that the poet had a strong hand in making such a gorgeous volume. Every book from Gaspereau Press is beautiful; that's a given. But this one takes the cake. There are so many fine details that even the digital warriors and mass-market gurus must take notice and stand abashed. The book as a physical whole resembles a small slab of basalt, the surface of which looks untouched until one gets close to hold it; then the light catches it a certain way, so that the shallow inscriptions on its face darkly flash forth. The way red and baby-blue inks are used to give Bringhurst's polyphonic poems more sensory life than print usually affords is an achievement in itself. To be frank, the nature of an omnibus review of this sort is such that the scope of this large-spirited but human-scaled book can only be gestured toward, with the anticipation that it will be attended to more appropriately elsewhere. One suggestion, though—get it.

Close on Bringhurst's heels in terms of necessity, and surpassing him in terms of settling in and cozying up in a chair with a book, is P.K. Page's *Coal and Roses*, also an anthology. Of what, you might ask, knowing full well that the volume is an original collection of twenty-one glosas. The answer? An anthology of quatrains, accompanied by biographies and pictures of their authors. Included are the following, attesting to Page's range and taste: Anna Akhmatova, John Ashbery, Jorge Luis Borges, Marilyn Bowering, Dionne Brand, Margaret Cavendish, e.e. cummings, Thom Gunn, Zbigniew Herbert, Gerard Manley Hopkins, Ted Hughes, Juan Ramón Jiménez, Federico García Lorca, Gwendolyn MacEwen, Don McKay, Theodore Roethke, Wallace Stevens, Philip Stratford, and Robert Penn Warren. In a world where, contrary to propaganda, there is no shortage of poetry, it is nice to have one of Canada's greatest poets select for us some fine stanzas amongst the noise.

Page gives the reader a definition at the start of the form she employs throughout: "The glosa form opens with a quatrain, borrowed from another poet, that is then followed by four ten-line stanzas terminating with the lines of the initial passage in consecutive order. The sixth and ninth lines rhyme with the borrowed tenth." In *Hologram*, her 1994 collection of the same form, she wrote in an introduction that "this book contains some...of the many songs I heard when, falteringly, I was searching for my own voice." Page's influence in that book, as well as the fact that this form is characterized by its relation to inspiration and creative repurposing, may explain why so many of the younger poets this year, poets perhaps searching for their own voices, turn on frequent occasion to the glosa. Even more than the epigraph, the glosa's four borrowed lines are like the already running car that jumpstarts the unresponsive poetic engine. Of course, as one with a distinguished and years-long career as a writer, Page does not warrant the simile. She passed away not long after the publication of *Coal and Roses*, adding until the end to her body of work. (In her last year she also saw published *Cullen*, a short poetic sequence about the female protagonist of the title; *The Sky Tree*, an illustrated trilogy of children's fables; and *The Golden Lillies*, a little book of eight more glosas.) Taking Roethke as her starting point, but also bringing Hopkins's "No worst, there is none" to bear, Page in "No Exit" suggests how dearly she holds human vitality, which also suggests to the reader something of the poet who made so much of her life: "The Dark Night of the soul, the darkest night. There is no darker. 'Pitched past pitch,' he said—/ Hopkins, that is. And Saint John of the Cross / knew equal suffering—a loss of faith / that nothing equals, so they say, but I / who lost my life—why can I not compare / my loss with theirs?"

There are also lighter moments, moments more free that float in the air like the birdsongs that she had used to explain the appeal and necessity of the glosa in *Hologram*'s introduction. Lorca spurs such a poem: "Come water, come springtime / come my green lover / with a whistle of grass / to call me to clover." One sees how the author of these bouncing lines might also write so frequently for children. Lines borrowed from Brand beginning *"some words can make you weep"* occasion verse that is aware of the power of incantation, no less adult in being just as fitting for a fairy tale world: "there is magic, of course, and among the many magics there are / words—spellbinders, but there is also sleight-of-hand, / and the magic of herbs." As she writes in another poem, insisting on the importance of verbal play in reaching for truth, "The literal is rarely true / for truth is old and truth is new / and faceted—a metaphor / for something higher than we are. / I play the truth of Everyman / I play the truth as best I can. / The things I play are better far / *when changed upon the blue guitar.*" Page takes Stevens's singular "The Blue Guitar" and makes of it something new that nevertheless encapsulates the spirit of the original.

The term *orphan works* has been bandied about quite a lot of late, given the Borgesian attempt to put everything ever written in the history of the world online. But that melancholy term would also be a fitting replacement for naming those final books that we now call "posthumous," insofar as the parent who brought them into being has passed on and left them to fend for themselves. The late Margaret Avison's *Listening* lends a reason for considering the substitution. This beautiful work was orphaned, in a sense, as the manuscript was left almost, but not quite, finished upon Avison's death. The manuscript was nurtured into a book by Stan Dragland and Joan Eichner, no doubt lovingly and doubtless delicately. There is a quietude to the book that is already characteristic of Avison, but there is an added magisterial austerity to *Listening* that is characteristic of the late style of many great poets with long and varied oeuvres. These are considerations that lead one to reminisce. One poem, "Architecture," seems to recall a past when things were quieter and when poetry perhaps could be heard a little better, not just reaching back to the Toronto of 1936 of the poem's story, but yet further back to the days when poems were read by the hearthside:

> The white and gold of a
> cold morning, with
> March through the door tomorrow's
> daybreak, sets
> the pulses throbbing.
> Oh I know the heaviest snowfalls
> have been March's. Nineteen
> thirty-six saw single-file
> foot traffic down
> Yonge Street. Many who went,
> set out to go, to
> work, walked all they could,
> wading thigh-deep at times
> until, in any
> coffee-shop or pub someone had managed to open by then,
> they met and talked with
> whatever other venturer
> chose to be stranded there.

The idiosyncratic enjambment is a joy, while the long *o*'s floating down through the lines keep the sound of snow falling, as if a silent occurrence could have an onomatopoeic existence in verse. The pleasing trick recalls the drifting periodic sentences of Longfellow's "Snow-flakes," another attempt to represent through form the nonverbal phenomena of nature, where "the poem of the air" is "[s]lowly in silent syllables recorded." The title and subject matter also recall Emerson's "The Snow-Storm," in which Nature, that "fierce artificer," "[l]eaves, when the sun appears, astonished Art / To mimic in slow structures, stone by stone, / Built in an age, the mad wind's night-work, / The frolic architecture of snow."

For Avison, in these minimalist poems of meditation and remembrance, it is possible to pull art from the air. Considering that in today's Toronto, "The birds seem few now," she recalls a moment years before when a flock of birds "breakfasting, / on their way south," perched in a tree, where they "twittered and piped and gurgled all / at once, each with its / colorful cravat or patch or / crest." That trio of verbs, that triplet of nouns allows for choice and for the pleasures of variation over singular rightness. And yet the scene occasions some strange crystallization of sight and sound into just the right, single word: "How still I sat! How a word formed / itself in air so gentled: / *zephyr* (stone-blue but soft)." From sight and sound to a word one can touch, this is a synesthetic epiphany prepared for by stillness and listening. In another poem, a spare disquisition on what she takes to be the "Misconstruing" (the poem's title) of the word *abominable*, Avison closes with a telling anecdote: "The misreading evokes a / thickening gentleman who / knew the tailor's / larger waist was a good / fit, but hankered / to try a smaller... // He was / misreading 'fit' because / he didn't want to face its / meaning, yet." Our contemporary situations are similar, at the level of wilfully misconstruing scale, or so it often seems. We try to fill more space and perform more acts and write more words and make more impact, out of social pressure and personal ambition, than our limited lives allow for with decency or comfort. Our lives don't always fit our lives. There is a nagging feeling a reader gets when, still in the thick of worldly things, he encounters the wisdom of an author who, writing late in life, has pulled away from those things, from that world. The reader feels chastened. But, as Avison kindly writes: "Distance / is not rebuke."

From here, having considered two books by masters who even at the end of their careers were working at the height of their powers, let us travel back to the beginning and consider this year's first books. Or are we travelling forward? Well, let's call it the circle of poetry and we will get there either way.

Among this year's debut volumes, one of my favourites was Sonja Ruth Greckol's *Gravity Matters*. Even to describe it as a "debut" is somewhat misleading. The poems in *Gravity Matters* radiate maturity, the powerful energy of the lived-in life. First book, second book, third book, last—one could hardly tell which of these was Greckol's without being told on the back of the book. Two poetic sequences define the volume, one of them more obviously a sequence than the other. The more clear-cut of the two, "Emilie Explains Newton to Voltaire," treats a fascinating subject, the learned and vivacious Emilie du Châtelet (1706–49), who died days after childbirth, having just completed her translation of and commentary on Newton's *Principia*, and whose work on Newton is described by Greckol as the most comprehensive in French. Compelling protagonist aside, the poem is also formally masterful. After a prologue in prose, we enter the series of fifteen poems, beginning, "Matter puzzled her—gravity, the universe." Some of the fifteen are sonnets, some just long or short enough to suggest that form. The group as a whole is a variation on the *sonnet redoublé*, or heroic crown, whereby the last line of each poem reappears as the first line of the next. The fifteenth poem is a sonnet made of the first lines of the preceding fourteen poems taken in consecutive order. The archaism, elegance, and nominal regality of the form seem chronologically and spiritually apposite, given the poem's eighteenth-century heroine, while its structural difficulty and complex organicism do honour to her mind and her work.

The other group of poems is a sequence only in a sense less contained, scattered as they are throughout. I have never read anything like them. With Sylvia Plath was encountered what before had hardly existed (having hardly before been allowed to), an expressive range of mother poems, not merely imagined but straight from a mother herself. (Perhaps I'm giving Anne Bradstreet short shrift.) There have since been numerous elaborations of tone and voice, updates that registered social changes, and expansions of viable subject-positions. Greckol's contribution is compellingly specific. What do you do when your daughter embarks on a career that you cannot help but admire, but which also causes you emotional pain? What do you do when your daughter undertakes the dangers of aid work in faraway, war-torn lands? Underneath the specificity, however, is also the lurking universality of the soul-harming paradox of the successful mother, whose hopes for her child are fulfilled: "That your appetites are large, I see / is redundant among my wishes. Your arc / is larger than the scripts I unfurled." In other words, how does one handle the pain that one inflicts on oneself by having reared the independent and ethically minded child that one always wanted into the well-adjusted adult that leaves one behind?

"A Girl Studies Genocide," "What She Learned," "What She Decided"—this is the start of the arc of the sequence. The last ends where many lesser parents would never have gone:

> Now we have taught ourselves what our daughter learned.
>     I grasp
> / structural adjustment / coffee markets / foreign currencies / planned genocide /
>     our complicity:
>
> And a daughter sets her radius to Kigali—declares her own
>
> *Never again*

After these lines follow three spare poems—"Mother Watch," "Skin of the Universe," "Small Disturbances"—that register Greckol's unease and her determination to remain even-keeled. In the poem after those, "Gravity and Flight," we enter by seeing the doorframe on which the daughter's height has been measured through the years. Strangely, the marks do not uniformly ascend. Mother and daughter "chuckle," but there is sadness tracked in the ebb and flow of those marks that also mark their relationship. What is so atypical of this parent-poet is how clearly Greckol shows the symbiotic nature of their love. Her daughter can be both teacher and taught. She herself can be made younger than her daughter when her daughter, although still and always her child, becomes an adult: "A week before you left, / we bought pillows on Spadina Ave: / you plumped and squeezed and giggling / lay your head down and buoyed your courage and my urge // to be the feathers that could hold you; smoothed my / frayed edges, / and I found my young feathers imped." A word worth looking up, that last one, as well as an occasion to add that Greckol's strength is not just in her fearless approach to meaningful subject matter, or in her idiosyncratic but in-the-pocket rhythms (established not only by impeccable enjambment but also by her use of indentation, of stanza breaks, and of the page as a field). Her strength is also her vocabulary.

Less impressive than Greckol's book, but nevertheless worth reading, is Christina McRae's first collection, *Next to Nothing*. It, too, considers the relationship of mother to daughter, but, at least at the start, from the other direction. In McRae's poems, being a daughter is painful, to put it mildly: "At six, taking a wet thumb from my mouth / to plug in the kettle for my mother / a swarm of skewers twists in through my thumb, / behind my head, and down the other arm. // A new pain, a whip cracked handle to tip / I scream and turn on her / so sure she's snuck from behind in slippers / and thrown boiling water down my neck." Such pain, distrust, and incipient paranoia is a product of living in a house where "hope [is] framed into moments on mantelpiece and wall." Here, a daughter who returns home from Bible camp to recite in bad faith songs that she feels are false is not truly heard, but blindly praised: "Surely she had to see it, to sense the lie / but she was chuffed and the warm Christian praise / for the good little girl / was cold comfort to me. / She'd seen what she wanted to see." There are thick sheets of scales over paternal and communal eyes, lots of determined make-believe. There is the "[s]mall town girl knocking at the townhouse / pretending to be warm in a skirt too short for January"; there is the wife, with her husband just home from work, cooking "in the kitchen smiling and stirring / looking like she still wants him." The distance from pretence and putting on a good face to well-meant verbal deception is short: "I said you can't help what you feel / it's what you do that counts / not believing a word of it." Ill-meant deceptions and hurtful acts done in darkness are not long to follow.

Such is the poet's picture of being an observant and sensitive child in a tiny burg in Nova Scotia. Growing up to adulthood is no easier. In "Small Town October," the boring loops of life there are depicted not with nostalgia, but in their detrimental essence: "Fall and everything changes / but this place repeating itself in pumpkins. / Every face is a friend of a friend / and being known is exhausting." Although she claims that "[w]hen I leave town I'm not coming back," she already imagines, without having yet left, the pressures of returning:

"Everyone knowing I'm back and waiting on something." This "daughter of perpetual hope / and disappointment" becomes a wife and mother, on both counts a predictably manic one. McRae writes of a woman "barely listening," who finds it "[s]trange how I feel so little in this scene / compelled only to detail // that is your mouth moving around words I've heard before"—words that repeat like those pumpkins every October. Beneath the lack of expressed feeling, which also renders inaudible the words of others, is a radically different internal voice: "I need calamity—a wreck, a crash / I can start there, close enough to feel it matters"; "Winter and I'm driving fast and / skiing straight down. / I think I'm thinking too much / and wanting that edge / to catch to fly up / a wreck of skis, arms, legs, poles / crashing into woods to the sound / of brush breaking"; "I'm inviting disaster."

The trouble with trouble is that, although it can be provoked, it hardly needs to be invited. It tends to welcome itself and doesn't knock before entering. When desire for drama "collapses into drama I no longer want to keep" and when "crawl[ing] / from the staleness you made for me" leads to a "[l]oneliness / [that] makes fools of us all," then the poet considers what it means to play "For Keeps": "I wish I could remember / more of those things / that come to mind / just when they're leaving." This poem reminds the reader that being abandoned by a husband may be a painful practice round for when one's children leave home. The paper being inked in "Conjugal" could be a college admission contract if it wasn't a document solidifying divorce: "You sign us away like a gift to yourself." If that is looking farther ahead than *Next to Nothing* looks, this introspective book has given us no reason not to anticipate the worst. With its nondescript diction and form, working quietly away at honest autobiography (albeit on occasion falling into a flatness not always counter-balanced by the flashes of internalized anger), the collection will not elicit wows for its verbal pyrotechnics. Its strength lies not in formal or sonic exuberance but in its self-focus and command of narrative.

Ilona Martonfi's *Blue Poppy* describes a different kind of life altogether. Far from staying in one place, Martonfi has moved around—born in Hungary, then spending part of childhood in a German refugee camp, then emigrating to Montreal, then, after getting married to a Sicilian, spending significant time in Italy. Being peripatetic hardly leads to happiness. In fact, to be frank, McRae's harsh poems are a walk in the park compared to Martonfi's. Hers are a catalogue of what are, alas, everyday and genuine horrors, committed by her monstrous husband, who is vile and almost inhuman: "You ordered me not to talk to my mother, / sister Erna, my friend Sylvia." "Our daughter was one week old, / you slapped me with the baby in my arms." "You slapped me three days / before the birth of our fourth child." "In the hotel room, you swirled the rum in your mouth. / Spat twice into my face: 'Now you can tell your friends, / I am not a violent man.'" "The only time my husband spoke directly to me / was to mock me." "He said: 'I could push these keys into your throat / and you'd be dead. Get back into the house.'" "'I'll throw you down the elevator shaft, if you divorce me!'" "He poured the wine on my head. I sat soaked. My hair. My / eyelids. My face. He stood over me and poured."

Like McRae's volume, Martonfi's has an arc. It begins with "The Apple Tree," which she plants on the same day that she loses her virginity to her husband-to-be; even then there is a hint of the violence to come. Next, for many pages, the unbroken circuit of abuse and domestic life continues, "twenty-four years of battering, four / children, and one granddaughter." After the divorce is finalized, the poems shift to remembering her mother, to whom the book is dedicated; in dealing with her mother's death, Martonfi goes back to her childhood. Around half of the volume's poems are in long lines from ten to sixteen syllables. This gives the perception of roominess, even though within that room there is a quality of confinement. Sentences of the starkest type alternate with names of objects and even starker sentence fragments. An incident will be described, then followed by locutions that recall the scene of a crime: "Soaked in wine. Until, I got up and washed my face and hair. / Scraped food from plates. Washed the dishes. Blue-painted / cupboard. Embroidered flower picture. The quilt patched / together." It sounds like a report written by an exhausted policeman or in the prose of a gifted automaton.

To encounter a happier account of the possibilities of family than Martonfi's and McRae's, as well as a wider (but not necessarily deeper) account of the world, Soraya Peerbaye's debut is recommended. *Poems for the Advisory Committee on Antarctic Names* is not a family story, exactly, but its lines contain many glancing mentions of a beloved older brother, Yousouf, with whom the poet travels to the Antarctic Peninsula; of a "mother's skirt" held by the young Soraya, as her parent "comes down to the parquet / knees smooth as opals" and gives her daughter the memory that elicits the poem "First memory of memory"; of a "great-aunt's cookbook" that "keeps a concoction / for cough syrup, made from garlic, fennel, sugar." Most prominent in these poems is the father, especially in the section called "Curios: Poems for K." The eleven titles there point to Peerbaye's Mauritian origins, for though she was born in London, Ontario, her father's past is present enough for her to hear him as a child, under "the sun-sequined shade / of the mango tree, he and his friends / arguing in Créole, playing in English." (They are playing Scrabble, sequestering themselves from more sporty engagements.) A loving man, he is also well-loved. Peerbaye prettily says that she has "learned to make my attention / gentle" when she listens to her father talk. She translates back to us much of what she has heard.

This is mainly a book of nouns, at least in its essence, concerned as it is with persons, persons as refracted through objects, objects as described by words, words as grounded in places. Peerbaye at one point responds to a baffled query about her interest in a "souvenir pen" by saying, "Because I believe in this, the object, quotidian, beloved. / What our hands have held." This is a little too much, the first sentence sounding like an over-expository voice-over, the fragment that follows too precious. But the moment is minor, one of few false notes. The lines are not needed, because the poems already embody and make the point. The father's (and thus the poet's) history lives in her titles and the lines that follow them, balancing the narrative and lyrical modes with an easy but finely calibrated lilt: "Caméra," "Armonica," "Stéthescope." This last is especially lovely, because what his daughter feels for the object is like the feeling that the father himself literally feels when he holds the object up to a chest: "teaches me heart sounds, lung sounds: / murmur, hum, crackle, / the terrifying heave, / arrhythmia of flutter and gallop, // thrill, the one he can feel / through his fingertips." My favourite of these poems is "Disque," which starts by hearkening back to a broken 78 rpm record and ends with father and daughter sitting "in the living room, as the needle / passes through its brief darkness, a cyclical / crackly creek." Although he owns CDs, he can't stand their "breathless perfection." He "misses the scratch, skip and stutter" of old vinyl. (One can only guess what he thinks about MP3s.) By the final stanzas the creek has travelled its distance, showing how well Peerbaye handles a conceit, as she considers the "gesture itself, / the needle carried to the record's surface, / a pond where the water ripples inward." Family is destiny, or the largest part of it. There is music everywhere here, not just in the poems but also in their stories. Her father sings Jacques Brel "in gruff giggles / so as not to weep"—an excellent observation of a man, sensitive to art, displaying while withholding emotion. When seeing Charles Aznavour perform in Toronto, he "turns away, wraps his arms / round himself, caresses / the nape of his neck."

But a poet by her vocation must also choose an alternative family. Peerbaye's parental figures in verse are not always apparent, except for Hopkins, who is everywhere: in the verbal and adjectival kennings ("We goat-head into the wind," "the cricket-quilted dark"); in the pregnant word from the poetic past ("shines with a curiosity vivid as a kingfisher," "kingfisher eye quicker than mine"); and in the propulsive rhythms, abrupt stops, elided articles, off-kilter negatives, thickets of sonic effect, and repetitions with a difference:

> He lifts it from ground,
> where it lies, hatched
> by hatchet of wind. It opens
> its beak: hisses: no song hinged
> on this breath.
>
> I knelt, nestled her between my thighs. She slipped, hopped away; I plopped her back, smoothed her taut ears. She darted. Claws rasped as I grasped her by the haunches. She bit, breaking skin. I squeezed her head down, spanked her across flank.

The former excerpt has a more compact energy, though the latter prose passage is probably a better mixture of Hopkins's rhythms with those Peerbaye elsewhere deploys. Either way, the influence only helps the poems, even if it is not fully assimilated. Other father and mother figures are harder to detect. One cannot point only to Hopkins for the way Peerbaye has with light, though his dappled things and dragonflies drawing fire do come to mind when reading her descriptions of it: "On the leaden sea, from each prism, a blue, luminous / hum"; "in the streets, young men, brown ankles bangled by sunlight / and rainwater"; "the seashells line the illuminated glass shelves"; "All the sky's greys mineralize to birds."

If one took the major concerns of Peerbaye's book and streamed them into two separate volumes, one might get (minus the overseas locales) something like *Inventory* by Marguerite Pigeon and *Never More There* by Stephen Rowe. The latter book deals with family stories, which often means conjuring "memory by proxy." Its many attempts to rearticulate "a name from the days of my father and father's father" is also tied to place, in this case Heart's Content, Newfoundland, the warmly named town where Rowe was born. The former book shares Peerbaye's interest in objects. Pigeon's volume is a virtual collection of them, fifty-eight poems in alphabetical order, the titles of which are the names of the objects being described, from "Apartment Block" and "Banana" to "Wings" and "Yucks" (as in laughs). The poems are hit-or-miss. "Cock" and "Cunt" are funny, gaining verve not just from the objects themselves, but from the vulgarisms chosen to name them. (The titles "Penis" and "Vagina" would doubtless yield different results.) Whereas the anaphora in "Television" leads to uninspired lines, the same rhetorical figure used in "Colony" leads into lines of fascinating strangeness and sadness: "Ant-girls chew the meat of leaves. / Ant-girls in an empire of females. / Ant-girls, only some, grow wings, and, in their myriad eyes, multiply visions of resistance[ ... ] / Ant Queens and the aunts know life in the colony is long, and the ghost of love is terrible." In the case of both poems the formal choice is fitting, since both television and an ant colony seem as repetitive as anaphora; only the latter object, though, provokes the kind of defamiliarizing observation that tends to give object poems their life.

The most extreme example of that mentally fracturing mode of refraction is Gertrude Stein in *Tender Buttons*, where an associative mode of irrationality is sung in sonic strings of prose of exhausting density. Another extreme example on the other end of the continuum is the prose poetry of Francis Ponge. Those poems instead confront one with hyper-rationality and are deliberately flat in their sonic and figurative effects. By giving us a range of rhythms and enough sounds in her sentences and decorous fragments to perk up the ear, as well as by trying to absent herself from the descriptions as living actor (as opposed to "author"—one of the best poems is called "Marguerite Pigeon"), Pigeon tends to split the difference of these extremes. Sometimes, this results in a more humanizing and likeable object poem than one might expect; at others, this balance paradoxically results in vitiating her attempts to enliven the object. In Frankenstein movies, doesn't the insentient creature have to be literally shocked into life?

The project of *Inventory* is a strange one, if you think about it, although we anthropomorphize all the time in our daily lives. But we think about such transmutations as infrequently as we meditate upon objects qua objects, which is where the interest of Pigeon's project lies. Perhaps the conceit itself is not enough. Given that both the cover and the title page picture a card catalogue, it is telling that the poem called "Library" ends with a kind of admission: "After lock-down, ideas mutter their blues, / earnestly pray for a revolutionary conceit // that would spell rebellion." This is not that conceit. There are times in this series of poems when an "exercise" quality obtains, without the formality, say, of the Oulipo group, where a kind of fundamental conservatism is pressed so hard in formal calisthenics as to re-emerge on the side of the radical. I wouldn't have thought from the outset that a more frequent recourse to narrative might be desirable for such a project as Pigeon's, given that narrative can often be a crutch in such poems. But when it comes to bringing objects to life, personal stories can admittedly help. (A comparison with Peerbaye's object poems is instructive.) That Pigeon won't rely on such stories is impressive in its own way—and in that sense she takes something from Ponge and Stein. There is still plenty here worth reading and enough times at which she crystallizes, either through sheer strangeness or astute observation, our unarticulated thoughts and feelings about something we see every day.

The only object-poem in Stephen Rowe's *Never More There* is called "The Wallet" and, like many of the book's lyrics, it is elegiac. Rowe holds its weathered leather in his hands, describes its folds and contents. He then describes one moment in the life of the man who used it, his father, who, after feeling a "grip on his chest," is "waiting for the doctor" with his wife and silently "turned to her / with his wallet, yellow eyes and all their weight." This is near the end of the book. Two poems later, in "The Hero Cometh," the lyric is not merely elegiac but outright elegy, taking its initial tone and diction from Auden's memorial for Yeats: "His heart seized up on a day like any other. / The sun smiled, no more, no less than usual, / no pigeons burst from perches." Cycles of filiation, both personal and poetic, are intriguing to Rowe. The father poems are long preceded in the collection by "Below the Spruce," a series of fourteen altered haibun that conveys in moving, briskly comprehensive fashion the life of Rowe's grandfather. Scenes of adventure—from "a cargo ship off Australia" the old man, now young, leans "on the white crusted rail. // whitecaps / crash the hull / men cheer // in a ring for two deckhands, wrists wrapped in rags. Their sweaty arms glisten at dusk. Someone stops the fight"—give way to moments of amused contemplation: "*Dad*. The vowel almost shouts affection. *Pop*. More reverence and awe." If that latter vowel signals awe, might not the consonants containing it plash and plop with plosive irreverence, creating a pleasing frisson? No matter—the poem is the heart of the book and beats strongly. Rowe's chosen form works well, moving us along through family stories and the poet's thoughts, speed and sound commensurate in the blocks of prose. Interrupting them, the tiny unpunctuated stanzas arrest us, almost emptying the page, thus carving out small spaces for silence where reverence can occur.

In addition to Auden, *Never More There* takes a touch of verse from Tennyson and Larkin from across the pond; from among Canadians, some lines of Lorna Crozier and Alden Nowlan and Patrick Lane are used. One poem, "A Pre-emptive Dirge of Sorts for My Grandfather," has a scene reminiscent of Frost's "'Out, Out,'" although unlike the boy in that cold-blooded story, Rowe's grandfather survives. The eternal return of the family is a theme throughout, as is the return of older art in the work of the newcomer. Rowe does not rely only on published poets to represent the poetic past. Unknown singers and bards are recalled in titles such as "The Blacksmith," "The Balladeer," and "I Knew a Maid," the last the finest of the lot. These have an old-fashioned feel that sits well here. Their surprising but cozy cohabitation suggests that even in those poems that are overtly contemporary, tones of the past resonate in their bones. Much of this, Rowe implies, is because all of the songs, both old and new, come from an actual place. His Newfoundland is personal and mythical, but also alive with the world of nature. He mixes these elements when he describes the cat, which "in all his slothful glory kneads your sweater / like a warm spread of dough." And he mixes them in a different arrangement in "Death Song for Crows": "Crows on a green gate, limp shrew in claws, beaks parted / to screak at seagulls, their eyes rolling up from the beach." And he mixes them all together in this tableau of two starlings frozen to death: "This denies / the idea of starling; she is the one you'll remember / of all the others swarming in a wing-blur. / There's a certain / preservation in the way the upper beak has been / snapped off, / its scraps like cracked almond shells." This last is from the well-titled "And You Were Never More There," with its rich ambiguity pointing toward both absence and presence.

As Rowe learns in that title and in the occasional minimalism of form taken from Japanese models, so likewise does Guy Ewing in another of the year's first books—but much more so, insofar as there is more of "less" found there. Ewing's *Hearing, and answering with music* strikes a balance between the absence of action (feel these quiet, calming poems) and the presence of production (acknowledge the actual making of these poems); between the activity of being aware and the passivity of remaining, in relative stasis, in the here and now; and between the natural and the urban worlds. This latter balance is the strong suit of the book. A tendency in writing a collection of minimal and meditative lyrics like these might be either to rely so heavily on anachronistic traditions of nature poetry that the real world of urban life—which is the strongest context of their making—would become unreal. Sometimes the book's effects are subtle and sometimes it seems devoid of any effects whatsoever. It is graceful, however, in the way that it incorporates into its lines elements that are in some senses incongruous, and in other senses yield up their incongruities through Ewing's poetic will. It is mental-palate-cleansing poetry, a sort of green-tea-sorbet in print that accentuates the pleasure of differing elements by tempering the starkness of their contrasts.

Like Williams and Moore and countless others, Ewing often lets his title serve as a first line in a gesture of demurral, as if the poem is not proud or loud enough to name itself. Yet there is no demurral from the assertion of value, as in the poem called "The best theory," which theory "is what we understand / in silence // reaching for a pen, / or watching clouds / billow over the lake." (This obviously does its work more effectively when spread vertically on a full page amid much white space.) Here the remnants of the august trope of reading nature as a book that is metaphorically "written" by the Great Author above melds with another (also essentially Romantic) trope whereby actual writing is figured as a "natural" act. In another poem, it is the absence of graffiti (another kind of writing) that provokes attention to, or the deliberate production of, other absences—of sight, of sound—in a synesthetic moment that is curious, for the senses seem to have been evacuated: "Brick washed clean—/ no graffiti. // My eyelid closes over / the sky. // No wind. // I am waiting,

waiting / for any // small sound."

If such quiet stillness suggests something of the therapeutic (insofar as meditative quietude is supposedly inextricable from getting oneself right, even if we never seem to achieve it and our world conspires against it), there are also reminders that where there is a need for therapy, there is likely a past of sadness, violence, trauma, or simply of desires unmet. This is suggested by questions that rise to a higher pitch than one has been led to expect, as in "Compressed": "That the mind needs the body / amazes the mind. // Why can't a thought break out, / blood scattering like leaves?" At other times, the balance achieved between the nature poem and the city poem is abruptly halted: "Birds fly into the light"—the reader feels: so far, so good—"necks snap, // rain of tiny bodies"—the reader sighs: not so good after all. Sometimes the therapeutic suggestion is simply, if metaphorically, made: "We've built / shelves for grief, // containers for need, // tried to stop wanting / more, // but we still want, / need, grieve." That last list of verbs is a Buddhist belief in a nutshell, a representation of the results of desire and of the unlikelihood of ever ridding ourselves of it.

Ewing's "Solace"— "fire in brick   solace of trees / ache of longing / anger in a small room"—reminded me in its finale of another first book this year with a therapeutic component, though in this case one not implied but explicit. Andrea Nicki's *Welcoming* contains critiques of a certain kind of therapeutic relationship. In "Therapist," after paying "22 dollars out of pocket" and watching the "therapist's face like a round clock" on which "the minutes tick away," the clock-face in question has "forgotten my story." The poem that precedes it, "Psychiatry," is intense: "The doctor questions whether I am paranoid / 15 framed degrees hanging behind him / like 15 pairs of eyes." No poem of three lines could take less from the tone of the typical haiku (which three-line poems always recall, and which Nicki's volume also contains). It is an interesting formal approach. Poems titled "Depression," "Suicidal Despair," and "Mental Illness" continue the theme, no less unhappily from no longer being under the professional's gaze.

So it is a therapeutic volume in being *about* therapeutic relationships and (at least as depicted in this cluster of poems) their lamentable failures. It is also a therapeutic volume in that it apparently means to do therapeutic work. It is dedicated "*to incest survivors*" and contains "Adult Survivors of Incest," an abecedarian poem, the form of which is effective for Nicki's greater purpose. From a critic's standpoint, the dedication somewhat forestalls criticism on "poetic" grounds, which in a way are rendered moot. If one were to critique *Welcoming* on other grounds, one might remark that the poems of professional frustration ("Adjunct," "Academia," "Rejected C.V.") make the exploitation by academic institutions felt by those attempting to rise through their ranks essentially, if inadvertently, commensurate with the trauma of incest. They are not the same (for starters, one of them begins with a choice and the other does not) and it is not probable that the poet thinks so. Yet the close proximity of these poems with others like "Reporting Rape," which are on radically different topics but which exhibit similar levels of disgust, gives one pause.

In a way, *Welcoming* embodies the interwoven nature of the personal, political, and aesthetic, even as it seems to resist it. The volume's complex confusion in its terms of what constitutes various levels of trauma is in part produced because Nicki tries to do such a wide range of formal work. This range of forms is a lot to pile on one's plate, even more so for a burgeoning poet. Some of these formal choices are failed and some are fruitful. The concrete-type poems don't pan out, nor do those that worry over a few syllables in repetitions of seventies-era sonic experiments. There is a good deal of pat comparison—"her eyes like two suns," "his eyes two moons," and the like. Yet there is also in the book a wonderful and reverent diptych, "Ode to a Moose" and "Moose I Have Lost You," the poetic panels of which are essentially beautiful prayers. I kept imagining while reading them that "moose" was a version of "Lord" or some similar word, given the poem's locutions—but Nicki's choice of "moose" is perfect, leading to moments of strangeness, of bafflement, to a sense of wistfulness, of mystery: "Moose, don't let me get lost in the matrices of your antlers." "Moose, you are not bothered by your enemies who ridicule you from afar, say you are stupid." "Moose, teach me to accept my own nature, my human head without antlers." "Moose, I have lost you / I cannot see you anywhere." "Moose, my love for you has become insecure." "Perhaps we are co-existing now, moose / Why do I need to see you to know you are real?" These two are strong poems, and those titled "Ravens" and "Prayer for the Bees" ("The bees are dying / Yellow gold butterscotch ripple / receive this honeyed thought") partake of the same strengths. *Welcoming* tries to do so much work of so many kinds that its burden is hard to bear. But then it is a book that means to speak to those who carry unspeakable burdens. If it offers any solace, it has fulfilled its truest purpose.

Michelle Muir's *Nuff Said* is also a book with a purpose and poses some similar problems for the critic. At the formal level, however, Muir is operating from the opposite end of the spectrum of Nicki. Rather than trying everything under the sun, she works mostly in a single mode—relatively long free-verse poems in the first-person, heavy with rhyme. In short, this is spoken-word poetry put on the page. As a fourth-grade teacher (as well as a two-time champion of CBC's *Poetry Face-Off*), Muir is often speaking to her students as they age into adolescence and beyond, while at the same time speaking from the stage and the page to her adult readers or listeners. Achieving balance in reaching such a multivalent audience is not easy. There is sometimes a sense of preaching to the converted, which can be either invigorating or patronizing, depending on one's mood as much as on anything else. Liberal values already agreed upon by most people who would pick up this book are rehearsed with performative vigour. I took pleasure in encountering a fellow traveller who is as paranoid as I am about Blackberrys and Facebooking and "tell-lie-vision" and the way that *they* try to track my whereabouts by asking me for my Air Miles number when I go to the Beer Store: "So indoctrinated are we / That we voluntarily / Offer our welts as ID / To anyone who demands it / Student number / Social insurance number / Health card number / Employee number / Driver's license number / Work number / Home number / Fax, blackberry and cell phone number. / PIN number / Air miles number / Credit card number / They got your number. / They got your number." The word "welts," with its blunt physicality and historical resonance, is good, as is the way "number" transforms through repetition from a numerical sign into something like "more numb," which is how "They got your number" in the first place.

As the above excerpt indicates, Muir is a fan of the list. There is a "To Do" list and a list of "A Few of My Favourite Things." There are also seven poems called "Mich-Understood" that list the different aspects of the poet's personality by embodying each aspect in a created character—for instance, Indigo is the artist, Mona is the militant, Shugga is sexy, and Ms Muir is a demure teacher: "Not wanting to commit to anything / Because secretly / She wants to do everything. / Trying to be everybody / for everybody / Until there is nobody left for her." (Alas, there is a Ms Muir in many of us.) There are also the ludic companion poems "Ain't That Some Shit?" and "Some More Shit," which are lists of pet peeves and other observations. I was feeling her when she says, "I've never liked moths, because when you kill one, it doesn't bleed... it just gets all chalky. *Ain't that some shit?*" But I had to pause at another peccadillo: "Ping-pong and the trampoline are Olympic sports... they eliminated softball but ping-pong and the trampoline are safe... *I mean really... why can you get a medal for that shit?*" I am as much for softball as the next person, but I stand neither pro nor con on trampoline, though it looks pretty hard to me; as for the worthiness of Ping-Pong, however, can its practitioners in other lands (to say nothing of Forrest Gump) be wrong? This comic piece of cultural insensitivity sits oddly but intriguingly in a volume that includes, in two iterations, this koan-like creed of pedagogy: "When I get into that classroom, we will be / Respecting difference / Protecting difference / And reflecting difference / Until difference doesn't make any difference."

But a teacher will try whatever works and Muir must be a good one. Poems such as "The Thread," "I Hope They Ask the Things I Didn't," and "Kidspeak Guru" all are concerned with problems of teaching and with what its goals and outcomes might be. As practical and personal expressions of classroom experience, these pedagogical poems are to my mind preferable to most pedagogical theory. As poems, more deliberation of structure would be welcome as a counterweight to their improvisational freedom. Granted, too much poetry being produced of late is so outside-edited and over-workshopped that structure and polish are practically gimmicks. In that sense there is a definite freshness to *Nuff Said*. Yet in an attempt to retain the performative power of the music Muir loves (names of great artists are scattered throughout), the poems as a collective whole might gain by considering different structures, or even by curtailing one level of formal freedom in the process of discovering others. This is not to say that the lyric "song" must be compromised. In "Jazzzzzzzzz," Muir writes that the music of the title is "Just the intense orgasmic coincidence / Of the right elements coming together," that "Jazz doesn't concern itself with the right note / It is brutally honest." Although jazz has a range of symbolic meanings to listeners, this might not fly if you were in Duke Ellington's Orchestra playing out of key. The right elements don't always come together merely by coincidence, nor is attaining the "right note" the opposite of being "honest." However, the performative mode of spoken word is steeped in an immediacy that calls into question certain notions of what constitutes a "successful" kind of structure or form. Furthermore, as a teacher, Muir is speaking from a position where even to open students up to their own suppressed potential, a whole host of calcified social, institutional, and even personal norms must be resisted. One assumes that she knows what methods work best in doing such work on the stage and in her classroom, and on these levels, one defers.

Given the kinds of phrases that appear on the back of Shaista Justin's debut, *Winter, the unwelcome visitor*—phrases such as "From brief and academic, to wordy and effusive," "Unstintingly political, unforgivingly critical of commonly held ideas," and "her fascination with colonization and the contemporary manifestations of historical tragedies"—I was expecting much more overt pedagogy than I ended up getting. That turned out to be a good thing for the poetry. Justin mostly manages to engage her aforementioned "fascination" without resorting to dry accounting or to slack historiography, which is to say she resists the quick turn from pedagogic to pedantic. The book's overall heaviness is leavened by the humanity of its love poems; although these are not the strongest poems in the book, they have a positive effect. Perhaps the best love poem is the one to her father, which begins strikingly—"My Dad still dreams like an immigrant"—and doesn't stint in recording the necessity (or is it the curse?) of having a chip on the shoulder when one is thrust into difficult circumstances: "Boy, did he prove that he wouldn't be defeated." "How he raised us to be better than those sluggards / in the schoolyard still slugging away in my dreams." You can see how, if this is the tone of a love poem—another one begins, unpromisingly: "Our love is conflicted like the Middle East"—that the dominant tone of the book might well be apocalyptic. And, so it is. There are remnants of early Eliot throughout, but especially in some of the glosas, where Justin attempts to channel Gwendolyn Brooks, Pablo Neruda, and W.B. Yeats, among others.

It is in the poems of South Africa that Justin is at her best. In them, she often achieves an effective mélange of approaches—there is a postcolonial political thread running through them that is strengthened by being interwoven with strains of the poem of local speech, as well as those of the landscape poem. These last strains are the volume's strongest, as in "On the Way," which begins: "In Hermanus, / where the whales never came, // the land reached out / to greet itself at every curve: / a floss of road / between ochre mountain and salty sea." This is quite a way to picture a coastline. In describing the title feature of Cape Town's "Table Mountain," she writes, "Shadows of jutting rock / false echoes of themselves... // Beaten by the sun / or polished by a rag of fog, / the sun breaking on it / or the fog caressing it, // she has surrendered to neither sky nor sea." In the missing comma after "rock" is found a touch of the inconsistent punctuation that pointlessly troubles the volume, but such matters are minor when weighed against the refinement of description by which Justin captures that massive but still invitingly human-scaled natural edifice that in its name is domestic, in its size is majestic, and in its location overlooks one of the world's most gorgeous coastlines, as well as one of its historically most-troubled countries.

In Gillian Sze's *Fish Bones* the reader finds little of politics. One does find much of love, or at least of eroticism: "The man I'm with likes to bite my hands, / leaves little red dashes on my knuckles / and along the bones of my fingers. // He pinches my breasts, / says they're so soft he only does it / to see if they're real." Elsewhere, in "The Kiss," a tiny blown-kiss of a poem, "eyelashes strain to meet." These eyes trying to touch each other are appropriate not only because there is romance in the air, but because Sze's poems are described by her as ekphrastic. We can imagine her getting close to, almost kissing (if not with her mouth, then with her eyes) a painting she admires. She writes that the book "emerges from my engagement with artworks" in a handful of museums named in the acknowledgements. But with the exception of "To John Lyman and the Portrait of His Father," the ekphrastic nature of the poems is more muted than in most ekphrases. The visual artwork that has provoked the poem is hidden behind the curtain of the page. This discretion works in favour of the eroticism that runs through the volume. Also accentuated is the way in which both erotic poems and ekphrastic poems can give voyeuristic pleasure.

There is no wasted meat in *Fish Bones*. Sze is often at her best when most withholding, a predominant mode being the elliptical, as in the entirety of part one of the six-part "I'll Make the Drinks Tonight": "My current lover—/ she is nothing like you." There is a dark (not morbid, but perhaps slightly mean) humour in these lines, as there is elsewhere in the volume. There is also an untold story lurking. Perhaps it is the one we hear in "Bird Watching": "*Love on a pedestal,* / you said when we first saw the birds. / Your voice broke the unerring quiet, // broke the same way when months later, / you told me that you were sorry / to have fallen in love with another woman." If one doesn't always get the full story, or see the painting behind the poem, one does pick up snatches of prior poems. Is that Pound's "River Merchant's Wife: A Letter" one hears in "She Has a Lovely Face"? The locution is similar. ("In the heat, / I thought you romantic, / that someone who still scythed / must also keep chickens. // Up the road, / your hair shone dark as blackcurrants. / I confused the barley you shook out / for strips of sun.") Perhaps Williams's "Sympathetic Portrait of a Child" inspired "The Jailer's Daughter"? These Modernists may be models, but only Stevens is named outright, both in an epigraph to the book and again in a poem called "The Rumored Jar," a nice work of expansion on his "Anecdote" of the same: "What is new / and what is ordered / is not in the jar, / but in how I've capped it / with an open mouth / and learned to swill the air." In fact, this poem and the two that follow it, "Playing Fish Bones" and "Lunacy," comprise an inspired bit of sequencing, so well do they fit together. But then, the book as a whole has an admirable coherency, a certainty of organization and tone.

Equally coherent, if not of the same calibre, is Nic Labriola's *Naming the Mannequins*. The book begins with a night watchman at a mannequin factory. It is midnight and he gives female names to the plastic bodies (they all end with *a*)—not a bad start. The conceit of the book is that we move in time, poem by poem, through the hours and minutes of the dingy night until 6:30 in the morning, following a cast of characters that float in and out of the poems. Beginning in the mannequin factory is a good idea, because it allows us to see that there is intention behind the caricatured nature of the figures that populate this imaginary Tom Waits-Charles Bukowski world. But Waits seems partly apart from the real or modern world in his arcanity and weirdness, while Bukowski wallows in his own literal and existential filth. Labriola's poems—which include a boxer, a ring girl (the boxer and the ring girl have sex in the dressing room after a bout), a bum, a psychic, a tattooist, a leather-wearing thug (he participates in a "rumble")—are too controlled to bring to life his squalid characters or the city they inhabit. The material, by choice, is hackneyed, as it would be in most gangster movies or tales of drunken sprees. The fact that such stories are hackneyed in outline is no mark against them (so is Keats's "To Autumn," *in outline*). The devil is in the details. *Naming the Mannequins* is a case in which the content would be better served by some wildness of form. Labriola's ability to control his lines and write in a variety of stanzas speaks well for his future projects, but in the present case it would be preferable to have more moments like his description of Henry (the tattooist) searching out "a plate of wet ham" (nicely gross), some formal equivalent of the "jagged open cans of sloppy beans" he invents. The book does begin to get there at the end, when Labriola switches to the second person and "you" are bitten by a panhandler in the hand, which over the final three poems swells up like a balloon. Then the balloon-hand lifts "you" up so that the wretched city beneath is visible. And then "I" help "you" cut off the bloated hand, then your arms, then the rest of your parts, then "I" put "you" and your pile of parts in a child's red wagon, pulling "you" along with some manuscripts and crossword puzzles. Strange and sordid stuff—now we're talking.

A more effective approach to the seedy side of life is taken by Jeremy Stewart in (*flood basement*, an oddly titled book that even in its half-bracketed title suggests something messy and perpetually unfinished, like the open-ended and practically uninhabitable lives he describes. Open-endedness in this case represents not possibility, but the inability of his characters to contain the boredom that swerves so frequently into chaos, which happens because these people with dead-end lives need to experience some action, even if it brings only additional trouble their way. Stewart's project is more successful than Labriola's, in part because the former is more wedded to the real. Even though Stewart also often works in archetypes, these are closely associated with places in Prince George, BC. The tendency toward broad brushstrokes, but also the connection to place, can be seen from the opening lines of the book: "Fort George Park is half graveyard   half love letter / to working mothers and blonde babies / stoned long hairs   as my Grandpa would call them[.]" The more personal Stewart gets, the better he writes. The snatches of graffiti (with explanations of their origins) that take up a single page each, helping to divide this long, unstructured ramble of a book, seem almost like negative mantras stuck in his head. Another technique of dividing the littered stream of the poem is with small running stories printed in italics about a friend-slash-nemesis named L., a native contemporary from a rougher side of the tracks and with violent cousins named B. and W.

In this world where a mall is "(The centre of it all)" and where "nothing is ready to happenherenothing ishappeninghereright now[,]" it was inevitable that a future poet would say to himself, "*I can escape / can I escape / can't I escape / I can't escape.*" There are compensations, or at least attempts to fit in and make the first attempts at art out of the environment. Some may nod with nostalgia at scenes like the one inside the 7th Avenue Legion Hall, where there is "long dark hair and denim / double-kick drums and floor toms / tremolo picking down-tuned XLS / slap-back drenched garage howls / 2 x15 bass cabs with horns / black Marshall stacks and heads / stereo QSC 2000 watt amps / mosh pit injuries and unsigned waivers." Some doing the nodding will also likely be glad not to be spending current weekends that way. The sometimes plodding, sometimes jumpy cacophony regurgitated here is like the formal design of the book as a whole. It is not the most pleasant stream of consciousness one can dip into, nor does it always seem as if Stewart is making every distinction he might between what is worth cutting and what is worth including. Yet that lack of discrimination or pleasantness does in its own loose and unspooling way provide fittingly unfit confines for the lives that Stewart describes.

The second, shorter part of (*flood basement* ends with a "crow song." Stephen Rowe's volume, too, has its "Death Song for Crows." But even considering among the genre Stevens and his "Thirteen Ways," there is nothing quite like the poem that begins Kate Hall's rightly well-received debut, *The Certainty Dream*, which Hall merely calls "A Few Words about the Sea": "The vastness of the sea is missing. It is called blackbird. / Blackbird recollects mast, rigging and hull floating out there intact. / Blackbird until a swarm of dragonfly-looking things. / Blackbird in the well. / Blackbird in a circle closes around and eyes a sandwich. / Blackbird, then the throat. / Blackbird loves the dog and hates the baby." By the end, as well as about the end, "Blackbird sums up the ending except for the guilt. / Blackbird is what blackbird wants." There is a lot of anaphora in Hall's book. It seems to mimic repetition compulsion, to represent how the same elements often appear in different dreams, and to produce the effect whereby saying the same word over and over without changing it leads to its changing.

There are also a whole lot of birds. Mostly they are not blackbirds, but mynahs. But just as the blackbird is the missing vastness of the sea and all the rest of it, the mynah can be many things: "mynah morphs into crow / stands in for nightingale / don't assume abandonment / he needs a new name / not being himself anymore." Even if he becomes a different bird, or remains himself, he may not be a bird and may not be himself: "I count the mynah birds overhead / as minutes. But they are not / really mynahs. In the empty dump box, they are // not even beautiful, not exactly / birds; they are so dark and distant / on the horizon." Sometimes a bird is not a bird because "he was flat, he was a tapestry." Sometimes a bird is not a living, breathing bird but a problem and a piece of paper: "The problem was folded neatly over itself into an origami bird." Sometimes a bird is not paper but stone, not a problem but something that takes the place of a kind of a house: "It's equally possible that the dream house is not really / a house at all, but a bird, folded stone." It's equally possible that in Hall's poems any element is equally possible, or possibly equal to any other element. *The Certainty Dream* is mesmerizing. It is even anger-provoking. What arrogance is this, this perpetual making of things from things? The reader is rendered a mere mortal buffeted on tempests of meaning being made and stolen back. It is as if there exists a generous (at times), mean-spirited (at times), demanding and arbitrary God making creative decisions on our behalf and on a whim that have an effect on us. And, so it is. This God is called author.

The L=A=N=G=U=A=G=E group put across the idea for poetry readers that the elements in poems that we believe to have an existence outside of the poem, and those meanings inside of them believed to be inherent, objective, and locatable, were really just products of their grammatical functions. This notion is insinuated rather deviously in Hall's work as well. But I would say that she takes the argument further. By mixing the strains of the philosopher and the prophet (there is just a touch of Michael Palmer's tone in some of these poems, which works well to leaven the manic and ludic moments), while also knocking over and over again on the surrealism of the dream world's door (asserted here as an alternative reality), Hall forces these conundrums of meaning outside of any reading that would be consistently logical, or that we might confuse as being intellectually objective. Because she always keeps us disoriented, the reader on occasion is even led to doubt—even if it is patently ridiculous to do so—the very existence of the poem one is reading; or perhaps it exists, but is not in fact a poem. Perhaps it is a bird. (Hall does title one poem "I Invented the Birdcall," after all.) There is little to no exposition in this volume, as there usually is in poetry that purports to be (rather than genuinely is) disorienting, few if any meta-moments at which the poet pulls back the curtain and shows you how the lady in the sequins and the plume was made to levitate. From time to time certain notions coalesce, such as in "As Though Sealed in a Glass Jar," where we see that even a series of sentences that are essentially non sequiturs will seem coherent as a group, as long as there are enough related images among the non sequiturs. In such a case, coherence or logic is not a given going into the poem, as it usually is; however it coheres, and whatever kind of (dream) logic is revealed, this revelation and coherence take time to become manifest, as the elements held in common by the sentences pile up. Here one also notices that the sentence, as a logic-machine made out of words, is crucial in producing the effect. Fragments wouldn't work, because then the friction between logic at the level of the unit, and illogic at the level of transitions between units, would be lost. That is a big reason that dreams can be so troubling, because they contain familiar elements placed in unfamiliar contexts or in anarchic arrangements. It is also why so many bad surrealistic poems turn out to be just a jumbled list of a bunch of pseudo-weirdo kind of stuff. Hall is up to something much more important, taking from and adding to the surrealistic tradition, developing a hermetic and philosophically leaning dream world that taps into numerous existential wells.

In *Our Extraordinary Monsters*, a book that—along with Hall's *Dream* and Greckol's *Gravity*—takes the laurel among the first books, Vanessa Moeller makes the reader feel strange in a differently surrealistic way. The long sentences that constitute her lines in the sonnets that open the book march forward in linguistic lockstep; they are structured as if inexorable: "Cirrus unicus, / feathers detached from the wings / of angels who crash to earth after rejecting the degeneration / of paradise, who learn to live under our altostratus ceilings, / walk the streets with charred nubs that protrude / hideously from shoulder blades they hide under / old coats and dirty sweaters." There is a no-nonsense, rational strain, yet it is combined with concerns with things mysterious. The language of angels mixes with that of meteorology. Talk of the soul melds with that of biological functions: "The mystery / at our centre a milky area in the human heart with no function / that some claim is the soul's physical manifestation." Perhaps such discursive mixtures are themselves surface manifestations of the fact that Moeller's English came after her German and that the two languages still claim (almost) equal space in her head. From another land she writes, "This city is not my home but my mother's. / It bears down with brick and traffic, / and it contains half my language / *halb meiner Sprache, halb meiner Stimme.*" "When I was six," she writes in another poem, "I learned / to unbraid my vocal chords, / weave them into an angular / pattern of English instead of the / familiar orbed syntax of German / that had sheltered me since birth … // Eventually I learned to untangle / the Gordian threads of breath and accent / until my voice became cobwebbed / enough to sift away the vaporous / and leave only the gracile syllables / and the definition of a loess." Here she mixes the language of inspiration and geology, punning on that Aeolian sediment that also represents a loss of purity, stability.

Something of being blown by the winds of contingency and time characterizes many of Moeller's poems. In addressing her imaginary daughter, she writes a self-elegy: "When my body begins to erode, age scuffing away / my surfaces, you will begin to fully inhabit / the chamber of your name, learn to siphon / knowledge from the world and rearrange it / to fit the nooks and alcoves of your character. // Eventually I will be disincarnated, reduced to / flecks and wind, but you will read me again / in the syntax of your own daughter's body[.]" In other poems, postcards stretch into letters. In some, her English of the present carries on a correspondence with the German of her father from letters written forty years ago. In others, the missives are made up, messages from a past that didn't quite materialize, by imaginary people writing from the dark side of actual existence. These dead letters from the never-living close out this spectral, loving, and tough-minded volume by a poet of promise.

That does it for the debuts; now for the next ones, which is to say, on to those who have published books before. One fun and witty entry in the catalogue of 2009 is Jason Guriel's second collection, *Pure Product*. The cover shows a red-and-white striped bendy straw divided into three parts; in a way, you can judge the book by it. The tripartite division suggests that the title is meant in three ways. First, there is a "pop" sensibility (toward which the plastic straw punningly points, down into the unseen soda) that accounts for the products our culture produces and ingests. Titles such as "Thinginess" (which describes "the pushback / of a Coke can / before it gives / way to your compacting grip"), "Assemblage" (pointing back to an earlier era's attempts to compose commercial objects as art), and "On Derek Jeter's Batting Stance" (a perfect picture of the Yankee's magnetic preening at the plate) follow this line of inquiry. Second, there is the sense in which one often hears "pure product" uttered—behind an open car trunk on a cop show, after either buyer or buster has sampled a sugar-like substance on the tip of the tongue or rubbed on the gums. (The straw in this case is also a visual pun.) The suggestion is that, like the pure cocaine that will later, under less austere care, be contaminated with talcum powder, Drano, baby formula, and rat poison to extend its life in dollars (if not the life of its users), these poems are the real stuff; here, what is most minimal means more. The first poem, "Less," tells us as much, as do the short lines, spare diction, and physical slimness of the volume. Third, "pure product" alludes to those "pure products" that "go crazy" as imagined by William Carlos Williams. (Perhaps this accounts for the wrenched bending at the head of the straw?) The final meaning of the title thus directs us to a strain of overt reference, to a roll call of major modernists, throughout: "No room of your own perhaps / but leaf by leaf you branched / out into the world." "Like frost / in spring or spring / pools in that poem by Frost." "Airbrushed, buffed to the point of abstraction, / the patient etherised on a table / in Milton Bradley's game *Operation* / is as everyman as every able- / bodied Prufrock stripped of hospital gown / and dissected in art, heart tweezed by hand." This last citation circles us back to the first meaning of the title described above. Many young poets treat the same materials as Guriel; many bloviate or over-theorize in an attempt to give them meaning, or evacuate them of meaning in an attempt to retain the cool-factor thought to accompany insouciance. His wit and his minimalism steer Guriel away from these dual threats.

Stretching out much more in time and space, while also setting himself more rigorous formal limits, is Richard Greene. His third book of poems, *Boxing the Compass*, is excellent. Much of the time we are ensconced in the present; poets, too, must earn their bread, as one title, "At the College," has it. In describing how he earns his, Greene avoids the mundane through the clarity of his observation, the ingenuity of his rhyme, and the modesty of his wisdom:

> Serpentine, the path unwinds its innocence
> from building to building in flickering shade
> where my students feed lazy raccoons muffins
> and glazed doughnuts, as if to domesticate

the last wild things on this suburban campus,
though nothing can make the few deer unafraid
of engines, words, footfalls, the human rumpus,
or subdue the fox's wily nonchalance
and teach him not to kill anything helpless.
Here, among these fierce and sentimental students,
I stand on the edge of a world not my own,
snatching small goods from the large irrelevance
of what we do, making the old sorrows known
to children bearing their first calamities,
teaching solitudes to the newly alone,
explaining writers' exile to refugees
and notions of intrinsic worth to half-fledged
bankers, already driving smart Mercedes.

The snaking path on which innocence will become experience, the way both poet and students encounter their allegorical doubles in the animals around them, the mild acceptance of one's inevitable resentments: there are multiple worlds in these straightforward words. Greene's rhythms, locutions, and tones are varied throughout. From these multi-clausal, modern-sounding sentences we may move to lines with more archaic majesty, such as when, in "Two Chronicles," the soon-to-be martyred Polycarp speaks of his devotion to Christ: "'Eighty and six years have I served Him, and He has done me no wrong,' / his answer to the governor, / and tied to a wood-pile he gave thanks for what he had come to." Another man who was murdered, the Jesuit priest Martin Royackers, is described in the sparest of terms in the elegy bearing his name: "A head full of books at nineteen, / his conversation was with hogs, / their cleanliness, their intelligence, / and the slanders against them." That final phrase shows the subject's capacity for empathy.

There is religiosity in these verses, but not preciosity. Death and destruction may lurk at every turn, but not fear in the face of them. Greene's great-grandfather, "whaler out of Nantucket," returned "one year / to find his land fenced / for ecclesiastical uses, / tore it all down, / told the priest to go to hell, / and would do his own praying / after that." He "[g]rew old jigging cod / on the southern shore, / then fell from a roof / and lingered days to tell / his last stories, / empty his mouth of good oaths." Greene tells some good stories himself, such as one recounted in a memorial to a friend. Having dropped five one-dollar bills into the Manhattan wind, Greene watched as five locals each retrieved one; all were returned to him, thus temporarily dispelling "the myth of the nasty New Yorker." The native New Yorker for whom the elegy is written was not so quick to be dissuaded: "Far from your bed and bones, / I heard you, still yourself, touching this milk / of kindness with your tongue: / 'Repeat the experiment. This time, use twenties!'" The book draws to an end with poems in flexible blank verse, a series of sonnets, and finally a long and brilliant poem, "Over the Border," that chronicles Greene's trips to various archives in the States while doing research for *Graham Greene: A Life in Letters*, which he edited. This scholar's road poem is an ironic variation on the genre, just as the breathing tightness of its lines suggests, contra Kerouac, that there is as much freedom in constraint as in spontaneous, unscrolling composition.

Both Greene's and Guriel's volumes were published by Signal Editions, and thus edited by Carmine Starnino, whose fourth book of poems, *This Way Out*, was also released in 2009. With Greene he shares a sureness of form, though his poems are less wide-ranging, except, of course, that several take place in Italy, which is fairly far afield—geographically, at any rate. Culturally, Starnino seems more than comfortable there. The nine epistolary sonnets sent from Rome are especially nice, more expansive than the postcard poems one often gets from abroad, less tediously touristy or educationally expansive than one also often gets, in the latter case from poets not close enough to the country by blood to allow them the luxury to focus on the everyday instead of the desiccated eternal. He writes to one friend, "Honestly? This rubble-gawking feels like duty, / and ancient history an abstraction sleeping off its particulars." Come to think of it, also august is the history of Italian craftsmanship; the usual (essentially moral) hierarchy of seeing the sights before hitting the stalls is reversed: "Ruins are a great place to catch your breath after shopping."

Starnino has a strong way with repetition, as in the prose poem "Heavenography," where what is written upon the heavens are iterations of "working-class clouds," or in "Squash Rackets," which one is surprised to hear echoing Christopher Smart's beautiful love song to his cat Geoffrey in *Jubilate Agno*. "Squash Rackets" also points to Starnino's interest in objects, which he often allows to speak. "Who'll have me, the wedding ring cried out. / Who'll rescue me now that I'm unwanted?" So starts the "Tale of the Wedding Ring." His favourite objects are those that get their meaning through humble use, as does the "Front Door." An "Abandoned Fence Post, North Hatley" demands, "Look at me when I talk to you." Also often noticed are people who do things for us, as in "Our Butcher," in which the poet imagines himself "bon[ing] up" for the job—Starnino likes puns in which a verb or adjective points toward the occupation or object being described—or "brows[ing] apart a chest's cardiac leafage." His own related occupations (critic, editor, poet) come through in that verb, as they do in other moments, such as when late-night mopeds affect one's heartbeat, sounding out "spondee of rev and roar," or when clementines are not harvested or picked, but instead are "deleted from tree." There are many such gratifying touches throughout from a writer who must value quiet, given the several times that he remarks on its absence. Renters everywhere will appreciate the angry words offered "To the Couple in Apartment 949"—"Stair-stompers, all-hour furniture-draggers"—and recognize in their own domestic arrangements how noise begets noise, or how one noise can't quite drown out what is noisier, because more disturbing, as in "Loud TV from Next Door, Notre-Dame-De-Grâce": "First order of business / is to get it off our chest. / Pissed, we pull out all the stops: slam doors, / scream. Hotheaded, / hair-trigger, we mistake / a short fuse / for signs of life, husband and wife."

Indeed, a good number of this year's books, as one would expect, take up the domestic life, but not always in the ways that one would expect. In some cases the matter at hand is less about living in romantic or no-longer-romantic partnership, or about parenthood and its discontents and malcontents, than it is about something more literally domestic, as in Michael Kenyon's *The Last House*. This third volume of his is also a kind of emigration collection that is different from what is typical in today's Canada, coming as the poet did from England. But Kenyon is very much an immigrant poet, and his poems have in common with his poetic cohort from other lands much of the same kinds of sadness regarding the loss of a world and of its loved ones left behind. There is confusion in nostalgia, however. On the one hand, the past seems like a dreamlife: "Dad planned the old stone pile from the top / down with a fine view of rolling hills / and woods in the distance, the village / spire fixed in clouds." But this poem is called "Broke" and begins with an epigraph from Yip Harburg's "Brother, Can You Spare a Dime?" There is a reason people leave their homeland—because being there is hard: "Fifty-three years of struggle since / our family blew west and off / the sea to the dust of this hill." Even what might be an innocuous memory of a childhood pet turns sour: "Back home my parents wait on the hillside / for a sign. Meanwhile the creditors play / poker. Meanwhile I grow older and cry / hard at night because a dog will not live / as long as a man." "Picker's Sons" bring the old world with them and much of life remains a struggle, where one is forced to play a new game of struggling but where winning propositions are few: "The beginning of a fight's a farewell: / if you win you lose. *And if you lose?*" If life remains a game whose results seem ever out of one's control, you wouldn't know it by Kenyon's adeptness with a range of forms: sonnets, glosas, tanka, haiku. And despite a certain dreariness, he rouses himself for some nice erotic passages.

In *Lousy Explorers*, Laisha Rosnau's second book of poetry (she also wrote a novel, *The Sudden Weight of Snow*), the eroticism resides not in a present partnership, but in some once-felt sexual desire that, even if long dormant, might flare up someday, a resting but titillating danger: "Hands clutched around mugs in the coffee shop, / we didn't talk, I wondered what it meant / to have borne my restraint through each country / without you. / ...There was no heat when / I returned, my mind spored with other men." And bored, one hears, with the current one. "I will never be an architect in Montreal," she writes in "Sister Life," wondering, "What beautiful sister life was elsewhere, / in a frost-etched city or held in the hand of a man / who didn't have my phone number?" As for the man who shares her phone number, "Here we are, you and I and a bi-level bungalow / in a town built on the milled trees of a forest / eaten by bugs that burrow into wood, / leave behind decay the colour of twilight." Now, I'm not a licensed exterminator, but I believe those termites represent more than the necessity of getting the bungalow sprayed with toxic dust. But the woman in the poems keeps it all together, despite her "mood" being "a pie on the counter, heat rising / off the surface" (or because her moods are starting to seem like things in the kitchen, which is as good a sign of "domestication" as one will find). After all, there is the baby to consider: "Soon, we will set up the nursery, swaddle the baby / then watch him grow, leave." Then it's back to the life of ambivalence in this book where mixed feelings are successfully recorded.

In Ronna Bloom's muted, moving, oft-wrenching *Permiso*, the life that was lived with another has not panned out as planned. The book is an embodied example of the distinction Freud draws between mourning and melancholia. No death has occurred, so this must be the latter: "One day I found a different life than I had before." So Bloom begins. This is not the kind of life-change urged by Rilke's archaic torso of Apollo. No, this one wasn't exactly chosen, even if there was a kind of choice: "Last night. He said. After I said. / He said: *if that's the case, I can't stay.*" "Rolling on the land. / Whose life is this?" Bloom's is a life lived with a number of tocks-and-ticks on the clock. There are thus crucial domestic decisions to be made with a significant other, who also lives in time—which is a roundabout way of saying that having children was at issue: "I kept trying all those years / to bring down the future. // Called up old friends, did surveys: *what is good about having children?*" Good question, followed by an even better one: "*Isn't wanting what you* want *labour enough / without trying to want what you don't?*" The answer to that rhetorical question does, in the end, precipitate a kind of death—"When we were dying, before we were dying," remembers Bloom near the end of the book—so maybe this is a manual of mourning after all. Whatever it may be, clinically speaking, it is an exceptional end-of-relationship book, an explanation in almost, but not quite anhedonic tones of how to take the breaking up of a relationship without breaking up your own relation to your Self.

The end of relationships is handled differently in Fiona Lam's Enter the Chrysanthemum and Pam Calabrese MacLean's The Dead Can't Dance. For Lam, the fact that the father of her child is no longer her partner is a given, although he still comes around from time to time, producing some difficult moments. For MacLean, there is not one definitive breakup, but a string of almost interchangeable ones. In the section of her book called "The Morning You Leave Me," men leave women and women leave men—or rather, a woman writes a "Dear John" letter explaining "not that I am leaving / but rather / that I am gone." There is a dog (there are lots of dogs, some of them canines; the rest are romantic bums) who "belongs to a man / whose wife left him so long ago / he remembers her by another's name. / In the night he cries out, *Olivia, Olivia* / but she was called Amanda." In one poem a woman is left every night, but only in her dreams: "I awoke crying so often, / angry at him still in my bed, / each time forgetting / there was no other woman, / no other house." Is it premeditated wish-fulfillment, or her unconscious, prodding toward a different kind of security? "Not being loved by him / began to feel right. / So with every trip / I set aside / a nail / a board / a need / for a house of my own." Not that these feelings of dissatisfaction can't be communicated. One woman kindly asks her paramour to "Tell me [about] the night you waited while I danced / with fifty or was it 100 other men / (so you said it seemed) / until the last dance." The nostalgic strains of "Thanks for the Memory" these ain't. Is it any wonder that the book's next section is all about MacLean's dead (i.e., absent) father? This bitterly funny collection is a perverse pleasure to read. The spareness of its diction is a manifestation of MacLean's no-nonsense relation to the world and to her apparent experience of it. There are probably more good jokes per line in *The Dead Can't Dance* than in any other of the year's books. The main character in "The Ida-Mae Poems" is a great source of them. Her husband, although perpetually cuckolded, does get some loving attention: "Nights like these / she disposes of Angus quickly. / Butter should churn / so fast." She certainly has her soft side: "Ida-Mae has pet names / for all her lovers, / helps keep straight / who belongs to who. / On each child's birthday / Ida-Mae spends time / remembering the father." Such humour doesn't come out of nowhere, naturally, so it goes without saying that there is a serious undertow to all of these waves of sardonic winking.

You won't find much that is funny from Fiona Lam. Being a single mother, which is the topic of most of the poems in *Enter the Chrysanthemum*, is hardly a barrel of laughs. Before we see Lam as a mother, however, we see her as dutiful daughter. In the poems that open the volume, she shows us scenes of her admirable, if imperfect, parents. There is poignancy in her depictions of the kind of family life we eventually come to realize is her model for what she wishes her own family might be; there is sadness as she recounts the death of her father, of her mother's slide into dotage. Nevertheless, there is something missing in this first section. "But I was mere spectator now," she writes in "Origami," and this bespeaks the problem. In looking back to a time before she had begun to experience her own adult difficulties, Lam seems merely to recount rather than to engage, as if her distant past existed primarily to have narrative poems written about it. Perhaps the lack of immediacy I felt early on was a matter of contrast, for the poems that fill out the rest of the book are deeply engaged indeed. Just home from the hospital, Lam writes of how "the baby's father, when he's there, / broods on the outskirts of love." He's not there much. The real couple in this book is mother and newborn son; her description of the latter when breastfeeding, as a "[s]mall, sweaty cannibal," is both loving and unsentimental. The child is ever-growing; he is taken to the "Beach," he is taken to the "Water Park," he is taken into the mind of his mother. The stories she tells him are infiltrating the titles of her poems: "Rapunzel," "Mermaid," "Jack's Mom" (of Beanstalk fame). In "Mother," there is no "I" or "she," only a robotic, insentient "it": "Smiling, almost alive, it marches / blank-eyed through the child's day... / When the child's away, / the switch flicks / off. It halts. Folds / itself into something very flat, / unites with the couch, mattress, / floor." Not every moment represents the loss of emotion and bodily motion. Meaning is retroactively added to Lam's earlier parent poems when her own son breaks a glass and she erupts: "Suddenly my son's face became mine as a child, frozen / before the contortions of my mother's fury. / My own face stiffened into its inheritance... / My son clung to me in terror—/ all those mothers shrieking through my skin." Taut turns of phrase such as this often sit beside those more slack or less felicitous, but this doesn't greatly diminish the strong-point of the poems, which is the story being told. As Lam does well to convey, one will push oneself through a good deal of difficulty to have a little moment like the one when her son, at breakfast, "stirs in the honey, licks the spoon, / says *Thank you bees.*"

A grown-up's place in this world of always working for one's kids is half the subject of Mike Boughn's double-whammy of a book, 22 *Skidoo/ SubTractions*. The other half is the historical world of words themselves. It is really two books under two covers. One cover recalls the madness of a Cold War sci-fi imaginary now made tame by newer realities; the other depicts the bygone days of pulp fiction through lurid red lips, blue blazers and blouses, impassioned and anguished beige faces, and a hypodermic needle containing the letters *o-r-p-y-e-t*. No matter how you scramble it, the link between the lyric poem and dangerous dope is secure. If "dope" is not your bag, perhaps one of the hundred-plus other synonyms for heroin (according to one thesaurus) will tickle your fancy. Lost to changing fashion as most of them are, they would tickle Boughn's, for a running conceit in the 22 *Skidoo* part of the book is to give each poem a one-word title, a piece of pleasing but outdated slang: cahoots, caboodle, oodles, coots, hoosegow, oomph, canoodle, smackeroo, and the eponymous skidoo all include what "Oodles" calls "wild bundles / of unexpected oo's"; yap, showdown, skedaddle, golly, breather, swell, gab, sock, gunk, dandy, beef, scram, and gumption round out the range of language mostly left behind. That adds up to twenty-two poems, with each poem having twenty-two lines.

A numerical arrangement also obtains in the *SubTractions* section. Its two epigraphs—Boughn is fond of, and astute at choosing, his; more than half the poems have them—tell the tale. Dickinson leads us to understand that what is under discussion are *"Life's little duties,"* while Deleuze and Guattari explain why each poem's title is indeed a "SubTraction" that contains the phrase "minus one": *"The multiple must be made, not by always adding a higher dimension, but rather in the simplest of ways, by dint of sobriety, with the number of dimensions one already has available, always* n -1 *(the only way the one belongs to the multiple: always subtracted)."* When the logic of this excerpt is applied again and again in poems about maintaining the life of a viable family, mathematics takes on an existential weight that might, were it not for Boughn's wit and his syntactical refractions deflecting stark exposition, be too heavy to bear without cracking. I was and remain a big fan of Boughn's 2003 book *Dislocations in Crystal*, which contained several marriage poems, including the multi-part masterpiece "Next." If in that collection domestic arrangements met philosophical engagement, here the new math may lead to active disengagement (oxymoron and narco-pun intended) in "Weed Minus One": "The door opens / neither in nor out so your choices / are unlimited arrangements / of whatever baggage gets hauled along / and set free from Calvin's / ever lingering distaste for small / mercies' surprising connections—/ world in the unmaking." "Marriage Minus One" records the "flawless / little confirmation of hermetic / completion's anticipated smile" just before having it fly away. Boughn's language itself is hermetic and shifty, suggesting that the normal course of domestic narrative as we tend to encounter it in poems is strategically naive, a falsification in its ostensible clarity and lack of indirection. To the strengths of his earlier *Dislocations* he adds in this volume an expansion of the parameters of family life: "Kids Minus One" lead to "Waiting Outside the School Minus One," "Soccer Minus One," "Orchestra Practice Minus One," "Karate Minus One," "Seven AM Hockey Arena Minus One," and "Strapping on the Goalie Pads Minus One."

One infers not only that Boughn is attuned to the nature of parenting (including its capacity to produce fear in the father), but also that he must be an incredibly attentive parent. If the ambivalence regarding his role leads someday to his children being slightly disturbed when they realize what their Dad was really thinking during all those hockey games, then even that will be a sign of the strength of his commitment to fatherhood, for such a realization will likely be contingent on his having helped them to learn to read poetry. In the end, the deeper if difficult pleasures are entwined in mixed feelings regarding parenting itself, which also amounts to an adult commitment to honesty, as against a perpetual cultural marketing campaign promoting domestic bliss. "Ongoing Offensive Operations to Eliminate All Pockets of Resistance Minus One" may be a political poem (the invasion of Iraq lurks in its lines); and it may be a poem about battle manoeuvres prosecuted at home against men by their children and wives; but most of all it seems to be about how we have warring aspects of ourselves, whereby we wage an internal counterinsurgency to quell a rebellious nature that was insufficient enough to have led us to our current state of affairs, which is more or less what we were looking for.

As in Boughn's book, in Angela Hibbs's *Wanton* we also get our oodles. Her "Rockland" contains the refrain "Just give me oodles," while the eye-like *o*'s of that weird word are ensconced, too, in "Circles," the poem that precedes it: "Two moose cross the road, / two wine barrels balanced on stilts, / those gangly high-school boys, / their green eyes glowing in our slowing headlights." The reader is headed to the psych ward, where "pill cups" are "pushed along by the hour hand" of a clock that "is the only perfect circle in sight." Unlike in Boughn's book, Hibbs's has some radically poorly-reared children. These are found in the long series that lends the book its title. ("Wanton" is the name of a town, as well as a description of the various characters that people it.) The back cover calls it "something like the bastard child of Harold Gray's *Little Orphan Annie* and Harmony Korine's *Gummo*." For once, one defers to the writer of copy, as that summary would be hard to top. There are twisted pleasures to be had in the decrepitude of others, alas, and it turns out that they are propulsive; it is hard to stop reading the sequence, although it is also hard to keep up with what all is happening to whom, and whenever it did when it does, and whether or not whoever it was really was the one that did it to 'em. One thing here is for certain, however: some folks talk funny, have shitloads of sex, and don't hardly give a damn about their kids. They cuss a fair bit, too.

It is not a happy place to have imagined, but "Wanton," even in its wilful confusions, is a coherent construction, a fairly well-made world of ill-makings and cosmic unfairness. It is all the better prepared for by the poems that precede it, which are also often about kinds of illness, but are less imaginary and thus more sympathetic. Poems titled "Cindy Sherman" and "Anne Sexton" suggest something of the aesthetic world we are in, and the daughter whose Daddy knocks her out while pitching her a ball (and then has her lie about it to the doctor) may be able to identify with Wanton's population. "Metronome," about an obsolete world of mix-tapes and Walkmans, is also a moving poem about being crazed by remembering: "We dumped dated technologies. / Made citizen's arrests on vow breakers. / My ability to hurt you flagged; / I failed to listen to your sleep. // Now that I would lie awake, exhausted, fascinated / by your cake-shaped face, // lunatic to your round white moon, / could you make your faithful listener a tape? / Whirring wheels distract from your absence, / another unstable medium, absent as the new moon." It suggests how Hibbs's diction stays stark, but also bounces about like troubled thoughts in the head.

Of the books this year that took domestic life as their subject, none is more surprising or satisfying than Tonja Gunvaldsen Klaassen's *Lean-To*. We begin, "After all" (in the poem of that title), with the lines: "After the wedding, after wearing white, after the guests and the fields gowned and flowered; gaillardia, badgerholes; // after you shot the thing that held me up, the light cleaving and clattering knife handles against fieldstone, // reaching out to catch what was thrown, reaching for what had been held and held and held." Klaassen works as often as not in lines of prose punctuated by dashes and double line breaks. This gives a sense of temporary expansion that at any moment may be sharply truncated. She is as easy with the fragment as with the sentence, although *easy* is not quite the right word. Hers is a book full of tension, although not the sort that leads to the luxury of exploding, before utterly shutting down. The feeling instead is one of stoicism, preparedness, alertness. Her methods of forming her poems are original, nonce forms that feel correct and keep one guessing within a general atmosphere of security.

In "August after August," a multi-part anniversary poem in which the different parts are named after the traditional gifts given for the various years of marriage (paper, cotton, leather, linen, etc.), Klaassen shows a prosodically lighter side when in "Wood" she makes sounds like those found in Dylan's "Subterranean Homesick Blues" or REM's "It's the End of the World as We Know It": "Pheromones. Something roan. Billy Bragg on the stereo. / Broom handle, collarbone. Just a lucky so-and-so. // Rough-jaw, U-haul, screw ball / bully in the butter." It is a strategy she repeats less playfully in the hellish "Sidhe of the City" (the Sidhe—pronounced "she"—are Celtic spirits of the underworld):

> hogs modified by hundreds and slaughtered
> buried uneaten; hurry the surgeons
> it's urgent, an emergency, a market collapse
> hurry the embryos, fly them from France
> *urgeon-say, etus-fay, Suidae*
> what the fuck, hey -

In "Ivory" she works over a single sound, letting it echo as it falls down her lines, as the end of her lines echo Plath: "[U]seless, too big, too nude. / I feel your eyes move, my breath // a notch truer to mute. This close / you're blue. One brow fused, nay-lipped, // all canine, uncouth. My eyelet tangled, blouse loose. / This close, this close // a kiss. / You're a brute // Picasso triangle of tooth, blunt rectangles, absolutes; / and, beside you, I'm rearranged." All the "oo" sounds—coupled with that "a kiss" and "you're a brute"—leave us hearing the "Daddy, Daddy, you're through" that never comes; the sounds of poetry past have indeed been "rearranged." The poems that centre the book are a series describing vacations and camping trips that represent one family's mode of resisting what is "[n]ormal ad nauseam." Observing sea-side dunes occasions more than observation of nature: "Dunes, barely rooted; not-grass. Greensward? Rust-flowered claymore sword grass, the three-pronged hilt heading out. A grazing, nagging guilt of wanting this lonely aimlessness, this loose sort of stasis: prolonged." The volume (and trip) comes to an early climax when a child takes ill—"it happens overnight: basins of bile, pillow-slip over lipids / the IV drips // all night, all night, the shivering rigid question that won't lie down"—and is taken to hospital. The rest is drawn-out denouement, but no less welcome for that. Not everything can or need be climax; this aspect of Klaassen's strong third volume is normal (but not ad nauseam), too.

Not every family story is a nuclear family story. Some stories are more extended, becoming virtual histories. In *God of Missed Connections*, Elizabeth Bachinsky delves into her own Ukrainian family's story and in doing so opens an inquiry into Ukrainians in Canada more generally, a story, as she notes, "fraught with tragedy, warfare, ethnic conflicts, racism, anti-Semitism, political intrigue, ecological disasters." There is a winsome humility to the book, insofar as Bachinsky seems, alongside the reader she leads, to be learning this history as she writes. "Why bother with history?" she asks in a prose poem to her sister. Not all of the answers would endear her to everyone: "Because we can. Because we're curious. Because we want to know." But this is just the beginning of inquiry. Later answers turn more serious: "Because one day you can be conscripted into one army and the next day another. Because extremism thrives." Probably somewhere between these two sets of answers is the basis for prolonged political engagement. Not wanting to be a "Goddess of Blissful Ignorance," as one poem has it, Bachinsky has educated herself on some facts. Poems such as "God of Mechanical Accidents," "To Ukraine," and "The Bread Basket of Europe" recount the horrors of forced starvation, economic devastation, and the irradiation resulting from the Chernobyl disaster that led to deaths and child deformity.

The book's best poem is the long centrepiece called "The Wax Ceremony," which does an excellent job of stretching out as it makes Ukrainian history come alive, but also of retracting back to Bachinsky's lived reality: "How does the girl work? Like this." This is not "like" how her ancestor worked in a Banff labour camp in the nineteen-teens. "How does the girl work?" "[S]he writes," a phrase scattered throughout, a refrain of truth that places the poet both inside and outside the story she recounts. I enjoyed Bachinsky's last book, *Home of Sudden Service*, full of strong sonnets, but here she has taken a leap forward. *God of Missed Connections* does a fine job of mixing the formal conservatism of the former book and the less conservative tendency of her first (*Curio*), all in service of trying to tell both a family and a national story while being true to the opportunities afforded a young woman in contemporary Canadian life. That is a lot of balls to juggle but she keeps them in the air. (It is worth noting too the simple but powerful illustrations by Michelle Winegar, which bluntly punctuate the poems.)

Bachinsky achieves her goals with concision; the book could be a beast, given its subject, but instead is small in size and slim in girth. Not every writer considers such close-honing as the ultimate in virtue, however. rob mclennan, for one, is known for being prolific and there is no dearth of material in his *gifts*, a book that runs to roughly 150 pages. It crossed my mind that less might be more. But because the book's quantity is in conversation with its notions of quality, having fewer poems would make the collection more precious, polished, and contained than mclennan means it to be; nor would it produce for the reader certain problems of attention that it addresses and enacts at the level of genre and form. At the generic level, *gifts* is dominated by occasional poems in which the occasions are not public but personal. When the personal becomes acceptable matter for occasional poetry on a par with the important public occasions, there is always an occasion to write it, and thus there is always a lot of it to read. Not skimping on this score, mclennan also means to represent spontaneity itself, while writing his lyrics of the average occasion.

The book is in four sections. The first, "gifts," is also a kind of re-gifting, for the fifty poems therein are styled as valentines, invitations, postcards, and other virtual epistolary forms, addressed to actual people, many of them contemporary poets, most of whose names are listed at the back of the book. So they go out to these worthies while the reader gets to glance at them too. The second section is subtitled "twenty-one (incomplete) poems," the third is called "weightless," and the fourth, which we are told was first drafted "on the VIA rail train from Winnipeg to Toronto, November 23-24, 2006," consists of both "letters to g" and "unfinished shield notes." Incomplete, weightless, unfinished; notes, letters, valentines; train trips and small gifts: this is a poetry of the transitory, casual, tossed-off—no doubt just as *felt*, for an author, as the ode or the epic, but born of different desires.

Such poetry might well emphasize directness of expression, but mclennan takes a different tack. Some parts of every poem do *seem* direct, but whatever is straightforward is compromised by persistent ambiguity and deliberate indirection. The dominant mode is the elliptical and it takes two forms: leaving out and crossing out. The former is a ghostlier demarcation than the latter, but the frequency of the latter reminds us of the editorial nature of our choices in life regarding what we elide. mclennan has various elliptical methods: one is punctuation preceded by blank space, suggesting that there is often a structure even to what is left unsaid; another is his multitudinous making of puns, which leaves out the "straight" original of the word that instigates the verbal swerve. Much of what is missing is time, as in the time one might expect it to take to make poems. That missing time may be found by the reader, for it paradoxically takes more time than usual to settle into an understanding of poems that took less time than usual to write. It is an interesting trick, a passive-aggressive poetic that yields to being returned to. The insouciance and promiscuous responsiveness of these poems made me think of Frank O'Hara, although they sound nothing like him. For one, they cannot replicate his charm—what poems could? Granted, those in *gifts* are written in the wake of years during which the lyric self that might conceivably have come off as charming has been deconstructed ever more starkly—or more theoretically—or at any rate, with greater frequency than when O'Hara wrote. The result here is a personism in shards, or in the fragments of a person who cultivates fragmentation: *"the speaker as a wholesale fragment."* That may sound like serious, blood-drawing business, but mclennan's are mostly playful (though also often melancholy) poems.

In her fourth collection, *Could Be*, Heather Cadsby does on occasion sound a little like O'Hara, at least in his anecdotal mode. In "Bridge over Mimico Creek" she gets the dry drollery of I-do-this, you-do-that down pat:

> A boy was throwing pieces of bread
> at the ducks. I said, "Excuse me but
> that is killing them." He turned and
> said, "Lady, these ain't stones."
> The confusion was clear. I cleared
> my throat and he spit on the ground.

In the end, the two can't even agree to disagree—so much for civilized discourse—and the narrator takes "off in a huff." Elsewhere, in "eau de parfum," because we can't get enough of random encounters (or of the "-uff" sound, for that matter), we find that

> A pretty girl was standing
> at the foot of the escalator. She was trying
> to give away smells. I knew she was going

to corner me because she smiled at my hat.
"No thanks," I said, "I never use that stuff."

The brisk pace, plain-style diction, and simple pleasures of sound heard here are consistent throughout the book; for the most part, though, the other poems are less directly narrative. Stories indeed abound, but there is a gentle surrealism, not so much like O'Hara as it is reminiscent of Ashbery. There is no anxiety of influence, however, for *Could Be* is just about the least anxious book one could imagine reading that takes Ashbery as one of its models—or if this is anxiety, it is incredibly transparent. Of the poem called "We see us as we truly behave," we are told at the bottom of the page that the title "is a line by John Ashbery" (indeed, it is the first line of his first book). "One way or another" is a call to the Muse, or as Cadsby styles her, "Bigwig of quirky wordthings." It is also a roll call of models: "O triangulate Courted One / of the Beckett jokes and diminishings / of the perhaps and wandering Ashbery / of the sonnetful Raymond Queneau / hit on Me."

I think Cadsby got her wish and that she accepted the overture. The lines quoted above constitute almost the full extent of her naming of names or showing her hand. It is just the right, light touch. Without bloating into a bibliography of influences, it frees the reader from that subconscious rumbling of wondering whether or not those echoes are really there, or of whether or not the poet expects us to hear them. The anecdotal mode and the "quirky wordthings" mode are afloat in a general lyricism that is sometimes distilled, but with impurities, as in the seven aubades. Placed through the volume like small shafts of light full of motes, with one exception they are a superstitiously numbered thirteen lines long, suggesting—what? That the act of waking is unlucky, which undercuts the genre with formal irony? Perhaps the suggestion instead is that here is yet another day during which we will not quite finish the things we set out to achieve, just as these aubades never quite grow into sonnets.

If we cite from the opening lines of these poems, we return to Cadsby's roll call of role models, for one hears Beckett in the pleasure taken in repetitions of reasons for despair, one sees Queneau in the serialism of the repeated attempts to awaken to life: "Praise be to the angels of morning breath. / A waft of nasty odor is a sign of life." "At first light / a veery's tumbling song / and everything

I knew was feared." "Between moonlight and sunlight / what lies in shadow is out of our hands." "At dawn / one toothache / and a couple of disappointing mutual funds / are sufficient collaboration / to spoil the sunrise." "Sunrise / and the most reliable thing / is the way you lose all courage." *Could Be* is a collection of anti-heroic, neurotic poems that perform equivocation throughout. Yet there is courage in Cadsby's use of humour, as well as in her open admission of influence (which is also a nod to the personal past), to forestall what one comes to realize could be an utter silencing: "On the brink, beyond itself / grief allows nothing." These final lines of "The work of mourning" are not the only ones that suggest a genuine pain. Almost too direct to bear are the first two (of sixteen) stanzas in the exquisite and horrible elegy "Single woman on the death of her mother":

> I grew impatient with waiting
> as my mother was dying.
> I stood rigid in elevators, a potential griever
> who allowed her mother to pull off the oxygen mask,
> by leaving the room, going down for coffee.
> And on returning, snapped the thing
> back into place as the mother winced.
> Who did I think I guarded.
>
> I grew mean with waiting
> as my mother was dying.
> She wasn't answering, seemed to be sleeping.
> I looked for stale-dating on the IV bag.
> I banged my leg into her bed,
> forced bad breath out of my mouth.
> I grabbed her thumb
> and was just about to yell mommy
> when she opened her eyes and was gone.

This takes the last line of Milton's sonnet on his blindness and injects it full of bile. It is brilliant: the contrast between the elderly "patient" and the "impatient" daughter (the kind of contrast in which Kenneth Burke used to see an ethical universe); the shifts from "my mother" to "her mother" to "the mother," with the mother figure ever-diminishing both in affection and in sentience; the cruel verbs ("snapped," "winced," "banged," "forced," "grabbed"); the cruellest verb of all, "allowed," where passivity is the enacted dream of a daughter's release from the debt or curse of having been born; and finally, the move from "impatient" to "mean" between stanzas. If there can be courage in poems, surely this collection exhibits it.

What *is* a "collection," after all? The same thing as a "volume" or "book"? One is drawn, it is true, to the meta-questions from time to time when called to plough through the year's field. As I read *Drive*, by Chris Pannell, there were reasons to consider the differences. Pannell, who lives in Hamilton, has been a driver there for DARTS (Disabled and Aged Regional Transit System), a worthy program if ever there was one. Here, I thought, looking at the title along with the author's occupation, was not a "collection," or even a "book," but something else altogether—a "project." Part of me didn't like the notion, but why was hard to say. Imagine the consternation, then, and the chastening turns of thought when I got to the end of the first of four sections of *Drive* and—beginning the second before then quickly flipping ahead to the third and the fourth to survey the scene—realized that only that first section of eighteen poems concerned Pannell's experience as a DARTS driver. The subject matter was deep, the approach to it intimate but unsentimental (or just sentimental enough), the formal handling deft and various—and I had just finished them. I wanted, nay, demanded more bus-driving poems! This was truly, or this truly should have been...yes...yes, of course it should be—a book-length *project*. But having turned tail on my own over-determined values, I was thus better prepared to continue reading Pannell, to see what kind of work he had really conceived.

*Drive* is a book about different kinds of travel, so that from the bus routes of Hamilton in the opening section we find ourselves, in the second section, "In the Air." The first poem there is called "At Wanuskewin, Saskatchewan" and the section ends with the poet and the reader "Taking Off from Regina." In between are some lovely images of night, even if the nocturnally beautiful poems reveal the mental corollary of the literal dark: "Another twelve hour trip to commuterville / has extinguished the sensational inner life / of every driver. No one had time to admire / the half-moon against that indigo drape."

(The immediacy of that final "that" lets the narrator partake both of the commuters' insensibility and the poet's observational acuity.) In section 3, "Long Distance," we find that taking off from Regina has landed us in London, after which we meet the poet's proud, octogenarian Aunt Doris in Devonshire. Between there and arriving in Lincolnshire, we come across quite a character, the roofer Mick, who, while dedicated to his craft of tops, also has opinions about the pipes beneath them, as the epigraph he speaks to "Plumbing and Roofs" suggests: *"The only good plumbing was what was left by the Romans."* Mick is observed observing on trips of his own, in a way that also calls into question what Pannell, the Canadian poet in his ancestral homeland, observes: "When my Mick goes abroad / 'e spends too much time lookin' at roofs / A-frame, flat, tile, shingle, or slate / It makes no difference / 'e's a roofer by trade / Gawd, lad, give it a rest, I say."

From these journeys Pannell then takes the abbreviated Grand Tour, stopping in Rome and Florence and, like his poetic forebears, writing about the Uffizi. (In a nice touch of diminution, he writes less about the artworks than about the labels that identify them.) From there he museum hops back across the pond to the Met. While in New York he sees Matthew Broderick outside the Tony Awards, but the real message of the poem is not about celebrity, but rather reveals a truth universally acknowledged—that one has not lived until one has been intimidated by a New York City cop. Nice to return after that to Toronto's Union Station and then back with "My Suitcase" to Hamilton. It has been quite a series of trips, with not only strong travel poems but a "temp pome" that takes on the linguistic banality of legalistic and instructional language in a battle it cannot win; a pleasing "Poem for a Dream Bookstore" that smartly extends the dream vision whereby one falls asleep on the book into a dreamy store full of shelves full of books. Pannell is good at nocturnes and dream poems; some "love talk" that proves once again that the legacy of bpNichol is a difficult one to navigate for twenty-first-century poets; and a range of other love and are-we-in-love poems, such as "Receiving an International Phone Call from Canada," which at first struck me as too flatly documentary, but the flatness of which grew to make perfect sense, both in the rendering of the traveller's mind and in the record of his end of the unwanted conversation: "You have the right to hear from me. You're phoning." "Meat and deep-fried veg twice a day. / Oh yeah, food's great, wash it down with beer."

Now back to what I assumed was the volume's reason for being, those opening bus-driving poems. They are a special group, just as Pannell sees the group of young and old men and women he conveys around town, some of them to school but mostly to St. Joseph's or Chedoke Hospital, some of them to dialysis, many of them not abstract entities but folks with proper names, like grinning Melvin Greenberg: "*I don't know much about dialysis, / but my friend refused it*, Melvin says, *and died*." Or Gavin MacKinnon, who "cannot restrain himself / despite wheelchair, lap table, seatbelt" and who, even with his difficulty speaking, lets his driver know that he knows a pretty girl outside the window when he sees one. Or Sam with his "gappy gums," elderly and trembling, who just by existing offends the sensibilities of patio diners in an upscale constructed "village" of the city: "If he could rise out of his wheelchair / what would they think of his grey cardigan / its gravy stains and open pockets / like nests, emptied of birds?" Pannell at one moment sees himself as Noah, trying to contain the wilderness in his wheeled ark. At other times he finds himself always already delinquent: "Three months into this job, and I am / years late, years behind / I know not what. / My frequent dreams of squandered time / are withering into a truth." Mostly, one feels, despite the rich depiction of roiling, troubled, discarded, surviving humanity, Pannell sees himself as alone, as when he looks back through the mirror at the last two kids on the bus, "anticipat[ing] their stops," "remembering how / thirty-six empty seats will / follow me all the way to sleep." And then he ends this moving group of poems with the words of another sort of soldier-poet, prepared to travel on: "Goodbye to all that."

Having been set in motion, perhaps the reader of poetry will, like Pannell, find it hard to stop moving. But if one is prepared to slow down, to be more solitary, and to work the land in lines, then there is another vehicle very unlike a bus that drives a volume of poems this year. That workhorse of the farm, the personality-filled tractor, is the subject of Saskatchewan poet Gerald Hill's amusing and heartfelt *14 Tractors*. The book begins with (and takes its name from) an exchange between Hill and Brother Bernard Lange, farm manager of St. Peter's Abbey, as well as dedicatee and hero (along with the tractors) of the collection:

The Poet: You must have, what, five or six tractors out here?
Brother Bernard, farm manager: We've got 14 tractors.

It is a nice start, suggesting, as it does, not the stance we are accustomed to—the poet as master observer—but rather the poet's humbling relationship to a humble man and the humble but vital machines he maintains.

Brother Bernard's voice is heard throughout the book's first part in italicized and prosaic descriptions of each of the tractors themselves, alongside tales of their origins, of their uses, and of those who drive them: *"When I got here in 1947 we had only two tractors, an old Case / and a W30 International / and 18 horses." "The Minneapolis-Moline Model RTU, 'Minnie,' / is a rowcropper with a hand clutch, / for orchard work, cultivation around trees / and for the bees. // It's the only tractor around here with a dynamo, / the only tractor with one headlight. / Father Xavier drove it for years, he lost the headlight. // Minnie was his legs. / If Minnie was on the fritz, so was Xavier. / If Xavier wasn't feeling well, / better go out and tune up Minnie."* These anecdotes are then answered by the poet in poems that are often equally prosaic, as in the lists of "Regional Headquarters of Minneapolis-Moline" or "As Long as You Have That Pocket Knife," the latter of which instructs: "Lance a boil on a calf / wipe the blade on your pants / peel an apple / wipe the blade on your pants / get the Model R started and / back it out of the shed." The repeated line recalls the "worried line" of a blues stanza, and indeed, that folk form associated (if not in Kansas City or Chicago, at least in the Mississippi Delta) with agricultural work appears just prior to the pocket knife in a "Two-Cylinder Blues" that refers to Robert Johnson's "Stop Breakin' Down": "Some day you gotta come / find me some day you gotta get / beyond this breaking down."

In part two of *14 Tractors* ("The Body of the Tractor"), Hill continues to balance a lyrical strain with the everydayness of prose narrative. There is a series of personal and local-colour stories running along the bottom of every page in small type under the rubric "In the City of Tractors." These are mostly humorous, but the kind of humour ranges from folksy—

Uncle drove a two-ton Ford truck with a grain box, small motor. *Couldn't pull the hat off your head,* was the standard line.

For fun, we buried a railway tie behind the truck, attached it to the axle with chains. When uncle was ready to head home, his truck wouldn't budge. We were waiting in the tavern when he showed up moaning that his axle was busted. Most fun of all, we made him buy beer until his story got all the way told

—to exceedingly dark: "Got run over, broke his hips and back and lived, or had a heart attack, fell off dead but the tractor dragged him around." These stories work in counterpoint to poems such as "A Few Words at First Light," a lovely aubade: "I can't say enough about light once / the dark's rubbed off... // I blame the light for what I see / I've got to get up and do." A poem titled "What You Think about out on the Tractor" illuminates the meditative space that is cleared in much of the work done away from a desk or a screen. There is also a series scattered throughout called "Chapter Quiz," which does similar work in reminding the reader that it is not only in school that we study; here on the farm, inattentiveness can lead to being crushed under a tipped tractor's weight.

When part three begins with an obituary for Brother Bernard adapted from the *Prairie Messenger* and continues a few pages later with a story about a shed fire at the abbey adapted from the *Humboldt Journal*, several impressions are made. The elegiac character of the book comes to the fore. What is being mourned and celebrated is not only the life of Brother Bernard, but something of the world of work he represents. The shed fire suggests—a "shed" being a little thing—that the days of the small farmer are as transient as the soul of the Brother. The local nature of the poems is emphasized by these stories in small papers, so that the importance of place and proper scale is increased. And in terms of poetic lineage—given this congruence between persons and place, given the prosimetric mélange of free-verse lyric, prose narrative, snatches of song, newspaper clippings, lists and instructions, and a rejection of over-abstraction—one sees that Hill is working in the mode of Williams's *Paterson*. The action has moved from New Jersey to Saskatchewan, and the approach is appropriately less epic. But if so much depends upon a red wheelbarrow, so much more depends upon fourteen tractors. If a poem is a machine made out of words, then many poems can be made out of attention paid to machines made out of rubber and metal parts. And if there shall be no ideas but in things, then Hill's volume, which claims that "[a] tractor in a shed is a working thought," both revises and epitomizes an aesthetic heritage that is often appropriated a bit too loosely.

By a strange Saskatchewan coincidence, "Tractor," a poem from Karen Solie's Griffin Prize-winning *Pigeon*, also contains the names of fourteen tractors. Thirteen of them are afterthoughts, though. There is only one tractor for Solie:

> More than a storey high and twice that long,
> it looks igneous, the Buhler Versatile 2360,
> possessed of the ecology of some hellacious
> minor island on which options
> are now standard. Cresting the sections
> in a corona part dirt, part heat, it appears
> risen full-blown from our deeper needs,
> aspirating its turbo-cooled air, articulated
> and fully compatible. What used to take a week
> it does in a day on approximately
> a half-mile to the gallon. It cost one hundred
> fifty grand. We hope to own it outright by 2017.
> Few things wrought by human hands
> are more sublime than the Buhler Versatile 2360.

Like the Buhler 2360, Solie is versatile with a capital *V*. She has many strengths, but it seems to me that her versatility is among them the primary. Normally when we speak of versatility in a poet, we mean that she can do a range of things across different poems, that she can write different kinds of poems with success. Certainly this characterizes Solie. But there is another sort of versatility she exhibits, much more difficult to achieve, that likely accounts in part for her popularity among such a wide range of readers. Her versatility is evident not only across poems, but within them. In a single poem she can include a range of demotic language, from the everydayness of cliché to specialized kinds of local talk; she employs the ecological strain that has evolved out of Canadian nature poetry, by which her poems produce both the pleasures of naturalistic description and the implication of political realities; she includes personal narratives and winsome stories, while also stepping back into a mode more abstract, even imperious; she is funny, but edgy; she is good at lists and piling up congeries of things, but she balances such moments of gross accumulation with Jamesian sentences of multiple clauses, thereby suggesting how different syntactic arrangements constitute different ways of making meaning; she mixes the languages of science and sublimity, the material and the spiritual; and she does this in lines that are rhythmically impeccable, easy to read without lulling the reader to sleep.

Solie is not the only poet to attempt such a range within single poems. Usually, however, even in successful cases, what one finds is a result that can best be described by such words as *pastiche* or *collage-like*. There is thus an implication that obtains from the formal results, which is that the "self" is always radically mixed in its modes and is thus fragmented, held together primarily by social agreement. (This *looks* like a poem [with "poem" as a figure for the '"self "]; thus the poem/self coheres as a unified "thing," even if its elements don't.) Solie instead mixes her elements just as radically as do the most brazenly po-mo of poets, yet the elements in her poems cohere. Thus the normal formal-cum-existential arguments feel out of place. There is a magic of competence to it and it is hard to explain how she does it. Suffice it to say that *Pigeon* is full of riches, from "Cave Bear," which begins as a political-archaeological poem before ending with the revivifying, ghostly force of Keats's "This Living Hand"; to "Air Show," which collapses the usual distinction between the transcendent and the sublunary; to "The Girls," which formalizes stasis, but a stasis that is its own kind of history. "Jesus Heals the Leopard" finds the spiritual in humour and memory, while "An Acolyte Reads *The Cloud of Unknowing*" finds it in doubt and attentiveness. The title poem sees the similarity of a pigeon to a human brain, while "Archive" is a long prose poem that extends the life of that most anthologized and read of Canadian poems, Atwood's "This Is a Photograph of Me." If you look long enough, eventually you will see that Solie has placed herself in a lineage of important national poets.

David Zieroth is also responding to a poet (and also has pigeons on the brain) in the last stanza of the last poem of his latest book in a long career. *The Fly in Autumn* is a great joy but one not unmitigated by darkness—a word that appears in the final line of Stevens's "Sunday Morning." In that poem's final lines Stevens also sees "in the isolation of the sky, / at evening, casual flocks of pigeons make / Ambiguous undulations as they sink, / Downward to darkness, on extended wings." Zieroth, walking on "The New Pier" that attracts few people, sees things differently:

> Over there, a solitary walker
> glides under windsocks that hang inert
> and though he ventures beyond our endpoint
> closer to ships, closer to the centre deep
> does he see anything more
> than a black cormorant on guard
> skimming the top inch of waves,
> one white gull floating in air different from his own,
> a tight flock of seven pigeons
> oblivious to beauty and heading downtown?

From the solitary walker to the oblivious city-bound pigeons, the critique of Romantic aestheticizing and meditating seems certain. Yet it ends with a question—what is seen is not known. This tendency to expose the sentimental urges while also acknowledging their pull and their possible relevance is characteristic of the volume. Zieroth's pose is often the curmudgeonly formalist, but like those before him, such as Larkin and Frost, he is far from a bore, because of his wit, his clear sight, and his willing lapses into a world of dreams where he sees through the other side of the glass. He is not devoid of human feeling, though one senses that time has rubbed his feelings raw enough that he knows how to resist them. When, in "Say Baghdad," he finds himself unable to rise to indignation about the latest overseas indignities, even in his defiance one senses sadness in his lost capacities: "so let the young accuse me / and children of the killed curse me / because it remains true: / I failed to maintain continuous hope." But the belief in better things is still there, even if the man who might so believe has been chastened enough by life that he figures himself as a fly in autumn, buzzing near the end, chastened by the years but not willing to accede to winter: "And even so, my wings / carry me, and what thinness / upon which to rely." No thinness, this; Zieroth's book is dense with thoughtfulness and wistfulness, with cutting wit and clear-eyed dreams—exceptional, beautiful work.

From the arc of oeuvres still unfolding and from the seasons always turning, we now proceed to tales of those who preceded us. Historical recreations continue to figure prominently in recent poetry, as poetry rightly remains unwilling to cede to its more popular relative—prose fiction—the right to use recorded facts (or at any rate, prior histories) to make things up that have the ring of veracity. Nor are poets so without savvy as to divest themselves of the right to piggyback on stories or subjects that might already maintain the public's interest, thus increasing the public's potential interest in their poems. That prior interest can cut both ways, though, given the expectations that readers bring to bear when a beloved story or character is getting the revisionary treatment.

Take Jesus, for instance—with apologies to Depeche Mode, "your own personal" version, whether religious or literary or otherwise, is likely to determine how you digest someone else's. The version in Brian Day's *Conjuring Jesus* is not to my taste, although I could not help but admire the conviction behind the attempt to understand and remake the title character. The formal range found there is also to be admired. In fact, Day's Jesus shares the quality of versatility with his poet-creator: "Jesus, slippery from the beginning, becomes the wholly versatile man: entering, entered, everywhere at once." Nor are forms uniform for this refigured figure—in "Reversals," we read that "[f]or Jesus the world is made of water / and what now holds one form will soon hold another. / The male will be female, the straight will be bent // ... Jesus coolly enacts the drama of his words, / taking the roles of eunuchs and girls." The adverbs in these excerpts epitomize the problematic aspect of their characterization—"wholly versatile," "perfectly permeable," "coolly enacts"— their dearth of tension and lack of intellectual and emotional torque. Despite its stanzaic and prosodic variety, Day's conjuration is consistent in tone, a smoothed-out and dreamy lyricism, or as "A Woman Caught in Adultery" puts it, "Languorous / as a poet recalling his beloved." She is describing Jesus, who elsewhere is "enchanted by a lily and / uttered his purest line of poetry: // how Solomon in all his glory / was not arrayed like one / of these." That is indeed a deathless verse; given its cultural iconoclasm and rhetorically purposeful aesthetic reversal, I don't know whether "purity" is one of its primary attributes.

Then again, this is Day's adaptation of scripture, not mine. There is something of interest in his attempt to fashion Jesus less as religious reformer or homespun scholar than as mystical poet. He begins the book by emphasizing as "Jesus' genetic allotment" the Davidic lineage and, with an unexpected qualification, he reminds us that "David is, perhaps worst of all, a poet." Jesus here is also sexually fluid, as a male poet figured in contemporary terms might be. In one instance he enters the dreams of Pilate's wife "like a lover, like a wound," with the entering as a sign of masculinity and the wound as a sign of womanhood. (That is, if you find convincing the art historian Caroline Walker Bynum's argument about the vaginal nature of wounds in depictions of the crucifixion, which I do.) The aforementioned adulterous woman believes Jesus eyes her "not like merely another / suitor, but like a woman who shares / my knowledge of men." The tone of most of these poems is reminiscent of the gauzy abstraction that one associates with a certain sort of late Victorian lyric, the lyric of a culture that preferred its Jesus effete and that Pound wrote his "Ballad of the Goodly Fere" to resist by insinuating instead (in anachronistic verse) an earthy, muscular Christ.

Pound wouldn't have liked Day's Jesus either, but then neither would have the enervated Christians that Pound was protesting. To Day's credit, there is too much (as he puts it) "bodily knowledge" here. On occasion, there is also too much Harlequin-Romantic verse: "Called back / to the place where I stand, he faces me, / me with sweet saliva still slick / on my skin, my lover's adoration / polishing my limbs." One wishes for more of those simple and unsentimental moments, those plain-spoken and direct statements suggesting inner conflict of which Day is also capable, such as the one at the end of "Jesus, Forsaken": "This is the closing tableau of his life. / Whatever he has done and said has been wrong." But the final fact is that if this interesting but sometimes cloying adaptation of the Gospels is unsatisfactory, if it is not the personal Jesus for you, then there are always other versions to turn to, as Day implies in the volume's last lyric, "Jesus Not Contained in His Book."

The importance of Jesus as a historical figure adds credence to the idea asserted in that title, but what about when it is applied to a figure known mainly for being a writer? Is there ever an instance when writers *should* be contained in their books, rather than repurposed for poetic reasons? The question came to mind when reading Carolyn Smart's *Hooked*, an impressive collection consisting of seven long poems about seven different women. In one of those poems, about the writer Jane Bowles, the subject speaks an apparent contradiction that dissolves when one stops to consider it: "I cannot be contained, I want to be contained." Because she cannot, she wants to. This causal relationship between lack and desire turns out to be a crucial line running through the book. Or is the first statement one of defiance, the second a submissive reversal in response to the silent disinterest that her defiance calls forth? The psychological possibilities in even so small a line as this show how empathetic an imaginer Smart is of the inner lives of her subjects. In the case of Bowles, despite a chaotic life, she did achieve containment in her stories. They are as reticent and finely wrought as any extant; in them, so much is being asserted by keeping so much at bay. They are like the interior parts of the Moroccan medinas that serve some of them as a source.

As it happens, I was reading Bowles several months before encountering Smart's rendition of her life. One story in particular, "Everything Is Nice," built to a stunning conclusion, to sentences that were so different, yet so of a piece with all those that had preceded them, that for a moment I literally lost my breath. Smart reproduces a version of those sentences (derived from an essay Bowles wrote, which she then turned into her story) as a stanza in lyric lines in *Hooked* (and in case you intend to read the original—spoiler alert): "Once I reached to touch a beautiful and powdered clown / because I felt such yearning / it was at a little circus / but I was not a child[.]" Smart does much work on her own and Bowles's behalf with these lines: she shows the exquisite balance in the sentences through her line breaks; she accentuates the running theme of desire; she illustrates the potentially terrifying nature of that desire, insofar as even as ostensibly rational adults we cannot arrest our irrational, child-like impulses; and she uses the words of the story as a bridge between a passage describing Bowles's first encounter with Tangier and her first encounter in its market with the mysterious Cherifa, the woman who would become her lover (and, as local apocrypha had it, the one who caused her death). Smart does much work—and yet taken from its original context, an important aspect is missing: the ability to take your breath away.

There is plenty of breath loss in *Hooked*, however, even if it is not found in final moments of pristine prose epiphany. Smart instead takes out the oxygen, breath by breath, in her first two sequences, harrowing accounts of the aristocratic Nazi-lover Unity Mitford and the murderous Myra Hindley. I did not recognize the name of the latter, although when I Googled it and saw her picture, I realized that this murderess of the Moors was already embedded in my mental bank of images. With baited breath I awaited coming to the end of these poems and was relieved to move on to people whom I could respect, even if their lives were not a bowl of cherries dipped out with silver spoons. The painter Dora Carrington I had first seen depicted in the movie that bears her name (with Emma Thompson playing the artist), but revisiting her through poems was a welcome experience. The rest of the volume is rounded out by writers; in addition to Bowles, there are sequences devoted to Zelda Fitzgerald, Carson McCullers, and Elizabeth Smart. The depiction of Zelda strikes just the right tone, irreverent in regards to the world but otherwise self-serious and self-dramatizing. Every experience (and the point is to acquire experiences) is grist for a future tall tale: "[W]e knew Picasso we knew Léger we knew Miro / we knew Joyce we knew Stein we knew Hemingway"; "Goofo wrote *Gatsby*, I let the sea exhaust me / we warmed our backs, invented cocktails / played in the sand / and once I turned my eyes sideways / couldn't help myself but stroke some creature there / we both told that tale so many times." Smart is revealing of the fallibilities of her subjects and still produces a sympathetic response. It is not as if we are unwarned to be wary. McCullers is heard to say, "I will eat up anyone who'll let me / there is so much on earth I crave," and indeed, the hunger here makes one's own stomach rumble, while the instinct of self-preservation urges one to make sure that the main course is not oneself.

Being a sucker for anything having to do with outlaws and gunslingers, I was enthusiastic upon coming across Kuldip Gill's thirty-page sequence "Bill Miner's Notebook," which makes up the latter half of the posthumously published *Valley Sutra*, Gill's second book. In "Bill Miner Explains," Bill Miner explains, "'If we had known then that we were Canada's first train robbery / we might have worked harder at setting the gold standard.'" Gill has chosen a fascinating figure in Miner, the "Gentleman Bandit," a well-mannered if preternaturally thievish native of Bowling Green, Kentucky, who made his way north across the border to rob the Canadian Pacific Railway. (Incidentally, he is buried in Milledgeville, Georgia's Memory Hill Cemetery, where Flannery O'Connor is also interred, and he is said to have coined the phrase, "Hands up!") Gill, who was born in Punjab, India, before coming to Canada at the age of five, creates a character named Amer Singh, an employee of the CPR who is on the robbed train and who has bestowed upon him by the ghost of Bill Miner the title "my agent in life for the rewrite." In her notes that close the book, Gill explains that in "Punjabi Sikh culture, storytelling in the evening is a very intimate, though formalized event. The words 'Ah mere vaht, utho paghi rathe' (This is my story, night has fallen over it)... are the words each storyteller recites at the end of his or her story. These words signal the end, but also encourage the next storyteller to begin to tell another story." Thus the pun in Singh's surname is meant to recall the beginning of the phrase that signals both a story's end and its new beginning (Ah mere), while the double entendre of "Singh" reminds us of the medium in which the current retelling takes place. It is an interesting addition to the historical story of Miner, but the poem in the end was disappointing. It didn't fulfil my hopes for a grand adventure story and was a bit flat in the telling. Given my predisposition toward tales of outlawry, I was surprised to find as my favourites instead the poems that make up the book's first half, recalling Gill's childhood in the Fraser Valley. In their depictions of the activity surrounding the local mill, as well as of cultural cross-pollinations rendered, years later, from a Punjabi-Canadian perspective, these poems have a fascinating vivacity and expand one's sense of what Canada looked and sounded like decades ago.

Another volume published posthumously that treats historical figures is *The Artist & the Moose*, a "fable of forget" (as the subtitle has it) by Roy K. Kiyooka, who died in 1994. A multi-talented writer and artist, Kiyooka left behind a manuscript (dated 1989) that is as various in its methods as he was in his art. Although it is a prose narrative, *The Artist & the Moose* is a kind of prose poetry that follows the history of Tom Aplomb, who stands in for the painter Tom Thomson. The nature of Thomson's 1917 death in Algonquin Park was unsatisfactorily explained, and Kiyooka's tale is not just a historical recreation, but an archival mystery story. It is also the fable it titles itself, for we experience "the fabulous effects of treating things and abstractions as characters." (This quote comes from Roy Miki's generous and educational afterword. He also edited the book.) In addition to Thomson, figures such as Margaret Atwood, Northrop Frye, Lester Pearson, and Al Purdy appear in slightly altered guise. The narrator is led to the case of Tom Aplomb after having been commissioned to write a white paper by a royal commission on "The Status of a Genuinely Multi-Cultural Aesthetic for Canadians in the 21st Century." He is helped by a mythical figure, Ol Moose, who represents a natural world under threat since seemingly forever.

Much history is recalled and many hypocrisies are skewered in the book, but all is treated with a touching wit and a tacit acknowledgement of the foibles of being human. The narrator's "prosody showed the riven seams of its hauntings," and this book is haunted by the past and emboldened by postmodernity, where artistic hybridity of tone and form makes sense in attempting to organize a multi-layered story. Books such as Ishmael Reed's *Flight to Canada* and *Mumbo Jumbo* came to my mind as being similar in strategy, as did Ed Dorn's *Gunslinger* (a book, incidentally, that Gill names as an influence on her Bill Miner poem). If you enjoyed any of those books, or take an interest in Canadian political and cultural history, or collect tales of Tom Thomson, or appreciate fine pastiche, *The Artist & the Moose* is up your alley. It also includes Kiyooka's serial poem, first published in *Artscanada* in 1972, titled "letters purporting to be abt tomthomson," which conveys something of the epiphanic quality that Thomson (and the Canadian natural landscape itself) had for Kiyooka: "and one day you'll come upon one of tom's paintings / it will F*L*A*S*H* in front of you— / when you miss the sharp turn going eighty / on the transcanada above lake superior. / it will be there HUGE as a technicolord billboard / before you disappear into the crack be- / between 2 brushstrokes."

For an example of postmodern pastiche meeting narrative with exuberating results, none better fits the bill than George Elliott Clarke's *I & I*. Clarke describes his book as a "pop-song opera" and a "comic-book ballad," with "grindhouse-dark origins" and phrases and images "cannibalized" from "adolescent inklings. Hence, it is Gothic in romance, grotesque in its depictions, and gaudy in plot." This story of two young lovers, the classy Betty Browning and the boxer Malcolm Miles, does not exactly go smoothly from the start. (Betty's father is verbally and physically adamant that Miles is not worthy of his daughter; but then, the father is not worthy of battling a boxer.) After leaving Halifax under pressure and in desperation, they end up in Corpus Christi, Texas. Betty enrols in the Baptist Bible College and that's where the worst of their troubles begin. The lecherous Professor Lowell Beardsley—it is always the professors—turns quickly from typical slimeball to sexual criminal. Degree is destiny—his PhD is from Harvard, of course, which has produced even more monstrous figures than himself; he believes self-servingly that a "cell exists for everyone, and his is *Lust.*" From mere lust, Lowell descends to rape, which results in his dismemberment by Malcolm, after which the "white stiff" is "slid / Into the white ass of an ambulance." (The "stiff" slid into "ass" alludes to one of the Professor's predations as a rapist, although Betty, his victim, is not white.) This "stunted stiff" will lie "[e]ncunted in a cool, wet grave."

Is it possible that events could turn worse? You bet. But let's leave the tragic ending untold. Clarke's dramatic skills are ratcheted up to melodrama and there is a sonic excess that elides with the action, as heard, for instance, in the *b*'s that bounce through these early couplets. It is as if Betty Browning, already "being bruised," is sonically scattered throughout the lines that first describe her, a deft device. The characterization of the two lovers is strong—much stronger than one might expect it to have been, given the broad, garish sketches that Clarke's prefatory material leads one to expect. (Speaking of "garish sketches," *I & I*'s balanced and flowing illustrations by Lateef Martin are impeccable companions to the story.) Probably if Betty and Miles were not so humanized, the reader's interest would flag before the last of the book's 230-plus pages. This reader's interest, at any rate, led to what instead could best be described as inexorably plowing through the book, a reminder that plot is momentum. What is most impressive may be how perverse it is; few new writers would have the nerve these days to attempt such studied sordidness. Even our creative writers are now expected to exhibit creative decorum, so as not to be too upsetting. Clarke can stretch boundaries with his status.

There were a handful of other long narrative book-length poems released in 2009, or at least long books of poems that evinced a narrative drive. The second part of Wayne Clifford's *The Exile's Papers*, subtitled *The Face as Its Thousand Ships*, is autobiography as sonnet sequence. From poems forming a piratical prologue, to those about a "Little Boy" who is "mystified by lust," and on to adulthood and fatherhood (the poems about his relationship with his daughters are of special interest, even when they morph into poems about his poems), this book is primarily about one aspect of Clifford's life—how women figure in it. Perhaps the nature of the sonnet sequence is relativist and Heraclitan, as each new sonnet constitutes a revision of the idea of the ideal form (there is no final or perfect form: "True love is only true when it's compared"; "Versions Are the Sole Truth"), as each new sonnet changes the sequence as a whole ("Meaning Haunts the About-to-Happen Moment"). Few of these sonnets are easy to read—their variety can be unsettling, their syntax labyrinthine, their attitude aggressive—but the sequence is hard to stop reading. Difficult or not, each sonnet, at least in size, is like one of those short chapters in a throwaway novel you read on the beach. Why would you stop at any given time, since you could stop at any time?

Some similar compulsion drove me over a long afternoon and late night through *Mosaic Orpheus* by Peter Dale Scott. However, the book is radically different in tone and form (for the most part; a few sonnets are included). There *are*, as in Clifford's book, many poems in Scott's that consider, from an older man's perspective, the role that women have played in his life. His reminiscences of cherished female figures from his young days give way to beautiful considerations of his current (and second) wife, as well as poignant poetry regarding the loving but problematic relationship he had with the first woman he married. So this is an extremely personal volume; yet it is also the most explicitly political book to come down the pike in 2009. These two tendencies are of a piece in *Mosaic Orpheus*, or perhaps one had better say that they are pieces of the same mosaic. Personal relationships are intertwined with political beliefs and commitments, which Scott is wonderful at showing; and one's sense of oneself as a person is inextricable from one's politics, as he also shows, sometimes in the same stanza: "Like the times in a bad marriage / good times flash back with pain / so in the midst of preemptive war / I remember loving this country." There is a vast amount of knowledge and commitment on display and the directness of the diction coupled with the size of the concerns suggest that Scott means to counteract "a shrinkage of our culture / towards the trivialities / of narcotic distractions undecipherable poets // and expansion of empire / with help from al Qaeda / until now there are American troops / from Kyrgyzstan to Kosovo." That's quite a leap between stanzas, but one feels in Scott the courage of conviction and the solid rock of knowledge. The rhythmic movement of his poems is an attractive balance of insistence and serenity. (In this they have much in common with Suwanda Sugunasiri's *Obama-Ji*, although in Sugunasiri one often finds a sort of humour of exasperation, an exuberance in the face of human foibles, different in tone than one finds in Scott. Like Scott, Sugunasiri crosses the supposed fault lines that would separate the political from the personal, although his manner of making political arguments is less scholastic than Scott's—though both poets, it should be said, are equally free in referring either to the external evidence of recorded fact or to the internal evidence of emotion to make a case for their beliefs.)

Scott's attention to others, as well as his spiritual searching, shadow and soften any propensity toward dogmatism: "Have I lived too long inside this brain?" One man's dogmatism may be another man's passion; while one man's passion may be that same man's own poison and antidote both. In the earlier poems in the collection of new and selected by Métis activist Gregory Scofield, called *Kipocihkân* (Cree slang for someone unable to talk), there is much impassioned speech. In the poem "Taste of Hatred," youthful anger is being reflected upon. At other times, the line between past and present is blurry: "From their cars / they were safe, those honkies. / We knew they were there / skulking around / like a weak species / trying to build themselves up." Grammatically we are in the past, but in the recounting is an immediacy that belies mere grammar. In "Mixed Breed Act," Scofield see-saws between resisting demands that he perform his marginalization and reinforcing his marginalization through his performance: "I'm not solely a First Nations act / or a Canadian act / But a mixed breed act / Acting out for equality // This is not some rebel halfbreed act / I just scribbled down for revenge / Besides / I don't need to be hung // For my mixed mouth blabbing / How they used their act / To cover up / Dirty goings-on in our country." Much of the power of the poems is in the pronouns. The movement from "I" to "we" suggests Scofield's dilemma, while the constant distinction between "we" and "they" suggests the reader's. On the one hand, identification with the poet is inevitable, no matter one's background—an "I" is an "I" in the mouth of a reader. Yet one will just as quickly find oneself on the other side of the equation, pushed (if only in the poem) into an outsider position vis-a-vis the poet and the "we" for whom he sometimes chooses to speak.

It is a volatile poetic from the reader's perspective, as the passion evidenced there means that at one moment we may be angry on the speaker's (and a people's) behalf, while at another we may be angry at that very same speaker; nor is it outside the realm of possibility that we will become angry at ourselves for being complicit in his anger or for being angry ourselves at all. But it's contagious, this version of passion, and can be used for a spectrum of purposes good, bad, and between. Although this is not all that Scofield is up to, it is one of the most interesting; in its roundabout and ambivalent way, it speaks to the range of personal, social, and political selves we must inhabit, usually with some discomfort. Given his beleaguered position, as he styles it, Scofield's self-habitation is necessarily more fraught than most. The frequent referral to the history of his people does not always have a stabilizing effect— this is not a storybook world where everyone is saddled with the burden of being perpetually noble—but when weighed in the balance, the past gives ballast to a roiling heart. The pronominal taking of sides is also counteracted by linguistic touches that suggest more cultural capaciousness than a surface reading reveals. Nor do the poems remain the same throughout the selections from his career, the range of approaches embodying a ranging mind. The selection of new poems begins with the lines: "The poet in him is an assassin, / a killer, cantankerous and absolute." That very well may be—in a particular poem. In another, "I'll Teach You Cree," one is offered instruction, while in the last, "This Is My Blanket," irony tempers anger like heat tempers steel. Even the form seems toughened and, if anything, the new poems cut more sharply by being more contained. But these, one must acknowledge, would lose some of their effectiveness if we had reached them without having passed through the arc of the poet's growth, without having passed through his process of living represented on the page.

In Fred Wah's *is a door* is a poem called "Opaque" that Scofield, who explores the Métis margins from their centre out, might find less opaque than most readers. It begins:

> Amalgam ache me -tis    rite to exit    syncrude

Perhaps this would count for the Scott of *Mosaic Orpheus* as one of his "undecipherable poets," but Wah here, and elsewhere in the section called "Discount Me In," touches on the challenges not only of being ethnically mixed in a world that would find singularity easier and simpler (not that singularity even exists), but also touches on the challenges of being a poet called upon by self or by others to account for one's own patch in the Canadian multicultural quilt. The "amalgam ache" is shown by splitting "Métis" into the doubleness by which it is generally characterized, but the division is difficult for the subject—almost literally in this case, as what we would expect to be the subject and verb agreement best representing identity—the "I am"— is a "me tis." Thus, although the "me" is still a "first person" (which could be a position of strength), the verb archaizes him, forcing him into a grammatically and temporally clumsy position outside of the linguistic (and cultural) norm. The "rite/ right to exit" pun can be taken as a kind of benediction bestowed by an experienced poet on his younger colleagues, while "syncrude" can be seen as a warning against over-blunt attempts to achieve a wishful syncretism. (There is also doubtless lurking there some remark about oil, given Wah's environmentalism.)

So *is a door* is the end of a statement (That is a door.), the end or beginning of an interrogation (What is a door? Is a door this or that?), and in the title poem, repeated twenty times, it becomes a mantra of mobility. In the book's opening section it is also "Isadora"—an allegorical muse (Isadora Blue) and an actual hurricane (Isadora blew)—and Wah throughout uses puns and other structures of multiple meaning as a way of telling us how mixed are our languages, and how our languages are ourselves, or the way that others see us: "She said 'spanner.' He knew he was dealing with a Brit." Humour, of course, is one way to tackle the subject. Wah's often comes in the form of dry observation. In one of the more personal (or at any rate, less opaque) poems, Wah records his own early experience with what in another land has been called "double consciousness": "Trust me, I was somewhere / else. In 1947 I don't think / I was counted. I must have / been Chinese. From the summit / of myself I was on the other side, / part of an exclusion act." Wah goes on to say, "I keep looking for a signifier/ to cling to." There are those, like "the click-clack/ of Mah-jong," that might be expected cultural markers, but are certainly linguistic self-stereotypers. Yet even the most basic, culturally neutral of signifiers are fraught: "Selves is a plural noun dormant within the outside though it is not a pronoun so when *I* chatter *we* don't get colder // it tricks language into an intense recitation of *I we I we I we* as a way to keep warm around the pockmarked tongues of other selves // a translation of winter that comes after winter // left holding the math of multiple history[.]" Left holding the math, left holding the bag, left holding the door—that last echo suggesting Wah's poetic chivalry, for *is a door*, even given its verbal density and its critical intensity, does not slam shut on the reader, but is an opening.

# Books Reviewed

Jordan Abel, *Injun*, 189

David Alexander, *After the Hatching Oven*, 140

Madhur Anand, *A New Index for Predicting Catastrophes*, 197

— ed. w/ Adam Dickinson, *Regreen: New Canadian Ecological Poetry*, 275

Amanda Anderson, *The Way We Argue Now*, 83

Larissa Andrusyshyn, *Mammoth*, 270

Tammy Armstrong, *The Scare in the Crow*, 247

John Ashbery, *Where Shall I Wander*, 85

Leanne Averbach, *Come Closer*, 256

Margaret Avison, *The Essential Margaret Avison*, ed. Robyn Sarah, 212

— *Listening*, 281

Elizabeth Bachinsky, *God of Missed Connections*, 317

Nelson Ball, *Certain Details: The Poetry of Nelson Ball*, ed. Stuart Ross, 158

Douglas Barbour, *Listen. If*, 177

Majlinda Bashllari, *Love Is a Very Long Word*, 181

Sarah Beaudin, ed. w/ Karen Correia Da Silva and Curran Folkers, *Gulch*, 273

Chad Bennett, *Word of Mouth: Gossip and American Poetry*, 87

Dominique Bernier-Cormier, *Correspondent*, 139

Lisa Bird-Wilson, *The Red Files*, 187

Juliane Okot Bitek, *100 Days*, 186

Sarah Blake, *Mister West*, 90

Yvonne Blomer, ed., *Refugium: Poems for the Pacific*, 178

Ronna Bloom, *Permiso*, 310

Christian Bök, *The Xenotext: Book 1*, 197

Michael Boughn, *Cosmographia*, 272

— *22 Skidoo/ SubTractions*, 313

George Bowering, *My Darling Nellie Grey*, 223

Tim Bowling, *The Annotated Bee & Me*, 231

Dionne Brand, *Ossuaries*, 207

— *Fierce Departures: The Poetry of Dionne Brand*, ed. Leslie C. Sanders, 277

Robert Bringhurst, *Selected Poems*, 278

Susan Briscoe, *The Crow's Vow*, 248

Stephen Brockwell, ed. w/ Stuart Ross, *Rogue Stimulus: The Stephen Harper Holiday Anthology for a Prorogued Parliament*, 276

Heather Cadsby, *Could Be*, 320

Tenille K. Campbell, *#IndianLovePoems*, 160

Domenico Capilongo, *send*, 178

Anne Carson, *Float*, 189

— *Nox*, 208

Tina Brown Celona, *The Real Moon of Poetry and Other Poems*, 117

Weyman Chan, *Human Tissue*, 191

Margaret Christakos, *Welling*, 241

George Elliott Clarke, *Canticles I*, 180

— *I & I*, 336

Wayne Clifford, *The Exile's Papers*, 337

Victor Coleman, *The Occasional Troubadour*, 225

Don Coles, *The Essential Don Coles*, ed. Robyn Sarah, 278

— *Where We Might Have Been*, 239

Stephen Collis, *On the Material*, 240

— *Once in Blockadia*, 190

Wayde Compton, ed. w/ Renée Sarojini Saklikar, *The Revolving City: 51 Poems and the Stories behind Them*, 194

Kevin Connolly, *Xiphoid Process*, 175

Lucas Crawford, *The High Line Scavenger Hunt*, 139

Amelia Curran, *Relics and Tunes: The Songs of Amelia Curran*, 17

Frank Davey, *Bardy Google*, 242

Jack Davis, *Faunics*, 167

Brian Day, *Conjuring Jesus*, 331

Adrian De Leon, *Rouge*, 144

Rosanna Deerchild, *Calling Down the Sky*, 200

Barry Dempster, *Blue Wherever*, 232

Robert D. Denham, *Northrop Frye and Others, Volume II: The Order of Words*, 93

Leanne Dunic, *To Love the Coming End*, 164

Paul Dutton, *Sonosyntactics*, ed. Gary Barwin, 193

Mercedes Eng, *Prison Industrial Complex Explodes*, 173

Karen Enns, *Cloud Physics*, 178

Joanne Epp, *Eigenheim*, 199

Roger Epp, *Only Leave a Trace*, 162

Guy Ewing, *Hearing, and answering with music*, 293

Triny Finlay, *Histories Haunt Us*, 261

Philip Fisher, *The Vehement Passions*, 95

Angus Fletcher, *A New Theory for American Poetry*, 97

Michael Fraser, *To Greet Yourself Arriving*, 183

Elee Kraljii Gardiner, *Trauma Head*, 153

Lise Gaston, *Cityscapes in Mating Season*, 161

Gary Geddes, *Swimming Ginger*, 238

— *The Terracotta Army*, 238

Kuldip Gill, *Valley Sutra*, 334

Lorri Neilsen Glenn, *Lost Gospels*, 234

Artie Gold, *The Collected Books of Artie Gold*, eds. Ken Norris and Endre Farkas, 220

Kevin González, *Cultural Studies*, 103

## BOOKS REVIEWED

Beth Goobie, *Breathing at Dusk*, 169

Ariel Gordon, *Hump*, 249

Catherine Graham, *The Celery Forest*, 170

Sonja Ruth Greckol, *Gravity Matters*, 283

— *No Line in Time*, 157

Elizabeth Greene, *Moving*, 258

Richard Greene, *Boxing the Compass*, 306

David Groulx, *The Windigo Chronicles*, 188

Jason Guriel, *Pure Product*, 305

Helen Hajnoczky, *Magyarázni*, 184

Louise Bernice Halfe, *Burning in This Midnight Dream*, 187

Kate Hall, *The Certainty Dream*, 302

Phil Hall, *Guthrie Clothing: A Selected Collage*, ed. rob mclennan, 194

— *The Little Seamstress*, 244

Steven Heighton, *Patient Frame*, 235

Angela Hibbs, *Wanton*, 315

Gerald Hill, *Hillsdale Book*, 201

— *14 Tractors*, 325

Liz Howard, *Infinite Citizen of the Shaking Tent*, 196

Ray Hsu, *Cold Sleep Permanent Afternoon*, 253

Nasser Hussain, *SKY WRI TEI NGS*, 147

Emily Izsak, *Whistle Stops: A Locomotive Serial Poem*, 161

Major Jackson, *Hoops*, 106

Sheniz Janmohamed, *Bleeding Light*, 265

Amanda Jernigan, *Years, Months, and Days*, 133

Tyehimba Jess, *leadbelly*, 124

Aisha Sasha John, *I want to live*, 171

D.G. Jones, *The Stream Exposed with All Its Stones*, 218

June Jordan, *Directed by Desire: The Collected Poems of June Jordan*, 108

Eve Joseph, *The Secret Signature of Things*, 233

Shaista Justin, *Winter, the unwelcome visitor*, 298

Adeena Karasick, *Checking In*, 136

Jake Kennedy, *Merz Structure No. 2 Burnt by Children at Play*, 204

Michael Kenyon, *The Last House*, 309

Roy K. Kiyooka, *The Artist & the Moose*, ed. Roy Miki, 335

Tonja Gunvaldsen Klaassen, *Lean-To*, 316

Robert Kroetsch, *Too Bad: Sketches Toward a Self-Portrait*, 237

Tiziana La Melia, *The Eyelash and the Monochrome*, 136

Nic Labriola, *Naming the Mannequins*, 300

Fiona Lam, *Enter the Chrysanthemum*, 312

Ted Landrum, *Midway Radicals & Archi-Poems*, 161

Patrick Lane, *Witness: Selected Poems 1962–2010*, 209

Genevieve Lehr, *Stomata*, 186

Joe LeSeuer, *Digressions on Some Poems by Frank O'Hara*, 110

Kenneth Leslie, *The Essential Kenneth Leslie*, ed. Zachariah Wells, 213

Tim Lilburn, *The House of Charlemagne*, 135

Gary Copeland Lilley, *Alpha Zulu*, 113

Michael Lista, *Bloom*, 271

Pat Lowther, *The Collected Works of Pat Lowther*, ed. Christine Wiesenthal, 219

Canisia Lubrin, *Voodoo Hypothesis*, 166

Randy Lundy, *Blackbird Song*, 143

Kathy Mac, *Human Misunderstanding*, 173

Pam Calabrese MacLean, *The Dead Can't Dance*, 311

Alice Major, *Memory's Daughter*, 240

— *Welcome to the Anthropocene*, 149

Pasha Malla, ed. w/ Jeff Parker, *Erratic Fire, Erratic Passion: The Poetry of Sportstalk*, 195

Daphne Marlatt, *Reading Sveva*, 182

Camille Martin, *Sonnets*, 267

David Martin, *Tar Swan*, 141

Ilona Martonfi, *Blue Poppy*, 286

Harry Mathews, *The Human Country: New and Collected Stories*, 115

Seymour Mayne, ed., *In Your Words: Translations from the Yiddish and the Hebrew*, 179

David McFadden, *Why Are You So Long and Sweet? Collected Long Poems of David W. McFadden*, ed. Stuart Ross, 216

Julie McIsaac, *We Like Feelings. We Are Serious*, 155

rob mclennan, *gifts*, 318

— *wild horses*, 221

Christina McRae, *Next to Nothing*, 285

Joyelle McSweeney, *The Red Bird*, 117

Vanessa Moeller, *Our Extraordinary Monsters*, 304

Pamela Mordecai, *de Book of Mary*, 201

Gustave Morin, *Clean Sails*, 206

Garry Thomas Morse, *After Jack*, 221

Michelle Muir, *Nuff Said*, 295

Jane Munro, *Active Pass*, 268

George Murray, *Quick*, 175

Les Murray, *Poems the Size of Photographs*, 120

Marion Mutala, *Ukrainian Daughter's Dance*, 184

Shane Neilson, *On Shaving Off His Face*, 202

Cecily Nicholson, *Wayside Sang*, 173

Andrea Nicki, *Welcoming*, 294

Emily Nilsen, *Otolith*, 159

E. Martin Nolan, *Still Point*, 166

Alden Nowlan, *Collected Poems*, ed. Brian Bartlett, 179

Merle Nudelman, *The He We Knew*, 259

Alexandra Oliver, *Let the Empire Down*, 181

P.K. Page, *Coal and Roses*, 279

— *Kaleidoscope: Selected Poems of P.K. Page*, ed. Zailig Pollock, 211

Chris Pannell, *Drive*, 323

Rebecca Păpucaru, *The Panic Room*, 167

Arleen Paré, *The Girls with Stone Faces*, 169

R.D. Patrick, *The Stonehaven Poems*, 268

## BOOKS REVIEWED

Soraya Peerbaye, *Poems for the Advisory Committee on Antarctic Names*, 287

Marjorie Perloff, *The Vienna Paradox*, 122

Caryl Phillips, *Dancing in the Dark*, 124

Marguerite Pigeon, *Inventory*, 289

Peter Quartermain, *Stubborn Poetries: Poetic Facticity and the Avant-Garde*, 126

Sina Queryas, *My Ariel*, 176

Shazia Hafiz Ramji, *Port of Being*, 154

James Reaney, *A Suit of Nettles*, 230

Ishmael Reed, *New and Collected Poems*, 109

Janet Rogers, *As Long as the Sun Shines*, 156

Laisha Rosnau, *Lousy Explorers*, 310

Stephen Rowe, *Never More There*, 291

Kerry Ryan, *Vs.*, 229

Gregory Scofield, *Kipocihkân*, 338

— *Witness, I Am*, 188

Peter Dale Scott, *Mosaic Orpheus*, 337

Johanna Skibsrud, *I Do Not Think That I Could Love a Human Being*, 256

Carolyn Smart, *Careen*, 202

— *Hooked*, 332

Karen Solie, *Pigeon*, 327

Kevin Spenst, *Jabbering with Bing Bong*, 199

Carmine Starnino, *This Way Out*, 308

Dean Steadman, *Après Satie—For Two and Four Hands*, 183

Christine Stewart, *Treaty 6 Deixis*, 157

Fenn Stewart, *Better Nature*, 165

Jeremy Stewart, *(flood basement*, 301

Catriona Strang, *Reveries of a Solitary Biker*, 168

Suwanda Sugunasiri, *Obama-Ji*, 338

Moez Surani, ة‎مل‎ح‎ *OPERACIÓN OPÉRATION OPERATION* 行动 *ОПЕРАЦИЯ*, 185

Fraser Sutherland, *The Philosophy of As If*, 244

Gillian Sze, *Fish Bones*, 299

Sharon Thesen, *The Receiver*, 177

John Thompson, *Collected Poems & Translations*, ed. Peter Sanger, 192

Aaron Tucker, *Irresponsible Mediums: the chess games of Marcel Duchamp*, 168

Michael Turner, *9×11*, 138

Priscilla Uppal, *Successful Tragedies: Poems 1998–2010*, 228

— *Traumatology*, 228

— *Winter Sports: Poems*, 226

Emily Ursuliak, *Throwing the Diamond Hitch*, 165

Paul Vermeersch, *The Reinvention of the Human Hand*, 246

Fred Wah, *is a door*, 340

Keith and Rosmarie Waldrop, *Ceci n'est pas Keith/Ceci n'est pas Rosmarie*, 127

Kathleen Wall and Veronica Geminder, *Visible Cities*, 137

Sheryda Warrener, *Floating Is Everything*, 203

Joshua Whitehead, *Full-Metal Indigiqueer*, 162

Ian Williams, *You Know Who You Are*, 250

Rob Winger, *The Chimney Stone*, 264

Rita Wong and Fred Wah, *beholden: a poem as long as the river*, 148

Liz Worth, *No Work Finished Here*, 205

Catriona Wright, *Table Manners*, 163

John Yau, *Borrowed Love Poems*, 129

Suzanne Zelazo, *Lances All Alike*, 151

David Zieroth, *The Fly in Autumn*, 329

Jan Zwicky, *Chamber Music: The Poetry of Jan Zwicky*, eds. Darren Bifford and Warren Heiti, 193

# About the Author

Andrew DuBois is Associate Professor of English at the University of Toronto Scarborough. He is the author of *Ashbery's Forms of Attention* and *He We Her / I Am White*, as well as co-editor of *The Anthology of Rap* and *Close Reading: The Reader*.